The War
Come Home

*Disabled Veterans in Britain
and Germany, 1914-1939*

D1713609

Deborah Cohen

UNIVERSITY OF CALIFORNIA PRESS
Berkeley · Los Angeles · London

Portions of this material have been previously published as "Civil Society in the Aftermath of the Great War," in *Paradoxes of Civil Society: New Perspectives on Modern German and British History,* ed. Frank Trentmann, © 1999 Berghahn Books; and "Will to Work: Disabled Veterans in Britain and Germany after the First World War," in *Disabled Veterans in History*, ed. David Gerber, © 2000 University of Michigan Press. Reprinted by permission of the publishers.

University of California Press
Berkeley and Los Angeles, California

University of California Press, Ltd.
London, England

Library of Congress Cataloging-in-Publication Data

Cohen, Deborah, 1968–.
   The war come home: disabled veterans in Britain and Germany, 1914–1939 / Deborah Cohen.

      p.   cm.
   Includes bibliographical references and index.
   ISBN 0-520-22008-0 (alk. paper)
   1. Veterans, Disabled—Great Britain—History—20th century.   2. Veterans, Disabled—Germany—History—20th century.   3. World War, 1914–1918—Veterans—Great Britain—Care.   4. World War, 1914–1918—Veterans—Germany—Care.   5. Great Britain—History—20th century.   6. Germany—History—20th century   I. Title.

UB359.G7 C59   2001
362.86'0941'09
41—dc21   2001027088

Manufactured in the United States of America
10 09 08 07 06 05 04 03 02 01
10 9 8 7 6 5 4 3 2 1

The paper used in this publication meets the minimum requirements of ANSI/NISO Z39.48-1992 (R 1997) (*Permanence of Paper*). ⊗

For Edwin and Helen Cohen
and Sarah Kasdan

And in memory
of Belle and Abe Cohen
and K. M. Kasdan

Contents

Illustrations

Acknowledgments

I would like to thank the institutions that made the research and writing of this book possible: the Mellon Foundation, the University of California at Berkeley, the Center for German and European Studies (Berkeley), the Council for European Studies (Columbia University), the German Historical Institute, the German Academic Exchange Service, the Center for European Studies at Harvard, and American University. A Conant Fellowship at the Center for European Studies made it possible for me to turn my dissertation into a book; a Senate Research Grant and a Mellon Grant from American University allowed me to finish final revisions of the manuscript. For their wisdom but also for their forbearance, I am deeply indebted to my advisers, Gerald Feldman and Thomas Laqueur, and to the other members of my dissertation committee, Thomas Brady, Carla Hesse, and Kim Voss. Richard Bessel, David Blackbourn, James Cronin, Thomas Ertman, Susan Pedersen, and Jean Quataert improved the final manuscript through their thoughtful criticism and encouragement; Seth Koven and the University of California Press's two anonymous reviewers will see how much I profited from their astute comments. To Susan Pedersen, Olwen Hufton, and Anne Higonnet, I owe (since my undergraduate days) the debt of inspiration and good advice. Sheila Levine, the Assistant Director of the University of California Press, ensured that this book saw the light of day.

I wish also to acknowledge the many archives and institutions that opened their records to me. In Britain, I would particularly like to thank the staff and residents of the Star and Garter Home, especially Mr. Charles Groves, Mr. Peter Hill, and Miss Jean Oliver, for their kindness; Dr. Andrew Bamji; Mr. Rick Brunwin and Mr. George Foster of the Sir Oswald Stoll Mansions; and the staffs of the Royal British Legion, Preston Hall, the Richmond Poppy Factory, the Enham Estate, the British Library, the British Red Cross Archives, the Hammersmith and Fulham Local Record Office, and the Wellcome Institute for the History of Medicine. Brunel Cohen gallantly permitted me to use the enormous newspaper clipping collections compiled by his father, Sir J. B. Brunel Cohen. H. L. C. Greig and Commander Langton Gowlland spoke to me about their fathers. Mrs. Clarice Gardner shared her unpublished memoirs with me.

In Germany, I would like to acknowledge the assistance of the late Dr. Lehmann of the Geheimes Staatsarchiv Preussischer Kulturbesitz for permitting me to read otherwise closed documents; Dr. Klaus-Dieter Thomann for sharing his expertise; the obliging staffs of the Bundesarchiv in Potsdam, Koblenz, and Freiburg; the Caritas Archive; the Innere Mission Archive; the Hessisches Hauptstaatsarchiv in Wiesbaden; the Sächsisches Hauptstaatsarchiv in Dresden; the Berlin Landesarchiv; the Humboldt University Library; the Invalidenhaus Siedlung; and especially Helmut Vietor of the Evangelische Stiftung Volmarstein.

I am grateful to Susan Ecklund, who copyedited the manuscript; to Lynn Meinhardt and Erika Büky, who shepherded it through production; and to Josh Greenberg, who prepared the index.

For their comments on my work along the way, I thank my colleagues in the Department of History at American University, especially Richard Breitman and Vanessa Schwartz, who read the final manuscript, Tim Alborn, Keith Allen, Roger Chickering, Martin Daunton, Belinda Davis, James Diehl, Greg Eghigian, the late David Englander, Stig Förster, David Gerber, Christian Gerlach, Martin Geyer, Michael Geyer, Kevin Grant, Susan Grayzel, Adrian Gregory, Liz Harvey, Maria Höhn, David Houts, Cathy Kerr, Paul Lerner, Anne Lipp, Charles Maier, Peter Mandler, Greg Moynihan, Jerry Muller, Jeffrey Reznick, Cara Robertson, Marya Schock, Richard Stites, Frank Trentmann, Lisa Trivedi, Bernd Ulrich, Jonathan Wiesen, Jay Winter, Louise Young, Benjamin Ziemann, and the members of the Institute for Historical Research's Social History Seminar, the British and German Seminars at Harvard University's Center for European Studies, the Standing Seminar in German History at Georgetown University, the Transatlantic Doctoral Seminar, and the History Department at Villanova University. Above all, I am grateful to my family, to whom this book is dedicated with love and great admiration.

Introduction

Reconciliation and Stability

This is a book about the First World War's aftermath in two belligerent nations. It tells of the war's most visible legacy, the nearly 6 million British and German men disabled by injury or disease in the years 1914 to 1918.[1] A study of reconstruction in the literal sense, this book examines the making of social peace in the shadow of war. Its subject is the reintegration of disabled veterans in Britain and Germany, its contention, that the war's burdens could not be met by states alone. Whether British or German, disabled veterans had endured much the same war, suffering wounds their fellow citizens found unimaginable. Unlikely members of a community of fate, the war's casualties returned to very different lands. Through analysis of provisions for disabled veterans in Great Britain and Germany, this book asks how states and their citizens came to terms with the First World War's costs and how they made, or tried to make, the peace.[2]

The First World War was murderous without precedent. More than 9.5 million soldiers died over a period of fifty-two months; on average, the war claimed the lives of 5,600 men every day that it continued.[3] Twenty million men were severely wounded; 8 million veterans returned home permanently disabled.[4] They had suffered the worst injuries ever seen. Shrapnel from exploding shells tore ragged paths through flesh and bone, leaving wounds, one British surgeon acknowledged, "from which the most hardened might well turn away in horror."[5] Under the threat of constant shellfire and ubiquitous death, some men lost their minds.[6] After months of exposure in rat-infested trenches, others contracted debilitat ing illnesses that stole their breath and shortened their lives. As many as 6 million children lost their fathers in the war, and perhaps another 3 million watched them die at home.[7] Few families were spared mourning.

In the aftermath of the Great War, social peace came, if at all, only slowly. For those who championed democracy, the end of the First World War had appeared the harbinger of a better era. Between 1917 and 1919, four empires crumbled; republics succeeded monarchies. Yet the new states inherited the burdens of the old. More than four years of war left treasuries deeply indebted and political capital sparse. Service on the national debt became the largest expenditure in many states' postwar budgets.[8] Currencies previously stable faltered; sometimes, as in Germany during 1922–1923, they collapsed altogether. Amid the postwar inflation and the resulting social dislocation, middle-class benefactors became welfare supplicants. Mass politics fed on the grievances of the dispossessed, and demonstrations became the emblems of the era. Within only a few years, many of the new republics had been replaced by dictatorships intent upon imperial expansion. Hardly had one peace treaty been concluded than another war threatened.

More than any other group, disabled veterans symbolized the First World War's burdens. Long after the Armistice, the sight of empty sleeves tucked into pockets recalled "sad memories of the war and its longdrawn suffering."[9] For the disabled themselves, as one veteran explained, the Great War "could never be over."[10] Years after their demobilization, disabled veterans bore the sufferings war inflicted. Like the bank clerk Erich Rehse, they lived with injuries that robbed independence. Both hands amputated, blind in one eye, Rehse found himself unable to hold even an umbrella.[11] The former infantryman Albert Bayliss, gassed in France, could not sleep for his racking cough. Unemployed for thirteen months, his rent severely in arrears, Bayliss despaired. "I am only 31," he wrote, "what will I be in a few years time."[12] Keen sportsmen became invalids unable to climb staircases. A drummer boy lost both hands. Each disabled veteran appeared to bring the war's horrors home with him.

Stark reminders of the war's sacrifices, disabled veterans also endangered the peace. No country was spared mass protests by disgruntled exservicemen in the immediate postwar years. Insufficient provisions for the disabled provided a rallying cry for veterans' organizations. In Britain and Germany, disabled veterans demonstrated in the streets for higher pensions and secure employment. To worried observers in Manchester as in Munich, veterans appeared disaffected, even brutalized—a constituency ripe for the picking from left or from right.[13] By the mid-1920s, however, the course of the veterans' movement had diverged decisively in the two countries. British veterans had become bulwarks of the established order, loyal to King and country. Their organization, the British Legion, preached an ethic of "Service, Not Self." The German disabled, by contrast, had joined the Republic's most visible enemies. In German cities, thousands of disabled veterans demonstrated to secure their rights; even the smallest towns witnessed protests. When the state failed to meet their demands, the German disabled turned to extremist politics.

In Great Britain, the state escaped the wrath of its veterans, whereas in Germany, a newly founded republic bore its heroes' full fury. Yet at the heart of this study is an apparent paradox. Contrary to historians' expectations, the state's largesse did not secure, nor did its absence preclude, the loyalty of veterans. Although Germany's postwar democracy, the Weimar Republic, accorded the disabled generous benefits, veterans came to despise the state that favored them. State-secured employment and the best social services in Europe did not foster disabled men's allegiance to the new Republic. In contrast, British ex-servicemen remained the Crown's loyal subjects though they received only meager material compensation. Despite the state's neglect, disabled veterans in Britain—alone among their European counterparts—retreated from politics.

So precarious throughout the 1920s and 1930s, social stability did not arise as a matter of course, but had to be created. Preeminent among accounts of postwar stabilization is Charles Maier's study of "new corporatism" in France, Germany, and Italy, complemented for Britain by Keith Middlemas's account of the rise of "corporate bias."[14] Stability, Maier and Middlemas agree, depended on new distributions of power. They trace a decisive shift in the locus of political decision making over the course of the 1920s from legislatures incapacitated by the burdens of total war and inflation to powerful interest groups of industry and labor bargaining directly through new and influential state ministries. Charged with the task of arbitrating between industry and labor, officials in government ministries in Britain, as on the Continent, gained unprecedented authority. Not the consensus of the voting public but collective bargaining among powerful interest groups characterized the postwar stabilization. Despite mass enfranchisement, stability depended on the concentration of power in fewer hands.

Corporatist explanations share a focus on the state. This book offers a different, if in some senses complementary, interpretation of stability in the Great War's aftermath. Rather than viewing stability solely as the *purpose of book →*

achievement of states and powerful interest groups, it investigates the role that the public played in the attainment and maintenance of social peace. By analyzing sources of instability, it considers, too, the unintended consequences of one state's attempt to create domestic harmony. Critical to successful postwar reconstruction, I will argue, was civil society, defined here as the dense network of voluntary, and especially philanthropic, organizations that mediated between the individual and the state. Stabilization required more than the machinations of experts. The peace this book will describe was forged not in back rooms and ministerial chambers but in arenas of broad public participation, in soup kitchens and makeshift local pension offices, homes for orphaned children and villas turned lazarets.

Reconstruction, no less than war, depended on the mobilization of civil society. The legacy of industrialized warfare was measured in decades, not in years. The care of disabled veterans, the war's most visible victims, provides a study in the management of postwar social problems. With more than 750,000 ex-servicemen permanently disabled in Britain and 1.5 million in Germany, observers recognized that their rehabilitation would require an extraordinary effort.[15] While commentators in both countries agreed that it was the responsibility of the state, supplemented by the efforts of its citizenry, to provide for the disabled, their treatment differed greatly in Britain and in Germany. In Britain, civil servants in the new ministry charged with their care sought to limit the state's obligations toward disabled veterans. They left the task to philanthropy and the grateful public. In Germany, by contrast, state officials embraced the rehabilitation of the disabled as, in the words of the Republic's first president, Weimar's "foremost duty."[16]

Despite high expectations raised during the war and promises of "a fit land for heroes," the British state offered only modest compensation to disabled veterans. Pleading fiscal stringency and adherence to the principles of sound governance, civil servants in the Ministry of Pensions, founded in 1917, sought to restrict the state's liability for wounded soldiers. Pensions assessments, carried out by panels of the Ministry's physicians, were based solely on the degree of physical disfigurement or illness and did not take account of a man's capacity to return to work. Even the seriously disabled received pensions below the minimum needed for survival. Most important, successive British governments proved notably reluctant to institute programs that provided disabled men with a chance at gainful employment. In early 1920, the British state had trained only

13,000 disabled men, while another 60,000 waited for placement.[17] Two years later, with an estimated 100,000 disabled ex-servicemen unemployed, the government closed admission to the training programs altogether.[18] If disabled veterans wished to work, and many had no other choice, they had to rely on their own wits or the mercy of their fellow citizens.[19]

Historians have often noted the unwillingness of the interwar British state to intervene in intractable social problems.[20] Less well understood, however, is the role that voluntarists played in assuming duties that contemporaries regarded as the state's responsibility.[21] In Britain, the reintegration of disabled veterans proceeded primarily through voluntary and philanthropic efforts. Philanthropists ran most initiatives for the long-term treatment or rehabilitation of wounded servicemen, from the country's largest artificial limb–fitting center at Roehampton to the comprehensive program for the war blinded administered through St. Dunstan's Hostel. Every home for the totally disabled, and there were eight such institutions in the London area alone, owed its founding to private munificence. Britain's sole employment scheme for the disabled relied on voluntary effort; inaugurated in 1918, the King's Roll appealed to employers' patriotism to induce them to offer jobs to disabled ex-servicemen. Philanthropists administered all organized employment for severely disabled men, whether in settlements for neurasthenics, through the ten local Lord Roberts Memorial Workshops, or in factories such as Bernard Oppenheimer's specially outfitted diamond-cutting facility in Brighton.

In contrast to Britain, where civil servants sought to divest the state of responsibility to the disabled, the Weimar Republic—a pioneer in the field of social welfare—regarded rehabilitation as its highest obligation. Pensions were intended to compensate men for the loss of earning capacity, as well as for the physical fact of disability. Pensions for the most severely disabled not only approximated the wages of skilled workmen but also included provisions for wives and children.[22] Unlike the British government, which limited its responsibilities to the distribution of pensions, German authorities aimed to return even the most incapacitated to work, preferably to their former occupations. Weimar's National Pension Law (1920) accorded the disabled more than a right to pensions; they were also entitled to an occupational retraining course and free medical care for all service-related ailments. By 1924, as many as half of the war-disabled had received career counseling or retraining.[23] Severely disabled veterans were practically assured work by the Labor Ministry. Under the Law of the Severely Disabled (1920), most employers were required to hire and keep them.[24] It was very difficult to fire a disabled man. At the height of the Great Depression, severely disabled workers were twice as likely as their able-bodied counterparts to retain their jobs.[25]

While the Weimar Republic later created Europe's most comprehensive programs for disabled veterans, for most of the war, Germany, like Britain, relied on voluntary effort. During the war, a dynamic charitable culture thrived in Germany, surviving, even briefly, the defeat. In most regions, voluntary and local organizations assumed the lion's share of responsibility for the disabled. To finance their efforts, charities collected enormous sums from the German public. Following a 1917 decree by the upper house of the German parliament, however, the state required charities that sought to raise funds or solicit new members to secure the permission of the authorities. Desperate for scarce resources, the rapidly expanding and militarized state demanded the thorough rationalization of philanthropic efforts.[26] Only a handful of selected charities were granted a permit to raise funds for the disabled, and only on the condition that they submit to government control of their expenditures.

Justified during the war as a necessary measure against waste, the regulation of charity became, in the early Weimar Republic, a means to establish the new state's authority. Drawing upon the example of the country's seven major private welfare organizations, scholars have suggested that philanthropy gained a privileged, quasi-public status in the Weimar Republic.[27] However, incorporation into the state's welfare apparatus was an option available only to the largest and best-organized associations. As Germany's authorities gained unprecedented control over charity, many new or small philanthropies folded, while their more prestigious and long-established counterparts entered into junior partnerships with the state. To win the allegiance of its skeptical citizenry, the Weimar Republic sought to establish a monopoly over benevolence. Unlike British civil servants in the Ministry of Pensions, who deemed disabled veterans an unnecessary burden for the state, German officials regarded the "war victims problem" as an opportunity. They envisioned programs for wounded soldiers, alongside those for youth and the unemployed, as showpieces of postwar social policy.[28] More than a hindrance, unregulated philanthropy threatened the state's legitimacy. In the early Republic, the regulation of charity proceeded dramatically; in Prussia alone, the newly appointed State Commissioner for the Regulation of Welfare Work refused more than 300 charities for the war's victims permission to collect in the years 1919–1924.[29]

Even before the war ended, care for the disabled diverged markedly in Great Britain and Germany. In Britain, the rehabilitation of the disabled remained largely the business of voluntarists, whereas in Germany, it became the cornerstone of the new democratic order. In the latter half of the 1920s, Germany's first democracy spent almost 20 percent of its annual budget on war victims' pensions; in Britain, by contrast, war pensions occupied less than 7 percent of the annual budget from 1923 onward.[30] The efforts of the German state to secure the reintegration of disabled veterans, like the British state's neglect, had paradoxical effects. Men whom the Weimar Republic had courted with sophisticated retraining programs and preferential employment turned against the new democracy, while Britain's heroes, slighted by a state that had promised to care for them, came to defend the established order.

How can we explain why those who had profited from a state's generosity became its implacable foes? Or why Britain's heroes, treated so shabbily by successive governments, never forced the state to pay for its negligence in the political sphere? The answers to these questions are complex. The consequences of victory and defeat, on the one hand, and the broader political cultures of interwar Germany and Britain, on the other, frame this study. Given the vulnerability of Germany's political institutions in the wake of 1918–1919 and the tradition of antiparliamentary politics, the barriers to entry into radical movements were far lower in the Weimar Republic than in interwar Britain. What this book suggests, however, is that the war's resolution and political culture cannot fully account for the very different responses of British and German veterans to their treatment. I will argue that veterans' attitudes toward the public left an indelible imprint on ex-servicemen's political movements.[31] Broad participation in the resolution of the war victims' problems—through voluntary organizations and charities—led veterans to believe that their fellow citizens had honored their sacrifices. Voluntarism brought about a reconciliation between disabled veterans and those for whom they had suffered.

If an "unusual social tranquillity" was the hallmark of interwar Britain, veterans epitomized this state of affairs.[32] Like the unemployed (among whom many ex-servicemen numbered), disabled veterans did not translate their grievances into political conflict. Historians have explained the comparative absence of unrest in interwar Britain by reference to relative prosperity with few exceptions. This book underscores the significance of voluntarism to Britain's interwar stability, while at the same time demonstrating the perils for individuals of social cohesion achieved without social integration.[33] In the face of state neglect, British philanthropists brokered a lasting social peace between a public eager to prove its gratitude to soldiers and a conservative ex-service movement looking for signs that the country cared. Shoddy treatment at the hands of the state did not shake disabled veterans' belief that the public had appreciated their sacrifices. Fearful of alienating their fellow citizens, British veterans vowed to remain "apolitical." And yet this peace—struck amid the war's immediate aftermath—had profound consequences for individual men. For decades after the Armistice, many disabled veterans in Britain, like their predecessors from earlier wars, were forced to live as the objects of charity. Shorn of their rights by a state that had promised to care for them, dependent on the goodwill of the charitable public, they learned to suffer in silence.

Voluntarism shielded the British state from the consequences of its unpopular policies, binding veterans closer to their society and diminishing their rightful claims on the victorious polity. This argument necessitates two revisions: first, of the prevailing view of charity; second, of the received wisdom about the war generation. Scholars have tended to dismiss philanthropists as condescending, antidemocratic, and of negligible significance after the First World War.[34] Yet voluntarism did not only enable civil servants in the Ministry of Pensions to extricate the state from difficult social problems. Philanthropy also provided important opportunities for social conciliation, as between disabled veterans and those for whom they had suffered. Historians have often written of British ex-servicemen's hostility toward their fellow citizens, drawing on the writings of the War Generation's literati, Siegfried Sassoon and Robert Graves among them.[35] However, my research does not support that conclusion. Soldier-poets may have scorned the Home Front, but British veterans viewed their fellow citizens sympathetically, especially after the munificent philanthropic campaigns begun on their behalf during 1915. Charity was, of course, far from adequate when it came to the real business of caring for disabled men. Philanthropists had their own, often unorthodox, stakes in the war's victims; they often blithely disregarded their charges' desires. Nonetheless, voluntarism served to convey the public's appreciation.

No less striking than the quiescence of the British disabled is the rage that their German counterparts displayed. Even as pensions swelled to 20 percent of the Republic's total expenditure, veterans took to the streets to protest state neglect. The historian Ewald Frie has called the antipathy of the German disabled to the Weimar Republic a "strange phenomenon"—"a group that in international comparison was quite well cared for, yet nevertheless remained alienated from the state that provided them with these benefits."[36] While lauding the state's material provisions as "exemplary," historians have blamed Weimar's welfare bureaucracy for veterans' alienation. If the state succeeded in the realm of material compensation, it failed, in Robert Whalen's words, "to show human sympathy"; to consider men's psychological needs, as James Diehl has argued; and, in Michael Geyer's formulation, to incorporate its intended clients in decision making.[37] Yet judged by any criterion, the British state was at least as inflexible, bureaucratic, stingy, and inhuman as its German counterpart. However, successive British governments not only dodged their responsibilities to the disabled but also remained largely immune to veterans' protests.

What was significant about German veterans' attitudes was not their anger toward the state but their antipathy toward the public. At the war's end, many disabled veterans in Germany still believed in the goodwill of their fellow citizens. The public might have to be "enlightened," but once people realized how soldiers were suffering, they would respond sympathetically. As early as the mid-1920s, hope had turned to hostility. The public, or so veterans believed, was not merely ungrateful; it grudged war victims their rightful due. The animosity became mutual, for most Germans thought that the disabled were the favored wards of the welfare state and failed to understand why they should complain so incessantly. Whereas the British disabled could take pride in their fellow citizens' gratitude, German veterans complained that the public did nothing to help them. "It will not be much longer," warned one severely war-disabled man, "and we will be complete outcasts and pariahs, although it was this ruthless society that sent our bodies to be smashed up."[38]

In Germany, the state's consolidation of welfare initiatives for the disabled elided gratitude and compensation. For disabled veterans, the granting of ever-higher pensions and better social services signified that the nation was grateful. When social services returned to the local level (after the hyperinflation), or pensions were cut (as in the Depression), veterans assumed that their fellow citizens had forgotten them, even spurned their sacrifices. In interwar Britain, pensions were nothing more than compensation, inadequate, as everyone acknowledged, to repay what had been lost; the nation's thanks were expressed in other ways, chiefly by means of philanthropy and sympathetic public opinion. When German authorities eliminated thousands of private and local initiatives for disabled veterans, they established a monopoly on much more than welfare programs. The state unwittingly ended up bearing the burden of thanks for the entire Fatherland.

The German state's monopoly on benevolence neither ensured a peaceful reconstruction nor won veterans' loyalty for the fragile Republic. The Weimar Republic's model welfare programs failed to buy it immunity from protest. While the British government's decision to absolve itself of responsibility for the disabled contributed to veterans' heralded apoliticism, the policies pursued in Germany from 1917 through 1924 brought veterans into constant conflict with the state that promised to integrate them. My argument is not that British veterans would have turned to extremist politics without voluntarism but, rather, that the public's benevolence fundamentally shaped the development of ex-service organizations. Conversely, the animosity between the German disabled and their fellow citizens, a critical factor in the radicalization of politics, might have been mitigated by precisely the kinds of private initiatives that the state chose to suppress. Because of the defeat, the revolution, and the catastrophic inflation, the chance for a rapprochement between the German public and disabled veterans was small, but real. Outright hostility was not the only possible outcome.

To compare victors to vanquished may appear an exercise in foregone conclusions. And yet, as distinct patterns of politicization evident during the war indicate, the fact of defeat or victory alone cannot account for the differences between veterans' movements. The German disabled had become discontented and disruptive well before November 1918.[39] Similarly, the high point of British veterans' agitation actually followed their victory.[40] Nor are the consequences of victory and defeat always straightforward. Scholars have argued that victory only exaggerated the disillusionment and despair that many people felt at the war's end.[41] For the German disabled, I argue, the stab-in-the-back legend (which accused the Home Front of having robbed the army of its victory) was insignificant compared with their perception that the public had failed to honor the wartime pledge of the "Fatherland's thanks."[42] In my analysis, the war's resolution forms a backdrop of critical, if by no means predictable, consequence.

In comparing Germany with Britain, this study follows a well-trod path.[43] While implicit comparison to Britain served in the years following the Second World War to expose the malignancy of the German *Sonderweg*, scholarship of the past two decades has tended to emphasize the similarities between the two countries, in order to identify those features that were truly distinctive. My purpose is neither to uncover national character nor to vindicate a country's history, but to understand the con-

sequences of two very different attempts to solve a common social problem. While acknowledging the persistence of tradition, and the specific
constraints of the immediate postwar years, this book emphasizes con-
tingency. The developments it chronicles were far from foregone conclusions. Although policies were influenced by past traditions, their results could not be anticipated in advance. By 1922, for instance, German
officials had begun to realize they could not pay for the welfare perfec-
tion they had envisioned as the Republic's showpiece. Unfortunately, the
Labor Ministry's change of heart came too late. Not only had the hyperinflation dramatically reduced the funds available for charity, but the
critical moment of thanksgiving had passed.

German soldiers lying in hospital during the war repeatedly heard that
"the thanks of the Fatherland was assured to them," while Lloyd George
pledged their British counterparts "a fit land for heroes to live in." In
neither country did the promised land come to pass, though one might
argue that Weimar's officials approached their task with more determi-
nation than was ever evident in Whitehall. After the toll that the First
World War had exacted, a land fit for heroes was an impossibility. The
Fatherland's thanks, however, was not. Richard Bessel has argued that
German citizens were eager to express their gratitude, and that it was
the soldiers, in many cases, who resisted their overtures.[44] Yet state policies ensured that the public's thanks was expressed less often than would
otherwise have been the case. If the land fit for heroes could become just
another broken promise, the Fatherland's gratitude proved, in the end,
not as negligible.

This book is divided into two parts, both comparative. Part I examines
parallel developments: in Britain, the evolution of a voluntarist system
for the care of disabled veterans; in Germany, the extension of state control over war victims' care. Each trajectory fostered, I will argue, a specific
brand of veterans' politics. Chapter 1 shows that despite considerable
public pressure to meet veterans' demands, the British state consistently
failed to fulfill its obligations to the nation's heroes. Civil servants in the
Ministry of Pensions left the tasks of rehabilitation and employment to
voluntary effort, with the result that veterans' organizations demanded
less, not more, from the negligent state. Chapter 2 analyzes the origins
and the consequences of the German state's monopoly on benevolence
for the disabled. To gain the loyalty of war victims, the Weimar state
sought to eliminate philanthropic competition, as well as to distribute the
best benefits possible. Yet, as the result of the regulation of charity, the
state came to the shoulder the full burden of the Fatherland's thanks.

Part II considers how individual veterans fared in Great Britain and Germany. Measures that preserved social peace came at the cost of individuals' lives. Chapter 3 demonstrates that in Britain individual ex-servicemen bore the burden of their country's policies of retrenchment. The British government's refusal to require the compulsory employment of the disabled condemned them to a marginal existence. Compared with their European counterparts, disabled veterans in Britain enjoyed few legal rights. Denied training, state-secured employment, and dependents' allowances, many found themselves reliant on charity. Although the charitable public championed the veterans' cause, philanthropy did little more than rescue men from penury; it did not secure their reintegration into society. Philanthropists had their own investment in the disabled: they sought to preserve a particular vision of the war's aftermath, in which courage allowed even the worst-off the possibility for cheerful survival. Excluded from victory parades, employed in segregated workshops, hidden away in homes on the outskirts of towns, disabled veterans lived literally, as well as figuratively, on the edges of their society.

While British veterans existed at the periphery of their society, unhappy reminders of a time best forgotten, the Weimar state's programs reintegrated the German disabled into the economy. As chapter 4 shows, the state provided even the severely incapacitated with the hallmarks of masculine independence. Beginning in 1920, the Law of the Severely Disabled ensured that disabled veterans remained in work even as millions of their able-bodied contemporaries lost their jobs. As the welfare state's favored wards, disabled veterans stood at the center of political life. They achieved a prominence unknown in Britain. Reports about their organizations and demonstrations appeared in newspapers of every political stripe. Politicians, centrist and extreme, courted them as a valuable constituency. They had the right to make demands on the state and to express their dissatisfaction. A source of comfort to the individual, their discontent was more than the Weimar Republic could bear.

PART I

Civil Society in the Great War's Aftermath

CHAPTER I

A Voluntary Peace

British Veterans, Philanthropy,
and the State

Everyone was in it [the war], and as a consequence you have
a public conscience, very much alive, and an alert press, and
thousands of the nation who are directly concerned in seeing
that the maimed soldier gets a fair do. In former wars the
broken skeletons of military service might be safely ignored
or permitted to creep to the workhouse without anyone
bothering very much. Times are different nowadays. The
community will not permit the war-shattered soldier to be
harshly treated.

> "Talk for the Times,"
> *Glasgow Evening Times,* 21 July 1919

At the same time every year, from 1919 to 1934, Miss Hilda Monamy King
mailed a donation of 1s. 6d. to the London War Seal Mansions for Disabled Ex-Servicemen. Miss King's check was a small one, in fact, one of
the most modest subscriptions that the War Seal Mansions received. By the
standards of the time it was trifling; by those of ours it may hardly seem
worth consideration. Miss King left no records about why she sent the
money every January. Perhaps the donation was her own private way of remembering someone who had died. It is also possible that she saw her
check, small though it was, as a payment against a debt of honor, a way of
doing her bit for the boys who went to the front. The fact that the checks
came so regularly, but that the amount never increased, suggests that Miss
King lived on a limited income; maybe she was a schoolteacher or a help-
meet to her ailing father or a seamstress who could not afford to contribute
as much as she would have liked. She probably gave until she died.[1]

In her impulse, Miss King resembled millions of other private citizens,
many of whom were more leisured or wealthier than she and hence gave
more. Reconstruction after the First World War was not solely the state's

task, though scholars have tended to approach the problem this way.[2] In the years that followed the Armistice, members of the British public did their part in the recovery as in the war, devoting spare hours to clubs for the unemployed and settlements of the neurasthenic, rest homes on behalf of widows and crèches for infants.[3] Most prominent among voluntarism's accomplishments was reconstruction in the literal sense: the care of the million men who returned home disabled by injury or disease. In the Great War's aftermath, philanthropists controlled every major initiative on behalf of disabled ex servicemen. Sent to London in 1927 to investigate British provisions for the war's victims, one German veteran (and Social Democrat) marveled at the voluntarists' success. For every enterprise he toured there were, he reported, many others like it all over the country: "It is impossible to outdo the goodness of this work."[4]

The predominance of British philanthropy reflected the state's failure to provide adequately for the disabled. While the German observer applauded charitable efforts, their provenance was not lost on him. "Because the state has refused to provide social welfare for veterans," he commented, "the care of the disabled…has become a job for charity."[5] Although all political parties advocated generous treatment for the war's victims, successive British governments—Labour as well as Conservative—limited the state's liability for the disabled, as for the unemployed.[6] Fearful of committing the state to open-ended expenditure, civil servants in the newly founded Ministry of Pensions aimed to delegate whatever tasks they could to voluntary effort. At issue was not simply the stranglehold that the powerful interwar Treasury, concerned above all to balance the budget after colossal wartime deficits, exercised over individual ministries' spending.[7] Just as significant, I will argue, was a philosophical reluctance on the part of prominent civil servants to involve the state in seemingly intractable social problems. Forced by wartime public opinion to finance disability pensions entirely from the Exchequer, civil servants in the Ministry of Pensions, allied with their colleagues in the Treasury, sought to restrict the state's responsibility for rehabilitation and employment.

Unlike in Germany, where the Weimar state sought to restore disabled men to the economic position they had held before the war, most British officials argued that the state had acquitted its obligations through the distribution of pensions. Interwar British governments refused to sanction any compulsory employment program, even for the severely disabled.[8] With more than 100,000 disabled ex-servicemen among the more than 2 million unemployed in 1921, Sir Robert Horne, chancellor of the

Exchequer in Lloyd George's postwar Coalition government, defended a policy of inaction: "It should be observed that so far as the grievance of these men is that they cannot find employment, their case is not different at the present time from that of an unprecedented number of other men and women, who do not draw pensions from the State."[9] Disabled ex-servicemen, in other words, were entitled only to a gratuity in respect of their injury; the state was not obliged to ensure the man's reintegration into society. Of all the major belligerent European states, only Great Britain relied on voluntary effort to employ disabled ex-servicemen.

A poor substitute for state assistance, the public's charity left a permanent mark on British ex-servicemen. British veterans were not revolutionaries, but their fellow citizens' benevolence, I will argue, helped to ensure their moderation. However much the disabled ex-serviceman distrusted the Ministry of Pensions or the government or the state, he believed the charitable public had done its best by him. The sums raised to build the Star and Garter Home for Disabled Sailors and Soldiers, the Roehampton Hospital, the War Seal Mansions, Lord Roberts Memorial Workshops, though insufficient to care for the majority of disabled men, nonetheless testified to the public's goodwill.[10] The literary lights of the 1920s and 1930s took as an article of faith the ex-serviceman's hostility to his fellow citizens, but it is doubtful this sentiment, which so aptly expressed modernism's disdain for the public, was broadly shared.[11] What anger disabled men expressed after the war was directed against the state, usually the Ministry of Pensions, rarely against their families, almost never against the public at large. To be sure, the Home Front could not understand what soldiers had endured in the trenches. However, that did not prevent devoted contributors like Miss Hilda Monamy King from helping them to rebuild their lives. Most men appreciated the distinction. They had not wanted charity, of course, but the state left them with little choice.[12] An aluminum leg was infinitely better than a wooden one, especially delivered in the name of the grateful public.

Alone among their European counterparts, British veterans retreated from politics. Neither the British Union of Fascists nor the Communist-inspired National Unemployed Workers' Movement succeeded in recruiting significant numbers of ex-servicemen to their cause.[13] Eschewing demonstrations and protests, the country's largest veterans' organization, the British Legion, placed its trust in the grateful public. Presented in 1929 with a resolution that asked the government to match receipts from its annual Armistice Day collection, delegates at the Legion's annual conference found themselves in a discussion about what their state and society could provide. The generosity of the public was unbounded, they agreed, whereas the state gave only if it got something in return. According to this logic, there was no choice but to reject the resolution, which they did. "They did not want charity from the Government," claimed the delegate from Duncannon, speaking on behalf of his comrades. "At present their funds were obtained from the benevolent British public, and so long as they supported the Legion they should not ask the Government for anything. When the public failed them, the Empire, and not only the Government would fall. (Hear, hear.)"[14]

This chapter explores the making of social peace in the Great War's aftermath. An analysis of the symbolic politics of gratitude, it assesses the significance of voluntarism for the course of the British veterans' movement and, by extension, the stability of interwar Britain. The first section of this chapter examines how the state's neglect of the disabled scandalized a society mobilized for war, considering especially the importance of public opinion in forcing Lloyd George's government to acknowledge full responsibility for pensions. The second section assesses efforts by Ministry of Pensions officials to delegate the provision of employment for the severely disabled to voluntary enterprise. In an era often seen as critical to the development of the modern welfare state, voluntarism proved a more significant force than is generally acknowledged. Not only did philanthropists take the lead in caring for disabled veterans, but their efforts provided the most tangible evidence of the public's appreciation. The third section offers an interpretation of the veterans' movement, and especially the British Legion, asking how the conviction that the public was on "their" side reconciled ex-servicemen to the established order.[15]

A LAND FIT FOR HEROES

Even before 1914, the beggared soldier was much more than a symbolic figure in Britain. Unlike in Germany, where the veterans of 1870–1871 were, on the whole, reasonably well provided for, most Britons could personally testify to the neglect of the disabled. Medals pinned to a tattered uniform, emptiness where an arm or leg had been: the man people remembered was the same. He sold matches, he told hard-luck stories, he begged to keep his family from the workhouse. These were the heroes of wars gone by, the Crimea, the Boer, relics of the military engagements that most Britons could afford to ignore. Not this man: he gave the lie to recruiting promises, he denied the fruits of victory. Like so many others, the music-hall impresario and philanthropist Oswald Stoll remembered him too well. "People with 'vision' have been hurt by the spectacle over and over again," Stoll confessed. "It has hurt me more than I would trust myself to say in a spoken word, and even to write of it gives me pain too sincere for ordinary expressions."[16]

The war that began in August 1914 promised a "spectacle," as Stoll put it, of a different sort. Public opinion, the wartime British press left no doubt, considered disabled men the state's responsibility, to be treated without stinginess or delay. Within a year of the war's outbreak, however, the hopes raised on recruiting platforms had been dashed. Prime Minister H. H. Asquith's Liberal government, in power since 1906 and responsible in the prewar years for the dramatic extension of social services financed by national taxation, had shirked its responsibility to the disabled. According to a 1915 leader in the *Morning Post,* "The principle undoubtedly approved by the nation is that the disabled sailor and soldier are the care of the State, and that the State should ensure their welfare and comfort for the remainder of their lives. The official practice is very different. It consists in trying to discover how little the State can do without incurring popular odium."[17] The formation of a Coalition government under Asquith in May 1915, after a succession of well-publicized scandals, did not improve matters. In June 1916, a tabloid expressed the same frustration as the *Morning Post* had a year earlier, only more intemperately: "The nation doesn't grudge the money. It is determined to save itself from the shame and disgrace that attended all the old wars. It is in an angry mood with tapeworms and bureaucrats who thwart its pity and baffle its sympathy."[18]

Despite the government's extravagant recruiting promises, the British state was woefully unprepared to meet the needs of discharged soldiers. Unlike France and Germany, which had long maintained conscripted armies, soldiers in Britain were paid volunteers treated as lives at the service of the state. According to the Royal Warrant of 1834, which still governed compensation at the outbreak of the Great War, pensions were conferred as a matter of royal favor, not as a legal right.[19] The distinction was important: until men were guaranteed a statutory right to a pension in 1919, they had no law-binding claim on the state, nor could they appeal to a neutral court. The medical invaliding boards that decided pensions were infamously harsh and tended to look on the men who came before them as shirkers intent upon a life at the expense of the public purse. Not that such a retirement would have allowed them to live high on the

hog; pensions were very low, calculated only to keep a man from destitution, and failed to make provision for his dependents.

To the badly injured soldier who returned home after the first Battle
of the Marne in the fall of 1914, it may have seemed that despite all of
the lofty pledges, his fate would not be much different from that of Rud-
yard Kipling's neglected Tommy: "It's Tommy this, and Tommy that, and
Tommy, go away, But it's 'Thank you, Mr. Atkins,' when the band begins to play." Not only were rates stingy and medical examining boards
intransigent, but the administration of pensions was itself a muddle. At
the beginning of the Great War, no less than four official bodies shared
responsibility for the disabled: the War Office, the Chelsea Commissioners, the Admiralty Commissioners (for naval pensions), and the
Royal Patriotic Fund Corporation. The War Office was charged with the
task of caring for army officers and their widows, as well as for the widows of ordinary soldiers, while the navy took care of its own in the Admiralty. The small staff at Chelsea, still operating out of quarters dating
from the seventeenth century, administered pensions for army men of all
other ranks in tandem with the Royal Patriotic Corporation, a voluntary
fund originally established during the Crimean War by the *Times of London*, which provided small supplementary grants to those in need. Even
in clear-cut cases, disabled soldiers had to wait months to receive their
pension; rehabilitation was not one of Chelsea's responsibilities.[20]

But what had been good enough for the "old army" would not at all
do for the 2.4 million volunteers recruited during the first two years of the
war. Even before conscription, introduced by Asquith beginning in January 1916, fundamentally changed the relation of the British state to its
male citizens, public opinion had called for a dramatic overhaul of the
pensions system. "To-day things are quite different," one reporter explained in 1915. "We have an altogether new interest in and new view of
the Army; our lads, our girls' boys, our neighbours' lads, our lads' friends
have gone either to the Front or prepare for going, and never again will
we be parties to the old brutal treatment of men who cheerfully volun-
teered to do and die for those of us who have to remain behind."[21] "Our
lads" could not be sent before medical examining boards that even the
former director-general of Army Medical Services described as "perhaps
somewhat hard," noting that they had "frequently" refused pensions to
men later recognized as deserving.[22] Nor, for that matter, could one of
"our lads" survive on the pittance paid to the army's severely wounded.
The discovery late in 1914 that the totally disabled pensioner received
only 17s. 6d. (and this at a time when a flank of beef cost 7d., a quart of

milk nearly 4d., and the average working-class expenditure on food *before* the war had run to 23s. 9d. a week) provoked outrage among those who had formerly ignored "the old brutal treatment."[23]

In spite of public sentiment on behalf of the disabled, Asquith's Coalition government refused to accept full responsibility for veterans' compensation. The government's reluctance was, in part, financial; with all casualty estimates far exceeded by the war's second year and a soaring national debt, the Exchequer was unwilling to commit to what appeared an infinitely expanding charge.[24] Just as significantly, however, officials regarded supplementary pensions as an appropriate sphere for local government and private charities, which despite the expansion of central government from the 1880s onward continued to provide key services. Beginning in 1915, the government endorsed the compromise solution put forth by the Select Committee on Pensions: a centralized pensions apparatus funded, in part, by voluntary contributions. In early 1916, the Naval and Military War Pensions Bill unified the pensions administration under the aegis of the Statutory Committee of the Royal Patriotic Fund. Charged with the duty of setting up Local War Pensions Committees in each county and large town, the Statutory Committee was to provide disabled men, widows, and orphans with treatment, rehabilitative training, and supplementary cash payments.[25]

By the summer of 1916, over 1,200 Local War Pensions Committees had been founded, a definite improvement except for the fact that their funding remained under dispute. The Coalition government had intended that the local committees survive on voluntary funds that they were to incorporate or collect, a solution that radical members of Parliament, along with the House of Lords, had opposed without success. Shortly after the formation of the Local Committees, however, twenty of the largest and wealthiest boroughs refused to finance supplementary assistance, claiming that it was the duty of the state and that they either could not or would not raise the money.[26] As Sir Archibald Salvidge, lord mayor of Liverpool, declared, "It was the sacred duty of the State to make adequate provision for all such cases.... Parliament should be asked to take the responsibility, and not to shoulder a national duty upon private philanthropy and charity."[27] Faced with widespread dissension, Parliament granted the Statutory Committee a million pounds on the condition that Local Committees also solicit donations and draw on county funds.

Although Asquith evidently hoped that Local War Pensions Committees would rally support for a local solution to the war victims problem, the opposite was true. The committees contributed to the general sense that primary responsibility rested with the central government. Convened by the mayor of the town and directed by men and (more often) women prominent in local voluntary work and politics, Local Committees were supposed to represent "all sides of local life," including delegates from the local council, employers, trade union representatives, philanthropists, and, from 1919 on, ex-servicemen themselves, in addition to a large number of volunteers who helped with everything from casework to soliciting donations.[28] The spirit that prevailed, especially in the larger towns, was the voluntary one, although as was frequently the case in Edwardian Britain, charitable and local political interests were often represented by the same person. The imposing secretary of the Birmingham War Pensions Committee, Ethel Shakespear, for example, came to her post by way of a place on the Citizens' Society and the local chairmanship of the private Soldiers' and Sailors' Families Association.[29]

If anything, the founding of the Local War Pensions Committees fueled, not quelled, public indignation. In a matter of months, the number of private citizens who understood war victims' problems had multiplied at least a hundredfold (between 1916 and 1919, 100,000 voluntary workers sat on or worked with local Committees), and the insight they acquired into Chelsea's modus operandi gave new meaning to the scandals they had read about in the press.[30] Although the Local Committees sought to provide treatment and training, most of their resources during and immediately after the war were devoted to supplementing the inadequate pensions that men received upon their discharge. Day after day, committee volunteers saw the misery that the pensions system had inflicted: one-armed carpenters lacking resources for retraining, widows unable to make ends meet, men ineligible for a pension because their diseases were judged to have been only "aggravated" by and not "attributable" to military service.

By the autumn of 1916, outrage over pensions had become a serious problem for Asquith's Coalition government, already reeling from the Easter Uprising in Dublin and the disastrous battles of the Somme.[31] Not only had Local Committees given tens of thousands of people firsthand knowledge of the scandalous treatment of the disabled, but the government's reluctance to fund their efforts also brought county councils all over the country into conflict with the state. As casualties from the Somme filled the halls of London hospitals, philanthropists stepped up their fund-raising, even while acknowledging that the state would eventually have to intervene. In the summer of 1916, James Hogge, a liberal member of Parliament from Edinburgh, began a much-publicized campaign to force the state to assume full responsibility for pensions. "The whole question of disablement pensions...was in a chaotic state, and the gravest dissatisfaction existed in the country," remembered Sir Arthur Griffith-Boscawen, first parliamentary secretary to the newly created Ministry of Pensions, which opened its doors in February 1917.[32]

Although it soon became the target of widespread hostility, the Ministry of Pensions, legislated as one of the first innovations of David Lloyd George's Coalition government, was actually a significant concession to public opinion. After dislodging Asquith in December 1916, Lloyd George—viewed as the man most likely to win the war on the strength of a brilliant performance at the Ministry of Munitions and the War Office—moved swiftly to reorganize the government. To gain Labour Party backing for his government, he agreed to create two new departments: the Ministry of Pensions and the Ministry of Labour. In the spring of 1917, the Statutory Committee dissolved itself, and the Ministry of Pensions took over the welfare duties that had formerly belonged to the War Office, Chelsea Commissioners, and the Admiralty. As stipulated in the Ministry of Pensions Bill, the Local War Pensions Committees were retained as the Ministry's agents in the countryside and were granted Parliamentary funding, a provision the Treasury later deplored. Although the Local Committees nominally came under the Ministry's control, they functioned in large measure independently, continuing to pay out allowances, handle appeals, and provide supplementary medical treatment and training until 1921.

By establishing a central ministry for the victims of the war, Lloyd George's Coalition acknowledged the state's responsibility to the disabled soldier and sailor. Yet as was the case with previous improvements, the creation of the Ministry of Pensions seemed to cause more dissatisfaction than it allayed. That was, of course, to some extent inevitable, if only because the Ministry drew all the criticism formerly shared among four separate bodies. However, the problem proved more serious: the Ministry's own administration was a shambles. Not only had the Statutory Committee and Chelsea bequeathed the new department stacks of unsorted claims, but also between 1917 and 1919 applications for pensions poured in faster than they could be sorted, let alone filled. Describing his first month in office, John Hodge, the second minister of pensions, echoed Griffith-Boscawen's judgment of a year before: "Very quickly I made the discovery that the administration of pensions was in a terrible mess," commenting particularly on the Lost Files Room with its tens of thousands of incomplete claims.[33] Until 1921, missing records and unanswered requests were common occurrences, and many disabled ex-servicemen had to wait a year or more to receive word about their pensions.[34]

Delays were damaging enough to the new department's reputation. Several public embarrassments only served to confirm the widespread suspicion that the state neglected its duties whenever possible. The most infamous involved George Barnes, the first minister of pensions and one of three Labour ministers in the Coalition government. Although Barnes managed to implement two of the most-requested pensions reforms during his ten months in office, his term was disgraced by an offhand comment that he made in Parliament.[35] Asked why the government refused to grant full pensions to men whose disability was aggravated by military service, he described some of the recruits as "veritable weeds," a widely disparaged pronouncement that he soon had cause to regret.[36] When the Ministry was not giving itself a black eye, there were plenty of prominents waiting in the wings to do it for them, including Field Marshal Earl Haig, who denounced pensions officers as ungenerous, incompetent, and ignorant, and let it be known that he refused to accept a viscountcy until the state took on more responsibility for the disabled.[37]

For officials at the Ministry of Pensions, there could be no doubt that the public had sided with the disabled ex-serviceman in his grievance against the state. Not only did private citizens deluge the Ministry with letters of complaint, but the civil servants in Whitehall clearly felt under siege, and very fearful of public criticism as a consequence. Ministry files preserved in the Public Record Office are filled with references to "popular sentiment"[38] and "the steps necessary to satisfy public opinion."[39] In their efforts to avoid scandal, the Ministry's officials displayed a remarkable consciousness of public opinion and took no step without first considering how it would play in the press.[40] The uproar over Barnes's comment and similar travesties had made it clear that "public opinion at the present time demands extreme generosity."[41] That meant, according to the Ministry's permanent secretary, Sir Matthew Nathan, it was "important that the Ministry should not appear against an applicant, and, to a certain extent, it was better to expend some money than to have the appearance of taking that attitude."[42]

As the case of "aggravated ailments" demonstrates, hostile public opinion could force the Ministry's hand. For the first two years of the war, servicemen discharged because of prewar illnesses were denied pensions. Despite evidence to the contrary, Chelsea's medical boards nearly always dismissed certain categories of disease, primary among them tuberculosis and rheumatism, as preexisting conditions, a prejudice that left men whose bodies had broken down in the waist-deep muck of the trenches without any claim on the state. In June 1916, largely in response to the public outcry, a Royal Warrant introduced a new category for illnesses "aggravated" by military service, which were to be compensated by an award equal to four-fifths of the pension normally granted for the condition. However, even that amendment did not quiet the government's critics, who demanded that a man receive the full pension—a provision that the Ministry of Pensions' Royal Warrant of 1917 finally granted.

Awarding full pensions for conditions not directly caused by military service was less a question of justice than an attempt to placate public opinion. In late 1916, the Ministry's predecessor in the Board of Pensions recommended the change, acknowledging that "the difficulty with these cases [of aggravated disease] is largely one of sentiment. The public which has heard something of the hardships of training...will simply not believe the medical verdict, and if the man is refused a pension on these grounds he will be regarded as a martyr. On grounds of policy, therefore, it would be cheap for the State to buy off the grievance."[43] However, for J. A. Flynn, the Ministry's first financial officer, and hence responsible to the Treasury, the revised warrant was a distressing example of the way that "public agitation" had obliterated the "distinction between compensation and charity," and he added: "I have had nearly 34 years in the public service, and I have met with no instance of such an indefensible expenditure of public money as this paragraph of our regulations leads to."[44]

Throughout the war and early years of the peace, the Ministry of Pensions sought to improve its image with the country at large. This was never more true than in 1918, when John Hodge, leader of the steel smelters' union and the first minister of labour, succeeded fellow Labourite George Barnes as minister of pensions.[45] A showman who preferred public appearances to desk work at the Ministry, Hodge viewed his department's poor reputation as a challenge to his ingenuity.[46] His methods were novel: within his first months at the Ministry he had commissioned press photographs, hosted a dinner for 250 reporters to woo the newspapers, and hired a publicity agent "who happened to be an ex–House of Commons reporter."[47] These stunts paled in comparison to what came later. In early 1918, he commissioned a film touting the Ministry with himself in the leading role, which was shown in every picture house in the United Kingdom.

Neither Hodge's keen sense for public relations nor his liberal interpretation of the Royal Warrants could redeem the state's reputation for
stinginess, a fact that he indirectly acknowledged when he stumped the
country boasting that he had been accused of acting ultra vires (outside
of the law) by the Public Accounts Committee.[48] In 1919, the Ministry's
reputation stood at its nadir. On 16 May a demonstration by disabled
veterans and their supporters in Hyde Park turned violent when police
erected barricades. In June, a Select Committee convened by Parliament
heard evidence on the administration of pensions, and the Ministry—
attacked by the Treasury for uncontrolled spending and by the country
at large for miserliness—received a public hiding from critics of all persuasions.[49] That summer, the *Times* joined the legion of faultfinders,
claiming that the "pensions muddle grows worse instead of better" and
accusing the Ministry of Pensions of displaying "the kind of attitude
which views a pensioner as a beggar at the gate."[50]

The Royal Warrant issued late in 1919 over Treasury objections reme-
died some of the worst injustices—making pensions a statutory right, in-
troducing appeals tribunals, and increasing rates—but it also made clear
the limits of state responsibility for the reintegration of disabled veterans.
The state would provide ex-servicemen with pensions, training allowances, and, for a limited time, a noncontributory "out-of-work donation" to tide over the unemployed, but it guaranteed little else.[51] Although the minister of pensions acknowledged the amount of the pension
"could never really be sufficient" to allow men to return to the standard
of living they had enjoyed before the war, neither the central office nor
the Local War Pensions Committees had taken the necessary steps to develop the retraining programs they knew were required.[52] The Local Employment Committees set up alongside the pensions committees in early
1918 had accomplished next to nothing.[53] As demobilization proceeded
apace and hospitals closed their doors, tens of thousands of disabled ex-
servicemen returned home uncertain how they would earn a living.

However unsatisfactory the pensions situation was, the state of vocational training and employment was still worse. The chaos in the pensions system had left the Ministry's officials with little inclination to
tackle the complicated problems that training programs presented. By
February 1919, the Ministry of Pensions had trained only 11,000 men.[54]
That month, the Ministry of Pensions transferred responsibility for this
area to the Ministry of Labour, but with little apparent improvement.
Not only were the civil servants there completely unprepared to carry
out the task, but those disabled men who had found jobs in the flush im-

mediate postwar economy were reportedly reluctant to abandon steady work for an uncertain course of rehabilitation. As its chief officer James Currie acknowledged in his testimony before the Select Committee on Pensions, progress in the program's first ten months had been "disappointingly slow," a fact that he blamed on the Treasury's obstruction, noting that with all the paperwork the government could not act quickly enough to buy suitable buildings.[55] In July 1919, Currie reported that of the 80,000 places the Training Department required, it had only 15,000 at its disposal.[56] Nearly four months later, the Ministry was training a mere 13,000 men, and 20,000 stood on its waiting lists; Curry estimated that at least 40,000 more were eligible and would come if the department advertised vacancies.[57]

In comparison with the Continental states, the British government did not rate as a priority the return of disabled men to the workforce. Acting on the assumption of a postwar labor surplus, officials delayed the establishment of training programs and looked to private enterprise to provide employment. Where the sole British wartime report on the subject advocated only "public or private appeals to employers to hire ex-servicemen," most of the German states had, by 1916, established employment bureaus for disabled men, as well as a number of rehabilitation and retraining programs. Despite the burdens the war had exacted, the French and Belgian states had begun even earlier; experts in the field cited as a model the settlement at Port-Villez that prepared men to return to work.[58] For the delegates who attended the inter-Allied conference on the "After-Care of Disabled Men," rehabilitation, training, and employment, not pensions, were of central concern.[59] Yet in Britain, the end of the war found the Coalition government—awash in high-minded reconstruction schemes for social reform—with practically no plans for this purpose, a state of affairs that led one philanthropist to warn of the "formation of an army of cripples in the country."[60]

While the next two years witnessed improvements in Britain's retraining program, the Ministry of Labour could not restore lost time. The second-largest interwar governmental department, the Ministry of Labour was charged with responsibility for industrial relations and unemployment relief; its capacity to stimulate employment was limited.[61] Between 1919 and 1921, the Ministry's Training Department established fifty-two instructional facilities. Yet hardly had the training scheme been implemented when the country sank into a severe trade depression in the autumn of 1920. Fearing an influx of disabled workers into already ravaged trades, union representatives restricted the numbers of new men admitted for training.[62] With so many healthy men out of work, the Ministry of Labour could not place those men who had already been trained in the "improverships" necessary for employment. While the Ministry eventually trained 82,000 men in receipt of a pension (most of whom were not severely disabled), it is doubtful that more than half of these found work in their trades. Citing the difficulty in placing men in improverships and employment, the Ministry of Labour closed the waiting list for training in September 1921, with an estimated 100,000 disabled ex-servicemen unemployed.

Although administrative disarray and the heavy hand of the Treasury undoubtedly contributed to what Sir Montagu Barlow, the chairman of the Select Committee on Pensions, called this "sad if not alarming state of affairs," the immediate postwar years illustrate what tasks—the employment of severely disabled men primary among them—the British government preferred to pass off to the generous public and voluntary organizations.[63] Scholars have rightly faulted the Treasury and the budgetary ax wielded in 1921–1922 by Sir Eric Geddes's Committee on National Expenditure for the failure of British reconstruction programs, but civil servants within the individual ministries also bore responsibility.[64] The civil servants who made policy in the Ministry of Pensions viewed it as their duty to avoid those commitments that could be handed over to charitable institutions. Their counterparts at the Ministry of Labour, recipients of "this heritage of woe," recognized that the state could not rely on "enthusiastic peeresses" alone, but they found their hands tied by the Treasury's reluctance to incur capital expenditure, as well as "the awful mess and chaos" they had inherited from the Ministry of Pensions.[65] As a result, the Ministry of Labour, too, came to depend on voluntary organizations far more than originally planned.

In an era often characterized in terms of the expansion of central government, the case of disabled ex-servicemen demonstrates that the ethos and practice of voluntarism remained important far longer than generally acknowledged. Not only did the institutions founded by philanthropists serve as models for the government's own programs, but they also bore a substantial portion of the burden of treatment, training, and employment, especially for the severely disabled. In many cases, those ex-servicemen to whom the state ostensibly owed the most—the paralyzed, the armless, the insane, the tubercular—instead found themselves dependent on the public's philanthropy. Yet as the next two sections shall suggest, the state's abdication of responsibility had a paradoxical effect. A serious blow for the individual ex-serviceman and his family, it nonetheless provided an opportunity for voluntarists. In 1919, the stage was set for a reconciliation between a public eager to demonstrate its gratitude and a veterans' movement looking for proof that their fellow citizens cared.

THE VOLUNTARISTS TAKE CHARGE

In October 1919, the third minister of pensions, Sir Laming Worthington-Evans, traveled to the Village Centre in the town of Enham near Andover. Founded in early 1917 by a committee of philanthropists led by the Quaker physician, Fortescue Fox, the Enham colony had received its first settlers shortly after the Armistice. By the time of Worthington-Evans's visit, the program of concurrent medical treatment and training that Fox had adapted from the Belgian and French models was in full swing, and the pensions minister's visit was as much a fact-finding mission as an official sanction for the new enterprise. Although rates had just been raised, Worthington-Evans—a Conservative in Lloyd George's Conservative-dominated postwar Coalition government—admitted that pensions "could never really be sufficient," acknowledging that "what the men wanted was not merely monetary compensation, but the opportunity to live their lives again." In conclusion, he noted, "They might ask what the Government was doing; well, the Government was doing something, but voluntary action could do so much more."[66]

The pensions minister's statement was not merely a cynical attempt to convince his audience of the virtues of retrenchment—the byword of a Coalition government that between 1920 and 1922 presided over the demise of proposals for social reform.[67] More immediately, Worthington-Evans provided an accurate description of care for disabled veterans at the end of the war. In 1918, nearly every prominent initiative for the long-term treatment or rehabilitation of disabled servicemen was in private hands, including the country's largest artificial limb–fitting center at Roehampton and St. Dunstan's Hostel, which provided care for the nation's war-blinded men.[68] One newspaper chided the government that a privately supported institution such as Enham was "so far ahead that it is doubtful if the Ministry could overtake it."[69] In settlements such as Enham and Preston Hall, through the ten local Lord Roberts Workshops, or in factories such as Bernard Oppenheimer's diamond-cutting plant in Brighton, voluntarists had taken charge of all organized employment for severely disabled men. Every home for the totally disabled relied on the public's charity.

The ambitious and successful philanthropic initiatives of the years 1915 to 1919 owed their existence to the government's persistent refusal to accept full responsibility for the disabled. Unlike the state, individual philanthropists welcomed the challenges that the war provided, and, once the specter of another generation of decorated beggars threatened, they found a public eager to support their efforts.[70] Most of the War Seal Foundation's donors undoubtedly agreed with its secretary that "it is not for us to allow these men to drift into slums and Workhouses, simply because we consider that their case is one only for the War Office."[71] By the winter of 1916, the coffers of charities were overflowing.[72] In just six months (July to November 1916), the British Women's Hospital Committee raised £150,000 to build a home for paralyzed men.[73] Despite competition from other wartime charities, both the War Seal Mansions founded by Oswald Stoll for disabled men and their families and the Roehampton limb-fitting center raised £100,000 from public subscriptions in the year 1917.[74]

These were unprecedentedly successful campaigns, all the more remarkable for the fact that they happened during the war, when most families' weekly budgets allowed for little extravagance and even the well-to-do struggled under the weight of a dramatically increased income tax.[75] In the popular press, the philanthropic effort, like the war, was presented as an emphatically national affair, and charities rushed to demonstrate that their support came from members of all classes. Their fund-raising campaigns provided a suitable means of contribution for every income level so that all segments of the population could participate. The generous sum of £2,000 allowed wealthy donors to endow a room at the Star and Garter, in exchange for which they received a commemorative bronze tablet affixed to the door, as well as the privilege of corresponding with their room's present inhabitant.[76] While endowing a room was clearly out of the question for all but the most prosperous, even the poorest of schoolchildren could afford the "Jack Cornwell" penny stamp that the hospital sold to build a ward named after the boy-hero of the Jutland.

Charities succeeded in building a broad base of support for their objectives. Among the poorer, as among the wealthier members of society, philanthropic campaigns were well received. Most donors gave less than £2; sales of £17,000 in 1917 indicate that many people seem to have caught the "War Seal habit," as Oswald Stoll's propaganda had urged (one woman wrote to thank him for "providing a 'way' for hum-drum people with no splendid gifts to give").[77] In 1918, the Star and Garter's

Figure 1.   An advertising poster for the War Seal Foundation. Undated. By
kind permission of the Sir Oswald Stoll Mansions.

Jack Cornwell fund raised £35,000 from over 7 million schoolchildren.[78]
Among those who sent along 1.12.0 were the "Laundry Girls" at the
Saint Helena's Home in West Ealing, who reported that they had earned
the money from recreation work in their spare time, and asked for a picture of Cornwell.[79] One small boy hand delivered his pocket money directly to the home, accompanied by a note that asked the recipient to
"please forgive the pennies he wouldn't let us change them I think he
feels the pennies are of more value."[80]

Feelings of gratitude, sorrow, and occasionally guilt inspired most
contributions. The safe return of a beloved son or husband occasioned

many a donation, while others not so fortunate commemorated their loss with the naming of a room. There were also those, such as Lady Wantage, whose gift was more self-referential; the rooms she endowed at the Star and Garter and Roehampton were intended as memorials to herself. Many of the smaller contributions that charities received were anonymous, often signed only "One who is grateful."[81] Women made up the majority of donors small and large, but men—especially those too old to fight—contributed, too. "I am just over the age," wrote one man, an architect, "but I would like to help in any cause that makes life more bearable for those, who have fought and suffered so horribly."[82] More often than not, donations arrived cloaked in the noncombatant's language of duty rather than grace.[83]

Rare was the disabled ex-serviceman who, by the end of the war, had not come into contact with some form of charitable enterprise. For the blind, those with amputated limbs, the paralyzed, the unemployed, and the neurasthenic, voluntary schemes proved crucial. At St. Dunstan's in London, the businessman Arthur Pearson (who had himself lost his sight as a young man) offered training and employment to every one of Great Britain's more than 2,000 blinded soldiers. Early in the war, Pearson had developed a comprehensive program that began with the soldier's hospitalization and continued until his death. Before his discharge from the hospital, every blinded soldier in the United Kingdom received a braille watch courtesy of Pearson and an invitation to receive training at St. Dunstan's. Those who accepted Pearson's offer—and nearly 70 percent of all blinded did—received instruction in occupations and trades, such as basket weaving or stenography, deemed suitable to their condition and background. Once the men had completed training, St. Dunstan's helped them to find jobs, provided a market for the goods they produced at home, and employed an After-Care Department to follow their progress.[84]

The largest rehabilitation center for amputees was the Queen Mary's Auxiliary Hospital at Roehampton. Founded in 1915 by Mrs. Gwynne Holford in response to one man's complaints about the wooden arm he had received from Chelsea, Roehampton developed during the war from a country house operation into the central limb-fitting center for all of England. Here artificial limbs were tested, refined, and maintained; patients carried out much of the labor in the hospital's workshops. More important, their wearers received instruction in everything from eating with an artificial arm to operating heavy machinery with one leg. By the time the Ministry of Pensions took over the hospital in 1920, nearly

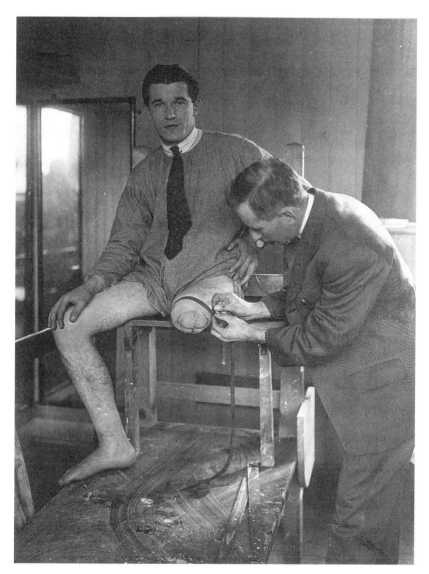

Figure 2.   The fitting for an artificial leg. Roehampton Hospital, undated. By permission of the Imperial War Museum.

20,000 men had received artificial arms and legs at Roehampton and its center at Brighton, 5,000 of whom were placed directly in jobs by the hospital's employment bureau, another 4,166 of whom went on to receive further training.[85]

Totally disabled men depended for their survival on philanthropists. Founded by the Actresses' Franchise League to honor women's contributions to the war effort, the Star and Garter Home for Disabled Sailors and Soldiers served as a memorial as well as a hospital, "a constant reminder of the havoc wrought by the War in countless British homes."[86] In 1916, the first patients, mostly paralyzed and incontinent men who could not be cared for at home, were brought to a once-renowned luxury hotel on Richmond Hill. Under the supervision of Sir Frederick Treves, the King's personal physician, they received expert nursing and massage to relieve the bedsores and circulatory ailments that accompany permanent immobility. By 1936, when the home celebrated its second decade, the Star and Garter had cared for nearly 2,000 "incurables."

The most innovative schemes owed their existence to philanthropy. Oswald Stoll's War Seal Mansions offer a case in point. A theatrical impresario who owned most of the music halls and picture houses in Britain, Stoll recognized that many badly disabled men were happiest at home, with their own families. In 1917, Stoll launched a campaign to build "Homes Fit for Heroes," where purpose-built apartments, as well as a masseur on the premises and a doctor on call, would provide some of the advantages of the hospital while also allowing a man to live in the company of his wife and children. Wide doorways for wheelchairs, elevators, running water, and special washing facilities made it possible for even paraplegics, including a few of the Star and Garter's former residents, to enjoy the comforts of domesticity. As of 1921, the Mansions were home to nearly 200 families, with a waiting list of more than 400.[87]

Voluntarists took the lead in the training and employment of disabled ex-servicemen.[88] What organized employment there was for the disabled in 1918 was privately run, a fact that the government acknowledged by hiring the voluntary Lord Roberts Memorial Workshops to train one-armed men. Founded in 1915 by the Boer War–era Soldiers' and Sailors' Help Society, the London headquarters of Lord Roberts and ten regional branches produced furniture, toys, and metalwork. Lord Roberts' trainees were guaranteed permanent employment in the shops; the highest-skilled among them received trade union wages. By 1918, Lord Roberts employed a total of 1,065 men, relying on donations to make up the difference between salaries and the diminished working capacity of their employees.[89]

Figure 3.   Queen Mary's visit to the War Seal Foundation, 5 June 1919. Sir Oswald Stoll stands to her left. By kind permission of the Sir Oswald Stoll Mansions.

Like Lord Roberts, the Village Centre Council at Enham conducted pioneer work in returning disabled men to work. One of two colonies for disabled veterans (the other was Preston Hall for the tubercular, after 1924 the property of the British Legion), Enham cared for those ex-servicemen who could not be accommodated elsewhere, either because they suffered from neurasthenia or because their health broke down under normal working conditions. According to its founder, Enham was to provide training while the man underwent medical treatment, a regime that the civil servants in Whitehall originally opposed as "impractica-ble" but that eventually became standard operating procedure in the Ministry of Pensions' own hospitals.[90] Between 1917 and 1926, 1,050 men settled at Enham, receiving instruction in everything from farming to blacksmithing.[91] About a quarter of those who came to Enham chose to stay there permanently.[92]

Enham, Lord Roberts, the War Seal Mansions, the Star and Garter, Roehampton, and St. Dunstan's were among the best-known charities for the disabled, but there were many more. In 1918, there were 6,000 char-ities for the disabled registered with the Charity Commissioners.[93] In 1936, the Ministry of Pensions compiled a directory listing more than

Figure 4.   Arriving at the "Not Forgotten" Association's annual garden party
at Buckingham Palace, undated. Miss Marta Cunningham, the founder of the
association, stands to the left.

500 war charities still operating on behalf of ex-servicemen and their dependents.[94] In addition to Lord Roberts and the Village Centre Councils,
there were at least twenty-five other workshops for the disabled in operation, including the Brighton diamond factory that Sir Bernard Oppenheimer started with £300,000 of his own money.[95] Severely disabled men
had the most contact with philanthropy; not only were the fourteen
British homes for disabled men privately run, but three national societies
(the "Not Forgotten" Association, Lest We Forget, and the Adair War
Wounded Fund) and countless local ones entertained hospitalized men.
    Whether large or small, these charities shared an emphatically private
quality. Each had been founded during the war, and most drew their
funds from public subscriptions. None were initiated by ex-servicemen's
associations, though the British Legion later assumed control of three.
Although the most prominent institutions, the Star and Garter and
Roehampton chief among them, received some support from long-
established organizations such as the Red Cross or the Soldiers' and
Sailors' Families Association, the impetus for their founding belonged to
individual men and (more often) women. For women, charity work of-

fered a highly visible means of contributing to the war effort, consonant with their roles as mothers, caretakers, and mourners.[96] While a few founders, including Annie Cowdray of the Star and Garter, were important in philanthropic circles before the war, the majority were not. The voluntarism that Worthington-Evans trumpeted so loudly at Enham in 1919 was spearheaded by people who were, for reasons of birth, religion, or occupation, outsiders. Jews, Quakers, members of the theatrical profession, and social climbers, these advocates for the disabled had their own and sometimes unorthodox stakes in the victims of the war.[97]

Through their work, philanthropists laid claim to a particular vision of the war. Voluntarists liked to contrast the "human" element of their initiatives to both the war's reckless disregard for individual life and the state's impersonal bureaucracy. Frustrated by Whitehall's stinginess and lethargy, they regarded the state with suspicion. Some of the "most resentful" of the Ministry of Pensions' critics, wrote the American journalist Katherine Mayo, were to be found among the voluntary workers, who "now and again [are] reduced to pulp by the Ministry's 'inhumanity.'"[98] Fortescue Fox agreed. According to the founder of the Village Centre Council, there was a "certain advantage in such an organization [as Enham] being voluntary, for without wishing to be disrespectful to the Government there was a touch of humanity in private organisations."[99] A few years later, he elaborated: "When an injured man is remaking his future, he wants more than the most benevolent State can give—a friend."[100]

Philanthropists did not see their work as a permanent substitute for government intervention. They were, after all, only private citizens doing their best to deal with the unprecedented problems of total war. Like many of the philanthropists active during the Depression of the 1880s, they urged a greater role for government. Most hoped that the state would copy their institutions, and a few even wanted the government to take over the work they had begun, though this was a minority position. Of the philanthropists discussed, Oswald Stoll was probably the most committed to the independence of his endeavor (he refused to apply to the Ministry of Pensions for grants that would have paid for the War Seal residents' treatment). However, he, too, hoped that the state would imitate his scheme. The committee that ran Roehampton was more amenable to state intervention. In 1920, it turned over responsibility for limb fitting to the Ministry of Pensions, while retaining control over the men's hospital treatment in the name of the "charitable public."[101]

As philanthropists recognized, charity was a poor substitute for state intervention. The yields of even the most successful philanthropic campaigns fell far short of the state's disbursements. Without adequate statistics, it is impossible to estimate charitable expenditures on behalf of the disabled, though Constance Braithwaite's careful study of the postwar philanthropic sector suggests a starting point. "It seems probable," Braithwaite observed for the year 1934–1935, "that the amount of receipts and expenditures of the public social services is about 10 times as great as the receipts and expenditures of charitable organizations—on my estimates it is between 8½ and 12½ times as great."[102] Whether, as Braithwaite's calculations would indicate, charitable expenditures for the war's victims averaged £6 million per year throughout the interwar period cannot be quantitatively verified. However, contemporary observers agreed that a disproportionately large amount of money relative to other charitable causes was expended for the disabled.[103] Writing in 1934, Elizabeth Macadam remarked, "Much money available to other purposes before the war was and is still ear-marked for war victims."[104]

Although philanthropists such as Stoll and Fox had no intention of replacing the state or even easing its burden, their successes affected policy. As the Lloyd George Coalition committed to deflationary policies and a steep reduction in government expenditure amid the severe economic slump of 1920–1922, Ministry of Pensions officials asked themselves why the state should become more deeply involved in providing for the disabled when private initiative had produced a Lord Roberts, a St. Dunstan's, and a Roehampton. Institutions that themselves reflected the state's unwillingness to provide for the disabled served to justify further governmental neglect. Nevertheless, the Ministry's civil servants believed that if charity could care for some of the most seriously injured men, then the state should share its duties with the private sector. Never eager to saddle their department with more responsibility, and after 1919 increasingly subject to tightened Treasury control, the Ministry of Pensions' senior officials decided to delegate whatever tasks they could to voluntary initiative.

In one sense, the Ministry's decision made sound financial policy, sparing an Exchequer drained by nearly four and a half years of war from further expenditure, but few outside of Whitehall saw it that way. Local officials, editorial writers, trade unions, and businessmen joined forces in condemning the state's opportunism, especially on the question of remunerative work for the badly disabled. At a 1919 hearing of the parliamentary Select Committee on Pensions, Ethel Shakespear of the Birmingham Local War Pensions Committee chastised the government for its failure to provide employment, claiming that "the State has failed to make the most of its opportunities and by hesitation—almost amounting to refusal—to incur capital expenditure, has endeavoured to shirk its responsibilities and to throw them on to the generosity of charitably-minded individuals."[105] While it applauded the Enham scheme as a bold start, the *Oxford Times* also reminded its readers: "The State has its duties towards disabled soldiers, and should not be allowed to pass them on to volunteers, however enthusiastic they may be."[106] A few months later, leader writers at the liberal *Manchester Guardian* confessed that they, too, viewed the ranks of voluntary organizations "a little anxiously," and urged "that this great work should be brought under the aegis of the Government."[107]

Because it defined the British state's obligations to its citizens, the question of employment for badly disabled ex-servicemen became one of the more contentious social issues that the government faced in the immediate postwar years. The problem rested on an assessment of responsibility. What were the state's obligations to the victims of the war? Was a pension fair compensation for permanent disability even if, as in the majority of cases, the rates paid were not sufficient to support a man and his family? Or was the state's responsibility even more profound, as most people seem to have believed, extending to an obligation to return the man to the position in civil life he had occupied before the war? The discussion was a theoretical, an economic, and finally a moral one, but its consequences for disabled veterans were eminently practical. Either the state would secure the compulsory employment of tens of thousands of injured men, or it would subject those who had suffered on the nation's behalf to the vagaries of the marketplace and the pity of their fellow citizens.

In marked contrast to Germany and Austria, which beginning in 1919 forced larger firms as well as government offices to hire men with a disability of 50 percent or more as 2 percent of their labor force, successive British governments proved reluctant to implement compulsory solutions of any kind.[108] Given widespread support for the policies of decontrol, the relatively circumscribed scope of central government in prewar Britain, as well as the comparatively minor role that work played in the country's rehabilitation programs, the decision was an uncontroversial one.[109] Even the largest veterans' organizations agreed (at least until the early 1920s) that a voluntary scheme should be tried before the introduction of compulsion.[110] In 1920, the Coalition government unveiled the voluntary King's Roll scheme, which appealed to employers' patriotism to induce them to offer jobs to disabled men.[111] Administered by the Ministry of Labour, the King's Roll attempted to place disabled veterans in employment. Firms whose workforces consisted of at least 5 percent disabled men were permitted to use the King's Roll seal on their letterhead and, as of 1920, were granted preference in obtaining government contracts.[112] To dramatize the plight of unemployed ex-servicemen, local King's Roll Committees printed advertisements, "giving brief details of particularly hard cases" for exhibition on trams, in cinemas, and by sandwich men.[113]

While the King's Roll enjoyed a measure of success, particularly considering its voluntary nature (in 1922, at the peak of the postwar slump, with 18 percent of the labor force unemployed, the Roll boasted 30,000 firms, employing 360,000 disabled), it alone was not enough.[114] However patriotic it was, no profit-making venture could afford to hire or retain men whose disabilities had significantly reduced their productive capacity. Yet most of these men could not survive without work, especially since a significant percentage of them had disabilities rated at less than 50 percent (mostly victims of disease or poison gas).[115] Unlike in Germany, where the assessment of pensions took into consideration a man's earning capacity, the British system awarded compensation based solely on physical disfigurement. Even before the King's Roll came into effect, the Select Committee on Pensions had already become acquainted with the difficulties that these men posed. In response to "repeated demands" for a solution to the problem of such "unemployables," the Ministry of Labour called the Committee on the Employment of Severely Disabled Ex-Servicemen into existence.

Upon hearing evidence in 1920, Committee members acknowledged that they faced a thorny dilemma. They did not, for example, even know how many "class c," or "unemployable," men there were in the country. Estimates ranged from 10,000 to 100,000, and regional figures depended on the calculations, and often also the political orientation of the local Employment Committees.[116] The renegade Labour borough of Poplar rated 15 percent of its disabled men "class c," while the Ministry's own figures for the neighboring district of East Ham put the number at 2 percent. If the scale of the problem was not clear, the range of possible solutions was. Over the course of its deliberations, the Committee considered everything from maintaining the status quo to instituting state-run workshops. Notably, it did not entertain compulsory employment as an option, perhaps because the government viewed employers' generosity as easily exhaustible.[117] Throughout the four months that the Committee met, the poles of the debate remained fixed between voluntarism and state control.

The evidence that the Committee members heard was striking in its unanimity. Each of the thirty witnesses who testified, trade unionists as well as employers, local councillors, and representatives of ex-servicemen's associations, disparaged the current state of affairs and demanded that the government take a greater role in the employment of disabled men. The Standing Joint Committee of the Mayors of London spoke for the other witnesses when it wrote that it was the state's duty "to provide these men with the means by which to enjoy a standard of comfort and living not less favourable than that which they enjoyed before the war."[118] How this was to be accomplished was disputed. Representatives of local government advocated the establishment of state-run workshops, as did trade unionists and employers, unlikely bedfellows brought together by their desire to reduce the burdens imposed on private workplaces.[119] Ex-servicemen's associations opposed state facilities on the grounds that men might be "herded" from their homes to work in national workshops, but they could not agree on an alternative.[120] While left-leaning organizations such as the National Association of Discharged Sailors and Soldiers tended to favor compulsory employment, the more conservative Comrades of the Great War dismissed it as "not practicable."[121]

Within the first month of its existence, the Committee had split into two opposing camps: those who, like its chairman, Sir Montague Barlow, parliamentary secretary of the Ministry of Labour and an advocate of comprehensive social security, favored some formal role for the state in disabled men's employment, and those who followed Adair Hore of the Ministry of Pensions in defending the status quo.[122] The majority of the Committee's eight members sided with Montague Barlow, agreeing that "the State could not refuse to recognize some liability."[123] That did not mean full liability. In light of evidence that appeared to confirm what its members were already inclined to believe—many of the so-called class c men were chronically unemployed even before the war—the Committee rejected the solution of state workshops as imposing a burden incommensurate with the government's obligations. Despite the evidence from the Committee's witnesses (and in direct opposition to the solution favored by powerful organized interests), the Committee's interim report admitted only partial responsibility. The task of founding workshops would be left to local government and voluntary initiative, with state grants to finance their efforts.

The Committee's most formidable member was in the minority. C. F. A. Hore (1874–1950) was the principle assistant secretary to the minister from 1919 to 1935, and minister of pensions from 1935 to 1941.[124] By the time Hore came to the Ministry, he had been in government service for more than twenty years, first at the Local Government Board, then at the Poor Law Commission, and, from 1912, at the National Health Insurance Commission. During his tenure at the Ministry of Pensions, he served as a liaison to every significant institution including Parliament and the Treasury, negotiated with veterans' associations, kept an official handle on the Local War Pensions Committees, commanded an army of civil servant underlings, spoke to the press, supervised the Pensions Appeals Tribunals, and briefed the pensions minister. In short, throughout the interwar period, Hore was among the most powerful officials in the Ministry.

Hore opposed any proposal that would admit even the slightest liability on the government's part. Sensing that his fellow members (including the Ministry of Labour's J. A. Barlow) were leaning toward state-assisted employment, Hore committed his views to paper, both in an attempt to persuade those who had not made up their minds and to exonerate his own role in the proceedings. Hore believed that the state could not acknowledge only partial responsibility for a social problem; it was accountable either fully or not at all. Hore asked his readers to take the example of the Local War Pensions Committees. Although the War Pensions Bill of 1915 had stipulated that local committees were to be financed through voluntary contributions, the largest and wealthiest districts had soon demanded that the government support their efforts. Because the state became involved, concluded Hore, the consequence was "that the State has had to find all the money."[125]

Hore's interpretation of the succession of events that led to the founding of his Ministry indicates that he did not believe that responsibility for disabled men's subsistence should have been entirely (or perhaps even mostly) left to the state. Coming from the leading civil servant in a department pledged to fulfill the nation's troth to the war victims, this was an unseemly, if not downright negligent, position, but Hore was not ashamed to admit it to his fellow Committee members. The fact that the government "has had to find all the money" indicated to Hore that the pensions questions had been badly handled, and he was determined that employment would not be resolved in the same way. While the other members of the Committee might have been willing to take "the man's point of view" in acknowledging the state's obligations to the long-term unemployed, Hore could only worry that the government would soon find itself saddled with another massive problem. It was his finger in the dike.

Noting that Committee members had not always been able to distinguish "unemployables" from those who could work only intermittently, Hore pointed out that they actually had no idea how many men the Exchequer might end up supporting. Moreover, if the state agreed to care for "unemployables," employers would have no incentive to hire other disabled workers, a point he claimed was "so obvious as not to need amplification."[126] By admitting an obligation to the disabled, the state would absolve employers and trade unionists of all responsibilities to the men who had defended British industry as well as Empire. Yet if state workshops were the worst evil, a system of contributions to voluntary and local enterprise was not much better, for in Hore's view, state subventions to philanthropic workshops would inevitably lead to a decline in charitable contributions.[127] Once the state intervened, the public would cease to do its part.

To Hore's way of thinking, the state did not "represent the nation," as the Joint Committee of the Mayors of London had claimed, but was only one actor among many, and a beleaguered one at that. It could not take on too much. Like J. A. Flynn, Hore had been distressed by John Hodge's extravagance, and especially by the way the second minister of pensions had broadened the definition of disability. The public, or so it seemed to Hore, wanted the state to accept an infinite amount of responsibility—whether or not it could afford to do. In contrast, his duty was to divest the state of as many tasks as he could and to avoid new areas of obligation such as employment that would result in "a heavy and increasing bill for the next twenty-five years."[128] All that the state could do for "unemployables" was to find a market for their goods. Instead of providing work, either directly or indirectly, Hore suggested that the state limit its involvement to distribution.

While Hore's proposal was surely the least expensive solution to the problem, there was more than money at stake. For Hore, the issue was one of justice. Since industry, organized labor, and the population in general had benefited from a soldier's sacrifices, they owed him compensation of a material as well as psychological sort. Although the state could pay a man a pension, only his fellow countrymen could return him to the social and economic position he had occupied before the war. Rehabilitation would have to be a broadly shared task; the state could not carry the entire nation's burden. At best, it might act as a middleman, organizing buyers for the products of disabled men's labor. Consistent with Gladstonian conceptions of governance, which dictated a minimal and neutral role for the state, Hore's solution represented a return to the nineteenth-century order: the state's "proper" sphere was to advise and to organize.

Although the Treasury's restraining hand undoubtedly influenced Hore's position, it by no means determined how he or his junior ministers thought. Widely blamed for the failure of postwar reconstruction programs, the Treasury's officials did not act alone. Civil servants within the individual ministries—in their desire to restrain spending and limit the state's role—also undermined plans for social reform.[129] Between the years 1920 and 1922, when tens of thousands of men waited on rehabilitation, the Ministry of Pensions underspent special Treasury grants by the purpose by more than one-third.[130] Not every department was as unwilling as Pensions to accept new obligations for the state. The Ministry of Labour's ranking officials, for instance, proved much more amenable to state intervention, in part because they feared that large numbers of unemployed and severely disabled men might further dislocate a marketplace already battered by the postwar trade depression.[131] Had the Ministry of Labour received responsibility for "unemployables" during the war, the state's role might have been greater, or at least the battle lines with the Treasury more clearly drawn.[132] But it came to the scene too late. By 1922, when a Conservative government led by Andrew Bonar Law succeeded Lloyd George's Coalition, the era of postwar stringency was in full force, and new programs were out of the question.

In contrast to their colleagues at the Ministry of Labour, Pensions officials such as Hore rarely came into conflict with the Treasury because they essentially shared the same conception of the state's "proper" role. Pensions' ranking civil servants received the Treasury's attack on John Hodge with approval, if not glee. On the question of the employment of disabled ex-servicemen, Hore and the Treasury's Frederick Phillips were of one mind. When the Committee on the Employment of Severely Disabled Ex-Servicemen issued its interim report recommending government subsidies to voluntary enterprises, the assistant secretary acknowledged that he shared most of the Treasury's objections.[133] But while Hore's memorandum had not swayed his fellow Committee members, he found solace in their proposal's likely failure: "The interim report won't be published, and I should imagine it highly improbable that the Cabinet would agree to find money for this class of case, in view of the more urgent demands for assistance towards the employment of the able-bodied."[134]

As Hore had predicted, the Treasury rejected the proposed scheme, though the Cabinet later decided to grant small per capita contributions to certain voluntary enterprises. However, the program's mandate owed much to Hore's intervention. Most important, he made certain that the state would not assist charitable employment schemes until absolutely necessary ("The question of Government aid should not be considered until organized voluntary work had been exhausted"), a principle that governed the awarding of capitation grants, as they were known, through the Second World War.[135] The assistance that workshops such as Lord Roberts received from the government depended on the amount they collected from charitable donations; the more the public gave, the less the workshop received from the state. The sums in question were relatively small, ranging from £25 to £35 annually, per man. Because Lord Roberts was well endowed by the public, it received only £25, while poorer enterprises got the full amount.

Not only had the Ministry of Pensions forfeited a potential opportunity to secure state-sponsored employment for the badly disabled, but Hore and his colleagues also left their successors at the Ministry of Labour in an isolated battle with the Treasury. After the Ministry of Labour received responsibility for "unemployables," civil servants there realized that the Treasury would do anything in its power to overturn the Inter-departmental Committee's recommendations.[136] Considering how little money was actually involved, the Treasury's stinginess infuriated J. A. Barlow, head of the Training Department: "Their present policy is to refuse grants where they can find any possible pretext, however unreasonable, and where they cannot decently refuse, to whittle away the grant by reducing its amount below the already inadequate sum of £25 per annum and by imposing unjustifiable and irritating conditions. Furthermore, they obviously intend to cut off the grant at the earliest possible moment, whatever the necessity for its continuance."[137] More often than not, Barlow sided with philanthropies in their attempts to gain adequate capitation grants, and he found himself in constant altercations with the Treasury.[138]

Aside from the "exiguous and inadequate" grants (Barlow's words) that the state granted philanthropy, employment for the severely disabled remained—in 1939 as in 1919—largely a task for voluntarism and the charitable public.[139] While some badly incapacitated men found work through the King's Roll, sheltered workshops offered the only option for many veterans. With the exception of Lord Roberts, most employment schemes for the disabled were local and relatively small; the Ministry of Labour distributed capitation grants to thirty separate enterprises. All told, the number of men employed in this way may have approached 2,000 at any one time; that was, of course, only a fraction of those who according to the

government's figures needed work.[140] Nevertheless, through private giving, as through the King's Roll, the public's role in the reintegration of the
disabled lasted longer than anyone had anticipated. Throughout the
1920s, donations to the charities for the disabled remained strong, and
while there was a general decline during the Slump, some institutions actually recorded improvements. In 1932, donations to Enham were higher
than they had been in 1921; at the height of the Slump in 1933, Enham
managed to collect more subscriptions than in the preceding year.[141] The
success of the British Legion's annual Armistice Day sale of commemorative poppies was undisputed, almost mythic: between 1921 and 1930, the
proceeds of Poppy Day quintupled, from £106,000 to £524,000; although
they declined slightly in 1931 and 1932, by the end of the decade, they
had again surpassed the half-million mark.[142]

Little wonder, then, that the British Legion members quoted at the
outset placed such trust in the public ("When the public failed them, the
Empire, and not only the Government would fall"). Not everyone cared
about the men's sacrifices, of course. Beginning in the mid-1920s, flap-
pers and their escorts, symbols of the changed gender order borne of the
Great War, started to dance Armistice Night away instead of spending it
in solemn contemplation of the nation's losses.[143] Yet on the whole, most
ex-servicemen could be satisfied with the role that the British public had
played, particularly in comparison to what they perceived as the state's
negligence. Disabled men had given the country their best, and their fellow citizens had not shirked from the task of repaying them, even after
(and because) the state had failed to do its part. This was the faith that
sustained the British veterans' movement and, despite small pensions, inadequate training, and high unemployment, helped to ensure their allegiance to the nation.

SERVICE, NOT SELF

In October 1929, Mr. J. J. McCoy decided to intervene on behalf of the
disabled. The narrow Labour Party victory at the general election meant
that for the first time since 1924, the minister of pensions, F. O. Roberts,
was a Labourite, and Mr. McCoy hoped that the change of governments
might improve the care of disabled men. There was little reason for optimism. In its first-ever government, Labour had—like the Conservative
government of Stanley Baldwin that followed from 1924 to 1929—done
little to assist these men. "Trusting that you will excuse me for being so
Impertient in writing you," McCoy began, "... it is Pitting to see those

men struggling to live." What disabled men needed, according to McCoy, was special allowances "so as to give them a chance of living in a little comfort for the short time that they have to live in this world." The rewards were substantial, noted McCoy, promising his correspondent benefits that no aspiring politician could afford to ignore. "I feel shur," he wrote, "that the Country will be greatfull for any measur of help for those men which has lost all."[144]

Mr. McCoy's certainty about the country's allegiances was widely shared in ex-servicemen's circles. In the years that followed the Armistice, returning soldiers placed faith in their fellow citizens, believing them as eager to acquit their debts as the state was intent upon shirking them. After previous wars, Britons had neglected to honor men's sacrifices, but that would not happen again. The public became the disabled veteran's best ally against the state. Newspapers claiming to speak on behalf of the "nation" attacked the state for its stinginess, its disorganization, or its moral failings. Local War Pensions Committees lambasted the government in the name of voluntary effort. As government departments balked at joining the King's Roll, private employers hired the requisite 5 percent of disabled men. In the meantime, private philanthropies collected hundreds of thousands of pounds for projects to benefit disabled men, from St. Dunstan's Hostel for the Blind to Oswald Stoll's "Homes Fit for Heroes," to the Lord Roberts Memorial Workshops.

To say that British ex-servicemen believed the public their best ally forces some reappraisal of the myth of the war generation. That is, after all, very different from what Robert Graves or Rebecca West or many of the other (especially modernist) writers of the later 1920s and 1930s had believed. Their opinion was that the returning soldier was suspicious, even hostile, toward his fellow citizens, an idea that scholars have tended to accept.[145] Yet my research in disabled men's own writings and, more broadly, in the documents of the veterans' movement, calls into question how widely such views were shared.[146] The figure of the disgruntled ex-serviceman aptly conveyed literary modernism's alienation from the postwar world, but it tells us much less about veterans' perceptions more generally. Ex-servicemen were angry at the state, that is indisputable— they despised generals in plush chairs behind the lines, Whitehall bureaucrats, profiteers—but their attitudes toward the general public were benign when not sympathetic. It was true that the war had resulted in an undefinable cleft of experience separating soldiers from those who had stayed at home, but that did not mean the public's benevolence was worth any less.

Ex-servicemen never received the "fit land for heroes" that Lloyd George had promised, but they blamed that on the government and economic exigencies. Individual philanthropists, supported by the charitable public, had done what they could. "To lose you, Sir, would be to lose the Greatest Friend the British Soldier ever had," wrote one man to Oswald Stoll, adding that "it is to me Sir very difficult to express in writing my appreciation for your kindness in thinking of my comfort and happiness, also that of my wife and children."[147] Only the wealthy could build "Homes for Heroes," but there were other sorts of voluntarism, equally appreciated if unspectacular. The highest praise in the *Star and Garter Magazine* went to the women of the Richmond Post Office, who organized a "Camel Corps" to accompany the men on their Sunday walks.[148] It was that kind of personal attention, said one disabled man, remembering seventy years later the care he had received in a private convalescent home, that made him believe "life was worth living again."[149]

While philanthropists occupied themselves with the most severely disabled veterans, the voluntary workers of the Local War Pensions Committees cared for those who returned home. Whether in moderating pensions disputes, providing emergency assistance, or organizing medical treatment, Local Committees earned praise for their sympathy and understanding. One member of Parliament, himself a veteran, credited local committees with relieving "a situation of chaos and distrust on the part of ex-service men who felt that they were out of touch."[150] For A. G. Webb, head of the British Legion Pension Department, the Local Committees were "always the human bulwark between the disabled man on the one hand and 'Departmentality' on the other."[151] Although men often regarded the Ministry's decisions with suspicion, Webb noted that when the claimant met with voluntary workers "whom he knows are anxious to help him," he went away satisfied even if the problem was not resolved in his favor.[152]

Gratitude and trust assumed a larger significance in the context of veterans' politics. Although the British veterans' movement was not radical during most of the interwar period, it did have the potential to disrupt the status quo. In comparison with their German counterparts, British ex-servicemen had organized quickly; as early as 1917, there were already three rival associations, each with its own political character, demanding pensions as a statutory right and priority for ex-servicemen in employment.[153] In the year after the Armistice, amid widespread labor unrest and the threat of a general strike, ex-servicemen became "political" as never before in the history of Great Britain. They demonstrated for better state provisions for wounded men (including one Hyde Park affair that ended in a clash with police), ran their own candidates in by-elections, and boycotted peace celebrations to call attention to the neglect of the disabled.[154] Between 1918 and 1919, no less than four new organizations were founded, including the Labour-affiliated National Union of Ex-Servicemen and the Communist International Union of Ex-Servicemen.[155]

Although ex-servicemen numbered among the disruptive elements of British society in 1919 (subject, along with other "revolutionary" movements, to constant police surveillance), by 1920, radicalism among ex-servicemen appeared to have dwindled away.[156] As Stephen Ward has argued, the Royal Pensions Warrant introduced late in 1919 stole much of the movement's thunder.[157] It cannot, however, be credited with the demise of radicalism. Pensions were still painfully low; the new total disablement pension of 40s. a week, though a distinct improvement over the 33s. granted in 1918, was still substantially less than what women cotton weavers (72s. 6d.) earned in 1920, not even half of what unskilled building (84s. 4d.) and coal mining laborers (99s. 3d.) could expect that year, and a third of the wages that skilled coalgetters (135s. 6d.) made.[158] Moreover, many of the government's wartime promises, especially in the fields of training and employment, were left unfulfilled, with little prospect of realization. Had ex-servicemen wanted to protest, they could have found ample grounds to do so, but much to the despair of those who presided over the veterans' associations ever-shrinking membership rolls, they showed little inclination. Most men wanted a steady job and a secure home life, not a revolution plotted in the East End. It was true that ex-servicemen bore serious grievances against their state. However, they were not embittered enough to want to destroy the established order.

The British Legion both reflected and perpetuated ex-servicemen's diffidence about politics. Created in 1921, the Legion unified four of the more moderate and conservative veterans' organizations. While its membership did not approach that of its French or German counterparts, the Legion was the largest, and for most of the 1920s the only, ex-servicemen's association in Britain.[159] Historians have treated it to very different receptions, either applauding the organization as a splendid accommodation to interest-group politics or condemning it as a sellout.[160] It was both, but at different times. Although the Legion's privileged relationship with the establishment eventually proved difficult to reconcile with rank-and-file opinions, the organization's early years were harmonious and productive. During the 1920s, the Legion's genius lay in its ability to contain men's anger toward the state within an "unpolitical" ideology that brought them closer to their society. It was a delicate balance that won the organization an unprecedented number of followers. From a membership of less than 18,000 men in 1921, the Legion had enlisted over 100,000 members a year later. By the early 1930s, over 300,000 ex-servicemen had joined its ranks.[161]

Within the first years of its existence, the British Legion had raised the public's gratitude to one of its foremost principles. However willing the individual ex-serviceman may have been to believe in the merits of his fellow citizenry, the British Legion offered him ample reassurance. "The nation is, as ever, determined to fulfill its obligations to those who served their country in its hour of danger," claimed John Smedley-Crooke, a member of the Legion's National Executive.[162] S. E. Perry shared Smedley-Crooke's confidence. A decade after the Armistice, the chairman of the National Pensions and Disablement Committee maintained that "the British public are definitely in favour of generous and sympathetic treatment for victims of the Great War."[163] While the organization's leaders encouraged their members to recognize what the public had done for them, the pages of the *British Legion Journal* resounded with praise for voluntary initiatives. Disclosing that the government awarded treatment allowances to only 36 percent of those men receiving outpatient hospital care, A. G. Webb asked his readers, "What would these poor fellows do but for the help of the various voluntary associations?"[164]

Explicit within the Legion's praise of the public was its critique of the state. In the first years of its existence, the Legion took up its members' grievances with vigor, sending deputations to the prime minister, establishing a department that advised men about their pensions rights, and arranging representation before the Pensions Appeals Tribunals. In Parliament, J. B. Brunel Cohen, a disabled member of Parliament and the Legion's honorary treasurer, condemned the "soulless bureaucracy," while Webb expressed his own frustration, borne of practical experience as the head of the Pensions Department: "Many years' experience of pensions problems has almost driven me to the conclusion that it's easier for a rich man to get into Heaven than for a poor man to ascertain his pension rights single-handedly."[165] According to Legion officials, the public had approved generous spending for the disabled, but the Ministry of Pensions and the Treasury had foiled their aims. Condemning "the officialness of officials and the Treasury point of view that places parsimony before humanity," Webb reminded the Ministry of Pensions that the public demanded that pensions be administered in a "sympathetic manner."[166]

Although the British Legion's criticisms were stinging, they were also narrowly focused on the pensions bureaucracy and the Treasury. According to Legion officials, the problem of obtaining just compensation was not "social" in nature. It did not, in other words, reflect a denial of their suffering but had to be attributed to administrative failure, bureaucratic red tape, and official hard-heartedness. By separating the state from the public and celebrating the unity of the British nation, the Legion sharpened its critique of the government without turning veterans against their society. The Legion's diagnosis of the problem implied its solution. Demonstrations, boycotts, and veterans' candidates would not improve ex-servicemen's lot because, as the Legion's officials emphasized, bureaucratic failings required bureaucratic remedies. If ex-servicemen sought justice from the government, the best they could do was to entrust their interests to a powerful organization that would press their claims within the context of parliamentary democracy.

The stabilization of pensions in 1923 under Bonar Law's Conservative government appeared to confirm the National Executive's policy. In 1919, the Royal Warrant had fixed pension rates to reflect wartime rises in prices, with the stipulation that pensions would be cut if the cost of living fell. In 1922, the *British Legion Journal* warned that officials at the Ministry of Pensions were contemplating a reduction in pension rates to match the significant drop in prices. In October, T. F. Lister, the Legion's chairman, led a deputation to the minister of pensions. If the Ministry cut pensions, Lister warned, the Legion would begin a blistering press campaign to influence public opinion against the reductions. Whether as a result of the Legion's threat, or the Ministry's own reservations about disabled men's ability to exist on less, pensions were spared the budgetary ax.[167] In the pages of the Legion's *Journal,* the stabilization was lauded as an example of what a powerful and moderate interest group could achieve with the public's support.

The Legion turned public opinion into an article of faith. Delegates at the Legion's annual conferences invoked the "generous public" in near-reverential tones.[168] Urging that the Legion's financial transactions be disclosed, the Southeastern Area delegate referred to the importance of "keeping faith" with the public: "It was impossible to tell the public too much, and the more they were allowed to know the more they would help."[169] Ex-servicemen broadly shared his confidence. In 1931, the Sandhurst delegate expressed the conviction that time limits on pensions claims might be overturned if the public were "rightly informed."[170] According to the Neath delegate, the Legion's very existence rested on the support of the public: "There must be public opinion behind the Legion to make it live."[171]

The knowledge that the country was on "their" side confirmed the moderate tendencies in veterans' politics. In contrast to those German organizations that aimed to create unity among their members by fanning hostility toward the public, the Legion brought ex-servicemen together by binding them closer to their society. According to the Legion's ethos, ex-servicemen occupied an honored position in their society, a product of service to King and country, but also of their special place in the hearts of a grateful public. In return, veterans owed the British public "Service, Not Self," as the Legion's motto proudly proclaimed. Only by defending their society's well-being in peace as in war could ex-servicemen maintain their privileged status. No less than in 1914–1918, a man's service to the nation proved his mettle. Instead of mere interest politics, then, the Legion promised ex-servicemen something higher: a moral and patriotic peacetime community.[172]

While the balance between advancing their members' interests and defending the established order was always fragile, the Legion faced an increasingly difficult situation as the 1920s progressed. At issue was the Legion's relationship with the Ministry of Pensions. Although the Legion had been avowedly "unpolitical" since its founding, officials such as Webb had not refrained from criticizing the Ministry of Pensions. However, by mid-decade the tenor within the leadership had changed. Whether because they feared the politicization of the rank and file or whether because they genuinely believed that the Ministry had made the necessary concessions to their members, Legion officials rarely spoke out against the Ministry of Pensions. Only on rare occasions did they complain about the Treasury. The conferring of the Royal Charter in 1925 confirmed their stance. In exchange for the honor of the King's patronage, the Legion's Executive Council vowed to reject any activity that might indicate political opposition to the government.

However honored ex-servicemen may have been by the King's patronage, a significant number, and perhaps even the majority, were unwilling to surrender the Legion's right to criticize the state and especially the Ministry of Pensions. Throughout the 1920s, delegates to the annual meetings urged the Executive Council to "adopt a more militant policy" toward pensions (1925), "severely" censuring it for failing to ensure that time limits imposed on postwar pensions claims were fought in Parliament (1927), and "expressing profound dissatisfaction" that a stronger pensions policy had not come to fruition (1929).[173] The failure of Brunel Cohen's 1925 petition to the House of Commons undoubtedly shook many Legionnaires' faith in the ability of public opinion to remedy their grievances.[174] In less than three months, Cohen collected 824,105 signatures on a petition—the largest since the Chartist effort of 1848—demanding the abolition of the seven-year time limit on pension claims. Not until six months later did the Ministry deign to reply.[175]

For the Legion's leaders, the public petition was a last-ditch effort to secure the changes in pensions policy demanded by rank-and-file members.[176] From 1925 onward, they reviewed "other means of entering the citadel," by which they meant meetings behind closed doors, the alleviation of individual complaints, and ultimately resigned inaction.[177] Members displayed a greater willingness to challenge the state, calling for the lobbying of individual members of Parliament, demonstrations, and press campaigns. There was even evidence that some of the rank and file wanted a political Legion. After members of Parliament pledged to the Legion's aims failed to initiate legislation on ex-servicemen's behalf, the 1926 annual meeting passed a resolution directing the Executive Council to delete that part of the charter which prohibited the Legion from engaging in political action. This prospect was as distressing to the conservative council as it was to the government. In an exchange of letters, Lord Haig and Stanley Baldwin settled the matter between themselves: there would be no constitutional amendment.[178]

For the first decade of the Legion's existence, conflict between the National Executive and the rank and file was sporadic and, for the most part, successfully suppressed. However, in 1933, with the country mired in the international Slump and unemployment at 3 million, a controversy that began in the Legion's *Journal* captured the attention of the national press. An article in the March edition of the *Journal* attacked the Ministry of Pensions with a venom unprecedented in the Legion's history, describing ex-servicemen's benefits as "at best a record of rights wrung only after the bitterest struggles from an unwilling hand."[179] Citing statistics that indicated that 34,202 of the 64,383 pensions appeals assisted by the Legion's experts had been overturned—"an astonishing indictment of the Ministry of Pensions"—the editors condemned that department for failing "signally to fulfill its trust."[180] The minister's response was not long in coming. In May, Major George Tryon, who had succeeded F. O. Roberts as minister of pensions in the Conservative-dominated National Government, told the House of Commons, "The assertions are not only incorrect, but the responsible leaders know they are."[181]

The *Journal*'s attack caught the Legion's officials off guard. Although Brunel Cohen at first denied Tryon's charge, claiming, "I thought the statements in the *Journal* were in accordance with the facts, and I am still sure they were," he quickly backed down. At the annual conference of the Women's Section of the Legion, where Tryon himself was present, Cohen claimed that "any concessions given by the Ministry—and there were many—had always been made willingly." As for the charge that the Ministry had failed to fulfill its trust, Cohen told his audience that it "had no foundation whatever." Colonel Crosfield, the Legion's former chairman, distanced the National Executive from the *Journal*, blaming the whole thing on a "brilliant young editor swept off his balance by a sudden gust of journalese imagery, and alas! he wrote things which were most unfair to the Ministry of Pensions and to our good friend, Major Tryon, whom we are delighted to see here this evening."

While the Legion's officials did their best to smooth the waters, the organization's membership welcomed the storm. Far from disavowing the "brilliant young editor," who, for his own part, acknowledged that he wanted to enliven the magazine by printing the "grouses," many of the local branches, led by the rebellious London Metropolitan Area, rushed to his support.[182] They criticized the Legion's leadership as well as the Ministry of Pensions. Major G. E. Cohen, chair of the Surrey Legion, claimed that the editor had expressed "the opinion of the majority of our members on pensions questions, which seem to fall into the background between the meetings of the annual blow-off of the safety valve at Whitsuntide."[183] That year's "annual blow-off" proved feistier than ever before. After a resolution calling on the council to refute Tryon's charges passed with an overwhelming majority, the Cardiff representative reproved the Legion's leaders for their conciliatory attitude toward the Ministry. When the newly elected chairman, Colonel John Brown, attempted to answer the charge, delegates shouted him down.[184]

The *Journal* scandal did not lead to the Legion's dissolution, in spite of what more than a few doomsayers had predicted. The dispute nonetheless drove a thicker wedge between the rank and file and the leadership. According to the Legion's official historian, the 1933 conflict exposed "a gap" between the rank and file, who "by no means regarded pensions as a dead issue," and the national leadership, who believed they had already achieved all that was possible.[185] Local Legion supplements published incendiary articles, while the organization found itself under increasing attack from ex-servicemen in the press. In 1936, an ex-serviceman who signed himself "Victimized" wrote to the *Glasgow Evening Times* to complain about the Legion's leadership: "A non-political Legion is use-less in protecting us from the attacks of any Government, and the Legion leaders know that, and they intend to keep the men politically dis-armed."[186] A year later, a disabled man berated the Legion for its "fail-ure...to do anything really worth while. The lack of leadership and ini-tiative has been appalling."[187] Ex-servicemen had joined the Legion because they believed it could represent their interests. That was the promise of the 1920s. When the Legion's critique of the state fell away, so, too, did its exclusive claim to represent the disabled soldier.

Although the National Executive embarked on another campaign to address pensions grievances, many of their dealings with the Ministry of Pensions were merely for show, as the officials there recognized. Ac-cording to Permanent Secretary Hore, the Legion's newest set of com-plaints "represents, I think, no more than an effort by H.Q. [headquar-ters] of the Legion to 'clean the slate.'...We have reason to know that this is not one of the points on which H.Q. feels at all strongly—and I think this is apparent from the tone of their memo."[188] A few years later, Hore's conviction was even stronger. He offered to preside over a collu-sion of inactivity, this time between the Legion and the Ministry of Labour. Reporting on a meeting with Hore about a conference that the British Legion had proposed, the Ministry of Labour's H.H. Wiles of-fered this analysis: "Sir Adair Hore continually impresses on me that the sole object...is to provide the Legion with an opportunity of convinc-ing their members of the strenuous efforts made by their officials to get the Government to do something... and he does not disguise that all he wants is to provide the British Legion with an opportunity for publicity which can only be described as eye-wash."[189]

Despite Hore's best efforts, no mere "eye-wash" would suffice. The Ministry's reputation among ex-servicemen remained dismal, while the Legion's policy of sending pro-Ministry speakers to local meetings had little effect on men's attitudes. On occasion, it even proved an embar-rassment. Captain Graves, the chairman of the Pensions and Disable-ment Committee of the British Legion, suffered such a setback in 1938 when he was asked to address a meeting organized by the Moulscombe and Farmer Branch. Although "there was a feeling that the Government was very hard-hearted in that matter," Graves claimed that was not his experience, arguing that there was only one case in 24,000 where he had failed to agree with the Ministry. So outraged were local branches by Graves's remark that they passed a special resolution at the annual conference of the Metropolitan British Legion, demanding that Graves's statement be repudiated in Parliament at the earliest possible moment.[190]

Ex-servicemen's discontent with the British Legion found expression in a new and radical organization of disabled veterans. In the course of the 1930s, the British Limbless Ex-Servicemen's Association (BLESMA) decisively broke the Legion's monopoly on the ex-service movement. Founded in 1932, BLESMA was a small organization, with only twelve branches and a paying membership of little more than 2,000 men, drawn from those who were either missing limbs or blinded.[191] However, its influence transcended its size. Due in large measure to the shenanigans of its indefatigable secretary, George Chandley, BLESMA was constantly in the press. It organized well-publicized deputations to members of Parliament and garnered their support for an investigation into ex-service unemployment.[192] Chandley himself provided fodder for scores of newspaper articles with a study about widespread poverty among disabled ex-servicemen. When the Ministry of Pensions disputed his results, his retort made headlines. Although the "address of the Ministry at Sanctuary Buildings suggested it was a haven of refuge for war-wrecked men... judging from the chilly epistles that emanated from the Ministry it would be more appropriately named 'Bleak House.'"[193]

The contrast with the Legion could not have been more apparent: until BLESMA, claimed one disabled man, there was "nobody to fight for us."[194] Moreover, much to the concern of the Ministry of Pensions, BLESMA appeared to be growing at the Legion's expense.[195] Although the Legion's leadership had distanced itself from BLESMA, local branches were often friendly, supporting, for instance, Chandley's call for pension increases. The Ministry's officer in Manchester noted that in "one or two districts the attitude of these bodies to each other is hostile, but in others, I have noticed indications of a disposition to 'fuse,' in the pursuit of objective, if not in fact." Limbless officers in the British Legion branch of Middleton had organized a branch of BLESMA and had secured the right to meet in the Legion's own rooms, a request approved on the condition that they retain their membership in the Legion. According to the Ministry's official, BLESMA succeeded because many ex-servicemen believed that the Legion was too closely allied with the pensions bureaucracy. He warned that "if the same process... spreads to other parts, either the British Legion may one day have to speak with another voice and in a way less friendly to us, or they may find themselves 'naked in the market place' and their clothes occupied by Mr. Chandley and his friends!"[196]

With the Legion's policy of apoliticism in disrepute, and BLESMA on the rise, ex-servicemen's hostility toward the Ministry of Pensions increased rather than declined during the 1930s. Legion speakers described the "general discontent and dissatisfaction with the Ministry of Pensions"—according to A. G. Webb, "so much inane criticism"—while ex-servicemen aired their own grievances in letters to the editor.[197] In its own defense, the Ministry began keeping a special press clippings file in 1936, which, though it ostensibly contained "letters of appreciation concerning the work of the Ministry," in fact consisted solely (when not of praise from Legion officials) of lukewarm statements such as "the Ministry of Pensions is not so black as it is sometimes painted."[198] Ex-servicemen were the most dissatisfied, but their fellow citizens were no more forgiving. According to the American journalist Katherine Mayo, "'Bureaucratic,' 'cold,' 'without generous impulses'—such phrases one hears applied on general principles to the Ministry of Pensions by good English citizens."[199]

In 1937, the Ministry was once more the object of a barrage of criticism, this time from an unexpected source: the National Union of Conservative and Unionist Associations. At their annual conference, deputies repudiated the minister's statement about his department's good work and called for an inquiry into the subject of pensions. E. J. Griffith, a member of the Public Assistance Committee of the West Riding County Council, described the plight of disabled men in the gloomiest possible terms. He alleged that 8,000 ex-servicemen had committed suicide in 1928 and 1929, one-third of whom were affected by poison gas.[200] By the end of the month, Labour M.P.s had taken up the Conservatives' charges in Parliament, noting, in the words of one, that "there must be something seriously wrong with the treatment of ex-service men when a complacent Conservative conference agrees to such a resolution."[201] For the umpteenth time in its short history, the Ministry of Pensions was on the defensive.

Yet there was an irony in the Ministry's apparently worsening reputation, for if anything, the monetary compensation that it provided was better than it had been in the early 1920s. Not only had the government continued to pay pensions at the 1919 levels though the cost of living and salaries had actually declined throughout the period, but Great Britain was the only country that did not reduce compensation to war victims during the worldwide Depression of the 1930s, despite cuts in unemployment benefits and the salaries of government employees.[202] Admittedly, the sums paid even to the totally disabled were barely sufficient for subsistence, but some improvement had been made relative to the average income of other Britons. Whereas a completely disabled man had received a little more than half of a female cotton weaver's weekly wage in 1920, by 1926, the difference was only three shillings. Without allowances for his wife or children, a totally disabled man received a pension of £104 per year in 1934–1935, compared with the £129 that an unskilled worker earned, the £195 that a skilled worker could expect, and the £273 paid foremen.[203]

The sources of the Ministry's increasing unpopularity are complex, owing as much to ex-servicemen's attitudes toward the public as to its own policies. By the mid-1930s, disabled veterans turned to the state because they believed they could no longer rely on the public's generosity. According to the ex-servicemen who joined BLESMA or turned disruptive in local Legion branches, only the state could fulfill their aims. That is not to say they were angry at the public, but they recognized that memories of the Great War, especially as another war threatened, would eventually fade. As the disabled treasurer of the Legion, Major J. B. Brunel Cohen, put it, "The public is not really neglectful, it is merely forgetful, and very busy with other problems which, to the life of the country, are at least equally important."[204] According to the Legion's Grimsby delegate, "The sentiment which existed in earlier days had gone."[205] Philanthropists who had devoted so much of their time and money to caring for the war's victims were aging and dying, while the public to which they had appealed had grown older. Speaking before the ex-servicemen of Halifax in 1936, J. V. Bell of BLESMA seemed almost to welcome the end of charity work. Noting that "as long as the ex-serviceman was supported by voluntary workers and the public, the Government would never accept its responsibility," Bell observed that as contributions declined, the state would have to play a larger role.[206]

As veterans' demands on the Ministry of Pensions increased, so, too, did their disappointment. By the mid-1930s, some ex-servicemen began to think that they had been wrong in eschewing politics. In a *Sunday Express* article of 1932, Viscount Castelrosse, who served with the Guards on the Western Front, condemned the state for neglecting ex-servicemen, but he acknowledged that he and his comrades had also failed: "We have never demanded our rights. The Americans, who never went through anything like what we did, are on a far better basis. Instead of demanding our rights, we went hat in hand asking for charity. We ought to have gone bayonet in hand demanding our rights. We behaved sweetly, and were swindled accordingly."[207] In comparison with their counterparts on the

Continent and in the Dominions, British ex-servicemen had not fared well. German and Italian veterans enjoyed secured employment and places of symbolic prominence under fascist regimes. Their counterparts in the United States received generous pensions.[208] Ex-servicemen in Australia and New Zealand could boast about their muscular politics.[209] Yet other than a vague contribution to the maintenance of social order, British veterans could show little for themselves. "Service, Not Self" had not even secured ex-servicemen's legitimate claims on their state.

Had the British veterans' movement gone "bayonet in hand," the history of the interwar period would have read differently. But ex-servicemen had not been angry enough at their fellow citizens to court the unrest that bayonets brought. The promise of a normal life had been too great. No one had realized that the state's neglect would make it so hard just to get by. While voluntarists succeeded in brokering a peace between returning soldiers and the millions of Britons who wanted to do their "bit," neither side knew at the time that the state would use charity as an excuse for inaction. The public's philanthropy could go a long way toward easing hard feelings, but it was never really enough to provide for even a minority of disabled men. It had kept them out of the revolutionary societies but not off the public assistance rolls.

Unlike on the Continent and in the United States, British veterans never became a political force. In most textbook accounts of the interwar period, they scarcely merit a mention. The significance of ex-servicemen lies not in the influence they wielded or the trouble they caused but in their quiescence. Denied state-secured employment, forced to survive on inadequate pensions, disabled veterans placed their faith in the public, refraining from demonstrations and eschewing politics. And yet, if their apoliticism contributed to the stability of interwar Britain, it also demonstrated the limits of social cohesion without social integration.[210] Reached in the early 1920s, this British settlement of the veterans question proved neither sufficient for the individual nor sustainable in the long term. For many disabled men, life as the object of charity became intolerable; they discovered that philanthropists had their own claims on the victims of war. Whereas in the 1920s British veterans had moderated their claims on the government, trusting in their fellow citizens' munificence, by the mid-1930s many began to regret their lack of political might. As another war threatened, they turned, in vain, to the state.

In 1938, the British Legion played host to a peculiar goodwill delegation composed of 900 of their once and future enemies. The German ex-servicemen had come to make peace in the name of their Führer. In the course of their stay, they also learned how Great Britain had cared for its ex-servicemen. They visited the Lord Roberts Workshops, chatted through translators with the disabled men who worked there, and expressed polite interest in the very different way that veterans' policy had developed in the two countries. The comparison was unavoidable. Triumphant heroes of Europe's bloodiest war, disabled veterans in Britain had become the objects of charity, relegated to the margins of their society and bound by desperation to a "grateful public" that diminished daily. The soldiers they had defeated were the honored citizens of Hitler's Thousand Year Reich, bemedaled, toasted, the leaders of the parades. "The miserable time is thankfully over," rejoiced one of their comrades in the Fatherland, "where soldiers could be scorned and insulted as ridiculous figures, cowards, and murderers, and where people dared to treat our disabled as burdensome petitioners."[211]

CHAPTER 2

The Nation Accused

*German Veterans and the State
Regulation of Charity*

Reverend Kreutz (Caritas)…demonstrated how in the course
of the decade, people had stopped caring about the welfare of
war victims…. Many people seem to have backed away from
their duty and shunned their "social conscience" because they
believe that national, personal, and collective obligations have
been fulfilled by the state's programs.

Benedict Kreutz, speech before the National
Committee for War Victims' Care, 1 April 1927.

Near the height of the German hyperinflation, Dr. Otto Wölz, an assistant secretary to the Labor Ministry and architect of the country's pioneering law for the employment of the severely disabled, drew a comparison. His subject was welfare provision; his cases, Germany and
England. To many, it no doubt appeared an unpropitious time for cross-
national reflection. In April 1923, when Wölz met with representatives
from the Labor Ministry, the Ministry of the Interior, and the country's
six leading private welfare organizations, the mark had sunk to 21,000
to the dollar; that spring, the Labor Ministry distributed welfare benefits
to 6.6 million people, or more than 10 percent of the population.[1]
Merely to calculate the supplemental allowances owed to war victims,
the chronically ill, and small rentiers required hours of additional labor.
Meanwhile, every day brought new petitioners.[2] For the assistant secretary, however, the English case proved of particular relevance to the social realities of 1923. "In England," Wölz observed, "charity is predominant, whereas in Germany large sections of the populace expect to
receive everything from the authorities."[3]

In the otherwise contentious literature on the Weimar welfare state, scholars have concurred in Wölz's assessment. Historians generally agree that many of Weimar's citizens, especially the unemployed, small rentiers, and war victims, had unrealistically high expectations of the new democracy. And yet we still know too little about *why* Germans expected so much from the state.[4] This chapter argues that veterans' demands on the state reflected more than the promises made in the Weimar constitution, the material facts of need, and Germany's tradition of welfare statism. Disabled veterans looked to the state because, in many cases, they had nowhere else to turn. Beginning in 1917, military authorities placed severe restrictions on charity, shutting down new and untested enterprises as a drain on the war effort. Initiated during the war, this regulation of charity proceeded even more dramatically in the early Weimar Republic. To gain a monopoly on benevolence for war victims, the Republic's civil servants sought to eliminate their philanthropic competitors. Prevented from raising funds or advertising for new members, most charities for disabled veterans had, by the early 1920s, folded.[5]

This chapter traces the origins and consequences of the *Verstaatlichung*, or state consolidation, of care for disabled veterans. In Germany, as in Britain, the treatment of the disabled remained for most of the war a task for voluntarism and local authorities. As the imperial state prevaricated, philanthropists founded homes for the severely incapacitated and implemented retraining programs for those men who could not return to their former occupations. With the imposition of state restrictions on fundraising in 1917, most philanthropists found their sphere of activity sharply circumscribed. To raise money or to advertise for members, charities had to secure the state's permission. What began during the war as a campaign to appropriate scarce resources became, in the early Weimar Republic, a means of establishing the state's authority. To win the loyalty of war victims, the Weimar state sought to dominate welfare provision. Yet in concentrating benevolence within the state's control, German officials created expectations that the new Republic could not fulfill.

Unlike in Britain, where civil servants sought to delegate responsibility for disabled veterans to voluntarism, Weimar's authorities viewed the care of war victims as a proving ground for the new Republic. As chapter 4 will demonstrate, their efforts yielded indisputable successes; innovative welfare programs enabled disabled men to return to the workplace and family life. Yet state-secured integration did not win for the Weimar Republic the loyalty of its veterans. However much the state could provide disabled veterans, it never seemed enough. Throughout the Weimar Republic, rival organizations of war victims made ever greater demands on the overburdened state. Carrying signs that read "Where Is the Fatherland's Thanks?" they demonstrated for higher pensions and improved benefits. The bitterness of war victims was infamous; as the state's favored wards, their discontent implicated the Republic. For Weimar's enemies, most prominent among them the National Socialists, disabled veterans became a vital constituency to be courted.

Scholars have attributed disabled veterans' discontent to their callous treatment at the hands of an unresponsive bureaucracy. However, veterans' attitudes reflected more than the state's policies toward them. Critical to disabled veterans' alienation from the Weimar Republic was their hostility toward their fellow citizens, whom they accused of neglecting soldiers' sacrifices. By consolidating welfare programs for the disabled within the state's control, Weimar's civil servants had institutionalized benevolence. Yet however generous the pension, it was never enough to compensate for a leg, the loss of vision, or a disfigured face.[6] Disabled veterans in Germany wanted public recognition of their losses. They wanted an honorary place in society. They sought respect and gratitude. Instead, the regulation of charity forced philanthropists and the public out of the field of social welfare for the disabled. Disabled veterans became convinced of the public's ingratitude, and they turned in desperation to the state. If the state could deliver legitimation in the form of improved benefits, the peace it bought was fragile, dependent on the Republic's always elusive financial prosperity. A decade after the war ended, the National Socialists capitalized on veterans' discontent.

Where British veterans viewed the public as their best ally, disabled veterans in Germany came to regard their fellow citizens with distrust and later enmity; the hostility became mutual. When the disabled and widows of the town of Fraustadt gathered in 1924 to protest their lot, they blamed the public as much as the state: "People have forgotten the solemn promises they made in 1914. They've absolved themselves of all responsibility."[7] At the same time, the perceived greed of the disabled turned their fellow citizens against them. However dissatisfied the disabled might be with their pensions, at the very least they had something, or so many people seemed to think. By the end of the decade, it was possible to believe that the disabled had profited from their injuries. In 1929, a man who had been blinded in the war reported that a gentleman "who counts himself among the educated" told him that he had been lucky to be blinded "because otherwise he would never have enjoyed such a 'luxurious pension.'"[8] By the early 1920s, what began as admiration and respect had been replaced by apathy, and later distrust. Disabled veterans had gone from being the honored victims of the nation to just another of the Weimar Republic's many supplicants.

In the aftermath of the Great War, stability depended, in part, on a reconciliation between the war's victims and those for whom they had suffered. This chapter begins with an examination of care for disabled veterans during the first years of war, considering especially the prominent role played by voluntarists. In the second section, I turn to an analysis of the state's consolidation of philanthropy. Implemented first by the militarized wartime state, the regulation of charity accelerated in the early Weimar Republic.[9] The unprecedentedly ambitious plans drawn up by officials in the National Committee, and later in the Labor Ministry, for the social welfare of the disabled hinged on a state monopoly over their care. Yet, as the third section of this chapter demonstrates, this *Verstaatlichung* held unintended consequences for the veterans' movement—and ultimately also for the Weimar Republic.

THE THANKS OF THE FATHERLAND

The success of the Reichstag Exhibition on the War-Time Care of Wounded and Sick Soldiers surprised even its enthusiastic supporters. In the two months between December 1914 and January 1915 as many as 100,000 people visited the exhibition hall in Germany's parliamentary building; on some days, attendance exceeded 6,000.[10] Courtesy of the Red Cross and the War Ministry, which sponsored the exhibition, visitors learned about developments in the treatment of war wounded.[11] They saw life-size models of new equipment, including one of a hospital ship complete with operating theater and dummies.[12] Placards informed the public that twelve field hospitals and three medical companies accompanied every army division into battle. For those who cared to hear more about the subject, eminences in the field of military medicine addressed the general public on the subjects of lazaret surgery, the control of epidemics, and the history of war victims' care.

Having heard "how varied, well-thought out, and effective" the German system of war victims' care was, many of those who visited the Reichstag hall undoubtedly left reassured.[13] Until the First World War, the decorated beggar, a common sight in nineteenth-century British cities, was almost an unknown figure in Germany. At the time of the Reichstag exhibition, German pensions for disabled veterans were the highest in Europe.[14] Administered entirely by the military, pensions were

Figure 5.   A disabled soldier with one leg practices jumping, 1917. By permission of Ullstein.

paid according to rank. However generous, the German system (like its European counterparts) was intended for a short war with limited casualties. Before 1919, all social services, including medical treatment after discharge from the army, rehabilitation, retraining, and employment, were administered regionally, locally, or voluntarily. Reporting for the Red Cross on European rehabilitation efforts, the American observer Ruth Underhill noted that "the German Government takes less part in the work than the government of any other nation."[15] The care that men received varied greatly, depending on where they lived. Although it was substantially better organized than comparable British efforts (by 1916, the German provinces had established employment bureaus for the disabled), there was little uniformity in the services offered. The Rhineland was often lauded as a model because of innovative retraining programs instituted while the veteran was still hospitalized. In contrast, Westphalia trailed far behind, providing the disabled with little more than a labor exchange.[16]

Not only the services offered but also the way that care was organized differed from region to region, and even sometimes from city to city, according to local administrative structures and the strength of volun-

Kriegsbeschädigte mit Beinprotesen
lernen das Gehen auf welligem Gelände.

Figure 6.   War-disabled men with prosthetic legs learn how to walk on hilly
surfaces, 1919. By permission of the Bildarchiv Preussischer Kulturbesitz.

tarism. Controlled directly by the provincial government in Munich,
Bavaria's system was far and away the most centralized and uniform,
while in Württemberg, a committee composed of city and state officials
as well as private charities directed a network of local efforts.[17] In East
Prussia, Brandenburg, Schleswig-Holstein, the Rhineland, and Hannover, responsibility for the care of the disabled fell to provincial welfare
associations, which before the war had provided treatment for the blind,
epileptic, and insane. In Saxony, the Ministry of the Interior administered the Home Front's Thanks, a public corporation that enlisted voluntary workers and local officials in the business of collecting donations
and organizing care in every area of the state—an idea copied in Baden
in 1916.

    While provincial governments bore much of the burden of providing
wartime social services for the disabled, care for war victims was widely
understood as an imperial responsibility, even, as one Frankfurt paper
claimed, an "honor" for the Reich.[18] It was, after all, the state that had
sent men to risk life and limb; in return, disabled soldiers deserved a national system of care. Yet despite pleas from local governments, experts
in the field of rehabilitation, and unions, which in 1915 threatened to

institute their own welfare programs for the disabled, the imperial state disclaimed action.[19] Even as wartime inflation diminished the value of pensions, the National Finance Office refused to initiate substantial reform in the laws governing compensation, arguing that only once the war was over (and presumably won) could the Reich take charge of war victims' care. The National Finance Office's stance not only caused hardship for individual disabled soldiers and war dependents; it also saddled localities with enormous expenditures that inadequate allocations from the Federal Council, or Bundesrat, composed of delegations from the separate German states, did little to assuage.[20]

If ultimate responsibility for the disabled belonged to the imperial government, most commentators emphasized that the public could not shirk its own obligations to the war's victims.[21] Cautioning that the disabled should not become objects of pity, local state organizations and charitable foundations urged the public to express its gratitude in deeds, rather than words, especially by helping the disabled to return to their former employment.[22] "Deep in your heart you know that this debt is not the Reich's alone, but your own as well," instructed one pamphlet distributed by the Baden Home Front's Thanks. "Silver and gold will not be enough to repay it. Above all, it requires warm-hearted love for one's fellow men!"[23] "Love for one's fellow men" connoted a solicitude that was familial in its scope: the public was called upon to do whatever it could to assist in reintegration, whether it was finding the disabled man a job, offering his family housing, or just listening sympathetically when he talked about his war experiences.

More than a moral imperative, some provincial officials construed broad public participation in war victims' care as a practical necessity. They believed that only voluntary involvement would ensure longstanding public sympathy for the disabled.[24] Urging that welfare programs for the disabled become "a matter for the people," the Saxon Minister-President von Welck explained the logic of the Home Front's Thanks: "The more members recruited for the task, and the wider the circles from which they are drawn, the broader will be the shoulders on which the responsibility for the care of war victims will rest."[25] According to the city committee in Cassel, "A satisfactory solution...can only be hoped for if the entire population demonstrates their sympathy and support."[26] That was the ethos that governed the work of the local state. Although it was most pronounced in those states such as Saxony and Baden, where the Home Front's Thanks sought to establish networks of support throughout the populace, voluntarism figured significantly in

Figure 7.   A meal at Frau von Ihne's Home for the War-Blinded in Berlin.
Frau von Ihne is in the back, dressed in dark clothing, 1917. By permission of
Ullstein.

every local system. In the city of Cassel, for example, citizens' committees found work for the disabled, while in Frankfurt am Main, a wartime
coalition of private charities directed vocational retraining efforts.

By any standard, the public's response was munificent, especially considering the hardships that the war imposed on the German Home
Front.[27] "Consciousness of the nation's debt to the disabled," the influential liberal daily *Vossische Zeitung* commented approvingly in 1915, "is
very much alive."[28] Charities opened in every city to serve wounded and
sick soldiers, the vast majority of them, as in Great Britain, amateur efforts organized outside of the purview of the prominent private welfare
associations. For blinded men, there were vacation homes and retraining
schools, among others, Berlin's School for the War-Blinded, founded by
the optician Paul Silex in October 1914. Those who had lost hands could
attend workshops for retraining, including the One-Armed School established in Saxony in 1915.[29] For the permanently disabled, facilities
like the Marburg Home for Disabled Privates and Riflemen promised
lifelong care. Those needing to convalesce could apply to the Fatherland
Fund for the Establishment of Convalescent Homes. In 1916, the au-

thoritative welfare periodical *Social Practice* reported that in the greater Berlin area alone, thirty-four new organizations had been founded to benefit the war disabled, a development that established philanthropists criticized from the standpoint of practicality, noting the fragmentation and inefficiency that resulted, but the fact of which nevertheless testified to public enthusiasm.[30]

Charities collected previously unheard of sums on behalf of the disabled. In 1915, the Foundation for the War-Blinded raised 4 million marks.[31] Even smaller charities, such as the Marburg Home, registered notable successes.[32] Launched by the town's most prominent citizens in 1915, the Home planned to provide a hundred rooms for war invalids. For soldiers who had learned the "dark side of human nature," the Home aimed, through "warm friendship and genuine love,...to lead them to believe again in the moral value of humanity."[33] Voluntarism promised to reconcile disabled men to their fate; it offered a means of spiritual reconstruction. In the first year of its campaign, the Home raised an enormous sum of 250,178 M. While most donors gave under 100 M, fifty private citizens contributed more than 1,000 M apiece, which entitled them to name a "hero's room" in memory of a fallen loved one.[34]

Although rising prices, food shortages, and declining real incomes severely reduced the amount that most Germans could afford to give in the later years of the war, charities nonetheless managed to raise money. In most cases, their yields did not approach those of 1915 and 1916, but the fact that they still collected substantial sums in the face of the gradual impoverishment of the German population testifies to widespread concern for the disabled.[35] During the harsh Turnip Winter of 1916–1917, when poor harvests caused hunger and suffering at home, donations to the Marburg Home declined by more than half (and were worth less as the rate of inflation rose); between December 1916 and the middle of May 1917, the Home raised just 37,655 M from 300 donors, 180 of whom gave less than one hundred marks, among them several three-mark contributions. Yet in the next five months some improvement was evident. Although small donations fell, the Home received larger gifts, including 20,000 M from the prince of tiny Schaumberg-Lippe. By the end of September 1917, donations had climbed again, to 65,576 M.[36]

Despite the economic and social burdens that total war imposed, public participation in the care of the disabled remained high. In 1917, the Home Front's Thanks recruited more new members in Saxony than it had in 1915, a striking result considering how dramatically the condi-

tions of everyday life had deteriorated for most Germans; in 1917, the
Saxon organization boasted more than 160,000 members.[37] To volunteer
in the Turnip Winter meant spending leisure moments poring over military compensation laws after standing in line for hours to obtain rations, but as membership figures for the Home Front's Thanks demonstrate, it was a sacrifice many citizens were eager to make. Indeed, the
zeal with which ordinary citizens gave their time and money to help disabled veterans confirmed the observation by the Catholic priest Benedict
Kreutz that programs for the war's victims occupied "pride of place" in
the public's heart. No matter how war weary they were themselves, Germans of all classes continued to do what they could for the disabled.

Commenting in 1915 on the variety of initiatives for war victims,
Social Practice noted: "For the war wounded and their dependents it is a
very comforting thought that everywhere people are working to help
them along."[38] Less than a decade later, however, little evidence remained
of the public's commitment to disabled veterans. By 1919, most citizens'
committees had handed over their work to the Reich; few private
charities for war victims remained in operation during the Weimar Republic.[39] Speaking in 1927, Kreutz—leader of the Catholic charity organization Caritas and a former army chaplain—complained of "the indifference toward war victims," all the more striking, he claimed, given
the enthusiasm for other sorts of charity work.[40] For Kreutz, it was no
wonder that the disabled felt neglected, and his comments echoed the
rhetoric that veterans deployed in the later 1920s. Whereas they had first
ascribed the public's apparent apathy to a "lack of understanding," by
the middle of the decade, the problem had assumed more sinister pro-
portions. It was not an oversight that the public ignored disabled veterans. The thanks of the Fatherland had never been delivered because their
fellow citizens no longer cared.

During the Weimar Republic, the public's ingratitude became legend,
a staple of the veterans' movement on the left as on the right. Historians
have largely acquitted the public of the charge, demonstrating the heart-
felt admiration and respect Germans paid their defeated army.[41] And
yet, as we shall see, disabled veterans were not entirely mistaken; because
of the state regulation of charity, the public's gratitude was expressed
much less often than would otherwise have been the case. Proposals to
open specially equipped workshops for the blind, plans to build convalescent homes, concerts to be given to benefit the disabled: in the years
between 1917 and 1922, the Prussian State Commissioner for the Regulation of Welfare Work received hundreds of applications from con-

cerned citizens who planned national projects to help wounded soldiers. Local authorities probably received thousands more requests from people whose ambitions were restricted to their own towns or cities. Whether the projects they envisioned were large or small, very few of these would-be philanthropists received the permission necessary to collect donations or solicit dues-paying members. Unless a project became part of the state's own machinery for disabled veterans, the chances of its survival were minimal at best.

This regulation of private charity work, the first national such effort in Germany's history, owed its origins to a decree issued by the Bundesrat in February 1917 and enforced vigorously throughout the early 1920s. Deployed first by military authorities to direct all available resources to the war effort, the decree later provided the legislative underpinnings for the consolidation of the Weimar welfare state. Between 1917 and 1922, German authorities quashed private initiative and public participation in the care of the disabled. In the early years of the Weimar Republic, the decree proved a powerful weapon against philanthropic work of all kinds. Everything from commemorative editions of books (a portion of the proceeds of which would have been given to charity) to Frau von Ihne's Berlin home for blinded soldiers was affected. Wielded by civil servants convinced of the necessity of generous and comprehensive programs controlled solely by the state, the power to regulate philanthropy ended up isolating the very ministries it was intended to protect.

BENEVOLENCE REGULATED

In the spring of 1917, Oskar Zill, a prosperous Berlin furniture manufacturer, decided to help blinded soldiers. On four acres of property near Potsdam, he planned a small settlement for artisans unable to practice their prewar trades. He would employ the men in his factory to make wooden forms for decorative furniture and placards. In addition to a salary, veterans and their families would receive purpose-built housing on the premises. Theirs would be a model community, with recycling facilities and access to the therapeutic powers of nature. Zill meant to ensure the dignity of the settlement's inhabitants. "The settlers," Zill proclaimed, "should be made to feel like free and independent citizens, not recipients of charity."[42] Although building could not begin until the war was over, Zill estimated that he would need 100,000 M to realize the proposed venture, 60,000 of which he planned to raise through donations from the public and the sale of postcards.

In accordance with the recently introduced February 1917 decree of the Bundesrat, Zill's application to raise funds for his settlement was passed from the Charlottenburg chief of police to his Potsdam equivalent. Two months later, it ended up in the office of the Prussian State Commissioner for the Regulation of Welfare Work. Zill's proposal arrived bolstered by testimonials that praised his character as well as the proposed endeavor. The Charlottenburg chief of police emphasized that Zill's factory was a venerable and well-regarded undertaking, while Zill enjoyed a reputation as a "responsible and skillful businessman."[43] He rated the prospects for the new settlement's success as "very good," given Zill's personal connections and his long years of experience in the trade. There was no need to worry that Zill's enterprise would interfere with existing welfare efforts for the disabled, because the would-be philanthropist and his brother stated that they wished to work closely with the authorities and hoped "only to put their knowledge and skill to use."[44]

Despite the police chief's endorsement, the State Commissioner denied Zill's petition. This decision reflected the advice of the National Committee for War Victims' Care. An alliance of provincial and imperial civil servants, the National Committee had coordinated welfare efforts on behalf of disabled veterans and war dependents since 1915; while it lacked formal jurisdiction, it functioned as a civil service in waiting on questions pertaining to war victims. However willing Zill was to cooperate with the authorities, the very essence of his plan violated the National Committee's principle that individual charities should not be permitted to solicit donations from the public. Writing on behalf of the National Committee, Dr. Hermann Geib (mayor of Regensburg and later assistant secretary to the Labor Ministry) further objected that Zill's purpose was not primarily to assist the state's authorities but to found a new business. Although he acknowledged that Zill's plan would assist the disabled, it could not be defended in terms of the "interests of official efforts."[45]

Faced with the rejection of a proposal he had considered unobjectionable, Zill suggested that the authorities had not understood what he had planned. Listing the advantages that his settlement would bring the state, he noted that the "founding principle of our enterprise is the desire to free the state from burdens."[46] If Zill could build his settlement, men for whom the state would otherwise have to provide would be able to earn their own living. "Considering how enormous people's needs will be after the war, we think that every citizen who can put a good idea into practice must be supported, especially when it doesn't cost the state anything."[47] Zill failed to persuade the authorities. The State Commissioner rejected his application. The settlement was never built, though Zill's factory operated until 1941. Zill became exasperated by the State Commissioner's refusals and returned to business as usual. Whatever he may have thought about citizens' responsibilities, the state had demonstrated it did not want his assistance.

The case of Zill's settlement is one of many thousands preserved in the Prussian State Commissioner's records.[48] Although more modest in scale than the majority of ventures, Zill's proposal is otherwise typical, as is the authorities' response to it. Whereas prewar institutions and venerable charitable societies could generally expect the State Commissioner to permit their fund-raising requests (albeit with restrictions), newcomers such as Zill had little chance of gaining approval. While it is difficult to trace the fate of proposed charitable projects after the State Commissioner's refusal, the majority, in all likelihood, abandoned their plans. Those who persisted in their quest, securing testimonials from local officials and tirelessly renewing their application, might succeed, but the proportion of philanthropic hopefuls willing to persevere despite the State Commissioner's rejection was small. Organizations that collected without permission risked substantial fines and, for their founders, prison sentences.

Until the First World War, the imperial state exercised little control over philanthropy; the Reich did not generally regulate how charities raised their funds or appealed to the public.[49] The task of coordinating voluntary and public services was left to local authorities and their philanthropic counterparts, who aimed, though not always successfully, to divide up the field. From the 1890s through the outbreak of war, poor-relief officials and welfare reformers from the private sector campaigned for greater state oversight of the charitable sphere, while the larger charity organizations centralized and sought to professionalize their own operations.[50] During the first year of the war, there were no restraints on collecting. In July 1915, the Bundesrat issued its first decree, prohibiting street collections unless first approved by local authorities.[51] However, in many parts of the country, it remained a dead letter, principally because there was neither the personnel nor the administrative will to enforce it. The decree published on 15 February 1917 was different. All organizations founded after the outbreak of the war were to be regulated, with the exception of those that collected for religious or political purposes.[52] The decree not only forbid membership campaigns as well as all forms of collecting (including direct solicitation) for such associations but also provided effective means of enforcement through local police headquarters, as well as State Commissioners. Throughout the Weimar Republic, this "wartime" measure remained in force. In November 1934, it was replaced by a stricter Nazi decree.[53]

During the war, the responsible authorities defended the February decree as a necessary measure against fraud. The streets of every German city, Berlin especially, swarmed with collectors of all stripes; the public could not distinguish the legitimate undertakings from the swindles. In a speech before representatives of the established charity organizations, Dr. Pokrantz, from police headquarters in Berlin, admitted that he, too, originally had "misgivings" about the regulation of philanthropy—that is, until he unmasked the Society of the Iron Cross.[54] Founded by a "Count" Wenzel zu Sternau und Hohenau, ostensibly to help wounded officers secure a home of their own, the organization existed principally to support its president, who paid himself a handsome salary of 500 M a month. For the benefit of his audience, Pokrantz depicted a philanthropic jungle populated by unsavory characters who preyed on the public's goodwill. Patronage by the wellborn and distinguished was no guarantee of legitimacy, while "homes" for the destitute were just as likely to serve the needs of lazy real estate speculators as their would-be inhabitants.[55]

Yet for all of Pokrantz's doomsaying, the Bundesrat decrees were in fact notable for how little fraud they exposed. In the fall of 1917, only five Prussian organizations had been placed under receivership, a negligible figure considering the thousands of philanthropies founded during the war years.[56] By 1921, the State Commissioner had assumed control of not more than twenty organizations nationwide, most of which had minimal assets.[57] There is no evidence that wartime philanthropy was more corrupt in Germany than elsewhere in western Europe. Judging from the report of a British Home Office Departmental Committee, which noted that 9 percent of all London philanthropies had been deemed fraudulent, it might well have been less so.[58] In Germany, as in Britain, there were notorious rackets, but the Count Wenzels were much the exception, not the rule. As even Pokrantz acknowledged, most organizations were founded by people like Oskar Zill, "kind-hearted" men and women who wanted to help.[59]

The Bundesrat decree testified not to the fraudulent nature of philanthropy but to the desperate state of the war effort. In the winter of 1916–1917, the production of steel and powder had plunged, forcing the High Command to retreat on the Western Front that March.[60] To increase production for the war, authorities in the newly created War

Office redirected all resources to military priorities. They urged a "Concentration of Forces," as the slogan propagated during the summer of 1917 went. No sphere of activity was exempt; along with efforts to rationalize and consolidate industry and agriculture came the regulation of welfare. Two weeks before the publication of the February decree, Wilhelm Groener, head of the War Office, condemned the proliferation of charities as an unjustifiable waste of funds and personnel. In a speech before the National Committee for Women's War Work, he called for the development of a national and unified welfare system in place of philanthropic "fragmentation." The true aim of welfare, he argued, should be to bolster production.[61]

Military exigencies explain the February decree's origins but do not account for its longevity. What began as an emergency policy to conserve resources for the war effort became, in the Weimar Republic, a means of ensuring the new state's authority. The interventionist German welfare state—in the late nineteenth century a model for other European reformers—reached its apotheosis in the Weimar Republic. War and revolution made the expansion of the welfare state not simply a possibility but a political necessity. To secure the loyalty of a skeptical citizenry, Weimar's framers sought to provide the best benefits possible; the constitution of the new Republic accorded each citizen an extensive list of social rights, including the right to work or maintenance. The centerpiece of a compromise among Social Democrats, the Catholic Center Party, and the left-liberal Democrats, Weimar's comprehensive welfare programs undergirded the state's claim to legitimacy.[62] Alongside comprehensive programs for war victims, delinquent youth, single mothers, and the victims of inflation came innovations in labor legislation, public housing, and unemployment insurance.

In a state that had constitutionally guaranteed the well-being of its citizenry, unregulated philanthropy, more than merely a hindrance, became a threat to authority. Largely overlooked by scholars, the state regulation of charity raises critical questions about the transformation of the voluntary sector in the period 1914–1933. Drawing from the example of the major private welfare organizations, scholars have argued that philanthropy gained a privileged, quasi-public status in the Weimar state.[63] Young-Sun Hong has demonstrated how national organizations such as the Catholic Caritasverband and the Protestant Inner Mission had, by the late 1920s, carved out a "semi-corporate" sphere within the welfare bureaucracy.[64] Not only did the National Youth Welfare Law (1922) and the National Welfare Decree (1924) institutionalize the

Catholic principle of subsidiarity, which instructed local authorities to delegate responsibility to existing philanthropies instead of founding their own initiatives, but the Labor Ministry granted the major private organizations substantial funds to underwrite their work.

And yet, corporatization was available only to the largest and best-organized private welfare associations. As a consequence of the Bundesrat decree, charities that were not chosen to or did not wish to, work within the state's welfare apparatus had no means of appealing to the public for funds or advertising for members. Historians have accepted the consolidation of charitable effort as self-evident, even ineluctable, a product of the socialist revolution and the economic exigencies of the 1920s.[65] However, the reasons for philanthropy's transformation are more complex. Although revolutionary demands for the socialization of charity gained new legitimacy in the early Republic, the threatened measure never came to pass.[66] Not only did the Social Democratic Party's stated opposition to charity fail to translate into a concrete socialization program, but the party proved, through its own voluntary association, the Arbeiterwohlfahrt, tolerant of philanthropy provided that it operated in concert with local welfare offices.[67] Similarly, the financial devastation inflicted by the inflationary decade of 1914–1924 severely hampered many philanthropies' activities, destroying their assets and reducing charitable giving.[68] Yet economic collapse does not fully explain philanthropy's loss of autonomy in the Republic. Neither political animosity nor economic exigency alone, but the policies implemented by state authorities diminished the independence of charities in the Weimar Republic.

The Weimar state's regulation of charity represented a fundamental intervention into society and the economy. Unlike the rationalization of industry, in which governmental ministries played a marginal role, the Bundesrat decree granted state authorities the initiative in charity regulation and—through the offices of the State Commissioner for the Regulation of Welfare Work—provided a means of institutional control.[69] While after the war the State Commissioner remained officially charged with the duty of approving charities, the real power lay with the architects of the Weimar welfare state, foremost among them officials of the Labor Ministry. Founded in 1919, the Labor Ministry formulated and implemented the social policies of the Weimar state, including programs for the unemployed, pensioners, and war victims. Willing and in some cases even eager to cooperate with established charity organizations, officials in the Labor Ministry regarded smaller philanthropies with suspicion and even hostility. Where the state could not or would not meet citizens' needs, officials encouraged charity work. However, in arenas the state had claimed as its own, authorities brooked no interference from amateur philanthropists, whose work challenged their own claim to competence.

In no case was the threat that unregulated private benevolence represented to state authorities more apparent than as regards charities for disabled veterans. As early as 1917, prominent officials of the National Committee for War Victims' Care had sought to restrict charitable fund-raising. Their stake in the problem was social rather than military: they believed that the care of the disabled would become an important task for the postwar state. Many of the National Committee's members, including its chairman, Joachim von Winterfeldt, the governor of Prussia, regarded the growing number of charities with scarcely less hostility than did Groener. Although von Winterfeldt did not criticize women directly, his denunciations of "vanity" and "dilettantism" in the charitable sector implicated their efforts. More often than not, wrote von Winterfeldt, philanthropists failed to accomplish their objectives because "alongside honorable intentions and practical sensibilities, dangerous, dilettantish utopias, vanity, and egoism, even criminal self-interest, made themselves felt."[70]

Until the nation's defeat, and the Revolution, the rehabilitation of the disabled remained a regional matter. The demilitarization of the pensions apparatus, mandated by the Treaty of Versailles, provided a foundation for the national system long endorsed by public opinion and urged by war victims themselves. Despite opposition from the state secretary of the Treasury Office, who maintained that the Republic could not "take on new financial burdens," and warned of the "paralysis of voluntary charitable activity," the Weimar state assumed responsibility for the care of disabled veterans and war dependents in February 1919.[71] Under the direction of the Social Democrat Gustav Bauer, the newly formed Labor Ministry, staffed in part by officials of the National Committee, took charge of rehabilitation and employment. Within the year, the voluntary and local edifice constructed in wartime had been almost completely dismantled. By 1921, reported the journal *Social Practice*, charitable organizations were engaged, if at all, only in an advisory capacity in war victims' care.[72]

At the heart of Weimar's comprehensive welfare state were programs for disabled veterans. To care for the disabled was, in the words of Chancellor Friedrich Ebert, the Republic's "foremost duty."[73] More than a duty, however, welfare initiatives for the war victims had symbolic im-port. The rehabilitation of disabled veterans stood as a metaphor for the reconstruction of the nation, and hence highlighted the skill of the Republic in solving pressing social problems even as the legitimacy of the new state was under siege. For Franz Schweyer, a permanent secretary in the Labor Ministry, the reintegration of disabled veterans was therefore not to be regarded "an economically sterile and unproductive field of work, which only burdens the budget, but a lively branch of state activity.... Care for the war victims is in a certain sense synonymous with self-preservation, renewal, reconstruction."[74] Between 1920 and 1932, war pensions accounted for nearly 20 percent of total governmental spending.[75]

The Weimar welfare state staked its reputation on the care of the disabled. Where some wartime local authorities had welcomed philanthropy as a means of sparing expenditure, civil servants in the Labor Ministry and its welfare offices tended to regard charity for disabled veterans as unwelcome competition. Not only did philanthropists distribute relief in a way that undermined the authorities' own vision, but their fund-raising campaigns called attention to the inadequacies of the state's programs. In 1919, the Hessian welfare office for war victims rejected out of hand a fund-raising proposal from a veterans' organization, fearing that "the appearance would be created that the official care of the disabled is insufficient."[76] Charities for disabled veterans served as an indictment of the government's policies. In a Republic that had constitutionally guaranteed its citizens' welfare, the existence of charities demonstrated that the state had failed, and their absence proved that it was functioning effectively. At best, philanthropy was unproductive; at worst, it threatened the state's claim to authority by highlighting the shortcomings of its services.

The February 1917 decree allowed the National Committee officials and their successors in the Labor Ministry to establish a virtual monopoly over the care of disabled veterans. During the years 1917 through 1924, they eliminated their philanthropic competitors either by ensuring that they did not receive permission to collect funds (a list of authorized collections was published weekly in local and national newspapers) or, failing that, by gaining decisive control over their administration. Faced with repeated rejections from the State Commissioner's office, the vast majority of small and untested enterprises folded. Yet even wealthy and prestigious organizations—bullied, harassed, and subjected to taxation—were forced to capitulate to Labor Ministry supervision. Many representatives of private welfare opposed the decree, but with little success.[77] Those who welcomed the state's supervision, like the prominent welfare reformer Siddy Wronsky of the Berlin Office for Private Welfare, long a critic of amateur efforts, saw their vision prevail.[78] The consolidation of philanthropy for the disabled proceeded in most cases by compulsion, not choice.

The case of the Foundation for the War-Blinded illustrates how even well-endowed and reputable organizations were rendered powerless in the face of state regulation. Founded in 1915, the Foundation first incurred the authorities' displeasure when its inaugural fund-raising campaign yielded the unprecedented sum of 4 million marks in donations. According to the newly formed National Committee, the Foundation had already raised enough money for the blind, and thus it directed the State Commissioner to prohibit all further appeals. The leaders of the National Committee feared that public sympathy for the war-blinded would limit local authorities' abilities to raise funds for other disabled men. As Prussia's minister-president later remarked, the war-blinded posed a "danger" because they could raise funds from all sides, a fact that made them a particular threat to civil servants attempting to establish hegemony in the field.[79]

A second, and more significant, intervention into the affairs of the Foundation for the War-Blinded came in 1919, after a revolutionary demand by blinded men for greater representation in the organization led to the resignation of most of its board members and the appointment of Dr. Paul Silex as its temporary chairman. The integrity of Silex, an eminent optical specialist and himself the founder of a school to retrain war-blinded men, was undisputed. However, civil servants in the Labor Ministry interpreted his appointment as a sign that the Foundation would pass "fully into the hands of the war-blinded, and that as a result, the competent state authorities would lose their influence over the organization."[80] Oskar Karstedt, the Labor Ministry official who became the most outspoken critic of unregulated voluntarism, spent the rest of the month attempting to rescind Silex's appointment, writing to the Ministry of the Interior and the police headquarters in Potsdam.[81] When that proved impossible, he set about implementing the most drastic provisions of the February 1917 decree: the seizure of the Foundation's assets.

What the Labor Ministry's officials phrased as concern over the future administration of the Foundation in fact reflected their desire to retain control of its assets. Karstedt and his colleagues had no intention of losing their authority over the Foundation. In a letter to Silex, Karstedt warned that the Labor Ministry "placed great weight on the fact that it previously had the necessary influence in the Foundation and that, moreover, the Foundation's funds had been dispensed in closest cooperation with official programs for the war victims."[82] Only after the new board agreed that the organization would be housed within the Labor Ministry's buildings on the Scharnhorststrasse was the forcible dissolution of the Foundation averted. Although some of the board members feared that this step would allow the Labor Ministry to gain too much control over the Foundation, Karstedt guaranteed the organization's independence, a curious promise in light of his role in the month's proceedings.[83]

Yet just what this "independence" entailed became clear four years later, when the Foundation applied for permission to solicit donations to replenish funds severely depleted by the hyperinflation. Although Ministerial Director Erwin Ritter of the Labor Ministry, a Catholic generally sympathetic to private charity, was inclined to support its September 1924 petition, citing the suffering of the blind during the inflation, information from the police headquarters in Potsdam brought the process to a halt.[84] According to the police chief, "in addition to completely unobjectionable people," the governing committee of the Foundation for the War-Blinded harbored—"as its treasurer no less"—a suspicious character by the name of Adolf Pochwadt. In the police report, Pochwadt was described as a "former variety artist, animal trainer, later a dentist, and today the owner of a factory for metalware and dentistry equipment, with a police record for violation of the patent law."[85] As if that were not enough to discredit him in the Labor Ministry's eyes, the report also accused him of peddling honors and titles.

The Labor Ministry rescinded its support. Until the Foundation rid itself of Pochwadt, it would not be allowed to collect. Therein ensued a bizarre correspondence between Pochwadt and the State Commissioner. Pochwadt refuted the charge that he was "a hairdresser, an animal trainer or a lion-tamer." True, as a young man, he had studied dentistry. And in 1904, he founded a dental and surgical tools business, a career move that he defended as "not at all unusual."[86] The police, he suggested, had the wrong Pochwadt. His brother, for many years a resident of Berlin, now dead, had indeed worked as an animal trainer and variety artist; their father had been a hairdresser. He went on to answer the police chief's other charges. He maintained that he had never been held in violation of the law, other than speeding. In conclusion, he noted that he had been awarded eighteen German orders, the Prussian Civil Service Cross, and the Red Cross Medal, second class.

Despite Pochwadt's attempt to set the record straight, the State Commissioner remained firm. A copy of a report from the police chief of Saxon-Weimar, who testified to Pochwadt's good reputation as a factory owner, adding that he was "very active" in charity organizations, most recently on behalf of the Red Cross, did not change matters.[87] So that the fund-raising campaign postponed six months could begin (albeit under the Labor Ministry's close supervision), Pochwadt resigned from the Foundation for the War-Blinded. He continued to correspond with the State Commissioner in an attempt to clear his name. Pochwadt maintained that he was the victim of a conspiracy engineered by the Sklarz brothers, intimate friends of Berlin's chief of police, and objected strongly to the police report that depicted him, in his words, as an "individual on the verge of the penitentiary."[88] The officials for the regulation of charities declined all his requests for interviews. In all likelihood, Pochwadt was neither as crooked as the State Commissioner painted him nor as upstanding as he claimed. However, there was nothing, such as criminal convictions or allegations of embezzlement, that obviously disqualified Pochwadt as a philanthropist.

Unlike philanthropists, who viewed the distribution of charity as an opportunity to moralize the giver, Labor Ministry officials perceived uncontrolled private benevolence as a threat to civil society from within. They viewed the charitable sector as a locus of fragmentation and discord, where private, not public, interest predominated. The State Commissioner thus required would-be philanthropists to meet the highest standards. They not only had to be of excellent repute, good family, and sound finances but also had to demonstrate pure motives. Any suspicion of financial interest in the proposed project resulted in automatic refusal. In 1919, the Labor Ministry rejected an application by Frau Schuller-Vedvy to institute a commemorative Flower Day on the grounds that she was "closely associated with the florist industry."[89] Nor could potential philanthropists expect to increase their own personal glory through their work. Artists who wished to stage benefit performances had first to prove to the State Commissioner that their primary interest was not the enhancement of their own reputation.[90] Among the allegations that discredited Pochwadt was the charge that he had become involved in charity work to gather honors and titles. Subjected to such stringent guidelines, few of the British philanthropists would have passed muster. Oswald Stoll, half-Australian proprietor of variety theaters—one step closer to the music-hall business than Pochwadt—would have appeared to the State Commissioner eminently unfit to serve. The suffragist women of the Actresses' Franchise League would have never received a hearing.

Through the regulation of charity, Labor Ministry officials sought to ensure that the rehabilitation of the disabled proceeded according to their plans. Aiming to return men to their own families and, whenever possible, the workplace, they vetoed proposals for homes or workshops for disabled—in Germany, as in Britain, the majority of charitable initiatives. Plans contrary to the Labor Ministry's own ideas had virtually no chance of survival. By the end of the war, the Marburg Home for Disabled Soldiers and Riflemen had raised enough money to buy a building. However, it could not accept patients until it had collected funds for an operating budget. On the recommendation of the National Committee, and later the Labor Ministry, the State Commissioner repeatedly denied the Home permission to collect. The early 1920s passed with it still lacking the necessary budget.[91] Discouraged by delays and red tape, the Home's original supporters dwindled away. By the time the hyperinflation destroyed the Home's capital, the necessary initiative was long since gone.

The Labor Ministry sought to control not only how charities for the disabled raised their money but also how they spent it. In 1919, the proposed law about the *Reichsnotopfer* (Federal Emergency Contribution) offered an opportunity to gain control over charities' disbursements. According to a proposal from the Finance Ministry, charitable organizations, including those that cared for the disabled, were to be exempt from taxation. The Labor Ministry, represented by Dr. Hermann Geib, objected. In a letter to the finance minister, Geib argued that the February 1917 decree had proven that these philanthropies could not "always be seen as helpful and appropriate."[92] Citing charities' high administrative costs, "dilettantish ways," and the potential for "socially damaging employment of their resources," Geib implied that the state's own efforts were endangered by feckless philanthropy. Although the State Commissioner had found very few fraudulent charities, Geib persisted in depicting the philanthropic sphere as a hotbed of criminality.[93] To safeguard the care of the disabled, Geib urged the finance minister to provide tax exemptions only to those organizations that promised to "disburse their funds in agreement with the state's administrative apparatus for war victims."[94]

Persuaded by Geib's rhetoric about the "fight against dubious enterprises," the Finance Ministry assented to the Labor Ministry's proposal. Dr. Dernburg reportedly stated that it was "regrettable that the govern-

ment had not yet intervened energetically enough."[95] In accordance with
Geib's suggestion, it amended the paragraph. For the rest of the Weimar
Republic, charities that sought to assist the war's victims were placed at
a disadvantage relative to institutions and organizations that cared for
the poor, the sick, the elderly, babies, children, and orphans. These institutions continued to enjoy tax-exempt status, no matter how they
spent their money. Charities for the disabled and the dependents of former soldiers were held to a different set of rules. Unless they agreed to
extensive state control over their expenditures, which in practical terms
meant the distribution of their funds through government offices and bureaus, they received no relief from taxation.

In the eyes of the National Committee and the Labor Ministry, the
only legitimate charities were those that gave the state extensive control
over the distribution of their funds. For that reason, Karstedt and Geib
heartily supported the Invalidendank (Thanks to the Invalids). Founded
in 1871 to benefit disabled soldiers from the Franco-Prussian War, the
Invalidendank was not subject to the decree of 15 February 1917. Nevertheless, it won the Labor Ministry's approval by agreeing to distribute
its grants through local welfare offices for the disabled. From April 1919
onward the Labor Ministry became the Invalidendank's firm ally. Despite criticism from the police chief, who in 1923 noted "considerable
reservations" about labeling the Invalidendank a benevolent concern,
given the fact that the organization's welfare expenditures represented
only a fraction of its receipts from donations, the Labor Ministry's support did not waver.[96] Throughout the Republic, the Invalidendank was
plagued by financial hardship and controversy.[97]

However straightforward the regulation of charity may have appeared
in 1917, it proved a tricky business. There was, for instance, the matter
of experts hired to judge whether new philanthropies were in the public
interest. On a recommendation from Geib and Karstedt, the State Commissioner appointed the businessman Fritz Maercker "chief expert" in
1919; his duties were to assist the police headquarters in their investigations and to testify in court against frauds. By 1920, the State Commissioner had two experts but nothing to pay them. There was no money
in the budget. After consulting the Ministry of the Interior, the State
Commissioner decided that their salaries should be paid from the funds
they seized. In other words, these ostensibly impartial experts were to
work on speculation, a fact of which they were clearly aware.[98] Unless
they shut down enough charities—with sizable enough assets—there
would be no money for their own salaries. While admitting to reserva-

tions about paying the experts from money collected for charity, the State Commissioner claimed that swindlers would have squandered more: "Objectively speaking, using a portion of this money for administrative purposes appears to me justified, because most of the organizations that were closed down...had administrations that were, without exception, very costly. However, by confiscating their assets, the cost of their administration is being spared, with considerable savings for the purposes of welfare."[99]

Despite the State Commissioner's happy rationalization, very little of the confiscated money went to charity. Most found its way into the chief experts' pockets, and what was left evaporated in the inflation. Financial dealings that in a charity would have been grounds for tirades about profit making—perhaps even for the seizure of its assets—became a daily routine in the offices of the State Commissioner for the Regulation of Welfare Work.[100] In 1922, the State Commissioner reported to the police chief that both a former official of the court and the public prosecutor's office had made serious charges against Maercker: "Maercker's written evaluations are completely lacking in objectivity," while his appearances in court "are remarkably clumsy and, in violation of the standards required of experts, display such prejudice that a judge has to fight the conviction that M. is motivated by personal interests."[101] His financial dealings were no less suspicious: "The excessive amounts that Maercker has charged for his expertise have also given rise to serious criticism. For his labors on seized records in the Schnabel case, which required studying a moderate number of files, he charged 1,500 M, for a written opinion in the case of Walter and Gen., 15,000 M!"[102] In the winter of 1922, the chief expert was fired.

The February decree allowed the Labor Ministry to gain unprecedented control over social welfare. Scholars have often debated Weimar's comprehensive welfare programs, asking whether costly social initiatives imperiled the Republic or prolonged its life span.[103] Yet in evaluating Germans' expectations of the Republic, the consequences of the state's consolidation of charity have gone unexamined. Never as comprehensive as the Republic's framers had hoped, the state's welfare programs, implemented amid the economic devastation of the postwar years, nonetheless shifted responsibility for care from voluntary and local organizations to the national authorities. Weimar could not deliver on its constitutional promises to safeguard its citizens' welfare, but by the mid-1920s there could be no doubt about the expectations it had raised. The vast majority of needy Germans looked to the state, not to philanthropy or religious institutions, to ameliorate hard times.

Devastated by the hyperinflation and the Depression, the Weimar state could not satisfy the expectations it had created. Under the leadership of Heinrich Brauns, a Catholic Center Party politician and priest, the Labor Ministry between 1924 and 1928 forged a close alliance with the National League for Private Charity, an umbrella organization representing the country's six leading private welfare associations. In the reorganization that followed the hyperinflation, the Labor Ministry mandated cooperation between the state and organized benevolence, according established charities such as the Red Cross, Catholic Caritas, and the Protestant Inner Mission quasi-public status and clearly delineated positions within the welfare apparatus.[104] Both the National Youth Welfare Law (1922) and the National Welfare Decree (1924) codified the "subsidiarity principle."[105] To ease this new arrangement, the Labor Ministry distributed substantial grants to the League's six members.[106] State grants to charity were not in themselves new, but the scale of the Labor Ministry's allocations far surpassed all precedents, undoubtedly helping private welfare organizations to recover from the ravages of hyperinflation, even to function more effectively.

Yet the Labor Ministry's generosity came at the cost of philanthropy's independence. Drawing on official homages and the massive sums allocated to the League, scholars have tended to conclude that Brauns's Labor Ministry aimed to preserve an autonomous philanthropic sphere.[107] However, this "corporatization of the welfare sector," as Young-Sun Hong has termed it, served to exclude amateurs such as Oskar Zill from the charitable field.[108] Only the leading private organizations were granted a privileged position in the welfare state—and only on the condition that they submit to considerable control over their activities. "In an alarming way," wrote the charity worker Else Wex in 1929, "the entire voluntary sector now resembles the large cartels of industry. In the leading private welfare organizations, rationalization, at least in idea and intention, has been taken too far. One is almost overcome by the feeling: What is actually left of charity?"[109] The Labor Ministry continued to guard its monopoly over the care of disabled veterans. Even as the State Commissioner eased fund-raising restrictions in other areas of private welfare work, many charities for the disabled were denied permission to collect, including the Foundation for the War-Blinded during the Pochwadt affair. While organizations of disabled veterans received important exemptions after 1924, the decree of February 1917 remained in force.

Oskar Karstedt retained his position in charge of "relations with charities," although his poor opinion of most philanthropy had not changed. In 1924, as in 1920, his ideal remained the unification of charities under the state's control: "The hypertrophic growth that characterizes certain branches of private charity work must finally submit to the knife and while in individual cases, the amputations will hurt, the whole will... eventually profit."[110] For Karstedt, most charities' postwar difficulties were largely of their own making—not attributable, in other words, to economic hardship or the state's own decrees. In the name of preserving "pioneer work," the philanthropic sector had tolerated too many new charities, which, in turn, had bred criminality. Although philanthropists had balked at the Bundesrat decrees, Karstedt expressed his hope that financial crisis might alert them to the errors of their ways. Karstedt persisted in his belief that "that are many people, especially in big cities, who... under the cover of charity have made millions of marks for themselves."[111] Karstedt's anxious vision of criminality thriving "under the cover of charity" legitimated any measure the state chose to take, however drastic. The state's knife was primed for body politic–saving amputations, and he was as ready as ever to wield it.

By 1924, the philanthropic moment had already passed, so far as disabled veterans were concerned. The hyperinflation left few with money to spare, while those who had resources showed little interest in the plight of disabled veterans. In 1924, other causes appeared more deserving, not least because the inflation had left new victims in its wake. In 1926, the Foundation for the War-Blinded, which in 1915 had collected 4 million marks, managed to raise only 436,909 RM.[112] Despite the Labor Ministry's apparently lenient policy, very few new charities for the disabled were founded after 1924. Five years of reassurances about the superior care available to the disabled had, in all likelihood, convinced many would-be founders to concentrate their resources elsewhere. As early as 1919, the Fatherland Fund's administrators informed the Labor Ministry that many of its members had canceled their subscriptions because they no longer saw the "necessity" of private charity work.[113] There was no reason for the public to support "charitable dilettantism" when the state could fund superior programs.

Whatever honorable intentions had prompted the decree of 15 February 1917, in practice, the state's attempt to regulate philanthropy for disabled veterans had proven a fiasco. Well-meaning people such as

Oskar Zill or the prominent citizens of Marburg, who had the ability to found private initiatives symbolic of the public's appreciation, were thwarted in their desire to help. At the same time, the Labor Ministry forged alliances with questionable organizations, such as the ineffectual Invalidendank, principally because its board agreed to submit to direct state control over the foundation's assets. The criminality that ostensibly "plagued" charities for war victims, so often deplored by the State Commissioner, the Labor Ministry, and police headquarters, either escaped detection or did not exist: fewer than twenty organizations had been closed down by 1922.[114] As if the failures in the decree's conception were not damaging enough, its implementation was little better than a farce, with confiscated charitable funds going to pay those charged with their regulation, and a supposed expert such as Fritz Maercker accused of incompetence.

Deprived of public expressions of gratitude, disabled veterans came to believe that their fellow citizens had scorned their sacrifices. During the mid-1920s, Benedict Kreutz, head of the Catholic charity organization Caritas, turned his considerable energy to the problems of war victims.[115] A chaplain during the war, Kreutz had become increasingly concerned by what he saw as the public's "indifference" to the disabled. Speaking in 1927 before the National Committee, he argued that the war victims' grievances were "partly real, partly alleged."[116] He acknowledged that many disabled had legitimate material complaints, but he believed their discontent owed more to "wounds of the soul" inflicted by the public's neglect than to pensions. As Kreutz put it, "War-widows and disabled veterans look at society differently from other people. They have sacrificed precious things for the community, the life of a beloved or their own health, and are therefore bound to their fellow citizens by blood, twice over. As a consequence, their eyes and ears are open, watching and listening to see if their cry for help echoes back an assurance of assistance."[117]

What the war victims wanted, claimed Kreutz, was the "so often-discussed Thanks of the Fatherland." Although he acknowledged that the disabled wanted to be regarded as "state pensioners," he did not believe that pensions could actually satisfy their grievances.[118] If the "spiritual dimensions" of care for the war victims were to be restored, "the people had to take a lively interest again" in the problem.[119] In a newspaper interview, Kreutz called on the public to return the war victims to "first place."[120] No longer could Germans neglect their duties and "shun their 'social conscience' because they believe that national, personal, and collective obligations have been fulfilled by the state's programs."[121] They had to take individual responsibility for the welfare of war victims. For Kreutz, who deplored the bureaucratization of welfare, charities provided one solution. He called for a "more forceful enlistment" of philanthropy to mediate a new understanding between the war victims and their public.

No such reconciliation happened in the last years of the Weimar Republic. If anything, the relationship between the disabled and their public deteriorated still further, as the relative prosperity of the years 1924–1928 gave way to the bitterness of the Depression. In the war's immediate aftermath, disabled veterans regarded their fellow citizens sympathetically; the German public, they believed, was eager to fulfill its duties. By the mid-1920s, however, accusations raged on both sides. Disabled veterans of all political persuasions charged that the public had neglected their needs, even forgotten them. For their part, many Germans viewed the disabled as greedy, even burdensome—an impression perpetuated by the Labor Ministry's own statements. Yet the less the disabled trusted their fellow citizens, the more they demanded from the state. As the next section indicates, this distrust had serious consequences for the Weimar Republic.

VETERANS VERSUS THE PUBLIC

Of all the Weimar Republic's sufferers—the unemployed, small pensioners who had lost their savings in the hyperinflation, the elderly and chronically ill dependent upon welfare—war victims were among the most prominent, and perhaps also the most embittered. In the years 1917–1919, disabled veterans, war widows, and orphans formed scores of local associations to represent their interests. By 1919, there were seven national organizations of war victims, with a total membership, at the high point in 1921, of nearly 1.4 million.[122] Ostensibly nonpartisan, war victims' organizations were thoroughly political, from the largest, the National Association of Disabled Soldiers, Veterans, and War Dependents (Reichsbund), which enjoyed close ties to the Social Democratic Party (SPD), to the conservative Central Association of Disabled German Veterans and War Dependents (Zentralverband). In the cities, thousands of disabled marched to secure their "rights." Even small towns witnessed protest marches.[123] Demonstration followed on demonstration: for higher pensions, for guaranteed employment, even for free or reduced fares on public transportation. In April 1919, as Free Corps

Figure 8.   A demonstration by the Internationaler Bund der Kriegsopfer and the Reichsverband deutscher Kriegsbeschädigter und Kriegshinterbliebener. Berlin, January 1923. By permission of the Landesbildstelle Berlin.

troops battled Communists across Germany, a mob of disabled veterans from a Dresden hospital, among them radical left-wing sympathizers, dragged the Social Democratic Saxon war minister Gustav Neuring from his office and through the streets, then flung him into the Elbe. As Neuring struggled to swim to the bank, a shot fired from the crowd killed him.[124]

The bitter discontent of German veterans has puzzled historians. Although disabled veterans received pensions that were as good as, if not better than, those of their European counterparts, superior social services, and secured employment, most came to despise the Republic that favored them. Even as pensions rose to 20 percent of the Republic's total yearly expenditure, veterans' organizations condemned the state for its neglect.[125] The politics of the disabled contributed to Weimar's weakness as much as their demonstrations reflected its illegitimacy. The Republic's ostensible friends behaved like its avowed enemies. The Social Democratic Reichsbund constantly denounced the state's failings, even in the years 1919–1920, when the Labor Ministry was in SPD hands.

Although historians have lauded the state's material provisions as "exemplary," they have judged the welfare bureaucracy more harshly.[126] In his book about the war victims, Robert Weldon Whalen condemns the pensions bureaucracy as "utterly arbitrary and capricious," charging that it alienated even those veterans inclined to support the Republic.[127] What disabled veterans wanted, argues James Diehl, was "a special place" in their society. By its refusal to issue commemorative medals to veterans and its failure to build a national monument to the war victims, the state ignored veterans' "psychological needs." The state's "bureaucratic impersonality and complexity" turned would-be heroes into "anxious supplicant[s]."[128] Similarly, Michael Geyer attributes German veterans' discontent to the origins of the pensions system. Because the welfare bureaucracy developed without political debate and the participation of war victims, its intended clients never felt represented by the state's institutions.[129] Instead, the disabled formed their own organizations, which entered into a perpetual "battle over resources" with the state.[130]

Historians have blamed the welfare policies of the Weimar state for veterans' hostility. And yet, veterans' movements reflected more than the state's failures and successes. The British state was no less bureaucratic, cruel, or unresponsive than its German counterpart; indeed, it may well have been more so. What was significant about German veterans' attitudes was not their anger toward the state but their antipathy toward the public. That was a critical difference. Whereas the British disabled could take pride in their fellow citizens' gratitude and respect, German veterans complained—accurately in the years after the regulation of charity—that the public did nothing to help them. After visiting a lazaret, one journalist commented on the consequences of the public's neglect: "A great many, perhaps most, men in hospital are suffering from the feeling that they are 'unpopular,' a burden to their fellow citizens and state."[131] Embittered by the public's "betrayal," disabled veterans demanded the "Thanks of the Fatherland" from the only source left to provide it: the state.

Veterans did not want to be dependent on philanthropy. In Germany as in Britain, veterans' organizations campaigned for "rights, not charity."[132] They expected a legal right to support; they wished, as Benedict Kreutz had noted, to be viewed as "state pensioners."[133] At the same time, however, disabled veterans demanded evidence of the gratitude of their fellow citizens: they wanted presents in hospital, celebrations in their honor, voluntary assistance to speed their reintegration into civilian life. It was a desire broadly shared on the left and on the right. Writing in the arch-conservative *Deutsche Tageszeitung,* one disabled man

observed that "while in earlier years there were donations and celebrations for the liberators of Berlin, for the miserable patients in lazaret,
there is nothing more left."[134] Erich Kuttner, leader of the Social Democratic Reichsbund, similarly deplored the neglect of the disabled: "In
months and years not one stranger has brought [the patients of the
lazaret] a single gift," noting that "the entire public has a serious moral
failure of duty to make good."[135]

By 1927, when Kreutz addressed the National Committee, the war
victims' animosity toward the public was a widely acknowledged fact.
That had not always been the case. Although veterans' organizations
later became the public's most severe critics, at the war's end, they were
conciliatory, even optimistic. In 1920, the conservative Zentralverband
observed that "the widest sections of the population have full sympathy
for the situation of war disabled and war dependents," commenting particularly on the public's "sense of honor and obligation, and their will"
to help war victims. "It is an inner satisfaction for us to know," wrote
the Social Democratic *Reichsbund* in 1921, "we do not stand alone in
our battle, that there are wide sections of the public that think and feel
as we do."[136] Every national organization of the disabled—from the
Communist Internationaler Bund (International League) to the Reichsbund to the conservative Zentralverband—agreed that war victims'
problems could only be solved with the public's help.[137] While they expected that the government would provide pensions and employment,
they urged Germans to support veterans in their claim against the state.

In the early 1920s the war victims' organizations courted the public.
In local meetings, such as one sponsored in the town of Wurzen by the
moderate Einheitsverband, they aimed to show the public how "great
was the misery of war disabled and war dependents."[138] Other organizations offered "honorary" memberships to sympathizers, while the
Reichsbund published scores of open letters in newspapers. Public relations formed the cornerstone of the conservative Zentralverband's plat-
form. Founded in 1919, the Zentralverband represented nationalist and
conservative veterans who opposed the Social Democratic Reichsbund;
by 1921, it was the third-largest war-victim organization, with 156,320
members.[139] To "prevail against the left-wing organizations" and "guide
the entire movement in a peaceful, objective direction," the Zentralverband's leadership sought to cultivate harmonious relations between the
disabled and their fellow citizens.[140]

By awakening "understanding" among Germans for the war victims'
plight, the Zentralverband—much like the British Legion—aimed to re-

assure veterans that the country appreciated their sacrifices.[141] According to the Zentralverband, war victims could not afford to become isolated from the public: "Everything that we demand and receive must be given by the entire German people."[142] Although the disabled often claimed that they wanted "rights," the Zentralverband's leadership reminded their members that the "evaluation of our rights is dependent on public opinion, whether we like it or not."[143] Better for the disabled to join forces with their fellow citizens than turn to violence like the Communist Internationaler Bund. In a speech before the Reichstag, Otto Thiel, the Zentralverband's president and a deputy of the conservative German People's Party (DVP), invited "the German people to join us in a comradeship in the best sense of the word, in the sense that the spirit of front-soldiers and the trenches demonstrated."[144]

To recruit the public to their cause, Thiel and his colleagues founded the Association for the Home Front's Thanks, an organization of "leading ladies and gentlemen" sympathetic to the Zentralverband's aims. Its governing board included, among others, two Reichstag deputies, an admiral, two generals, a writer, a university dean, and a newspaper editor. The Association intended to "keep awareness alive among the public that the war disabled and war dependents have suffered, and continue to suffer immensely for the German people and their country."[145] In addition, it pledged to support the war victims' demands and wishes before the public and state authorities. Finally, it aimed to encourage the disabled and dependents to "love their fellow citizens and their country."[146] In 1921, it began preparations for a national campaign to publicize its work.[147]

In compliance with the February decree, the Association for the Home Front's Thanks applied for permission to collect.[148] The State Commissioner denied their request. Despite this refusal, the Association proceeded with the collection, though on a more limited scale. In April 1921, the Association's secretary, Karl Butterbrodt, was brought up before the lower district court of Berlin on charges of violation of the Bundesrat decree.[149] In Berlin, as in the Stuttgart regional court of appeal two years later, the Zentralverband won a victory. For both courts, the deciding factor was the nature of the Zentralverband's campaign; the Association sought not only money but also, as the Stuttgart court commented, "other forms of support, especially the employment of the disabled in trade and industry."[150] The Berlin court, especially, noted with approval the Zentralverband's attempt to "depoliticize" care for the disabled.[151]

In 1924, the Labor Ministry reversed its previous stance and permitted war victims' organizations the right to solicit donations.[152] However, the Ministry's decision was a hollow victory. By 1924, there were few Germans able—or willing—to contribute to the Zentralverband's campaign. According to a Freiburg daily paper, the public no longer displayed even "the newspaper reader's casual interest" in the war victims.[153] In December 1923, the president of the Dresden Reichsbund complained that the "public responds to the demands of the disabled and war-dependents with...cool caution and indifference, indeed often even with aversion."[154] Even Otto Thiel was discouraged. In 1922, he had written that the "wide public knows very little about the miserable conditions that prevail among the war victims."[155] Two years later, he condemned "the unbelievable lack of consideration that people demonstrate when it comes to the fate of war victims."[156] Not even the blinded, formerly assured of the population's compassion, could count on assistance. In 1926, the Foundation for the War-Blinded reported that only one in a hundred collection cards was returned with a donation.[157]

By the hyperinflation, relations between the war-disabled and their fellow citizens had soured. Veterans bitterly accused Germans of shirking their duties to the nation's heroes. The animosity between veterans and the public became reciprocal, one of many rifts left in the aftermath of a catastrophic inflation that deepened class antagonism and strengthened interest-group politics at the expense of the older liberal and bourgeois parties. Although many disabled veterans had suffered badly during the hyperinflation, people believed otherwise. According to the public perception, the disabled still had a reliable source of income, in comparison with the millions who had lost their savings and employment.[158] In reality, only the sums paid to the severely disabled approached the minimum needed for survival; those with disabilities valued under 40 percent (which included such serious injuries as an amputated arm or diseases such as tuberculosis) saw their pensions dwindle away to nothing during 1922 and 1923. However, in the jealous insecurity of the time, it was easy for each to believe that the other had profited from his misery.[159]

No less damningly, the disabled were widely regarded as the favored wards of the Weimar welfare state. The publication of the revised pensions rates in 1924, like the original Pension Law of 1920, had been accompanied by a barrage of Labor Ministry propaganda attesting to the superiority of care that the Republic provided the disabled. Not only were the disabled economically privileged, but their organizations appeared well positioned to wring more concessions from the government. While the economic victims of the hyperinflation had to build their associations from the ground up, the war victims' organizations already occupied pride of place in the social welfare bureaucracy. According to Kreutz, the existence of so many "self-help" organizations seemed to indicate that "the people no longer needed to care" for the war victims.[160] The fact that the war victims' organizations appeared insatiable did not win them any admirers. The Internationaler Bund's violence made it difficult to see the disabled as victims.

While the inflation's casualties regarded veterans with envy, the disabled saw their own position as catastrophic. In the aftermath of the hyperinflation, the Reich transferred responsibility for welfare programs, including employment retraining for the disabled, to individual states and municipalities.[161] War victims condemned this move as an attempt to force them onto poor relief and deny them the honor to which they were entitled.[162] Across the country, disabled veterans and war dependents turned out by the thousands to protest "the systematic destruction of our legal claim to support."[163] As the war victims saw it, their sacrifices entitled them to a special status in society, symbolic of the country's gratitude. The fact that other Germans also faced financial ruin did not explain to them why they should "suffer twice over." The war victims blamed their fellow citizens, as well as their state. According to a 1924 resolution by the moderate Dresden Reichsverband: "The entire national community [*Volksgemeinschaft*] approaches the war victims' movement without understanding, as if it were something foreign."[164]

Even as compensation improved markedly during 1924–1929, as the Republic took its first tottering steps toward economic and political stabilization, the war victims remained disgruntled and, on occasion, disruptive.[165] In the latter years of the decade, pensions spending increased significantly, as the Labor Ministry restored benefits cut in 1923 and, in 1927, returned many men with disabilities of 20 percent to the pension rolls; by contrast, in Britain, France, and the United States, pensions budgets for war victims declined. However, the Labor Ministry's concessions won it few admirers. If anything, war victims' organizations, like other special interest groups, exerted more, not less, pressure on the state in the late 1920s. Each pension budget set the stage for a pitched battle, with the organizations demanding increases and amendments, most of which the state could not afford to fund. Reviewing the 1927 campaign, the Reichsbund's leaders acknowledged that they had learned from their fellow citizens' neglect. War victims were on their own: they could not rely on the public to protect their rights.

The onset of the Depression in the winter of 1929 heightened antagonism between disabled veterans and their fellow citizens. By September

1931, 4.3 million Germans were out of work; a year later, 5.1 million were unemployed. It has been estimated that the unemployed, with their dependents, constituted nearly a fifth of the total population during the years 1932–1933.[166] The emergency decrees of 1930, 1931, and 1932 reduced war pensions, in some cases drastically, to offset the fall in prices.[167] Even as the war victims' organizations demonstrated by the thousands to preserve the system they once criticized as insufficient, public opinion deplored the "burden" that disabled veterans and war dependents imposed on the nation.[168] In a National Committee meeting with the war victims' associations, Labor Undersecretary Griessmeyer observed that the German public was critical of the entire pensions system: "People are asking if money is being spent correctly on pensions, and if it can actually be afforded in the future."[169] According to the war victims' organizations, the public regarded the disabled as "double earners," whose pensions were sufficient for their maintenance, and who therefore had no right to employment.[170] Even the 1932 cuts in pensions garnered little sympathy for the disabled. Commenting on the protest by the League of Blinded Soldiers, one newspaper acknowledged that the reductions were "unfortunate," but it objected that the real income of the blinded "would not be so bad as [the Association] portrayed it."[171]

For disabled veterans, their fellow citizens' ingratitude served to indict not only the Weimar state and the political system but also the entire, morally degenerate, society. "There was a time after the war," wrote one severely disabled veteran in 1931, "when [our] sacrifices found thankful recognition in broad segments of the public.... There was a time when war victims were spoken of with the highest respect. Today, in our fast-living time, that has all now been forgotten.... With uncaring envy people point to our pensions and try to represent matters as if we war victims were responsible for the poor financial and economic situation of the German people."[172] Where the war's victims had once been promised honor, wrote one blinded man, envy had prevailed: "Today the public's duty of honor looks very different from what we were told it would be. Today the blinded man is the burdensome competition, for whom there is neither understanding nor morality."[173] For those who had sacrificed their health and vitality for the Fatherland, to be regarded as a burden was the most bitter insult imaginable. According to the Zentralverband, "It is a sure indication of the cultural downfall of the German people that...the war-disabled and war-dependents are seen as nothing other and nothing higher than objects of a financial speculation."[174]

Staking its legitimacy on welfare programs for the war's victims, the Labor Ministry sought to reassure the public in newspaper articles and in radio addresses that disabled veterans were well compensated.[175] In material terms, that was largely true, especially given the many demands on the Republic's meager resources. However, the disabled wanted more than pensions and welfare programs. They demanded gratitude, respect, and honor—emotional compensation that their fellow citizens did not provide. In the public's eyes, the war victims had become a privileged class to be resented. The public's rancor deepened the war victims' bitterness. To demonstrate that their claim on the Fatherland was justified, the war victims' organizations lobbied the state continuously, for higher pensions, better social services, and legal rights, battling for what they believed had been promised them and refusing to acknowledge the facts of scarcity. Yet the more the war victims demanded, the more animosity they provoked in their fellow citizens, whose own livelihoods had been shaken by hyperinflation and the Depression.

Frustrated by the insatiable demands of their ostensible protégés and fearful of public condemnation, the Labor Ministry's officials exploited the hostility between the disabled and their fellow citizens. In press notices about the revised goldmark pensions, the Ministry exaggerated the average amounts paid to the disabled, counting supplementary pensions (which few men received in 1924) along with ordinary pensions.[176] Later in the decade, Labor Ministry officials publicly denounced the war victims as greedy and inconsiderate. In 1929, Oskar Karstedt condemned war victims' "sense of entitlement to support, which makes a mockery both of reason and of consideration for others."[177] As examples, he offered three rejected cases, calculated to reinforce negative stereotypes: an imprisoned disabled veteran, who threatened violence unless he received money; a war-blinded man with a monthly pension of 479.60 RM who tried to publicize his rejection, while hiding his income; and a disabled officer who demanded 10,000 RM "to buy a summer house!"[178]

As the press disparaged "pensions scroungers," and war victims protested the "murderous Emergency Decree," the National Socialists took note.[179] In September 1930, the party established a special section for war victims in its directorate and began a concerted effort to recruit disabled and war dependents. Under the slogan "Even a poor Fatherland can be grateful," the National Socialists attacked the "pensions psychosis" that the welfare state had purportedly engendered, blaming the suffering of the disabled and war dependents on the Republic and the alienation of veterans from their public on the established war victims' organizations.[180] In 1932, the Zentralverband merged with the formerly more moderate Reichsverband, which itself sidled closer to the Nazi organization. Only the Reichsbund remained loyal to the Republic, though it also warned: "Even the most faithful of republicans can become unfaithful when instead of redeemed promises he receives blows to his grumbling stomach."[181] Neither the Reichsbund nor the Internationaler Bund survived the first six months of the National Socialist regime. By April 1933, both had been closed down. Other organizations were forcibly united into the million-strong National Socialist War Victims' Association.[182] The problem of war victims' protest, so injurious to the Republic, had finally been resolved.

The National Socialists honored the disabled as the "first citizens of the nation."[183] Festooned with badges, saluted, entitled to the best seats in theaters and priority in shops, celebrated in the press, disabled veterans basked in their newfound glory.[184] In material terms, the financial circumstances of most war victims did not improve significantly. Although pensions rose slightly, and front soldiers were granted a small supplementary allowance, the bureaucracy remained as intransigent as ever. Nevertheless, the state had brought the public to heel. By the millions, Germans attended ceremony after ceremony honoring the First World War's heroes. On one "Day to Honor War Victims" in October 1933, 300,000 citizens came to pay their respects in the port city of Stettin; war disabled veterans, proclaimed Hanns Oberlindober, head of the Nazi war victims' association, were "finally assured of the Fatherland's thanks."[185] "Unified under Adolf Hitler," Oberlindober declared the following year, "the German people have now become aware of their duties to the war victims."[186] The National Socialists gave veterans everything they believed Weimar had taken away: honor, gratitude, and respect. The Thousand Year Reich's munificence would not long be theirs to enjoy alone.

PART II

The War's Returns

CHAPTER 3

Life as a Memorial

Ex-Servicemen at the
Margins of British Society

For disabled men the War did not end in 1918. It was
a long and tragic serial lasting, for many, for a lifetime.

Mr. Baxter, president of British
Limbless Ex-Servicemen's Association,
16 December 1938

The Peace Procession of July 1919 was the largest parade London had ever witnessed. More than 400,000 servicemen, along with military policemen and members of the medical corps, joined the parade. Spectators had lined up the previous night, long before the streetlamps went out. By early morning, Trafalgar Square was impassable.[1] Regiment by regiment, division by division, the parade wound from exclusive Knightsbridge to the slums of Lambeth, past the newly erected Cenotaph, and down the Mall. Shortly after noon, the procession reached the Victoria Memorial, where King George stood at the salute to the roaring cheers of the crowd. "It was," observed the *Times,* "the greatest ritual day in all our history," remarkable for its inclusivity.[2] "Greeks, Czechoslovakians, Serbs, Rumanian, Italians, China, Siam and Japan passed before our eyes, acclaimed again and again."[3]

Disabled veterans watched the parade from the sidelines. Instead of an invitation to march in the procession, men in hospital blue were relegated to special grandstands not far from widows and orphans. For those who had lost limbs, there was an "alternative privilege": a paid trip home, with ten shillings allowance for expenses.[4] To the government's undoubted relief, most availed themselves of the opportunity. J. B. Brunel Cohen, a newly elected member of Parliament, himself a double amputee, spoke for many that day when he condemned the disabled's exclusion: "The Dead are brought to memory by the noble Cenotaph, the

lucky living are in the procession, but where are the wounded? Surely it
would not have been too much to have had even one lorry load just to
have given the crowd an opportunity of showing their appreciation." He
compared his country unfavorably with France, where *mutilés de guer-
res* had led the victory parade the previous week: "Our friends across
the water have a deeper understanding. There the wounded were given
a place of honour."[5]

Exclusion from the victory parade was the least of many indignities
disabled veterans suffered in postwar Britain. Compared with their counterparts in Europe and the Dominions, British veterans enjoyed few legal
rights. Forsaken by the state that had pledged to care for them, ex-
servicemen were denied state-secured employment and, in most cases,
supplementary pensions for their wives and children. If self-sufficiency
was a man's most treasured quality, the disabled had to endure dependence. Precariously employed, insufficiently pensioned, they scraped together a living and prayed for good health. Although their fellow citizens had honored soldiers' sacrifices, the disabled could not expect the
public's continual assistance. As the British Legion *Journal* observed in
1934, "A man who wears a V.C. on his coat lapel, or an empty sleeve,
or a sagging trousers leg, or whose lungs are still racked by the effects of
enemy gas, is of far less account to the community in which he dwells
than one who has a two-seater car in his garage and the money to pay
his domestic bills on the nail. That is War."[6] The problem was not
"War," or the nation's victory, though the disabled always figured as uneasy reminders of the war's costs. The reconstruction—not the war's
resolution—condemned the British disabled to a life on the periphery.

Although the charitable public championed the veteran's cause, philanthropy did little more than rescue men from penury. It did not promote
their return to society. Disabled veterans were segregated: in sheltered
workshops, in homes in outlying suburbs, in rehabilitation centers. They
rarely took part in the Armistice Day parades. Disabled veterans in Britain
were not forgotten. Loyal subscribers like Miss Hilda Monamy King continued to remember them with monthly checks. However, they were never
fully rehabilitated either as workers or as citizens. The Great War's most
conspicuous legacy, they became its living memorials: "If anyone wants
to read history, to read the 'Journey's End' of life, it is an open book at the
War Seal Foundation."[7] When journalists wanted to write about the war's
aftermath, they visited the disabled—but not otherwise. Veterans' stories
were feature articles, not front-page news. Touching, occasionally also up-
lifting, they were irrelevant to the economy and high politics.

WILLS'S CIGARETTES

THIS SURFACE IS ADHESIVE. ASK YOUR
TOBACCONIST FOR THE ATTRACTIVE
ALBUM (PRICE ONE PENNY) SPECIALLY
PREPARED TO HOLD THE COMPLETE SERIES

OUR KING
AND QUEEN
A SERIES OF 50

12

WITH DISABLED
EX-SERVICE MEN, 1922

No one has shown a deeper
sympathy with disabled ex-Service men than the King, who,
when Duke of York, worked
unceasingly on their behalf. The
picture shows His Majesty greeting some of them at the English
versus Scottish schoolboys'
football match, Stamford Bridge,
May, 1922. The King's sympathy
with the youth of the nation, too,
has always been manifest. When,
in June, 1935, he became Chairman of the Advisory Council
formed to assist in administering
King George's Jubilee Trust for
the encouragement of youth in
distressed areas, his duties gave
him great satisfaction.

W. D. & H. O. WILLS
ISSUED BY THE IMPERIAL TOBACCO CO,
(OF GREAT BRITAIN & IRELAND), LTD.

WITH DISABLED EX-SERVICE MEN

Figure 9.   King George V greets disabled ex-servicemen at a Stamford Bridge football match, May 1922. Advertising sticker for Wills's Tobacco. By kind permission
of the Sir Oswald Stoll Mansions.

Never systematically reintegrated into the economy or political culture, disabled ex-servicemen existed figuratively, as well as literally, on
the margins of British society. This chapter begins with an account of the
obstacles the disabled faced upon their return home. Deprived of guaranteed jobs and marriage allowances, disabled veterans were thrown on
their own resources, the goodwill of a previous employer, or the benevolence of the patriotic. When all else failed them, they turned to philanthropy and to poor relief. Yet, as the next section demonstrates, the objects of charity faced new indignities. Some discovered they could not live
as they liked; others came into conflict with philanthropists intent upon
the realization of their own utopian visions. Reporters and visitors mar-

veled at their cheerfulness, which they took as proof of manhood restored. For the severely disabled veterans of the Star and Garter Home, with whom this chapter ends, the stoic pose was all that remained.

SEEKING WORK

In late September 1933, Colonel Edward Gowlland, commandant of the Star and Garter Home, wrote to the War Seal Mansions' administrators. His purpose was to inform them of a misdeed committed by one of their charges. The day before, Gowlland had received a personal visit from a prewar patient of his. The lady, a hard-up widow, was distraught. At the beginning of the week, Charles William Neal, a tenant of the War Seal Mansions, had called on her to sell stationery he engraved himself. She declined his offer on the grounds of economy and told him she regretted that her weekly budget would not allow for writing paper. The next day, she found Neal's circular, "Stationery by a Disabled Man," in her mailbox. On the flyer, scratched in pencil, was a note: "Common courtesy becometh even on behalf of the Disabled Man."[8] Gowlland knew the lady well and was convinced she had done nothing to provoke Neal. Gowlland felt certain that the disabled man was solely at fault. "We both know the ex-service man," the Star and Garter's commandant wrote his fellow administrator, "and many of them are pretty troublesome." Neal's ploy for sympathy as a "Disabled Man" repelled Gowlland. He asked the War Seal Mansions to take immediate action against the writing paper peddler and suggested his own remedy, born of more than a decade of experience in veterans' homes: "If any of my patients did this sort of thing I should sack them."[9]

Ex-private Charles Neal applied for admission to the War Seal Mansions in 1926 and was accepted the next year.[10] He suffered from chronic infective arthritis, onset 1918, which left both his legs nearly immobile and movement in his right arm severely restricted. For his pains, the former milkman, aged twenty-four at the war's end, received a total disablement pension of £2 per week. He was lucky to have anything at all. In the years after the Armistice, ex-servicemen crippled by disease had little chance at a full pension. Neither the army's medical discharge boards nor the Ministry of Pensions looked sympathetically on arthritis claims. Disregarding weeks of exposure and nights spent in waterlogged trenches, the authorities dismissed these illnesses as "pre-war weaknesses."[11] Neal was one of the fortunates: his disease had become unbearable long before he was discharged.

While the British economy boomed in the war's immediate aftermath, Neal found odd jobs that, together with his pension, ensured a decent standard of living.[12] He married in 1919 and began a family. His first son was born in 1920, and three other children quickly followed. By the mid-1920s, however, his condition had deteriorated. Between 1922 and 1925, he spent nearly six months in the hospital. Without explanation, the Ministry of Pensions canceled his treatment allowance, paid to compensate for the disabled man's lack of earnings while hospitalized; his wife and children were to survive on Neal's pension alone. In the meantime, Neal had become virtually unemployable, unable to find even part-time work. With healthy men on the dole and almost 10 percent of the insured workforce unemployed, most employers were unwilling to hire a disabled man, whose condition might keep him in bed two days a week or force a prolonged hospital stay. "Owing to my condition," Neal explained, "no employer will look at me."[13]

In view of the family's desperate circumstances, the War Seal Foundation accepted Neal, his wife, and their four children for placement in the Fulham Road Mansions. In 1927, they moved into a second-floor apartment with two bedrooms and a large sitting room, complete with a hat stand, wireless hookups, flower boxes, and a combined scullery, bathroom, and kitchen. Although the improvement in their living conditions undoubtedly came as a relief, it was not enough to mend their fortunes. Neal was still out of work. Two years after their arrival in the Mansions, their rent seriously in arrears, Mrs. Neal wrote to ask whether the Foundation could arrange for her three boys to be placed in orphanages. She and her husband could no longer keep them. When the War Seal's administrators denied their request, Neal made a last attempt to earn money. Using the Mansions' printing press at night, he began to peddle stationery from door to door.

In Lloyd George's "fit land for heroes," Neal's predicament was anything but unusual. As soldiers, Neal and his fellow War Seal residents had young men's expectations. They looked forward to the hallmarks of masculine independence: a steady job, a home of their own, a wife, and perhaps even children.[14] For disabled ex-servicemen, the most modest of aspirations became unattainable, self-sufficiency foreclosed.[15] Long rides on crowded public transportation exhausted those able to find work, while spells of illness jeopardized even apparently secure employment. Men confined to wheelchairs were forced either to spend days on end cooped up in their apartments or to live apart from their families in veterans' homes outfitted with elevators. Even the easiest of tasks proved daunting, and the simplest of pleasures were denied them. By 1937, Arthur Pool, a chartered surveyor who had been gassed in France, had accepted a constrained life: "I am of course unable to take part in any sport, to walk any distance in the winter, or to hurry, and at times it is practically impossible to walk upstairs."[16]

More than anything else, soldiers looked forward to domestic life, to a reunion with their wives and girlfriends or to a new romance. After the horrors of the trenches, men eagerly anticipated the comforts of home.[17] For disabled veterans, the majority of whom were unmarried at the war's end, the search for a spouse caused great anxiety. Nurses in military hospitals reported that many wounded soldiers dreaded the once-longed-for reunions with sweethearts. They did not know how their loved ones would respond to their injuries. To "take on" a severely disabled man, a woman had to be "brave."[18] At the same time, most ex-servicemen realized that they needed someone to care for them. According to the British Limbless Ex-Servicemen's Association (BLESMA), disabled men were "more in need of a wife than the average man."[19] Even if a disabled man could work, he could not manage a household alone. At the Ministry of Pensions, officials discussed the "cases of single men who had lost both arms and who wanted to marry in order to secure the requisite assistance."[20]

As most women realized, marriage to a disabled man was fraught with difficulties. There were, first of all, daunting financial problems. The British state compensated men only for those familial "responsibilities" they had incurred before disablement. Unlike in France or Germany, where a man's pension was raised when he married and had children, the British veteran received no extra allowances once he was invalided out of the services. Even after his family circumstances changed, the state offered the disabled ex-serviceman no additional assistance. Despite marriage and four children, Charles Neal, declared 100 percent disabled, received a single man's pension of £2. His wife was not eligible for widow's compensation.[21] Had he started his family before he became ill, Neal's pension would have been more than £3, enough to allow him to live, if not luxuriously, then with a measure of security.

The Ministry of Pensions denied ex-servicemen's repeated demands for marriage allowances.[22] According to BLESMA fewer than one-third of all married pensioners in 1938 received supplementary allowances for their wives.[23] It was a question of money as well as principle. To pay pensions and allowances to men who married after disablement would, in the minister of pensions' estimation, "involve an exceedingly heavy expenditure" of £30 million per year.[24] According to the Ministry of Pensions' officials, the state was not obligated to assume responsibility for liabilities a disabled man had contracted after his injuries, any more than it should be forced to repay his debts. If all disabled men were granted wives' allowances, Ministry officials feared that ex-servicemen would soon fall into the clutches of "veteran-marrying speculators" out to retire on the state's benevolence.[25]

Even those women prepared to marry for love rather than money found domestic life more arduous than they had imagined. The care of a badly disabled man required tremendous stamina. Women not only nursed their disabled husbands and took exclusive responsibility for housework and children but also, if the family budget required, went out to work.[26] Before she and her husband moved to the War Seal Mansions, Mrs. Ripley held down a job, cared for the couple's young daughter, and carried her wheelchair-bound spouse up two steep flights of stairs every day—on her back.[27] "The women suffer almost as much as the men," claimed W. J. Roberts, secretary of the War Seal Foundation. "They undergo great nerve-strain, and everything must be done to alleviate their cases as well as their husbands."[28] In 1938, the Pilgrim Trust visited the wife of a disabled man: "The woman is in a broken-down state of health. 'Feels she is finished' and unsuitable for further work."[29] More than one-third of the War Seal Foundation's wives predeceased their severely disabled husbands. They were, according to the Mansions' nurse, "literally worked to death."[30]

Disabled ex-servicemen began their families in straitened circumstances, often in slums. While some cities accorded the disabled preference in council housing, others gave them no special treatment.[31] Many in interwar Britain had cause to complain about substandard dwellings.[32] However, for disabled veterans, ill health made the problem intolerable. George Foote was one of the first 100,000 volunteers, a soldier in Lord Kitchener's army.[33] On the Marne, in 1915, he was severely injured and taken prisoner of war. Until 1921, he was in and out of the hospital. When the stump of his amputated left foot healed, his paralyzed right arm began to bother him. Then came chest trouble. When he could, he worked as an elevator attendant to supplement his partial pension of 24s. a week. The state's compensation was not enough to support himself or the wife he married in 1925, much less the three children who followed. In 1933, when Foote petitioned for an apartment in the War Seal Mansions, his family was at the end of its resources. After an illness that had lasted four months, Foote, his wife, and their children lived in one basement room. That he could not provide for his family caused Foote to worry: "The cellar is so damp that even the mice have left it in disgust, in fact…the place shakes so much that there is an iron girder right through the house to hold it up. I did not mind these conditions in Belgium, but now I have got a jolly good wife and three grand kiddies to look after, I am trying to get a decent place for them to lie in." Although he wanted "to keep as fit as my wounds will allow me for my wife & kiddies sake," the damp basement made it impossible. "I often think of that saying 'HOMES FIT FOR HEROES TO LIVE IN,' well Madam this house is not one of them. I know my letter is rather a long one, but I always try & get a laugh under any conditions."[34]

For skeptics, Foote added a note to his application: "I trust Sir, I am not making my case too pathetic, but I can vouch for the truth of it, and more."[35] There was no need. Every week between 1921 and 1939, the War Seal Mansions received two or three such letters from men like Foote, relegated to "some miserable tenement in a noisome slum."[36] Only the worst-off could be placed; the rest joined waiting lists numbering in the hundreds. Many of the War Seal's petitioners, like David Lalis, a 1922 applicant, lived "penned up" in a single room with their families. As he wrote, "At present I have one room to sleep, cook, and do everything in, and as I have a wife and one child it isn't very nice, especially so, as I have a badly wounded elbow which is continually being knocked owing to the smallness of our accommodation."[37] With his wife and two children, Edward Jenkins, a woodworker at the Lord Roberts Workshops, rented a room so small "that when there are both he and his wife in it, one has to sit on the bed."[38]

Disabled veterans' apartments were small, crowded, and inconveniently located, requiring men who could barely stand to commute hours each day to work. For the badly incapacitated, they were completely unnavigable. Ex-private Robert Greig, totally disabled with a fracture dislocation of the spine, was forced to use a bedpan unless his wife was home: "The man is…much distressed because the only sanitary accommodation in a house full of tenants has to be reached by three staircases."[39] Other men, especially those confined to wheelchairs, became virtual shut-ins. So that he could live with his wife, Frederick Lewis left the Star and Garter Home, but there was a price to pay: "I am not able to get out at all now, as we live right at the top of the house and I can't manage the stairs."[40] Herbert Swann, a double amputee, occupied an apartment with doorways too narrow to negotiate in a wheelchair. As the Charity Organisation Society's visitor reported: "He can very seldom get out of his own apartment and his life is consequently extremely monotonous and dull."[41]

Financial exigency and crowded quarters forced disabled ex-servicemen to make unhappy choices. Until he was shot in the elbow, Edward Lifford was a regular soldier with long years of service in India. After the war, he and his wife had two children, a boy and a girl. Despite constant treatment, his wound eventually broke down and his entire arm had to be amputated. Lifford lost his job, and the couple could no longer keep the family together. When he wrote the War Seal Foundation, his daughter was in an orphanage: "Until just before Christmas my two children were put out, but unfortunately for us my Boy aged 5 years was knocked down on Sat Dec 15th by a motor car and received injuries from which he succumbed. The idea of course of not having our children with us has made this loss more hard to bear.... I was one of the first contingent that landed in France in 1914 and fought from 'Mons' downward being in all the engagements until finally being wounded in 1916."[42]

Had Edward Lifford been able to keep his job, he could have provided for his family. For disabled veterans, a good job was hard to come by—and harder to keep. Unlike in France, Germany, or Italy, where the state mandated the compulsory employment of severely disabled veterans, successive British governments largely disavowed responsibility. In matters of employment, as in housing, disabled veterans were left to their own wits and the goodwill of their fellow citizens. If a man was lucky, he could return to his prewar employer, though in most cases with a lower salary and a less prestigious position. Other men received training, either from the Ministry of Labour or from charities such as Roehampton, that allowed them a foot in the door. Just as often, men such as Charles Neal found employment immediately after the war and lost it as the economy slumped at the end of 1920. They joined the long-term unemployed.[43] To scrape together a living, disabled veterans took on piecework and odd jobs. Formerly skilled laborers supplemented their pensions with embroidery work.[44]

Other than the voluntary King's Roll scheme, there was no comprehensive state program for the employment of disabled veterans.[45] While the King's Roll enjoyed indisputable success—in 1926, it boasted 27,592 employers, in 1936, 23,586—it was the "lightly disabled" who most often profited.[46] The King's Roll offered employers little incentive to hire badly incapacitated men: any man who received a pension or a gratuity in respect of disablement, no matter how minor, counted toward the

Roll's 5 percent quota. Even those men who had passed off of the pension rolls, but were hired when still in possession of a pension, qualified.[47] Frustrated by the difficulty of placing severely disabled men in work, the secretary of the Edinburgh Local Employment Committee in 1921 condemned the Roll's wide definition of disability as "capable of much misconstruction, and even abuse," adding that "it is probable that, if all the cases operating under the present arrangement of the Scheme were classified, only a trifling percentage of really disabled men would be found."[48]

Throughout the 1920s and 1930s, tens of thousands of disabled veterans waited on live employment registers. The number of men on special registers for disabled ex-servicemen never dropped below 24,000 in the interwar period; in 1923, it rose as high as 65,000, and it climbed again to 41,000 in 1931; how many were placed on the ordinary register cannot be traced.[49] Countless men, having exhausted their unemployment benefit, failed to sign on.[50] According to the government's conservative estimates, there were at least 20,000 "unemployable" disabled veterans. Local Committees had little to offer them. Speaking at a conference of London King's Roll Committees in 1927, G.H. Heilbuth, deputy mayor of Westminister, admitted that though his committee "had been working for some four years, very little had been done towards solving the problem of the disabled ex-Service man who found difficulty in securing employment."[51] Most employers were reluctant to hire the severely disabled, given the large numbers of able-bodied men out of work throughout the interwar years.[52] It was not simply a matter of the bottom line, though few firms were willing to hire an unprofitable worker. Businesses also feared that disabled employees might injure themselves further or endanger their coworkers. "Doomed to go through life now wearing a boot with a twist in it like a cork-screw and about as much steel on it as would build a boat," one man wrote, "I rise in the morning and go out looking for work. A few minutes' interview soon convinces the most optimistic employer that I am of no use."[53]

Denied the state-secured employment provided their German counterparts, disabled ex-servicemen were thrown upon their own devices. Many could return to their prewar employers, albeit with the understanding that they might have to accept a demotion and a salary cut.[54] On his return from France, Bill Towers found that concrete had rendered his stonemasonry trade nearly obsolete.[55] Fitted with an artificial leg at Roehampton, Samuel Pears returned home to his guaranteed job only to hear that "there was nothing to suit him."[56] When he wrote to the minister of labour in 1921, George Ayling had lost the temporary pension granted him upon discharge because of deafness, and he was waiting upon training in the vehicle building trade: "I have made an application for training as a disabled soldier in a trade last March and have called at Whitehall Gardens every week since and receive the same answer that I shall be called the end of the month now some months have past and I am still waiting I cannot get any nearer I am absolutely destitute.... I should not appeal in this manner if I was earning ever so little instead of sheer poverty."[57]

Men who managed to secure a trainingship through the Ministry of Labour felt lucky. However, because of the severe depression of 1920–1922, only a minority could actually be placed in the trades they had learned; thousands of others were consigned to waiting lists. On the recommendation of his Local Employment Committee, Bill Towers enrolled in a yearlong course in hand tailoring. It was for naught because there were no more jobs. Like Towers, John Bennett completed one course of training; sent down to London from the Ministry of Pensions' Plymouth Convalescent Center, he discovered that his chosen career was closed to him: "Reported Ministry of Labour, and they could do nothing for me; Trade Unions refuse to sanction further training of exservice men; thousands of skilled men out of work, ect. ect." Although he received the one pound out-of-work donation granted ex-servicemen, he wanted to work: "I am steady, willing, active, abstainer, ect.... I cannot stand the awful depression much longer; surely I can be of use to somebody.... I *hate* charity, all I want is reasonable employment; will you please help a despairing man."[58]

Despite the obstacles, most men persevered, found employment, and made careers for themselves. Those who stayed healthy had the best chance, though even for them, the future was anything but smooth. To find work, men had to walk very long distances, sometimes four or five miles in a day. In London, only blinded ex-servicemen received discounted fares on public transportation; all other disabled were expected to pay their own way.[59] Among the most fortunate were those who secured employment in government offices, replacing the women workers who had staffed wartime posts; in 1928, nearly 15 percent of the total staff in government departments were disabled ex-servicemen.[60] After a trade turned obsolete and one useless training course, Bill Towers, an economic as well as military casualty, found work in an engineering firm. The manager warned him that he would receive no special treatment: "And I said that would suit me fine. Just treat me as a normal person."

To retain his post as a milk inspector, the one-armed Jack Hogg agreed to work for only a partial wage.[61] Gassed in France, repeatedly denied a pension, Arthur Pool struggled to keep his job as a chartered surveyor despite breathing difficulties and worsening eyesight. So that he would not be absent from work, he ruled out all leisure activities and "systematically tried to regain as much strength as possible by spending weekends in bed."[62]

Not every disabled man could accommodate himself to the labor market. Some were too ill, others lacked training. For six years, William Parrott worked as an elevator attendant. In 1926, the stump of his amputated leg broke down, and he had to return to the hospital. When he returned, his job was gone. He found another position later on but lost it when the firm went bankrupt. In 1932, after four years on the dole, he applied for training at Lord Roberts Workshops. The Ministry of Labour denied his petition on the grounds that he had once held "normal employment."[63] Another four months of fruitless job hunting convinced civil servants to approve Parrott's application. Many others were denied.[64] In 1921, George Foote applied to the Ministry of Pensions for training, "but they informed me that owing to my wounds I was not fit to learn anything whatever, so for the next four years I was out of work."[65]

For "unemployables" such as George Foote, there remained only life on the dole or the mercy of charity.[66] Yet as Sidney Webb observed in 1923, disabled men could not count on unemployment benefits or poor-law relief. When labor exchanges considered a disabled man incapable of work, they withheld unemployment.[67] In some districts, the Guardians of the Poor refused outdoor relief to single men.[68] Testifying before the interdepartmental Committee on Public Assistance, Webb remarked: "I consider that the partially disabled man is now suffering very severely—to the extent of tens of thousands of them—and the State is failing in respect of those men."[69] Awarded as compensation for physical disfigurement, disablement pensions disqualified men from other benefits.[70] The majority of Public Assistance Committees (PACs) took disability pensions into consideration when means tests were levied; most PACs counted at least 50 percent of the pension in calculating total household income.[71] Because of their pensions, some disabled men were also declared ineligible for old-age pensions.[72]

Aside from small grants to sheltered workshops that hired the disabled, the state did very little for "unemployables." Officials at the Ministry of Labour and Ministry of Pensions insisted that a pension was fair compensation for disability, distinguishing themselves from those such as

Figure 10.   At the Poppy Factory, a disabled ex-serviceman and his creations. Undated.

"Mr. Webb," who believed that "every person in need is entitled to look to the State for either work or maintenance."[73] Few "unemployables" could have survived without the assistance of their fellow citizens. In any given year, as many as 2,000 badly disabled veterans depended on sheltered workshops for their daily bread.[74] They found employment at Lord Roberts Workshops as cabinetmakers and woodworkers. Or the British Legion Poppy Factory hired them to make the millions of red paper flowers sold on Armistice Day. At the Ashtead Potteries, they produced Mediterranean-inspired ceramics, brightly colored and cheerful. In Sheffield, the Painted Fabrics Factory turned out tablecloths and curtains. Blinded men from St. Dunstan's Hostel relied on Sir Arthur Pearson to sell the baskets and brooms they wove at home.

Sheltered workshops offered stable employment to men whom no one else would hire. As workplaces, they were far from ideal. There was little room for promotion, and the skills taught did not prepare men for a return to the open labor market. At Lord Roberts Memorial Workshops and the Poppy Factory, production was organized around the assembly-line principle. On a machine specially designed for a man in a wheelchair, James Pegrum cut out thousands of red paper flowers every month.[75] Before the war, he had been an electrician, but a bullet in the spine left both legs paralyzed. Although men were grateful for the income, they found the work "monotonous."[76] To produce the maximum number of goods, the workshops relied on a high degree of division of labor; Lord Roberts' employees learned not a trade but a single process. At work nine hours a day, for eight pence an hour, on the mass production of beds, the trainee John Hudson complained to the Ministry of Labour that his "disability [was] being exploited."[77]

Most men would have preferred other employment to jobs in sheltered workshops. Not only were disabled workers isolated from their able-bodied contemporaries, but philanthropic factories suffered the stigma of charity. Although some disabled preferred to work among their comrades, others undoubtedly found the atmosphere depressing. If work conferred dignity on a man, a position in the Poppy Factory acknowledged that he could not be "treated as a normal person." Formerly skilled laborers who had taken pride in their craft viewed piecework as "debasing and humiliating."[78] Moreover, there was always the possibility that contributions would dry up, forcing immediate layoffs.[79] Even more than profit-making enterprises, sheltered workshops operated on a shoestring budget with little room for error. After a precipitous decline in donations, the Lord Roberts Workshops closed their branches in Cardiff and Leeds for two years. The Brighton Diamond Factory, with its 500 disabled cutters and polishers, did not survive its founder's death.

For those who refused sheltered workplaces, the prospect of employment was slim. In 1936, W. J. Roberts, secretary of the War Seal Foundation, received a letter from the newest supplicant. Crippled with arthritis and confined to a wheelchair, William Lea had turned down a job at Lord Roberts Workshops. His disability, he claimed, made it impossible for him to maintain regular working hours. Instead, Lea had chosen to make his own way. What Roberts heard displeased him: "I will be candid in telling you that I have been trying to do a little job on my own, that of selling sweets from a tray on my tricycle and unfortunately it is not a success, as I thought that by doing a little job, I could help my wife a little more by giving her some of the money I earned, as you see it is a failure."[80]

If Lea wanted to gain admission to the War Seal Mansions, Roberts informed him, he would have to abandon his enterprise. The secretary would not allow peddlers on the premises. Lea consented. With a sick wife, two small children, and a single man's pension, he had little choice. The War Seal Foundation could rescue him from destitution; however, there were rules to be followed. As we shall see, philanthropists had high expectations of their charges. Through the rehabilitation of disabled veterans, they sought to remake society—in their own, often unconventional, image. The objects of their benevolence expected nothing so spectacular. Above all, disabled veterans wanted to return to everyday life. If their injuries allowed them to work, they wanted jobs. If they could marry and have children, they wanted to live with their families. But the state's negligence left them dependent on philanthropists' good graces. Shorn of their hero's bounty, disabled men suffered the indignities that those without rights bear.

THE OBJECTS OF CHARITY

Edward Gowlland's letter came as an unpleasant surprise, but not as a shock. Charles Neal had been in trouble before. In 1931, W. J. Roberts found a circular Neal had printed on the Mansions' press offering private greeting cards and calendars at "below shop prices." Called in to explain, Neal claimed that he had used the printing press just twice, and only since he fell ill. He had no other way to make money. Employers would not look at him. Roberts expressed his sympathy but nonetheless directed the printer to his lease. No businesses were permitted on the War Seal premises—especially not those that promised to undercut local tradesmen. Although Sir Oswald Stoll had outfitted a machine shop on the first floor, he had not intended that men begin their own companies. The Mansions' press was meant for hobbyists, not for trade. If Neal continued his enterprise, he and his family would be evicted.

Angered by Roberts's ultimatum, Neal appealed to Sir Oswald Stoll and his wife. When they sided with the secretary, the printer took his case to a higher authority: the Prince of Wales. He asked the Prince, himself a veteran of the Great War, to intercede on his behalf.[81] Neal dismissed the Foundation's concerns about unfair trade practices: "As I am disabled in both legs and partly disabled in both arms, I could not compete against fit men." According to the printer, Roberts had it out for him. "I can assure Your Royal Highness, my sole object is to occupy my time and thereby prevent myself becoming morbid and depressed and slightly augment my pension to enable me to keep my wife and children properly." He had tried to obtain work, but without luck. Neal confessed that if he could, he would prefer to leave the War Seal Mansions: "I am not in a financial position to move or I would do so to a country village where my wife and eldest son could help me."

Neal's petition did not endear him to the War Seal Foundation's administrators. Within the month, Sir Oswald Stoll received a letter from the Prince's Equerry inquiring into Neal's case. Stoll stood by his decision. He would not allow Neal to operate a business from the Foundation. The Mansions were presently taxed as residential property; the scheme could not survive if the buildings were rated for trade. Despite the Foundation's efforts, the printer had proven himself "incorrigible."[82] Neal did not even have the decency to be thankful: "He is in no way grateful for the benefits which he has derived from his admittance to War Seal Mansions." The entire business had taken its toll on Roberts's health: "The Secretary is away for a few days at present owing to his being rather run down, largely through the constant anxiety caused by this man Neal." The Prince's Equerry had heard all he needed to know. The Prince of Wales, he informed Neal, could not help him.

Whether it was because he could not find other work or only because he was "incorrigible," Neal continued to use the Mansions' press, only at night and in secret. He journeyed farther afield to peddle his wares. Gowlland's letter exposed his deception. The War Seal Foundation sent him a notice of eviction. In December 1933, Neal's case went to court. The printer testified on his own behalf: "I am one of the worst disabled cases at War Seal Mansions. My will-power and the will to work has prevented me from being bedridden for three years. I have a wife and four children. My sole object is to look after my family."[83] Despite Neal's entreaty, the judge ruled in favor of the War Seal Foundation: "One sympathises with his desire to earn money to help his wife and children but for years he has disregarded the rules that are of vital importance." After his court case failed, Neal pled with Roberts personally, but to no avail. By the New Year, the printer and his family were finally gone.

Disabled ex-servicemen turned to philanthropy when the state failed to provide for them. Yet as Charles Neal discovered, the objects of charity could not live as they liked. Their conduct was proscribed. There were standards to be met. On the "outside," as Neal put it, a man could peddle stationery without fear of the consequences. However, as a tenant at the War Seal Mansions, Neal had to abide by a different set of rules or face eviction. To live in the War Seal Mansions, Neal had to surrender a measure of freedom. It was not that he wanted to gamble, drink in excess, or quarrel with other tenants. Neal asked only for the capacity to provide for his family. The Mansions' press might have been intended for hobbyists, but he had to support a wife and four children: "My main thoughts all along have been to ensure my wife and family having at least a small income should anything happen to me."[84]

Stoll and his fellow philanthropists were well-intentioned; they saved many men from destitution. At the same time, the rehabilitation of individuals was not their only priority. They had loftier ambitions. Above all, they viewed charity work as a means of social reform, the practical incarnation of their (often unorthodox) principles. Whether the cause was the revival of rural industry (Enham), the sanctity of the liberal individual (War Seal Mansions), or even women's suffrage (the Star and Garter), disabled men soon found themselves entangled in the philanthropists' schemes. Their own needs became a means to a larger end. Although Roberts and Stoll recognized Neal's dilemma, they intended that the War Seal's residents become self-supporting citizens, not peddlers. There was no reason to tolerate the printer's disobedience. The Mansions' waiting list numbered in the hundreds.

Although there were those who lived contentedly as the recipients of benevolence, grateful for the opportunities given them, for many others, as for Charles Neal, life as the object of charity proved intolerable. They clashed with those who provided for them. Troubles began when disabled men asserted demands at odds with the philanthropist's own objectives. They founded self-help societies, went on strike, disobeyed eviction orders. Treated as disciplinary infractions and punished accordingly, these conflicts exposed problems fundamental to the nature of philanthropy. To succeed as the objects of charity, disabled men had to remain compliant, appreciative, and cheerful—even when the philanthropist's rules violated their own aspirations. There was no recourse available to the "incorrigible." Unlike the state, philanthropists owed nothing to their charges. All that was given voluntarily could also be taken away.

Buoyed by idealism, filled with utopian visions, philanthropists began their work with great hopes. Before the Great War was a year old, the music-hall magnate Oswald Stoll had decided to provide personally for wounded soldiers. Happily married and the father of four children, Stoll wanted to ensure that even badly disabled men could live with their families. "The spiritual driving force of the War Seal Foundation," wrote W. J. Roberts, "is the feeling that the home life of our incapacitated heroes should be sacredly preserved."[85] With £40,000 of his own funds, Stoll commissioned a purpose-built, two-story red brick housing estate across the street from Lord Roberts's Fulham Workshops. According to Roberts, the War Seal Mansions offered genuine domesticity: "Model

homes these flats are to be, without any quote marks round the word
'Homes.' "[86] In 1915, Stoll launched a national appeal on behalf of the
disabled.

A retiring showman, Stoll was a man of contradictions. Australian-
born, he moved to England as a boy, when his Irish mother remarried a
Liverpool music-hall proprietor. His stepfather died when Stoll was fourteen, and the young Oswald took over the business. But the scholarly
Stoll was temperamentally unsuited to the music-hall business of the Gay
Nineties, with its scantily clad showgirls, lewd tunes, and riotous drink-
ing. According to Herbert Grimsditch, "Apart from the wearing of a tall
hat, Stoll had none of the characteristics of the impresario. He neither
smoked nor drank and, outside business, his interests were in philosophy
and economics."[87] His great happiness "was to wander in and out of the
second-hand bookshops.... I bought John Locke 'On the Human Understanding,' and read him. I was always interested in books. I wanted
to know things. All my spare time and all my spare money went in the
pursuit of knowledge."[88]

Under Stoll's proprietorship, the Coliseum and Empire Theatres became "respectable," places where a man could take his wife and even
his older children for an evening out. Alcohol was permitted only in
moderation, and hard liquor was never served. At Stoll's orders, risqué
scenes were toned down or omitted altogether, and woe was he who
transgressed the house rules. "There can, I think, be no question that the
evolution of the music-hall 'from pot-house to Palace' to use a well-worn
phrase was in great measure due to Sir Oswald."[89] If the new regime left
the former clientele mourning music hall's racier days, it nonetheless paid
dividends. Within a decade, Stoll had built an empire of variety theaters
across Britain, including the London Hippodrome and Coliseum, and
launched some of music hall's biggest stars. The first moving pictures in
the United Kingdom were shown at Stoll's theaters.

Stoll believed that it was every citizen's responsibility to ensure the
welfare of the disabled: "It is a national disgrace—a national sin—that
men should be condemned to slumdom.... Merely talking about the matter will not carry us very far. Something worth while in the way of work
and personal service is necessary."[90] He remembered the begging soldiers of past wars with shame. As a boy, he had seen them outside his
mother's Liverpool music hall, after Charles Godfrey performed "Here
upon Guard Am I," a song about the mistreatment of the Crimean veterans: " 'I've done this for my Country / But what has she done for
me.' "[91] He was determined that history not repeat itself. In 1919, the

Daily Telegraph estimated that a total of £260,993 had been raised through Stoll's war-charity work.[92] Wounded soldiers were admitted free to his theaters.[93] On average, he lent his theaters once per week for charity performances.

More than an "obligation," the War Seal Mansions were above all a "work of love."[94] No detail escaped Stoll's attention. A trellised rose loggia, flanked by pillars inscribed with the Great War's most famous land and sea battles, marked the Mansions' entrance. Wheelchair-accessible elevators took the tenant to his apartment. A rubber pad deadened the noise of every door knocker. The apartments themselves, painted a soothing shade of blue with walnut trim, had two bedrooms, a large living room, and a combined scullery, bathroom, and kitchen. The kitchen table was hinged to the wall to allow room for a tub, and flower boxes graced each windowsill. Stoll even made arrangements for tenants who were incontinent. There was a special washing room where soiled items could be washed in copper pots "without any objectionable odours."[95]

The overworked proprietor of forty music halls and cinemas, Stoll devoted countless hours and a small fortune to disabled men. Their plight moved him. It was human tragedy—and a matter of symbolic importance. Stoll was shocked by the war's reckless disregard for human life. He saw the War Seal Foundation as an opportunity to reassert the value of the individual: "Early in the career of the War Seal Foundation...I was met by people who thought that sorely-wounded men, regardless of the nature of their wounds, were 'better dead.' These people, thus callous in regard to human life and human relationships and sympathies, I invariably found did not agree with my views on industrial finance."[96] The rehabilitation of the disabled was a social necessity, not a luxury. According to Stoll, it was as essential to the "well-being of the state" as the wise cultivation of natural resources. No man could be wasted, no matter how badly he was injured.

On the outside, the War Seal Mansions was a war memorial, on the inside, a monument to the individual. "Cripples May Be Real Citizens," read one newspaper headline about Stoll's scheme.[97] That is, if they lived by the tenets of liberal individualism dear to the founder's heart. Above all, Stoll intended that War Seal men regain independence, the defining characteristic of middle-class Victorian masculinity.[98] The War Seal's residents were to practice self-help, to work, if they could, either in their homes or at Lord Roberts Workshops across the street. For their apartments they paid modest rents. Although Stoll aimed to "right the imbalance" that the war had created, he did not want the Foundation's tenants to suffer the stigma of charity. By fostering "the men's spirit of independence," Stoll aimed to create men of rational, provident, and ambitious character—emphatically liberal entities.[99] His War Seal scheme would allow the disabled to become, or so he hoped, exemplary individuals.

If the disabled seem curious standard-bearers for a brave new world, it is only because we do not see them as the philanthropists did—as emblems of an exhausted, war-scarred nation. They were broken down but were capable of "salvage," with the "glorious chance" to assume their part "in the great reformation of our national life."[100] For Oswald Stoll, every disabled tenant installed in the War Seal Mansions meant new respect for the individual. His vision was personal. If the disabled man could be rehabilitated, returned to his family and the workforce, then the nation, too, could be reconstructed. The government might be content to "throw the disabled on the salvage heap," but philanthropists recognized their potential. Where the state saw a pensions burden, the philanthropists found an opportunity for social reform, a chance to demonstrate where the world had gone wrong and how it should be rebuilt.

Yet if it was difficult to do good, as Stoll liked to say, it was still more difficult to live as the object of do-goodism. Soon after their arrival in the Mansions, many men realized that they would either have to behave as the administration expected or find a new home. What had been daily life became transgression. To drink in excess was to face Roberts's reprimands. Late nights were prohibited. At 10:30 P.M., the elevators were turned off; disabled men who stayed out had to find another way to reach apartments on the top floors. Despite the Mansions' rhetoric about the "unbroken family circle," children could serve as grounds for dismissal. In 1924, the War Seal Mansions attempted to evict Walter Witchell—paralyzed, mute, confined to bed—because his sons made too much noise. After other tenants appealed on Witchell's behalf, the administration conceded. If the disabled man's adolescent children would vacate the building, their father could stay.[101]

Until 1932, conflicts between the Mansions' administration and its tenants could be dismissed as the grievances of disgruntled individuals. With the feud over a burial society, matters took a new turn. By the time Stoll learned of its existence, the Independent Self-Help Society was five years old. Founded by four War Seal tenants, the "Self-Helpers" offered mutual aid in the form of a friendly society.[102] Members paid a weekly premium. In exchange, the Independent Self-Help Society promised them a respectable funeral and burial, complete with music, flowers, and a plot in the Fulham cemetery. Its service was greatly needed. Although working-class families placed high priority on dignified burial, the Ministry of Pensions provided only a pittance toward heroes' funerals. The option of burial insurance was foreclosed. As the organizers themselves discovered, no insurance company would sell to a badly disabled man. Most widows, themselves deprived of pensions, could not afford the price of a burial.

In 1932, the Independent Self-Help Society claimed ninety-two members, or more than three-quarters of the War Seal's tenants.[103] Like Henry Mitchell, most had married after the war. Wed in 1924, the former grocer had a wife and one child to support on his single man's pension. He suffered from debilitating arthritis. According to W. J. Roberts, Mitchell was "quite a helpless cripple…in great need of attendance."[104] Unable to travel to the clinic, "he has taught his wife how to massage him and she seemed quite pleased to be able to do it." Although Mitchell's health improved at the War Seal Mansions, his worries did not subside. He had no savings, and nothing to provide for the wife who had cared for him. Not only could Mrs. Mitchell expect no pension but, according to the Mansions' rules, she would be forced to vacate her apartment after her husband's death. To ensure himself a decent burial, Mitchell joined the Independent Self-Help Society.

Yet what seemed to the "Self-Helpers" an expression of providence appeared to Stoll the height of irresponsibility. The founder was livid. Not only did the Self-Help Society threaten to undercut local tradesmen. As he explained to the Foundation's Council, he doubted that the Self-Help Society would have the resources to meet its obligations. He suggested that its founders were insane: "It is palpably wrong for men regrettably unbalanced (possibly mentally) through their war disablements, and with an income of about 3 pounds a week or less, to be allowed to operate a Society such as the one in question."[105] According to Stoll, the founders of the Independent Self-Help Society had intimidated other tenants into joining the organization. They had illegally operated a business on the Mansions' premises. He ordered the members of the Self-Help Society's board to disband the organization—or to vacate their apartments within the month.

Although Stoll had intended that the War Seal residents practice self-help, he meant them to achieve independence as individuals. In an open letter to the Mansions' tenants, he restated his principles: "Every tenant should be independent of every other."[106] He found the idea of collective self-help abhorrent. To Stoll, it smacked of communism: "It is impossible to countenance this communistic element with its wide notions of what comprises Independent Self-Help." He interpreted the Self-Help Society as an attack on the Foundation's principles. If disabled men could become independent only through mutual aid, Stoll's cherished ideal of self-sufficiency would be discredited. What began with self-help could only end with a struggle for control over the War Seal Mansions: "The attempts being made by a few of the tenants to defy the management and under the name of an Independent Self-Help Society convert the whole scheme into a communistic one...cannot be sanctioned."

The Self-Helpers were astonished by Stoll's response. They had no idea that the founder would punish their efforts. They asked that their eviction orders be reconsidered: "We cannot conceive that you would be so harsh as to turn into the street, disabled men, many of whom are unable to walk, solely because they are members of a mutual aid society, membership of which is quite voluntary."[107] They offered to move the Self-Help Society's headquarters out of the Mansions, but Stoll was not placated. He would be satisfied with nothing less than the Society's dissolution. As he reminded his tenants, the War Seal Mansions was his scheme "upon which I personally expended 40,000 pounds in the hope that I was doing something really helpful for deserving people."[108] He held all the cards. Unless the men repudiated the Self-Helpers, he would turn the War Seal Mansions over to the Charity Commissioners. "Failing this," he said, "I intend to wash my hands of the whole affair."

Mitchell resigned his membership the next day. However committed he was to the notion of self-help and a decent funeral, he could not afford to lose his apartment. The Self-Help Society was disbanded, its principles disgraced. By the end of the week, Stoll had received the assurances he demanded. In their letters, War Seal tenants repudiated more than the Independent Self-Help Society. They also scorned the notion of solidarity. As R. Wheeler wrote, "I think this communistic element should be removed from here, for myself and family we make no friends here. But keep ourselves to ourselves."[109] J. R. Lund wrote to express his "sympathy with Sir Oswald Stoll...for all the unnecessary trouble you have been given by a number of ignorant, dissatisfied men who seem to think that they can demand all they want because they are disabled. We do not mix with any of the tenants except just to pass the time and day."[110]

To preserve his scheme, Stoll had evicted disabled men whose principal crime was a different understanding of the meaning of independence. He created rifts among his tenants. That was the philanthropist's prerogative. Because of the state's neglect, there were always more tenants to be found, and many of them would be grateful for whatever they received. Stoll was a warmhearted, generous man. Disgusted by the stinginess of the Ministry of Pensions, he rescued disabled men from penury—and demanded that they be treated with respect: "You require to be very patient and to reason gently with these men. The iron has entered into their soul; their bitterness brings out the worst in them. . . . Our discipline though firm should be very gentle and tactful."[111] But the assistance that the philanthropist offered was always conditional, dependent on the man's allegiance. Benevolence did not come with a guarantee.

However graciously delivered, charity was no substitute for rights. That was true for the most egalitarian of charities. Founded in 1919 by the Quaker physician Fortescue Fox on a 1,032-acre estate in Hampshire, the Village Centre at Enham was a model settlement. Fox intended to demonstrate that with the proper training and atmosphere, any disabled man—even the "unemployables"—could return to work. Enham welcomed "difficult" cases, even those with shell shock. Most men came to the Hampshire estate for a year of rehabilitative training and treatment. For a nominal price, married men could rent cottages around a village green; single men were assigned private rooms in a dormitory. If a man was pronounced suitable, as a quarter of all trainees were, he was permitted to remain at Enham as a permanent employee. Settlers shared in the village's profits and were accorded a role in its management.

Through the rehabilitation of "unemployables," Enham intended to demonstrate the virtues of country life. As one newspaper reported, "There will be little enough of pills and potions."[112] Instead, Enham's physicians prescribed a program of fresh air and physical labor, a movement back to the land. Following Fox's production principles, Enham trained disabled men in traditional village crafts—farming, carpentry, poultry rearing, boot and shoe repairing. Such small-scale collective enterprise was particularly suited to neurasthenics, whose nerves would not tolerate repetitious piecework or "Fordism."[113] As the *Lancet* noted approvingly, Enham's ambitions were not limited to the rehabilitation of ex-servicemen. Its founders anticipated "the advent of rural colonization, when the village settlement, with permanent institutions, interests, and a corporate life of its own, will restore to the country something of that combination of simplicity and efficiency which is associated with the popular view of the 'good old days.' "

Enham promised to bring "the next generation back to the purer, saner life of the villages."[114] Who was better suited to fuel England's "regeneration" than the modern age's quintessential victim, the war-disabled man?

Although Fox advertised his scheme as a restoration, he had something altogether more revolutionary in mind. To achieve the highest-quality goods, Fox planned "self-governing" workshops, where every man would reap the fruits of his labor.[115] Some settlers would have the "Utopian joy of being allocated a small-holding of their own."[116] "The great idea," as Enham's administrator told the press, "is that of the communistic spirit—we shall be a great big family, all doing our best to help each other."[117] From model bungalows to the "absence of harassing regulations," Enham sought to foster individual initiative and collective life. Like Stoll, Fox pledged to restore in his charges masculine virtues, to "bring back self-control and courage, in the unspeakable desolation and despair left by the war."[118]

Yet a decade after Enham accepted its first settlers, Fox's rural idyll was in an uproar. The trouble began in 1929, when a trainee named Spicer posted a notice for the newly organized branch of the Enham British Legion.[119] When the manager, Mr. Tallyn, ordered him to remove the sign, purportedly because it was too large, Spicer refused and instead wrote Tallyn to demand an explanation. Insulted by Spicer's "challenge to his authority," Enham's manager dismissed the Legion man for insubordination. A taxi arrived to take Spicer to the station. Word of Tallyn's actions spread quickly. Before noon, the permanent settlers and the trainees had proclaimed a strike to protest Spicer's summary dismissal. Despite Tallyn's threats, neither the settlers nor the trainees returned to work. For two days, the Enham workshops were at a standstill. On the third morning of the strike, Enham's manager fired the strikers and ordered them to quit the estate.

Until the strike, Enham's settlers had believed that they had rights; the events of February 1929 proved them wrong. As they discovered, the only way they could retain their jobs was to ask for Tallyn's forgiveness. Once the settlers apologized for their misbehavior, Enham's managers agreed to reinstate them, with the exception of ten firebrands who would be dismissed. As for the trainees, Tallyn refused to rehire them, and they refused to leave. Settlers sympathetic to the trainees' cause intervened on their behalf. They took the renegades into their homes. When management charged that the settlers had violated their agreement, Enham's disabled men claimed that it was their prerogative to house whomever they pleased. Tallyn threatened to evict the entire population of the village. The Governing Committee was hastily convened in London, and it invited Colonel Crosfield, chairman of the British Legion, to attend.

The Legion wanted the strike, which had become an embarrassment to headquarters, resolved. Although Crosfield noted that Spicer's summary dismissal had been "highly provocative," he assured Enham's governors that the estate would soon return to order if the trainees were reengaged.[120] After a week of discussion—and no sign that the trainees would leave Enham without force—the Governing Committee backed down, ordering that the men be reinstated. At the same time, Enham's governors demanded that the British Legion issue a statement that the ex-servicemen's organization would not interfere with the management of the village, even to prevent further dismissals.[121] Crosfield gave the Governing Committee his word. He hoped that the authorities at Enham would take a "generous view" of the situation but reassured them that the Legion did not wish to meddle in the estate. The purpose of the Enham branch, he wrote, was to "instill" its members "with the spirit of the Legion, which is 'Service' and not 'Self.'"[122]

The trainees' victory proved hollow. Despite the settlers' best efforts, Spicer and another founding member of the British Legion branch were not rehired.[123] Two months after the showdown, Enham's delegate returned to the Legion's annual conference to plead for assistance. "The lives of the men at the Village Centre," he said, "were hell. Recent events had played upon the minds of the men so that they did not know whether they stood upon their heads or their heels, and unless something was done by the Legion, and done quickly, he could not say what would happen."[124] He attributed the ex-servicemen's misery to a change in management. In violation of the Village Centre's founding principles, Enham's new managers had "endeavoured to commercialise the place." The Enham delegate charged that salaries had been cut, and the men's governing role in the workshops eliminated.[125] To add insult to injury, Enham's management accused the strikers of being "unclean and unfit for village life."[126]

Enham's governors denied that the Village Centre had broken with its founding ideals. But even if Enham had radically changed course, the settlers had no say in the matter. They participated in the estate's management only at the management's pleasure. True to its word, if not to its constituency, the British Legion did not intervene in Enham's affairs. By the end of the year, the worldwide economic Slump had taken hold. As Enham's management noted with satisfaction, those who remained did not dare to risk their jobs: "This depression has had one good effect, it has brought home to the men very forcibly how great is the advantage they are receiving by being at Enham."[127] To emphasize the point, the Governing Committee decided to include letters of gratitude from its settlers along with the annual report.

Neglected by the state, spurned by philanthropists, Enham's settlers asked the British Legion to safeguard their rights. Their confidence was misplaced. As their counterparts at the Legion's Preston Hall settlement could have told them, the ex-servicemen's organization proved no more indulgent toward the objects of its benevolence than any other philanthropy. At its owner's request, the Legion had assumed control of the Preston Hall settlement in 1927. The estate was insolvent, and the Legion's headquarters, unable to wring more concessions from the Ministry of Pensions, was eager to demonstrate the organization's commitment to the disabled. In its form and aims, Preston Hall resembled Enham. Located on an Andover estate, it provided medical treatment and rehabilitative training for tubercular ex-servicemen and their families. Men came to Preston Hall as trainees. Those deemed suitable were permitted to stay on as settlers; between 1925 and 1928, 16 percent of trainees qualified as settlers.[128] Once accepted as a settler, a man was provided with work, a cottage, and the promise of a normal civilian life.

When the Legion took over Preston Hall, sixty-five men had settled there with their families, each promised tenure of residence by the estate's founders. Although Preston Hall's settlers initially welcomed the Legion's management, they soon found cause for complaint. Within two years of the Legion's accession, the settlement's medical director had ordered the dismissal of five men he judged "unfit" for village life, a contravention of the settlement terms. The settlers passed a vote of no confidence in the medical director, but without effect. Headquarters did not even acknowledge their motion. In protest, Preston Hall's settlers boycotted all Legion activities. In 1930, the secretary of the local branch reported "a woeful lack of enthusiasm in all that appertains to the Legion."[129] Settlers refused to attend meetings and shunned even normally popular services for Armistice Day.

In 1934, the Andover magistrate witnessed a peculiar suit. The British Legion, guardian of ex-servicemen's interests, faced one of its own charges in court.[130] Ex-private William Lee had lived on the Preston Hall estate for nine years, since 1927, as a settler. In 1931, he was appointed manager of the workshops. Although free of tuberculosis for four years, he was, by his own account, still in delicate health. He received other job offers but did not accept them. He wanted to remain at Preston Hall. In 1933, the British Legion claimed that his apartment was needed for another tenant, and it asked him to leave. When Lee refused to move, the Legion sent him a notice of eviction. Lee's lawyer argued that as a disabled ex-serviceman his client had "vested interests" in Preston Hall, where he had lived and worked for almost a decade. Ruling in the Legion's favor, the judge decided that the settlement was a charity. Lee had no right to stay.

Lawsuits, strikes, "communistic" schemes: charities for disabled ex-servicemen were fractious places. None, not even the most idealistic, were free from strife. Yet with a few exceptions, conflict between philanthropists and their charges was a private matter, settled within the charities' own walls, usually to the disabled man's disadvantage. Sir Walter Lawrence visited the Star and Garter Home in the afternoon and came away "much struck by the happy and cheery demeanour of the men."[131] That night, the bedridden Private Byng abused the orderlies with "filthy" language; he was removed from the Home the same week. The grievances of individuals rarely came to the public's attention. They were situational and specific; they did not provide a basis for collective organization. Unlike the state, philanthropists were not accountable for the plight of disabled ex-servicemen. They did what they could, and that was usually enough. Their visions took precedence over the disabled man's needs. Most donors agreed on the importance of "rules."

Philanthropists liked to imagine that they had created homes for their charges, free of charity's odium. According to W. J. Roberts, the War Seal Mansions provided "model homes," with "nothing of that abomination known as 'the institution' about them."[132] At Enham, "the keynote struck …is that patients, doctors, administration, and staff are a family."[133] But familial ties are based on dependence and subordination, as well as love and respect. In the philanthropists' homes, ex-servicemen were cast as children, subject to the aspirations and discipline of their elders. Their financial burdens were alleviated, but the advantages they enjoyed were never secure. They had to behave themselves, express their gratitude, and live according to the rules. The philanthropists were not easy to please. From the neurasthenic they would make a spokesman for rural settlement. The paraplegic could demonstrate the virtues of self-reliance.

Disabled veterans correctly perceived that their own needs were frequently relegated to second place. For two decades, the paraplegic Bill Foster chronicled the daily life of the Star and Garter Home in his satiric "Epistle of Imahlia to the Kroks." He told the story of the Spinekaces' life under "a sect called the KOMITI," who though they were "rich and can do things," knew little about their charges' lives.[134] They founded hospitals for paraplegics on the summits of hills too steep for wheelchairs: "Now inasmuch as the spinekaces know not how to walk, but perforce have to ride in chariots, it is always necessary that their palaces be at the top of a hill, for of a surety it would be too easy on level ground."[135] They built grand marble entrance halls and forbade patients to enter them in their motorized tricycles: "Tarry ye not in the halls lest ye wear out the marble, then shall we have nothing to show to those that be not of the spinekaces."[136]

Unless they wrote in codes, the Spine Cases had no choice but gratitude. The object of charity had to get along the best he could, keep to himself, and bury his emotions. Most important, he had to remain cheerful when reporters came around. After all, he owed his livelihood to philanthropy, and the public did not want to support the disconsolate. In private, disabled ex-servicemen might despair, rage, or weep, but the image they presented to the world was uniformly good-humored. "Cheerful after 15 Years of Pain," as one headline about Roehampton read.[137] Or: "Shattered Soldier Laughs at Fate, Life Invalid Says He's Happy."[138] In a life lived as a memorial, a smile did not always signify what onlookers assumed.

SHATTERED SOLDIER LAUGHS AT FATE

In November 1934, the American novelist Mary Borden set out from London to visit the Great War's casualties.[139] The day was gray and bitter, the Thames River valley, which Turner had rendered in lush tones, appeared desolate. At the summit of Richmond Hill, steeper than she had remembered, Borden paused to catch her breath. Before her stood an imposing red-brick structure, four stories high, trimmed in Portland stone. It was an architectural sore thumb, out of character with the fancifully turreted Victorian hotels that lined the park. A small sign announced that Borden had arrived at the Star and Garter Home for Ex-Sailors and Soldiers. She shivered "with apprehension." Her motivation, she admitted, was curiosity. "I had heard so much of this home for disabled sailors and soldiers that I wanted to see it. 'It will be such a sad place,' I said to myself, 'All these men, crippled, paralysed, blind.'"

Borden was no stranger to disability. During the First World War, she had served as a nurse in a French clearing station. *The New Statesman* called her memoir, *The Forbidden Zone* (1929), "a moving and rather painful book to read."[140] She knew about the horrors of the operating room, gangrene, and deathbed laments. Men in hospital, Borden had written, "are no longer men." She described her patients in the clearing station as broken, incorporeal body parts: "There are heads and knees and mangled testicles. There are chests with holes as big as our fist, and

Figure 11.   The Star and Garter Home, 1931. By kind permission of the Royal Star and Garter Home for Disabled Ex-Servicemen and Women.

pulpy thighs, shapeless; and stumps where legs once were fastened. There are eyes—eyes of sick dogs, sick cats, blind eyes, eyes of delirium; and mouths that cannot articulate; and parts of faces—the nose gone, or the jaw. There are these things, but no men."[141]

But the Star and Garter proved a far different place than Borden had imagined. It had, first of all, a reassuringly masculine ambience.[142] "A spacious, comfortable men's club," there was "nothing to suggest an institution; no uniforms." In the common room, a fire crackled in a tiled hearth. Carefully dressed men gathered around circular wooden tables. All were cheerful. One had "a jolly red face and laughing brown eyes," another "gave a fat chortle." "What a lot of jokes seemed to be going about," she recalled. A few of the men huddled over a chessboard, while others made stuffed toys for an upcoming bazaar. Her spirits lifted, she ventured upstairs to where the "bed cases" lay. It was anything but depressing. In a ward "all gay with flowers," beds bedecked with bright pink blankets, she met the Home's drummer boy, paralyzed in October 1914. He "grinned all over." Her apprehension vanished. Much to her surprise, Borden realized that she had come to "one place in the world where men didn't worry, where they were at peace...one place where they were happy."

Between 1916, when the old hotel received its first patients, and 1934, when Borden visited, the Star and Garter housed 850 totally disabled inhabitants.[143] Before the war, they were farmers and shipyard laborers, clerks and school teachers, miners and boot makers, lift attendants and cotton spinners, crane drivers and chauffeurs. Like Joe Richards, the majority had worked with their hands. Richards had been a patient since 1917. On the Somme, the former postal worker was hit high in the spine by a piece of shrapnel and was left paralyzed from the neck down. The Star and Garter's patients were mostly enlisted men, privates, drivers, riflemen, and sailors. At Messines, Gallipoli, Ypres, the Marne, Suvla Bay, the Somme, a gunshot or a fragment of shrapnel cut short their war service—and their lives. A third of the Star and Garter's patients died there, most before their thirty-fifth birthday.

In 1914, Borden's description of jolly paraplegics would have been unthinkable. Paraplegia, most people agreed, was the worst of fates.[144] Asked by philanthropists to imagine an immobile life, a day without legs or arms, a minute deprived of sight and touch, Britons reached deep into their pocketbooks to provide for the severely disabled. At the same time, they expected something for their money. As one journalist noted, "Although the spontaneously kind-hearted passer-by can easily be harrowed by any beggar...into bestowing his sympathy and his small change, the solid English well-to-do public that keeps things going is not easily moved to sink its money in a desperate cause."[145] Above all, the objects of charity had to eschew bitterness and remain cheerful, at least publicly. Philanthropists might appeal on behalf of the war's "human wreckage," but when visitors arrived, the wreckage had to behave like the brave Tommies of 1914. No one wanted to support a malcontent, a depressive, or an amputee who mourned his lost limb.

In the years after the Great War, disabled ex-servicemen were portrayed as unfailingly cheerful. Their high spirits not only gratified donors but also demonstrated that victory, however terrible the price, had been worth it. No matter how badly injured, the war's casualties did not regret their sacrifices. According to the *Evening News* reporter, "There was not a sign nor a word of regret for the manhood left behind on a stricken field."[146] Stripped of youth's callow vigor, disabled veterans exemplified a higher ideal. Their masculinity, forged amid suffering, was expressed through self-control and the denial of pain. This vision of manliness was not new. Victorians had prized a man's stiff upper lip, judging his imperturbable reserve an important counterpoint to feminine emotion.[147] Disabled men's good cheer proved that their tragedy had ennobled them; their manhood had been strengthened, not sapped, by adversity. In a speech to her "dear friends" at the Star and Garter, the

Marchioness of Townshend praised them as "the highest type of British gentlemen."[148]

By the 1920s, the smiling bed-case had replaced the "human wreckage" in representations of the disabled. It was in large measure wishful thinking, a reassuring portrait for the generous British public. Some men were in fact good-humored. Although they had lost the physical and financial independence that defined manhood, they took pride in their plucky endurance. Undaunted cheerfulness signified a masculine autonomy that transcended physical limitations. Their emblem was W. E. Henley's "Invictus," written during the author's hospital stay: "In the fell clutch of circumstance / I have not winced nor cried aloud. / Under the bludgeonings of chance / My head is bloody, but unbowed." But those who thanked "whatever gods may be" for their "unconquerable soul" were probably in the minority. There were many others for whom helplessness, institutional life, and separation from their families proved intolerable. They got drunk and violent or retreated into an embittered isolation. Unless they committed suicide, no one outside of the Home knew about them. The unrepentantly disgruntled were discharged.

High atop Richmond Hill, disabled men became curiosities, living symbols of the war. "Legion of the Broken: Indelible Mark of War Inscribed on All Hearts," read one headline in the *Daily Sketch*.[149] When sympathetic thoughts turned to the "sad remaining memories of the war" on Armistice Day and Christmas, reporters came to see "how the men were getting on."[150] Like Mary Borden, they toured the Home, always in the company of a nurse or an administrator; spoke to a few patients; and filed their copy. As one patient observed, "Occasionally we are discovered by journalists who display the requisite journalistic surprise at their discovery in a feature article."[151] The visit was pro forma. Reporters described the Home's luxuries and reported about patients' cheerfulness. They interviewed the same handful of men: Joe Richards, paralyzed from the neck down; Charles Whittaker, the Home's first patient; Bunny Hunt, the grinning drummer boy.

Yet to believe that there was "not a happier family in England than the patients of the Star and Garter Home" required more than an act of imagination.[152] During the war, newspapers had reported that disablement and the loss of independence, not death, was the soldier's greatest fear. " 'The only thing I dread is losing a limb—I'd rather be killed!' These words must have been echoed a thousand times by our gallant fighting men who, while willing and ready to lay down life itself…have, very naturally, shrunk with horror from the terrible prospect of a helpless existence and the utter lack of previous independence which the loss of a limb suggests."[153] Heroic death was celebrated in poetry and consecrated in stone. Growing old in a wheelchair, deprived of a man's prerogatives, was not. Parents who lost their sons in the Great War's killing fields took comfort in the thought that they had not returned disabled. "My only son, Captain C. Harold Bass, Lancashire Fusiliers, fell on August 26 '14 after three days in France, and I have often thanked God that he was spared disablement or disfigurement, blindness or lack of reason. Those who fell are not to be pitied, only those who are left behind," wrote one woman as she contributed to the War Seal Mansions.[154]

Of all those "left behind," paraplegics inspired the most sorrow. Amputees might be rehabilitated, even returned to their prewar jobs. With seeing-eye dogs, blind men could move about town. Plastic surgery promised wonders for men with facial injuries. But paralyzed men were helpless, dependent on others for the most intimate care. Few families could afford to provide for them. They had to be bathed, dressed, bandaged. Only conscientious, laborious nursing kept them alive. Many men were incontinent. Without enemas two to three times a week, pyelitis threatened death by the body's own poisons. Bedsores were a constant worry. Many paraplegic patients had open wounds on their backs or sides so large that "you could put your hands in."[155] Twice a day, their bodies had to be rubbed with methylated spirits. Where bones protruded, extra layers of bandages were added to dressings.

The Star and Garter Home owed its origins to pity. As a field surgeon in the Boer War, Sir Frederick Treves had treated every sort of battlefield injury, but he judged paraplegia the most horrible: "There is no more piteous spectacle of human wreckage than this nerveless body, abject in its impotence and decrepitude, linked with the restless and imperious spirit of sturdy manhood."[156] One of the most celebrated medical men in Edwardian Britain, personal physician to King Edward VII, and a founder of the British Red Cross, Treves knew about the suffering caused by disfigurement: he had discovered the Elephant Man in a London freak show. The Elephant Man he granted hope; for the paraplegic, "it would have been easier to give life itself." The "vigorous" mind was imprisoned in the "listless" body, the young man instantly aged. The War Office would not provide for the hopelessly disabled, and their families could not care for them: "One knows what happens—the patient is moved to the wards of a workhouse infirmary, and there his career comes to an end with little glory to those who say that the wounded soldier shall lack for nothing."[157]

Disgusted by the state's indolence, Treves turned to philanthropy. Believing that it rested with the "well-to-do to mend this matter, to rid the country of reproach, and to perform, not merely an act of kindness, but an act of justice," he urged the Auctioneers' and Estate Agents' Institute to advance the purchase price for the old Star and Garter Hotel. Their president, L'Anson Breach, issued a public appeal for a charity auction to finance a home for "totally disabled ex-servicemen." From the drawing rooms, silver chests, and attics of Britain's well-heeled issued a century's worth of collectibles for the auctioneers' Star and Garter sale, luxury goods contributed to extend heroes' lives: "a set of handsome tiger claw ornaments in chased gold work"; "a valuable collection of point d'Argenton lace about 1780 period"; "a characteristic Letter from W. E. Gladstone to Mr. Justin McCarthy, dated from Hawarden Castle, 17 December, 1887"; "a splendid collection of frank autographs of Queen Victoria"; Shetland ponies, an Italian mandoline, and a cricket bat by B. Warsop.[158] The auction, which lasted for a full week in the Knightsbridge Hall, earned a profit of £22,000.

At its heyday, in the mid–nineteenth century, the Star and Garter was an elegant resort, symbolic of Great Britain's prosperity in the first fruitful decades of the Industrial Revolution. Its front building, four turreted stories high, was outfitted with opulent suites for the affluent city dwellers who resided there during the summer months. Located in the rear building were banqueting halls and a grand ballroom, crowned with elaborate cornices and intricately carved wainscoting. Thackeray, Dickens, Ruskin, and Tennyson were frequent visitors. After the Revolution of 1848, Louis Philippe sought refuge in a second-floor suite. In the Star and Garter's oak-paneled banqueting hall, Becky Sharp was the Marquess of Steyne's dinner guest. The view from its windows was legendary. From the peak of Richmond Park, the hotel overlooked the Thames River and the luxuriant wooded valley below. Turner had painted from its terrace.

Long before its ballroom was lined with hospital beds, the Star and Garter had lost its former glory. In the 1890s, ladies of leisure and their gentlemen deserted the hotel for smarter watering holes farther afield. Despite buckets of paint attesting to its " 'palatial' and 'desirable' features," the property went unsold at consecutive auctions.[159] Its grand entrances were boarded over. When a committee of philanthropists, led by Treves, toured the premises in 1915, the hotel's owners were willing to part with the property for a fraction of the original selling price. With sick and wounded soldiers crowded into hospital corridors and country houses converted into convalescent homes, even white elephants such as the Star and Garter could be put to good use. The hotel's banqueting hall and ballroom, emptied of heavy oak furniture and crystal chandeliers, would serve as wards. In the marbled foyer, a hundred cases of rare wine and liqueur were auctioned to make room for the first shipment of patients.[160]

For those who hoped that the war would usher in a new era of self-restraint and modesty, the Star and Garter's transformation offered an irresistible symbol. The Victorian pleasure palace was to be filled with the nation's martyrs. The *Evening News* judged the "once-famous hotel… now a nobler thing to look on than ever it was in the days of its riot of reckless hospitality, in the spendthrift 'glories' of the 'sixties.'"[161] In place of "the shrine of Bacchus," wrote the *Times* correspondent, "a temple of healing" had been constructed. An opportunity for national moral regeneration was at hand. "Here will come no idle pleasure-seekers, bent on self-indulgence, but men who have made sacrifice and suffered for a great cause, whose offering is to pain, not pleasure. Let it keep the old swaggering name for remembrance, to commemorate forever the exchange. And let it stand for a general change from frivolity and folly to a serious and worthy purpose in life."[162]

The old hotel received its first ten patients in January 1916. They were young men, all but one in their twenties, and most were unmarried. Three were regular army men, the rest volunteers. At thirty-four, Sergeant Charles Whittaker was the oldest. A hardworking career military man, Whittaker had married just before war was declared. On 30 September 1914, in Ypres, a shrapnel fragment in the first clavicle paralyzed his legs and his left arm. He was a brave soldier, mentioned in Despatches for the rescue of an injured man in No Man's Land. He did not want to come to the Home, away from his young wife in Ryegate, but his measly pension of 27s. 6d. left him little choice. Before the year was out, five of the first nine patients deemed "incurable" had demonstrated considerable improvement. Four even managed to return home. Two, aged twenty-three and twenty-nine, died. Three men, Charlie Whittaker among them, remained in the Star and Garter for the next two decades.

Despite its parquet floors and frescoed walls, the Star and Garter was not a comfortable place for paraplegics. The banqueting hall's enormous windows "would either keep the rooms airless or let in a gale."[163] Although some men were too sick to leave their beds, others recovered and became restless. If they wanted to leave the wards, orderlies had to carry them down the flight of stairs. The famous vista over Richmond Park, praised as the Home's "greatest asset," emphasized its inhabitants' isolation. "Man cannot live by view alone," complained the Home's first commandant.[164] Architects were summoned to calculate the cost of renovations to the old hotel. For the price of modernization, an entirely new building could be constructed. Treves gave his approval; as soon as the war was over, the old hotel would be razed, and a new Star and Garter built in its place.

The need for a new Home led Treves to unlikely allies. Not long after the purchase of the hotel, he heard about the Actresses' Franchise League. The 900-member strong League of suffragist actresses wanted to equip a British Women's Hospital in France, to be directed, staffed, and funded entirely by women. After the War Office refused their request, Treves suggested a collaboration. It was a gamble for the prominent surgeon. The Red Cross disapproved of the League's politics. Under the chairmanship of May Whitty, the suffragist actresses agreed to redirect their energies. In the summer of 1915, they formed the British Women's Hospital Committee, dropped "actresses" and "franchise" from their name if not from their aims, and recruited Annie, Viscountess Cowdray, as their treasurer. Queen Mary, who "had taken most grievously to heart those cases where the men were totally disabled by paralysis," pronounced herself "graciously pleased" to become patroness.[165]

As chairwoman of the British Women's Hospital Committee, May Whitty supervised the hundreds of charity theatricals, benefit performances, and appeal concerts at the heart of the Star and Garter campaign. A distinguished stage actress and in her old age a screen star (*Mrs. Miniver, The Thirteenth Chair, The Lady Vanishes*), Whitty (1865–1948) was a founding member of British Actors' Equity and a convinced pacifist. Always an energetic organizer, she found hospital work a consuming passion, an antidote to the helplessness she felt at the war's outbreak. Whitty's daughter described her mother writing appeals letters late into the night: "The dining room practically became an office. I was always surprised that we still managed to eat there, the table was so littered with pamphlets and leaflets and stacks of writing paper with boldly printed letterheads."[166] Despite lunches with "her mortal enemy," Asquith, and hobnobbing with royalty, she never gave up her "'agin the government'" activities and was accused ("to some extent justifiably," according to her daughter) of being a Bolshevik and Sinn Feiner. But no one disputed her success. Within a month, the Women's Hospital Committee had raised £20,000, nearly twice what Treves had expected.

Judged by outward appearances, Annie, Viscountess Cowdray, was a far more conventional character than Madame Chairman. Whitty's dress was eccentric, flowing where it should have been restricted, fringed with extravagant tassels. Her smile did not conceal "her keen eye for humbug"; her plumed headdress winked at polite society.[167] Lady Cowdray (1862–1932), on the other hand, was wire-spectacled, proper, even severe. In her own way, though, she was just as unorthodox as the theatrical Whitty. Openly ambitious, she presided over the dramatic expansion of her husband's contracting business and their hard-fought ascension up the social scale. She was, according to her own description, a "wily old cat."[168] She was also a great philanthropist, an ardent liberal, a member of the Executive of the Women's Liberal Federation, a suffragist, and a bereaved mother.[169] Shortly after the viscountess agreed to join the British Women's Hospital Committee, her youngest son was killed at Ypres.

The suffragist actresses and the viscountess made a peculiar but undeniably successful committee. From their handsomely appointed offices in central London, donated by the art dealer Louis Duveen, they broadcast appeals to their audiences, patrons, business leaders, trade unionists, and the Girl's Patriotic League: "Even if it only be as the widow's mite it will help to further this splendid work."[170] Within eleven months, they had raised £150,000; within a year and a half, £225,000. Gertrude Forbes-Robertson, the American-born president of the Actresses' Franchise League and an acclaimed Shakespearian actress, was the organization's public face. She conveyed the tragedy of disabled men's predicament. "Think of these men," she exhorted her audiences, "think of their helplessness, think of the spirit imprisoned in them."[171] She promised donors that the Star and Garter would be a "foretaste of Heaven," with "lifts to take patients to the gardens, verandah and the loggia with the southern aspect, where they can lie in all weathers." In closing, she pleaded, "Will everyone who has lunched or dined at the old Star and Garter Hotel give a guinea!"

"Everyone talked Star and Garter and encouraged other people to talk Star and Garter," wrote the *Woman at Home* in 1917.[172] Despite fierce competition from the hundreds of other war charities for disabled veterans, the Women's Hospital Committee's campaign blossomed. Every week the papers were full of the latest charity entertainment. A matinee all-star performance in Oswald Stoll's Coliseum Theatre raised £5,000 in one afternoon. In the press, the acclaimed literary men of the day—

among them the novelist John Galsworthy—appealed on behalf of the Home. "Who really grasps what it's like to lie like a log dependent for everything on others?" The "hopelessly disabled" had missed the "enfranchisement" of death, observed Galsworthy, but they had the "chance to prove the metal of the human soul."[173] It was the public's duty to ensure that the Star and Garter's patients lacked nothing. The morning after Galsworthy's piece ran in the *Sunday Observer,* the committee received £3,000 in donations.

Lady Fulton's overseas appeal yielded even more spectacular results. As the British government turned to the Empire for troops to fight the war, philanthropists campaigned abroad for aid in the reconstruction. Acknowledging the Empire's generosity in "men and money," Lady Fulton confessed that she would be "more diffident, except that the need for which I ask is so great."[174] Into the offices of the Women's Hospital Committee flowed contributions from all parts of the globe, foreign countries as well as British colonies. To the committee's satisfaction, "native ladies" responded to Lady Fulton's appeal enthusiastically: "A list of contributors forwarded from Penang, Strait Settlements, contains handsome sums opposite names such as Mrs. Khaw Sum Bee, Mrs. Heah Swee Lee and Mrs. Lim Hin Leong."[175] Under the patronage of Viscountess Buxton, a South African 6d. Fund collected £10,655.[176] The British Women of South America and Singapore contributed £3,000 apiece. The money the women gathered benefited the residents of the metropole; the vast majority of the Home's patients were native-born.

By January 1916, when the old hotel received its first patients, the Star and Garter was widely known as the Women's Memorial. That was May Whitty's idea, and Frederick Treves approved. Her committee directed its appeals toward women, urging them to "make" the Home. Women could not match men's physical sacrifices, but by alleviating the suffering of disabled soldiers they made a valuable contribution to the war effort: " 'What have *I* done' is the anguished cry of every true woman's heart in these times—'what have *I* done that these broken men should have given all that life is worth to fight for me?' Women—British Women—all the World over—it is not any longer a question of what you *have done*, but what you are ready *now* to do."[177] What exactly the Women's Memorial commemorated was left intentionally vague. Treves described it as a "Permanent Memorial of the Great War," dedicated to the disabled.[178] Whitty referred to it as the Women's Memorial to their own patriotic war work; the suffragist actresses intended to honor

women's service to the nation. Queen Mary called it a memorial of
women's gratitude to "those who have suffered in the service of their
King and Country."[179]

The Star and Garter was never one memorial, but many. Four hundred
separate inscriptions "in memoriam" were contained within its portals.
For the sum of £2,000, donors could endow a bed in perpetuity; a small
bronze tablet placed at the foot of the bed marked their gift. A contribution of £200 built a room. Mary Baillie, a vicar's wife from North Devon,
pledged £2,000 to endow a bed in honor of her son, killed on the Somme;
her donation reconstituted a family the war had torn apart: "Our first idea
was to build a room as well, but a cousin whose son has been killed wished
to do this in memory of her son. Our idea is that *our* bed shall be in *her*
room, as our boys spent so much time in each others' company."[180] In
1918, Mrs. Gladys Street donated £2,000 after a visit to the Home:
"Somehow I feel especially if there was any Gunner in my husband's
Brigade I heard of, he would so like to know him so well cared for. Yes-
terday I felt it all too much to even try and say anything of this sort."[181]

Bereaved donors often sought a "personal interest" in the Home. "I
shall be glad to know when it is finished so that I may take a personal
interest in the occupant," wrote one mother. "Had my own son recovered from his terrible wound he would have had the same fate."[182] Only
a few donors wanted to visit; most simply asked for pictures of the men
in their beds. Mrs. Violet Loring, widowed after the first battle of Ypres,
contributed £200 toward the cost of a bed: "There is nothing that I
would like better to give as a memorial to my husband.... I do not know
if I shall be able to afford it for I have 10 children and expenses are very
heavy, but if I could not manage it I and my children...would so like to
have some personal interest in the hospital."[183] One woman wrote that
she had sold her diamond necklace to pay for a bed "so that this might
be a real gift, not just money, to help one poor man who had given so
very very much for his country."[184]

With beds financed by diamond necklaces, the Star and Garter had a
certain "romance" about it, or so claimed the glossy magazine *Woman
at Home*. One page was illustrated with photos of tidy ballroom wards.
On the next appeared cameos of a bejeweled young actress with bobbed
hair and a pensive marchioness "who has also shown her interest in the
scheme."[185] The Star and Garter was not the only romantic institution;
others, including Bernard Oppenheimer's Brighton diamond factory and
Oswald Stoll's War Seal Mansions, also earned the sobriquet.[186] In
wartime, romance edged toward pathos, a drama of reconciliation staged

by survivors. The fate of the battlefield bound mourners to paralyzed soldiers. Philanthropy linked titled ladies to radical actresses. Other men's widows tended dying soldiers who lay in hospital beds that bore the names of the fallen. Wards for the doubly incontinent were built in the banqueting halls of dilapidated society hotels.

"There were kings in the old days whose subjects...bled for them," commented the *Richmond and Twickenham Times*. "But they never dreamed of providing so liberally for those who were permanently injured in the wars as the British people have now done for those who will make their home in the Star and Garter."[187] Like Oswald Stoll's War Seal Mansions, the new Star and Garter was a labor of love. Treves chose the building materials himself from the finest possible sources. Subiaco marble was sent from Italian quarries. Annie Cowdray took charge of interior design. Every aspect of the building was investigated, reviewed, redrawn. When Treves discovered flaws in Sir Gilbert Scott's plans, he dismissed the celebrated architect and brought in Edwin Cooper instead. Cooper undertook the work voluntarily and spent a year on the blueprints alone. Building began shortly after the Armistice. In 1920, three charabancs transported the Star and Garter's patients to their temporary accommodations in Sandgate.

Nine years after fund-raising began, Queen Mary and King George opened the Home in July 1924. Their Majesties toured the premises and commented on the Home's "light, airiness, space and cheerfulness."[188] They enjoyed themselves more than they had "for many a day."[189] Although the event was by invitation only, the building was full. Three hundred sightseers waited outside, while dignitaries and important donors crowded into the Star and Garter's public rooms. "Most of the women had honoured the occasion by wearing picturesque dresses."[190] After the official opening, members of the public were invited to view the Star and Garter, advertised in the London papers. On Tuesday, admission cost 2s. 6d., on Saturday and Wednesday, 1s. "In response to many requests," two further dates were added. On five separate occasions, more than 8,000 people visited the Star and Garter.[191]

Most observers agreed that the final product, which took four years to build, had been well worth the wait. The *Lancet* called it "sumptuous, ...a palace rather than a mere hospital."[192] In the *Birmingham Post*'s judgment, there was "no such perfect and restful a haven for the wreckage of war anywhere."[193] Polished marble adorned the entrance hallway. The wards overlooked the Thames. Single rooms afforded privacy for those men who wanted it. With its enormous fireplace and overstuffed chairs, the downstairs reading room was "as comfortable and well-furnished as the members' smoking room in a good club."[194] Annie Cowdray personally selected the furniture and linen. To give the Star and Garter "a homey feel," she brought knickknacks from her own house in Carlton Place. Even the normally reserved *Times* was favorably impressed: "The Home has the dignity and charm which are associated with the halls of such a place as Hampton Court Palace."[195]

No patients attended the opening-day festivities. The munificence of the public, not disabled men's suffering, was on display. The Star and Garter's patients did not come until the end of the summer. Although reporters flocked to the official opening of the Home, they were slower to visit once the patients had arrived. Like the *Yorkshire Post*'s London correspondent, they feared what they would find. "I had always wanted to go in [the Star and Garter]...but until the other day, I have always been afraid to."[196] In normal hospitals, patients might recover, return home to their families and work. Most of the Star and Garter's inmates were incurables. In Treves's description, "He has lost everything but bare life, and, saddest of all, there is taken from him the dearest of all treasures—Hope."[197] Rendered in rich colors, the stained glass windows in the Home's grand entrance hallway depicted three robed figures, identified by placards below: Faith, Charity—and Saint George, the patron saint of England. Hope, the customary third member of the trio, was noticeably absent.

Effaced from the Home's interior, hope thrived in the depictions of its inhabitants. To their amazement, visitors found that permanently disabled men, even paralytics, were cheerful. The *Evening Standard*'s reporter marveled at the "inexplicable, unbelievable wonder of it."[198] Although the gaiety of wounded soldiers had been a staple of wartime literature, their good cheer was understandable.[199] They had survived the trenches and would soon recover from their "Blighty wounds." Not the Star and Garter's patients. The *Standard*'s reporter met a man who had lost a leg, an arm, and part of another hand: "This extraordinary fellow was running himself around the place in a wheel chair, apparently as happy as a sandboy, cheering the rest with his gaiety." At a Star and Garter singing contest, a man rendered speechless by war service, but able to whistle songs, was "obviously one of the most happy and cheerful" of the competitors.[200] Not only reporters but also donors and volunteers commented on the men's high spirits. Mr. Innes, vice-consul of the British Bilbas, noted with pleasure that the men appeared " 'extremely happy and cheerful.' "[201]

These were heartening stories. Life was not as bad as the British public might expect; depictions of men's cheerfulness assuaged what guilt
people may have felt. "One would imagine that such a collection of men
...would be among the saddest it is possible to conceive," observed a reporter in the *Standard*. "On the contrary, Roehampton House is a place
of smiles and cheerfulness."[202] Disabled men's "cheery optimism," years
after the Armistice, proved that the public's money had been well spent.
At the Star and Garter, "sad memories of the war...gave place to a ra-
diant pride of spirit in the wonderful palace of healing on the hill."[203]
After a conversation with a man she identified only as "Wheel Chair,"
substituting his most visible attribute for a name, the columnist Norah
Hill commented approvingly: "Eight years in a chair have not dampened
his enthusiasm or embittered his outlook."[204] Even those who suffered
most for Britannia had managed to rise above their injuries. The obituary of a "Man Who Lay Still for 20 Years" noted that he never "lost his
cheerfulness," though "the tragic realisation" that he could never leave
the hospital occasionally depressed him. In time, however, "he conquered his mental anguish."[205]

Disabled men's cheerfulness was anything but "natural." It attested
to a resolute masculinity distinguished by the control of emotions; it
reflected great courage. The *Evening Standard*'s reporter returned from
the Star and Garter Home convinced: "I believe that to-day I have met
courage in its highest form."[206] The will to live impressed more than did
a willingness to die: "Employers, heads of organisations, friends, and
even wives seem to be unanimous in their tribute to this remarkable
courage which has outlasted war."[207] Battlefield bravery was fleeting,
days and months rather than years. In hospitals, the clock ticked
slowly.[208] "Their gaiety is the gaiety of the trenches—it's genuine, not
ghoulish—but it requires even more courage now than then."[209] After he
learned to paint with a brush in his mouth, Joe Richards, paralyzed from
the neck down, talked to reporters: "A press representative discovered in
Richmond on Thursday the perfect story of the havoc of war and of the
courage that turns the living hell of existence with a shattered body into
something pleasant to smile upon."[210]

Much as Galsworthy had hoped, the disabled offered an inspirational
tale. Theirs was the greatest misfortune. If they could reconcile themselves
to their fate, every problem could be overcome. The British Legion found
"encouragement for everyone in the record of the blinded soldiers, so
heroic and so invincible."[211] They proved the "resilience of human nature." Mourners, among them Queen Amelie of Portugal, visited the

Figure 12.   On the grounds of the Fourth London General Hospital, undated.
By permission of the Imperial War Museum.

disabled for consolation. After her fiancé died, Clarice Pound went up to the Star and Garter Home: "It was a new life for me."[212] Even men in the hospital, reported the papers, looked to their fellow patients for inspiration.[213] There was always someone worse off. Blind men and amputees joked about who was most incapacitated; it was always the other fellow. As a Roehampton patient observed, "The more hopeless his case, the more cheerful the man."[214]

The men's "gay nonchalance" defied their physical suffering. Their spirits transcended their injured bodies. The disabled demonstrated the essence of masculine perseverance, independent of physical strength. They represented manhood as nineteenth-century Evangelical reformers had imagined it, an expression of inner moral substance.[215] The war's "wreckage," so fearful to look upon, had souls that saved them: "These disabled ex-Service men may be maimed in body, but assuredly they are not maimed in spirit."[216] Their injuries had not damaged their character. Far from the labor unrest and economic uncertainties of the postwar world, the Star and Garter men preserved the "still invincible spirit of the Old Contemptibles."[217] They demonstrated "that spirit of quiet, patient optimism which was such a great factor in the winning of the war."[218] Their generation was the best that England had produced, buried in the fields of Flanders, or crippled, hidden away on the top of Richmond Hill: "Here are the last companies of the vast Army of 1914–1918, still living in the spirit of those days."[219]

Despite the men's gaiety, for a visitor it was not always "so easy to feel cheerful."[220] As one reporter acknowledged, the sight of so many injured men inflicted a "stab in the heart." Even familiarity with casualty statistics did not prepare George Barnes, the first minister of pensions, for a hospital visit. "I shall never forget the occasion when the Rt. Hon. G. N. Barnes came down to talk to us about pensions etc.," wrote J. B. Middlebrooks, a patient at Roehampton. "We were gathered on a lawn—invalid chairs, crutches, and empty sleeves, and Mr. Barnes was invited to address. He rose to do so, but there was a long silence, and the tears ran down his face, and he returned to London having said nothing at all."[221]

Visitors freely acknowledged their sadness. However, whatever bitterness and depression the Home's residents felt went unmentioned. Some disabled men preferred it this way. Cheerfulness was a sign that they had the strength to overcome their injuries.[222] Despite their pain, they had not lost control of their demeanor. Where reintegration into the workforce proved a German veteran's self-worth, the British disabled measured their manhood by fortitude in the face of adversity. The most manly veteran was the one who suffered without complaint. It was a matter of self-preservation as well as personal pride. Mindful of the public's interest, dependent on its benevolence, disabled ex-servicemen recognized that people wanted to think of them as brave and cheerful, not morose or resentful. On her visit to the Star and Garter, the Marchioness of Townshend complimented the patients' good humor: "Perhaps the great thing to do was to forget the past."[223]

For more than three decades, the *Star and Garter Magazine* testified to its inhabitants' cheerfulness. Founded and edited by the Home's patients, the publication boasted hundreds of subscribers outside the Star and Garter's walls. Its purpose was to chronicle the "inner life" of the Home, and to that end it printed articles by patients and staff, doggerel and jokes, reportage from the outside ("How Others See Us"), and obituaries. Its tone was resolutely optimistic: "In spite of physical disabilities, life can be a cheery affair, and in the pages of the Star and Garter Magazine we try to dwell on the highlights rather than on the shadows of life."[224] The war's "postscripts" rarely wrote about their service experiences. Most of the articles were humorous. Sex and marital relations provided a favorite source of jokes, proving that disablement had not extinguished men's interest in the opposite sex. In "The Convenience of Cousins," R.I.P. documented "Clarence's" extended "family" of attractive female visitors, while the long-running correspondence between 'Erb and his wife Polly lampooned a soured marriage.[225]

The *Magazine* reflected the philosophy of its editor, Clifford Hill. A former clerk, Hill spent most of his life in veterans' homes, at St. David's in Cheltenham, the Star and Garter, and later, when he married, the War Seal Mansions.[226] Although his injury had rendered him a paraplegic and doubly incontinent at the age of nineteen, he was not regretful. He cherished what remained to him and appreciated his advantages: "My invalid chair has enabled me to meet many interesting people whom I know I should not have met otherwise."[227] During the Depression, he noted the "happy position we patients in the Star and Garter enjoy," free of financial worries.[228] He delighted in the prosaic. In essays titled "The Decay of Jollity" and "The Beauty of the Commonplace," he celebrated small pleasures: "No one will deny that there is beauty in the commonplace, but it is one of the tragedies of life that few see that beauty."[229]

A popular subject for reporters who visited the Home, Hill personified the disabled ex-serviceman's virtues. He was amiable, unas-

suming, content with his lot. He compared himself not to "normal people" but to those worse off: to Joe Richards, paralyzed from the neck
downward, or to the arthritic George Breen, unable even to turn the
pages of his books. Disabled men could not follow the "pursuits of normal people," but "life had still much to offer if you were prepared to . . .
take it."[230] For those men who could no longer work, Hill—an amateur
photographer, tenor in the Star and Garter Quartet, founder of the chess
club—prescribed hobbies.[231] Those inclined to despair he reminded of
their advantages: a roof over their head, plenty of food, and free entertainment. The "virile personality" never questioned fate. Hill found his
ideal in the life of Harry Franklin, a fellow patient and friend, dead at the
age of thirty-eight: "Like Henley, he did not 'wince or cry aloud.' Circumstance did not conquer him; he conquered circumstance."[232]

Hill's account was by no means complete. There were, of course,
many other stories that could have been told about the Star and Garter.
In the *Magazine*, the Home's suicides received no obituaries. Cases of
"mental deterioration" went unmentioned, as did any record of theft,
violence, and loneliness.[233] The behavior of the inmates often displeased
the commandant. They insulted the orderlies and criticized the nurses.[234]
They refused medical treatment.[235] They "cadged" for drinks in pubs.[236]
Like Edward Wiles, the men drank their pensions on the day the money
arrived and returned to the Home belligerent and even dangerous. Ordered to quiet down and return to the ward, Wiles "threatened to bash
Orderly White's brains out."[237] After the commandant severely reprimanded ex-private William Macey, a miner with three children, for rudeness to a nurse, he responded with "insolence"—"They'd better put me
where they want us all to go: the Workhouse."[238]

At the Star and Garter, sadness remained individual, and grievances private. Those who openly aired complaints faced expulsion. Ex-private Dinham repeatedly refused treatment, drank, and "rambled on in [a] . . .
maudlin kind of way."[239] After he spent one evening camped out in the
hall, unwilling to return to bed, the Home prepared to discharge him. With
the loan of a bath chair and a catheter, Dinham, a paraplegic and former
prisoner of war, was given seven days to find a new place to live. William
Betts—paralyzed at Gallipoli, confined to a wheelchair—threatened two
orderlies with a three-feet-long plank after they refused to let him enter the
building in his tricycle chair. Three months later, an inebriated Betts attempted to kill the night orderly with a kitchen knife.[240] Called in to explain
his rage, Betts said only that "he was fed up with everything."[241] He offered nothing more, and the House Committee did not inquire further. As

the rules stipulated, Betts would be discharged for his misbehavior, and the Home's authorities could feel sure that they had done their best. There were activities to fill men's spare hours, and hobbies to occupy their minds. The food surpassed institutional standards. Men were allowed to come and go as they pleased, providing they obtained late passes and the commandant's permission. Still a young man and unmarried, Betts had been a farmer and a keen sportsman. That the Home's activities (Patients: Smelling Competition; Orderlies: Egg and Spoon Race; Patients: Needle Threading and Button Sewing; Orderlies: Sack Race; Patients: Pinning on the Donkey's Tail; Nurses: 100 Yards Race) could not assuage his sorrow was a possibility never acknowledged.[242]

Even the Home's vaunted cheerfulness was far more ambiguous than visitors acknowledged. It was gallows humor more often than light-hearted gaiety. In their first week, new patients were called upon to subscribe to the "wreath fund" so that those who died would have decorated graves.[243] The completely incapacitated Joe Richards, celebrated in the press for his ability to write with his teeth, sardonically referred to himself as a "well-known helpless man."[244] Unable to move from his bed or avoid visitors' stares, he wrote an article titled "The Invisible Man": "For weeks on end I had been endeavouring to solve the problem of how to make myself invisible."[245] In an essay on his outdoor treatment, "H.B." compared himself to a dog leashed on a porch, subject to the unwelcome attention of visitors such as Mary Borden: "It will not be many months before I shall be able to do all the tricks and work of a good dog, or, if there is no work to be done, I can try 'begging.'"[246]

Of all the Home's humorists, Bill Foster was the darkest. His pencil sketches, reproduced in the *Magazine*, depicted the patient's pre-amputation nightmare: a doctor in a Tarzan outfit with a club. In his "Imahlia's Epistles to the Kroks," no subject was sacred, even loneliness and disfigurement. He likened the Home's patients to the goldfish they watched in the patio fountain; both were confined to small spaces and subject to stares. "And these fishes were exceedingly wise fishes, and the sages and philosophers of Starungarta were wont to visit them and stand in solemn conclave or awful contemplation thereof. And if, peradventure, there was a bond of sympathy between philosophers and fishes who shall say which felt the greater pity for the other?"[247] In another epistle, he described an outing to Madame Tussaud's: "When [the guard] was about to lock the door of the 'Chamber of Horrors' a great shout went up, and the man was quite upset on finding that what he thought were the worst exhibits were members of the order of 'Same Old Faces.'"[248]

Reporters who expected the worst could have found it. However, stories of depression and bitterness found no place in narratives of cheerfulness. That was the way visitors—and a number of patients—wanted to represent the Home's "inner life." Despite the strength of pacifist sentiment in the 1930s, most people were not prepared to read that the war's casualties regretted their sacrifices. Like the author John Buchan, who visited in 1935, they preferred to see the Star and Garter as a "romance," the "raw material of a thousand dramas—dramas of fate defied and beaten and of the patently impossible achieved."[249] It was a romance with a happy, or at worst a bittersweet, ending. Reconciled to their "unalterable lot," disabled veterans made the most of what was left.[250] Despite physical pain, unemployment, and separation from their families, they displayed an "unquenchable zest for life."[251] All the war's victims were turned into survivors.

Despite the state's neglect, and the philanthropists' rules, disabled veterans continued to smile. If their smiles were forced, ironic, or pained, the reporters who discovered them failed to recognize it. Disabled ex-servicemen kept up cheerful appearances or faced the consequences. If they could work, they stayed in bed on the weekends to conserve their strength. If no one would hire them, they found consolation in hobbies. As much as was possible, they tried to forget their disabilities: "The innermost tragedy . . . is for ourselves; it is not for the face we turn to the world."[252] Yet there were many others who could not forget. They raged against the philanthropists who provided for them. They remained in their rooms rather than participate in the Smelling Competition. Cheerfulness was a mask that they took on and off. Much of the time, they buried their sorrows in drink, turned violent, and stared blankly at the walls.

Dependent on the public's generosity, disabled ex-servicemen were always in a perilous position. For them, the war could never be over. However, they recognized that "after four terrifying years the stricken world had but one thought—to forget the terrible experience."[253] In the *Star and Garter Magazine*, Clifford Hill asked his readers to remember the war's casualties: "Acutely as the disabled soldier in hospital may feel his disability and his exile from home, the crowning bitterness would be to think he had been forgotten by his countrymen."[254] Less than four years later, Hill acknowledged that the severely disabled were "forgotten men." The philanthropists who had cared for them were dead, the donors they had relied on were aging, the younger generation knew little about those "segregated in places like the Star and Garter." "We are 'forgotten men' because the great mass of our countrymen do not know we exist."[255]

As the charitable public grew smaller and as the memory of the Great War receded and another war threatened, disabled veterans looked to the state. They demanded rights instead of charity: compulsory employment, early retirement, higher pensions. Beginning in the mid-1930s, some joined the British Limbless Ex-Service Men's Association. As one totally disabled ex-serviceman explained, he and his comrades wanted "a little extra...so we could feel more like citizens than the position we are placed in now: paupers."[256] In the *Star and Garter Magazine*, Bill Foster agreed: "The amount we receive practically forces us to live in an institution....We are 'hors de combat,' but our motto is 'nil desperandum.' Notwithstanding the fact we have to bury our ambition, we are always hoping the Government will award us with some additional pension—some day."[257] A voluntary peace had been made at the expense of individual men. Their demands came twenty years too late.

CHAPTER 4

Life Reconstructed

The Reintegration of German Veterans

When we muster the iron will to overcome it, the era of
cripples will finally be behind us.

> Konrad Biesalski, *Kriegskrüppelfürsorge:Ein*
> *Aufklärungswort zum Troste und zur Mahnung,*
> 1915

By 1921, the Dadaist artist George Grosz had perfected his trademark
scene.[1] On the frenzied streets of Berlin, Grosz's bypassers crisscross,
double back, are superimposed. Observed from half-shuttered windows,
bowler-hatted gentlemen stride past. A peddler plies his wares. Yet in the
hubbub, a stationary figure commands the viewer's attention. At a
crowded intersection, a double amputee begs for change. The man's eyes
are downcast, an Iron Cross is pinned to his chest. His very presence is
an indictment, as essential to Grosz's polemic as fleshy trollops and smug
businessmen. Not only does the decorated invalid testify to the follies of
war, a favorite subject for the Communist Grosz, whose own military
career began with the volunteer's naïveté and ended with a trial for de-
sertion. The beggared hero also demonstrates the failure of the new Republic to provide adequately for its victims.

Cited in standard histories and reproduced in picture books, Grosz's
bemedaled beggar has passed into the iconography of the Weimar Republic. On the streets of Germany's larger cities, especially Berlin, disabled paupers in army uniforms were a common sight. During the Revolution, they multiplied "like mushrooms after a warm rain."[2] The
spectacle of "shiverers," or men who shook uncontrollably, brought
traffic to a halt.[3] They could count on the public's charity. As the *Berliner
Tageblatt*'s reporter explained, many passersby—unaccustomed to the
sight of decorated beggars—gave generously. It was a matter of honor,

Figure 13. George Grosz, "You can be sure of the thanks of the Fatherland."
By permission of American University.

the least that the nation could do for its victims.[4] So inflamed was public sympathy that most panhandlers could ply their trade without interference. To the police's despair, members of the public foiled attempts to round up beggars.[5]

Sent to investigate the "mass epidemic" of military beggars in 1919–1920, welfare officials discovered that many would-be wounded servicemen were peacetime handicapped, who found that their takings increased substantially when they donned an army uniform. Others simply feigned ailments.[6] There were a few genuine war-disabled among the mendicants, but not because they were destitute. Begging brought in more than they could have earned otherwise; for some, panhandling was even a weekend pursuit.[7] Skeptical of official findings, the Social Democratic Reichsbund and the conservative Zentralverband launched independent investigations. War-disabled members toured streets, spoke to beggars, and came away convinced.[8] The vast majority had never seen combat, and those few who had been disabled in the war were not too ill to work. At the Labor Ministry's invitation, war victims' organizations joined official efforts to eradicate begging.

Contrary to the impression left by Dadaist images, the vast majority of German disabled veterans returned to work. In contrast to their British counterparts, segregated in sheltered workshops and isolated in veterans' homes, even badly disabled veterans in Germany found employment. Through monumental economic and political turmoil, the war's victims held down jobs and raised their families. What they had they owed to the state. In retraining programs praised throughout Europe, Germany's disabled learned to adapt to their injuries. The pathbreaking Law of the Severely Disabled (1920) provided a measure of protection against layoffs and unemployment.[9] A familiar presence in most workplaces, the severely disabled became self-sufficient citizens through their labor. Disabled men's productivity attested to their manhood, demonstrating their independence. For those veterans too badly disabled to work, the state provided pensions that allowed their recipients to live at home with their families.

The Weimar state's programs secured veterans' reintegration into the economy, but not society. Economically reconstructed, disabled veterans nevertheless became socially isolated. Institutionalized generosity did not buy social peace. On the contrary, the state's dominance of social policy encouraged the disabled to feel that their fellow citizens had scorned their sacrifices. Everywhere there were cripples, wrote the ex-officer Ernst Wiechert, "who looked dully or full of hate at the healthy;

they had been told that they were heroes, and in the looks of the others now believed they could see that they were considered poor fools."[10] "Abandoned" by the public, disabled veterans joined mass organizations pledged to achieve their rights. As a direct consequence of its monopoly on benevolence, the Weimar state bore the full burden of the nation's gratitude.

To compensate for their sacrifices, Germany's disabled veterans gained the right to labor—and to protest. This chapter explores the paradoxi cal consequences of state-sponsored social integration. It begins with an analysis of the state's material provisions for veterans, arguing that welfare programs created in the first years of the Republic allowed the disabled to weather Weimar's economic storms better than most Germans. Comprehensive welfare programs nonetheless failed to win disabled veterans' allegiance. The disabled turned against the state that favored them. The second section analyzes disabled veterans' contentious relationship with the welfare bureaucracy charged with their care. Veterans expected civil servants to provide them with the respect they had been denied in public life. They anticipated a new age in welfare, when they would make the policies that affected them.

The Invalidenhaus Berlin, explored in the last section of this chapter, exemplified the failed promise of republican war victims' care. For more than two centuries, the Invalidenhaus had housed Prussia's superannuated military elite. In 1919, it became a laboratory for the Labor Ministry's policies. Most of the badly disabled men who moved there held full-time employment. Yet to the Labor Ministry's chagrin, the Invalidenhaus's residents were never content with their advantages. From their early calls for self-governance to the formation of a local Nazi Party branch, the politics of the Invalidenhaus anticipated those of the country at large. As individuals, the Invalidenhaus's residents profited from their persistence. And yet their self-realization contributed to the failure of Germany's new democracy.

THE IRON WILL TO WORK

At the height of the Depression, in the spring of 1932, the war-disabled Augsburger Christian Wilhelm documented his triumph over adversity. Drafted at the age of twenty, Wilhelm served fourteen months with a Bavarian infantry unit. For seven months he fought in Verdun, where the Kaiser had promised the war would end. At the end of the slaughter, what remained of his regiment was transferred to the Eastern Front. Wilhelm did not last long. In the July 1917 offensive in eastern Galicia, he was hit by a Russian hand grenade. He suffered a severe head injury and for three weeks lay unconscious in a Munich lazaret. When he awoke, permanently blinded in both eyes, Wilhelm despaired: "I thought that the world and everything that it had to offer, were lost to me. I could not comprehend what it was like to be condemned to complete inactivity, not to be able to move about freely."[11]

Wilhelm's recovery was slow. However, by the end of 1918, he could leave his bed. To occupy his days, he took up brush making in the lazaret's workshop. To pass sleepless nights, he learned braille. His local welfare office arranged for a career counselor to visit the young man in the hospital. Because Wilhelm's head injury made it difficult for him to concentrate, he was judged unfit to pursue any highly skilled occupation. When he was well enough to leave the hospital, he was transferred to a state trade school in Lichtenfels. For thirteen months, he learned basket making, yet the work, "too mechanical and boring," did not satisfy him. In 1919, Wilhelm requested that he be sent to the Berlin School for the War-Blinded to study stenography and typing.[12] The welfare office's response must have pleased him. Not only would the state pay for Wilhelm's training, but if he proved capable, the office promised to hire him after the course ended.

At the School for the War-Blinded, Wilhelm excelled, and the Augsburg welfare office offered him a position in 1920. At first, his duties were restricted to taking dictation on a machine specially equipped with braille keys. The farm boy was quickly promoted through the ranks, assuming ever more responsibility and attaining the valued status of tenured civil servant. He married and had children. By 1932, Wilhelm had become one of the highest-ranked officials in the welfare office, entrusted with the management of career counseling, job retraining, medical care, and housing for his fellow war victims. He also directed care for the war-blinded in Augsburg and surrounding towns. As he proudly acknowledged in an article detailing his accomplishments, he had proven his "independence to the greatest possible extent."[13] All of the law books he consulted were in braille. He required an assistant only to read incoming and outgoing mail.

Wilhelm's career was notable, but not unique. Most disabled veterans in Germany—even the severely incapacitated—held down jobs, among them positions of responsibility. Despite the massive upheaval caused by the hyperinflation and the Depression, the Labor Ministry and its local welfare offices succeeded in returning the disabled to self-sufficiency and family life. In state-sponsored rehabilitative training programs, they learned the skills they needed to return to their prewar occupations or, if necessary, to embark on another career. Local welfare offices ensured that their severely disabled clients secured and kept jobs. No man, not even a striker, could be fired without the welfare office's consent. For those veterans too badly disabled to work, the state provided pensions that allowed their recipients to live at home with their families.

To live with a margin of comfort, men had to work. As conceived during the war and implemented in the Weimar Republic, pensions functioned principally as a safety net for those whose health did not permit steady employment.[14] In most years they were sufficient for survival, but little else.[15] With his 90 percent pension, a man with an amputated leg could afford to pay rent and feed his two children, if not to replace old clothes.[16] Potentially worse off were the so-called lightly disabled, men with disabilities rated 40 percent or less.[17] Although their injuries might be considerable (the loss of a foot, for example, was rated at 30 percent), they received little compensation. With a few exceptions, they did not qualify for the protection of the Law of the Severely Disabled. In times of economic crisis, their pensions were the first to be cut.

Praised by historians as "one of the most progressive of the day," the National Pension Law (1920) sought to protect the weakest in society at the cost of the better situated.[18] The state compensated men not simply for the fact of disability but also for the economic disadvantage they had suffered as a result.[19] Disabled veterans deemed unable to help themselves received the highest compensation, including access to emergency funds distributed by local welfare offices. Men who prospered in their careers, on the other hand, faced reductions in their pensions. When a man's after-tax income exceeded a state-established limit, the welfare office withheld a part of his pension.[20] Similarly, in times of economic exigency, the Labor Ministry defended the living standards of the severely disabled to the detriment of their "lightly" disabled comrades. During the inflationary years of 1921–1923, only those unemployed veterans with disabilities rated 50 percent and higher received cost-of-living adjustments.[21]

Unlike in Britain, where ex-servicemen received no additional compensation for families begun after disablement, the National Pension Law ensured that German veterans could marry without courting pauperhood. For every dependent child, whether born before or after the man's discharge, pensions rose an additional 10 percent. Severely disabled men also received a supplement for their wives.[22] A married veteran with two children drew a pension 40 percent larger than a single man's. As the testimony of newly wedded veterans demonstrates, family provisions not only protected disabled men's social status but also allowed them central hallmarks of a normal life: a wife and children, evidence of the orderly reproduction of the family. "Since I married, peace and tranquility have come to me," wrote a war-blinded man in 1923. "Life has now taken its normal course."[23] Another graduate of Dr. Silex's School reported with pleasure that his new wife had said "even for lots of money she wouldn't trade me for a sighted man."[24]

While pensions protected men from poverty, the central objective of German welfare programs for the disabled was rehabilitation. The nation's debt to its wounded, experts agreed, could not be discharged by cash payments alone. Disabled veterans were entitled to the restoration of self-sufficiency. Unlike the British government, which largely limited its responsibilities to the distribution of pensions, German authorities sought from the beginning of the war to return even the most severely disabled to work, preferably to their former occupations. Weimar's National Pension Law accorded the disabled more than a right to pensions; they were also entitled to an occupational retraining course and free medical care for their service-related ailments. In 1920, there were over 300 separate welfare offices charged with the implementation of the Labor Ministry's war victims' program.

Duty as well as right, work was theorized as the necessary condition for a man's membership in society.[25] For the disabled, work was not to be simply a means of material subsistence or a general constitutional right. Employment conferred therapeutic benefits; it was the way to rebuild men: "Even the best care cannot replace the blessing of one's own act of labor."[26] According to one rehabilitation expert, only employment could make a man feel "whole" again: "For the war-disabled man, work is an especially exquisite and valuable life-property."[27] At work, a disabled man became self-reliant and fulfilled, secure in his sense of purpose.[28] He no longer "dwelt morbidly" on his injury or succumbed to depression. The "pleasure of working," claimed the Labor Ministry's Otto Wölz, "would change their state of mind and restore to them the feeling of their usefulness and the consciousness of their dignity."[29] The ability to earn a living dignified a man in his own eyes, as well as those around him. No matter how badly disabled, the working man received his fellow citizens' regard. Work ensured a man's integration into his community.

Figure 14.   Disabled men at work in the School for the Wounded, Bochum,
1915. By permission of Ullstein.

The significance accorded work predated the Republic.[30] Even before
the war ended, rehabilitation efforts were well under way. By 1915, military lazarets were outfitted with workshops intended to revive "an interest in productive occupation" and fill idle hours.[31] In a voluminous
pamphlet literature, experts on the subject demonstrated how men without arms could be taught to operate machines, and the tubercular rein-
vigorated at the plow. The exhortation of the renowned orthopedist Konrad Biesalski, founder of the German Organization for the Care of
Cripples, became dogma: "When we muster the iron will to overcome it,
the era of cripples will finally be behind us."[32] At the end of the war,
most German cities and towns could boast bureaus for career counseling, in addition to special retraining schools for amputees, the epileptic,
and the blind.[33] By 1919, local authorities in the Rhineland had provided 14,500 disabled men with career counseling, 3,600 with a retraining course, and 647 with small plots of land.[34]

    Yet as welfare experts recognized, retraining alone would not suffice
to return men to work. Although most wounded had found jobs easily because of wartime labor shortages, employers made clear their

preference to hire able-bodied men after the demobilization.[35] Without compulsion, few of the disabled would be able to work steadily. At the new Labor Ministry's urging, the Republic's National Assembly sanctioned a fundamental intervention into private enterprise. From 1920 onward, the Law of the Severely Disabled required businesses and government offices that employed twenty-five or more people to hire the incapacitated as at least 2 percent of their workforce.[36] The law not only established hiring quotas but also provided local welfare authorities with the means of enforcement. Businesses that failed to comply voluntarily with the law's provisions could be forced to hire extra workers. Without the welfare office's consent, no severely disabled man could be fired.

The Law of the Severely Disabled provided steady jobs for men who would otherwise have suffered extended bouts of unemployment. Evidence from welfare offices indicates that compulsion, while reluctantly invoked in many areas, was necessary to maintain the severely disabled in work.[37] As the historian Ewald Frie has documented, Westphalian officials resorted to compulsion only rarely, forcing the placement of only 6 severely disabled men in the years 1927–1929, as opposed to 239 such interventions in Social Democratic Saxony during the same period.[38] While the Saxon policy undoubtedly antagonized some employers, it produced results. During the Depression, there were half as many unemployed disabled in Saxony as in Westphalia.

Although employers often complained about the law, most adhered to its principles. Meeting in 1925, welfare officials "unanimously expressed their satisfaction with the Law of the Severely Disabled, which had passed the acid test."[39] By most accounts, businesses and government offices treated their severely disabled workers well.[40] According to a 1929 study by the Zentralverband, a conservative veterans' organization, private employers complied with the law and attempted to accommodate their disabled workers with additional breaks and sickness leave.[41] The vast majority of graduates of the School for the War-Blinded reported satisfaction with their employers. Several noted that they and their comrades were paid more than the average rate, while others related with pleasure the consideration that their bosses showed them.[42] Treated as a "seeing person," Erich Heinen expressed his gratitude: "One feels like a human being once again."[43] Hermann Kramer remarked on his supervisor's tact in seating him near a graduate civil servant instead of the lowly lady typists: "They treat me not simply as a typist, but rather as a kind of colleague."[44]

At its apex, in 1931, more than 350,000 severely war-disabled men profited from the law's protection.[45] For most men, as for the graduates of the School for the War-Blinded, work was not simply a means of sustenance. More than marriage or even physical recuperation, they credited employment with the restoration of their well-being. Employed by a "humane government office," Karl Noack wrote: "Now that I have steady work again, I feel happy and fortunate. It's hard for me to understand that I could have been idle for so long. Work is the only thing that can help us to overcome our hard lot."[46] Returned to his classroom, one primary school teacher reported that his "difficulties were now all overcome. My old balance has returned, so that I'm no longer the pitiable invalid of last summer."[47] As a telephonist wrote Hirsch, "With this job I've finally regained my sense of happiness. I feel best and most content when I'm at work."[48]

Like the civil servants responsible for their welfare, disabled veterans subscribed to the restorative value of work. In contrast to the British Legion, which argued that the severely disabled should be exempt from work, German veterans' organizations agreed that employment was the best remedy for disability. The Social Democratic Reichsbund approved the priority accorded state-secured employment over pensions as a "thoroughly sound notion."[49] For the conservative Zentralverband, work was "our reason for being. Only work can restore us."[50] At work, men like Karl Junghanns, whose "greatest wish was to be a useful member of humanity despite [his] blindness," could be like anyone else.[51] Newly hired as a typist, the twenty-three-year-old Willi Hemeyer exulted that he "worked as though he wasn't blinded at all."[52] Employment mitigated blindness, and "work is the only thing that makes a person forget his fate."[53] With work, the disabled man could "look with full confidence in the future."[54] He had overcome his disability: "Ever since I've had a job like everyone else I've felt like a complete person."[55] Unemployed for four months, a Leipzig man delighted in his newfound occupation: "Since the day I began work I've become an entirely different person. I feel so well and carefree as never before, freed from tedium and boredom."[56]

In contrast to Great Britain, where many severely disabled ex-servicemen joined the long-term jobless, unemployment among the badly incapacitated remained low during the Weimar Republic.[57] In 1922, the Labor Ministry reported that more than 250,000 severely disabled veterans had found work. Only 17,000 (or 6.2 percent) were unemployed, a percentage similar to that recorded in 1928.[58] In cities, the number of jobs reserved for invalids consistently exceeded the supply of eligible workers. Although a number of disabled men received nothing more than "invalid posts," others, like Christian Wilhelm, were entrusted with considerable responsibility.[59] Government offices took on a disproportionate share of the severely disabled. In Germany's welfare offices, more than 8 percent of all civil servants—and 34 percent of white-collar workers—were disabled veterans.[60] At the Labor Ministry, the severely disabled constituted 10 percent of all employees and 6 percent of its civil servants.[61]

With the law's protection, many of the severely disabled retained the social position they had achieved before the war. In 1926, the Hamburg welfare office's Dr. Gustav Tonkow undertook an investigation into the social conditions of severely disabled veterans resident in the city and the surrounding countryside. Based on a sample of 500 men chosen to reflect national averages, Tonkow demonstrated that 60 percent of the severely disabled had maintained or improved their prewar social standing, while 40 percent—8 percent of whom were "unemployable," 5 percent of whom were unemployed—had suffered a decline in status.[62] Civil servants and office workers fared best, with 75 percent of their number in the same position as before the war. Worse off among the severely disabled, as in the country as a whole, were artisans and the prewar self-employed, most of whom had been forced to abandon their old occupations.[63] Unskilled laborers faced mixed prospects. Most remained in their prewar social position, a small minority (12.4 percent) succeeded in improving their lot, and 35 percent suffered a reverse.

As the Hamburg statistics demonstrated, a man's age, the type of disability he had suffered, and his postwar occupational history all influenced employment prospects. Those most likely to prosper were young men like Christian Wilhelm, aged twenty to twenty-four at the beginning of the war, more amenable to retraining, and generally favored by employers over their older comrades.[64] Men afflicted with diseases suffered reverses more often than did than the injured. Because they were unable to work regularly, 38 percent of sick men—as opposed to 25 percent of all amputees—sustained a loss in prewar status.[65] The more a man changed jobs, the less likely he was to maintain his social position. Although only 21 percent of Hamburg's severely disabled had held more than two posts since their disability (and 62 percent had changed jobs not at all or only once), frequent job changes were correlated with a decline in status, especially among artisans.[66]

For the study's author, the Hamburg statistics proved "less promising" than experts had hoped. The hopes that Biesalski raised were disappointed. The age of cripples, Tonkow noted, could not be overcome simply by an iron will: "All of the legal measures cannot restore a severely disabled man's full capacity to work."[67] Despite the millions of marks spent on rehabilitation, those men whose jobs required little physical effort had the best chance of keeping them. While most white-collar employees were able to return to their business jobs, half of all unskilled workers were forced to find other means of support. Before their enlistment, 36 percent of Hamburg's severely disabled had been artisans; in 1925, only 10 percent were so employed.[68] To remain employed, formerly skilled workers in many cases had no choice but to leave their trades. In 1925, 23 percent of Hamburg's severely disabled were employed as civil servants and office workers (as opposed to 5.6 percent before enlistment), while 12 percent held invalid posts.

Despite its successes, the law could not help everyone. Formerly highly skilled workers could not always content themselves with menial positions, and some employers proved reluctant to entrust badly disabled men with important jobs. War victims' associations complained that private employers often placed the severely disabled "where they would not be so disruptive," as doorkeepers or elevator attendants.[69] Even the fine reputation of the School for the War-Blinded did not prevent disappointments. Idle most of the day, the blinded Hans Weber quit his job as a stenographer because he could not find "the necessary satisfaction" in his work.[70] To his chagrin, the blinded typist Kurt Neuwiller discovered that his supervisors considered him only a "50 percent worker" because he could not read the incoming mail. "With such a salary...a war-blinded man can never ever attain his highest goal—to have a wife and a home of his own."[71]

As welfare officials acknowledged by the mid-1920s, they could not return every man to his prewar social position. In a defeated and bankrupt society, their goal was unattainable.[72] That a majority of war-disabled men retained their prewar social position was an accomplishment. As many as one-quarter of disabled veterans returned to their prewar workplaces, if not to their old occupations. They changed jobs infrequently and, until the Depression, were rarely unemployed—security unknown in Great Britain. Although the severely disabled were not entirely spared layoffs in the public sector, they were much more likely than their able-bodied colleagues to retain their jobs.[73] As the Hamburg welfare office noted with pride, only a handful of severely disabled had been discharged from government jobs during the 1923 cutbacks, most of whom had been reemployed.[74]

Even during the Depression, the Law of the Severely Disabled continued to provide most of the badly incapacitated with steady work.[75] While the number of out-of-work disabled more than doubled from 1929 to 1933, their rate of unemployment was a fraction of that suffered by the able-bodied population.[76] In 1933, 12 percent of the severely disabled were unemployed, as opposed to nearly 30 percent of German workers as a whole.[77] In Bavaria, Brandenburg, Hamburg, the Rhineland, Thuringia, and Württemberg, welfare offices persuaded many employers to retain their severely disabled workers.[78] In 1931, Nuremberg businesses employed 690 more severely disabled than required by law.[79] Despite half a million unemployed, Berlin's welfare office maintained 30,000 of the severely disabled in work. In 1932, 28 percent of the capital's male workers were unemployed, as opposed to 15 percent of its severely disabled.[80]

There was a limit to what welfare offices could do. Where plants closed down or industries went bankrupt, as in Saxony during the year 1930–1931, local officials were powerless to stem the tide of layoffs.[81] Words of comfort meant little to those affected. Unemployment devastated the able-bodied, but it was still worse for the severely disabled. According to Dr. Bruno Jung, mayor of the town of Göttingen and a former Westphalian welfare official, unemployment "embittered the severely disabled more than other workers, for in addition to his physical suffering, he now has the uneasy feeling that his remaining capacity for work is undervalued."[82] Independence was hard-won, its sacrifice deeply resented. In an appeal to President Hindenburg, the unemployed war-disabled man August Cook deplored his diminished status: "Formerly young, a naturelover, filled with the joy of life, today—shut off from others—I burden myself, even in my family's eyes I am not a full person."[83]

The National Pension Law and the Law of the Severely Disabled shielded the war's unfortunates from some of the worst postwar economic hardships. They retained jobs when millions of their ablebodied contemporaries lost them. With work, many otherwise "unemployables" became in their own estimation "full men again," able to provide for their families, even to return to their prewar occupations. Unlike in Britain, where a disabled man's masculinity was measured by his stoicism, German veterans proved their manhood through their labor. "I've now been a stenotypist for eleven years, and know to appreciate what it means to be equal to others in professional life," wrote one disabled man in 1927.[84] The state's programs gave veterans the chance to demonstrate their independence. The war-blinded teacher

Herr Becker found the return to the classroom more difficult than he had imagined. He confused boys and girls and could not always match names to voices. Nonetheless, he wrote Hirsch: "No one here should be able to say that I'm pitied because of my disability. Respect is what I want, the highest respect."[85]

Measured in strictly economic terms, disabled veterans were well cared for by successive governments eager to secure their loyalty. Their rehabilitation was a feat unmatched in Europe. Hundreds of thousands of employers joined their goodwill to the state's resources to ensure that the war's victims could gain dignity through work. Yet despite material successes, disabled veterans were never reintegrated into their society. Convinced of the public's neglect, they developed an identity based on their isolation, hostile not only to their fellow citizens but also to the bureaucrats charged with their care. As the next section will demonstrate, disabled veterans turned to the new state with great hopes. They sought an unprecedented identity for themselves. In the new democracy, the disabled would become the subjects of their own destiny, equal participants in their own care.

THE SUBJECTS OF WELFARE

The graduates of Berlin's School for the War-Blinded never forgot their old teacher. Nearly every week, Betty Hirsch received a letter from one of her former pupils, who wrote from Frankfurt and Augsburg, Posen and Rügen. In braille and in type, in letters penned by another hand, they told her good news and bad: a promotion, a baby, a death in the family. They solicited her advice about difficult employers or typewriters that no longer functioned, importuned her with political diatribes, and asked about her health. Above all, they paid tribute to the training that allowed them to "live again." Stenographers, typists, doctors, students, and factory workers, the school's graduates demonstrated the marvels of rehabilitation. Their letters shared an affection for "Aunt Betty" and—without fail—a common signature. After their name, Hirsch's students added the label "War-blinded."[86]

The era of cripples was not quite over. For wartime welfare officials, such signatures were anathema. As the leader of the Rhineland government's welfare efforts noted in 1917, "It should not come to pass . . . that the war-disabled man, when asked what he is, answers not 'locksmith' or 'plowman' but proudly replies: 'I am war-disabled.' "[87] If disability became more than a physical description, the National Committee's civil servants warned, the war's victims might think of themselves as a "special class in society," separate from their countrymen.[88] Only reintegration among the able-bodied would prevent their segregation; sheltered workshops could not be tolerated. In accordance with the National Committee's principles, the War Ministry ordered its officials to refrain from using "the expression 'war disabled,' 'war invalid,' or similar declarations as professional or occupational terms."[89]

As the National Committee's officials had intended, disabled men returned to work and to the families they had left behind. Buttressed by a formidable array of state programs, they survived Weimar's economic convulsions better than their fellow citizens. Yet despite material reintegration into their society, the disabled retained the sense of separateness that wartime officials deplored. Rather than locksmiths or plowmen, they identified themselves as war-disabled. It was more than a practical matter. When writing to their former teacher, Betty Hirsch's pupils did not need to describe themselves as "war-blinded." But their disability—not their hard-won occupation, marital status, or class—proved the most compelling identity. The best-paying job and happiest marriage could not transcend disability. They remained "war-blinded," a class apart, members in "a community of fate."[90]

Disability was both a physical fact and an identity that men chose for themselves. In the years 1918–1920, disabled veterans across the political spectrum sought a special status based on their suffering and their "unparalleled service to the state." Distinguishing themselves from other welfare recipients, they noted that they were in no way responsible for their condition.[91] Their sacrifices entitled them to more than poor relief and the meddling of welfare officials. They demanded the right to fashion policies that affected them and to participate in decisions about their care. According to a Zentralverband official, "War victims, who underwent the purifying fire of the trenches, no longer wanted to be simply the object of the state and its welfare programs."[92] "From our own bitter experiences," noted the war-blinded Josef Meister, "we know most clearly, and feel most acutely, what is wrong, where amendments or assistance must come."[93] They would not tolerate the condescension of "minor officials," nor would they surrender control over their futures. "People don't feel like objects any more, they want to have a say in the matter," explained a reporter who visited the hospital-bound wounded.[94]

As disabled men recognized, theirs was a revolutionary demand. When workers' and soldiers' councils called for the right to participate in management, they drew on a legacy of radical political agitation and trade unionism.[95] For welfare recipients to speak of codetermination was another matter altogether; their claims were unprecedented. They insisted not only that pensions and employment be granted "as a right, not a favor," but also that they be accorded equal representation on all committees that dealt with their care. If the war's victims were to be more than "objects to which something happened," they needed the "help to help themselves."[96] In demonstrations and petitions, disabled veterans called for equal representation on the governing boards of local welfare offices. For their mass organizations, they demanded a decisive role in the state's policy making; for their severely disabled members, priority in civil service employment.

By 1919, under the pressure of revolution, war victims achieved most of the reforms they wanted.[97] At all levels of governance—federal, provincial, and municipal—representatives of war-disabled and dependents gained the right of participation. Under the Labor Ministry, the National Committee was reorganized to include representatives from the national war victims' associations along with leaders of the welfare offices and civil servants. Decisions passed with a two-thirds majority and approved by the Labor Minister became official policy.[98] Through advisory boards, the war-disabled participated in the administration of local welfare offices and the implementation of state-secured employment. Composed of equal numbers of war victims' representatives, employees, civil servants, and local businessmen, the welfare office's advisory board decided on guidelines for administration, passed final judgment on complaints, and handled violations of the Law of the Severely Disabled.[99]

For the Labor Ministry's other supplicants, the war victims' gains provided a model.[100] Peacetime invalids, the aged, and casualties of the inflation clamored for the "right of participation" accorded to the disabled and war dependents. Even those civil servants who had at first disdained the intrusion of "council ideas" into welfare acknowledged disabled veterans' wish to "be the subject and not the object" of their fate.[101] Experts proclaimed a new age of welfare provision, characterized by the participation of the needy in their own care. In 1928, Franz Rappenecker, leader of a Zentralverband chapter, secretary of the Catholic charity organization Caritas, and himself a disabled veteran, declared that the principle of "Help to Help Yourself" had become "ever more productive over the years." "Welfare programs for the war's victims have developed so successfully...because war-disabled and war-dependents are no longer seen only as objects of welfare, but their own participation conditions their care."[102]

New rights did not improve veterans' relations with the welfare bureaucracy. Despite the fact that the severely disabled constituted more than a third of welfare office employees and veterans' organizations served on advisory boards, veterans' hostility toward the state increased after the war.[103] In the eyes of the disabled, the bureaucracy was intractable. The Labor Ministry deprived men of their rightful dues. Its officials were at best inconsiderate, at times even hateful. "Time and Again," ran the headline under which the Social Democratic *Reichsbund* detailed the "scandalous proceedings" at local welfare offices. Every edition of each of the six other national war victims' newspapers printed similar stories; the fact that so many welfare officials were themselves severely disabled was never mentioned.[104] On the failings of the welfare bureaucracy, if on little else, the war victims' associations could agree.

The conflict between war victims and Weimar's welfare bureaucracy was not entirely the fault of officials. Not malice, but severe structural problems delayed the granting of pensions. In Germany, as in Great Britain, the administrative apparatus responsible for the calculation of pensions could not keep apace with the vast numbers of cases. In the early years of the Weimar Republic, the crisis was made all the more acute by the reassessments required for the new National Pension Law, the confiscation of pension documents by the Entente, and mandated reductions in the bureaucracy.[105] After a medical examination to determine their disability, many men had to wait over a year and a half for their pensions to be recalculated.[106] In the meantime, they had to depend on emergency allowances distributed by the local welfare offices. Between July 1921 and February 1923, more than 3 million applications were processed, an average of 169,814 per month; in March 1922 alone, civil servants reassessed 211,825 pensions.[107]

Although the National Pension Law's flexibility allowed officials to tailor pensions, taking into account family size, home, prewar occupation, and physical disability, reassessment also involved substantial intrusion into an individual's private affairs. To many disabled veterans, the new Pension Law resembled old-fashioned poor relief rather than the harbinger of a new order. The reassessment questionnaire required that a man not only specify his income but also calculate dependents' allowances; it also asked him to list any illegitimate children he might have sired along the way.[108] According to the officials in the Brandenburg Main Welfare Office, "It is not rare that war-disabled or war-dependents who have to be reassessed...go away angrily because they don't believe that all of this information on the questionnaire is required simply to establish their pension rates."[109] To receive supplementary allowances, men had to endure home visits twice a year. As one man complained, "The war victims should finally be left in peace. They already know what our apartments look like."[110]

Amid the turmoil of reassessment, disabled men felt acutely their impotence in the face of bureaucratic and medical "expertise." Men who had received pensions under the old guidelines submitted to reexamination only reluctantly, fearful that the Labor Ministry's doctors would reduce their pensions—as indeed sometimes happened—on the grounds that their condition had improved. Disabled veterans directed their anger at the doctors employed in pensions offices, questioning the impartiality of physicians in the pay of the state. According to Georg Panzer, a leader of the Zentralverband, doctors counted among war victims' "opponents." In an article published in 1927, Panzer charged that physicians aimed, above all, to protect the populace from war victims' claims. They viewed disabled veterans as "a burdensome element whose effects on the public at large had to be reduced to a minimum."[111]

Delays and invasive questioning exposed the limits of codetermination, causing many veterans to regard the welfare system with suspicion. Chief among veterans' objections, however, was the lack of consideration civil servants showed them.[112] Disabled veterans complained that welfare officials treated them as wards, not as partners in their own care. Thrown out of his local welfare bureau after he requested to see a supervisor, one severely disabled man deplored official rudeness: "One should be able to expect that the office set up for war disabled would be able to treat us poorest of the poor considerately."[113] In "their" office, they could not even count on respect. Instead, the war's heroes were handled like scroungers on the public purse. "Assume official mistrust of your honor as the necessary precondition," began one man's account of the difficulty involved in obtaining another artificial leg. Because he forgot to obtain a receipt for his train trip, the welfare office at first refused to reimburse him. It eventually conceded, but grudgingly, in his words, "although knowing your severely disabled criminal nature, you would have walked the entire way in order to obtain the state's money illegally."[114] In 1927, the head of the Social Democratic Reichsbund complained that "in the last few years the authorities' sympathy for war victims has diminished notably. Today they do not talk any more about social duties, but about social burdens."[115]

Disabled veterans claimed that civil servants believed it their principal duty not to help deserving clients but to guard the treasury "against exploitation by the war's victims."[116] As one war-blinded man wrote Betty Hirsch, "In our good Germany the authorities seem to try ever harder to cause trouble and difficulties for the disabled."[117] After the welfare office docked 2,000 M from one of her old pupils upon hearing that he had received 11,000 M from the School for the War-Blinded to start his cigarette shop, Hirsch demanded an explanation: "There are always complaints about the war-blinded...but no one asks about why they're so excitable and so forth. A lack of understanding can itself drive these people to despair...then they really begin to feel their misfortune, which for most of them wasn't necessary."[118] Recounting his tribulations with the Main Pension Office, a war-blinded masseur wrote Hirsch that it had become apparent "what the authorities would like to do with us."[119]

While local welfare officials were not responsible for delays or the complexity of forms, they failed to accord disabled veterans the necessary respect. Harassed and overworked officials made little effort to soothe tempers or accommodate difficult cases. Where they could not spare money, they saved on politeness. In 1925, the Labor Ministry acknowledged the war victims' dissatisfaction with a decree to its departments: "Beyond a formal legal claim, those who sacrificed their health or their breadwinner for the Fatherland have the right to assistance." Civil servants especially, the decree urged, should attempt to imagine what the war victims had endured. "Even the reception, the greeting or response, the address and so on removes self-consciousness and leads to freer discussion....It is the civil servant's duty of honor to soothe anger with level-headedness and calm. Even those who are in the wrong need not be treated curtly."[120]

Yet if civil servants were unnecessarily rude, the war's victims also expected a great deal from them. Beyond the prompt payment of emergency allowances, disabled veterans expected welfare officials to accord them the respect they felt denied in public life. Deprived of their fellow citizens' gratitude, they turned to the welfare bureaucracy to provide the Fatherland's thanks. Unlike philanthropists, who spoke readily of men "who had given their best for the Fatherland," civil servants were not accustomed to extol their clients' sacrifices.[121] More than a mere right, however, disabled men conceived of their care as a sacred contract. Their sacrifices "could not be measured solely with an accountant's pen."[122] It was the welfare office's moral duty to ensure their well-being, a small remittance against the Fatherland's unpaid debt, "levied not only in the dry letter of the law, but from the great, eternal moral right that forms the foundation of humanity and humaneness."[123] By their callousness,

the welfare office's employees not only aroused the disabled man's indignation: they "shocked him deeply in his soul."[124]

Although the welfare office's bureaucrats aimed to meet their clients'
demands, they did not think of their task in terms of morality. They were
not concerned only with the bottom line, as the war victims' associations charged. Welfare officials recognized that they had to do more than
distribute emergency allowances; they also needed to win their clients'
trust.[125] Yet not least because of the economic crises, the war victims'
confidence proved more difficult to obtain than they had imagined, and
they lost patience. For those, such as the war-blinded Karl Oehme, who
entered the welfare bureaucracy with the zeal to help, public service
yielded little satisfaction: "In the past, one thought that to be employed
as a welfare official, to help needy fellow citizens with advice and deeds,
would be a pleasant and rewarding job. These days it's nothing to envy.
Day in and day out one has to hear complaints and threats because the
limited means at our disposal cannot satisfy the demands of the countless who seek our help."[126]

During the Weimar Republic, the welfare bureaucracy's accomplishments remained hidden, its failures magnified. The state's successes, particularly the Law of the Severely Disabled, received only
grudging acknowledgment. Cases of officials who helped their clients
generally went unrecorded.[127] If, on the other hand, welfare bureaucrats behaved badly, the incident found certain hearing in the war victims' press, occasionally even in mainstream newspapers. Whether the
story was verifiable mattered very little.[128] It was, after all, the "unjust
wrong that united us ever stronger," as one Reichsbund poem read.[129]
That is not to exonerate the welfare bureaucracy's civil servants, a
number of whom undoubtedly treated very badly men who deserved
much better. But without an evenhanded assessment of the welfare
state's record—and on this count, civil servants looked in vain to the
war victims' associations—mutual bitterness was inevitable.

Whatever trust welfare bureaucrats had hoped to gain, little remained
by the late 1920s. Each side had its reliable scandals, tales of outrage
that confirmed what people sympathetic to the cause already believed.
For the war-disabled, it was stories like that of the pensions doctor in
Berlin, quoted as saying, "It makes absolutely no sense that the war disabled receive pensions, because they defended their own lives after all,
not the Fatherland."[130] The Labor Ministry's civil servants had their own
calumnies, proffered by the senior official Griessmeyer in a December
1929 radio broadcast: well-off disabled veterans who posed as paupers,

threatened welfare officials, and squandered the state's funds on luxury purchases.[131] There was no mention of the disabled veteran who worked despite pain or the weary civil servant who did his best.

Despite the right to participate in advisory councils and jobs in welfare offices, codetermination proved elusive for the war-disabled. Many concluded bitterly that "they are not *your* civil servants, but you are *their* war-disabled."[132] The war's victims had rights only insofar as they could defend them. In the heady days of revolution, codetermination seemed possible, but their model was wrong. Workers could walk off the job, soldiers could mutiny, but welfare recipients had little with which to bargain. Their only recourse lay in protest and sympathetic public opinion. By the mid-1920s, disabled veterans had lost faith in their fellow citizens' goodwill, and though cripples in wheelchairs could damage the state's reputation, they could not protect their own rights. Their powerlessness bred desperation and bitterness. The war's victims were not the subjects of their own destiny, but "an uncomfortable army, to be dragged along the way to a new destination."[133]

Codetermination discredited, war-disabled men resorted to the only identity left them: victims.[134] Deprived of the nation's gratitude, they had been victimized twice over. Not only had they sacrificed their health for the Fatherland, but the state spared where its petitioners were too weak to protest. Protesting the emergency decrees, the Zentralverband claimed, "The life of the war victim since the end of the war is a victim's life."[135] Whether disabled veterans were in fact "the poorest of the poor" is doubtful. Even after the 1931 cuts, pensions paid to the most severely disabled still exceeded the maximum benefit paid in unemployment insurance.[136] Despite massive unemployment, only 12 percent of the severely disabled lost their jobs. Yet suffering is not a relative concept. The amputee who walked to work every day despite his "open, burning stump" took little comfort in the fact that others suffered still more.[137]

Weimar's victims proved susceptible to the Nazi appeal.[138] According to National Socialist propaganda, disabled veterans had the Weimar Republic to blame for their suffering. Just as the traitorous Home Front had deprived soldiers of their rightful victory in the war, so, too, had it denied disabled veterans their due: "In the last fourteen years the victims of the war have been forgotten, even derided. Only with National Socialism did the Führer gain for these first citizens of the state the place of honor they deserved among the German people."[139] Their sacrifices had been scorned, their compensation reduced to the "crude materialist principle." By failing to recognize "their spiritual predicament," the National Pension Law had reduced the war's proudest heroes to the status of "paupers."[140] Common was the sentiment expressed by Hamburg's representative: "We did not enlist in 1914 to gain a pension.... We enlisted in the knowledge of our duty toward the Heimat."[141] Despite their unparalleled service to the nation, the nation's heroes had been treated no differently from other welfare recipients. Honor had taken a backseat to material welfare, which, "somewhat shamefully called social policy, had been thrust ever more into the foreground."[142]

In the Thousand Year Reich, the long-overdue Fatherland's thanks became a matter of daily life, disbursed in parades and movie theaters, badges and salutes. Even as the National Socialists implemented programs of compulsory sterilization and euthanasia to eliminate the "hereditary" handicapped, they extolled the sacrifices of the battlefield.[143] For a time, the honors accorded disabled veterans were extended even to Jews, who received the "front fighter" allowances paid their Aryan counterparts and discounts on public transportation.[144] In material terms, compensation for war victims did not improve markedly under National Socialism, though unemployment among the disabled dropped again after reaching its highest levels in early 1933.[145] Those disabled veterans who had hoped to win their never-ending conflict with welfare officials were disappointed. To their disgust, they discovered that medical reassessments carried out by Jewish doctors were permitted to stand.[146] "Are such things still possible in the National Socialist state?" asked the war-disabled Johann Stasch, protesting the rejection of his pension petition. "Does it matter to the state whether we get on miserably or what happens to us? That is absolutely not a *Volksgemeinschaft*.... I never dreamed I would have to suffer such a thing in the new state."[147] The bureaucracy was the same as ever. Only now, its foibles found no hearing.

After the First World War, German veterans expected what no state could give them: the right to define the terms of their own care. They envisioned their relationship with the state as a partnership, cemented in advisory councils and personified by the welfare office's severely disabled employees. Measured in material terms, the severely disabled fared relatively well in the Weimar Republic. However, they remained the objects, not the subjects of their own care. The inevitable limits of codetermination became painfully obvious. Whatever privileges the war-disabled enjoyed, they owed to the state's good graces. Unlike workers and soldiers, they had nothing but their loyalty to withhold. Yet not even the allegiance of the Labor Ministry's most privileged wards, as we shall see in the next section, could be bought for money.

Figure 15.   Official ceremony for War Heroes Day. After laying a wreath at the Neue Wache, Hitler greets disabled veterans. Berlin, 12 March 1939. By permission of AKG London.

FOR WOUNDED AND UNCONQUERED SOLDIERS

In 1937, the Labor Ministry surrendered without argument an acquisition celebrated seventeen years earlier. Amid fanfare and pomp, the nearly 200-year-old Invalidenhaus of Berlin returned to the army's control, courtesy of the Führer's order. The promised day that General Hans

Figure 16.   The Invalidenhaus before the First World War. By permission of
the Landesbildstelle Berlin.

von Seeckt, chief of Army Command, had predicted for the war's victims in 1920 had finally come, and Germany was "once again great and
free."[148] For the Labor Ministry's civil servants, who turned out to witness the transfer, the glorious day had not come soon enough. Exhausted
by the "well-known difficult relations in the House," they were relieved
to see it leave their hands.[149] Seventeen years earlier, the Ministry had entertained great hopes for the Invalidenhaus. In the place of the re-
doubtable military installation would arise a model community of severely disabled veterans, self-sufficient despite their ailments. In the
Labor Ministry's laboratory, as in the country at large, the state's aspirations were thwarted by the resistance of its charges.

Berlin's Invalidenhaus numbered among Prussia's best-known military institutions. In 1748, Frederick the Great ordered his architect to
build a suitable resting place for injured and retired soldiers on the model
of the Paris Hotel d'Invalides: "Ingratitude is an ugly vice in private life;
when princes or states lack thankfulness it is abominable."[150] The old
warlord wished to be remembered for his benevolence to the fighting
men. Inside the home's entrance hall stood a marble statue of the elderly
Frederick in his dressing gown, one hand resting protectively on his dog's

head.[151] "Laeso et Invicto Militi" (To Wounded and Unconquered Soldiers) read the motto carved above the entrance. In the House's graveyard rested Prussia's most highly esteemed eminences of the sword, including the military reformers Gerhard von Scharnhorst and Hermann von Boyen; General Field Marshal Helmuth von Moltke, the victor of Königgrätz; and the author of the disastrous Schlieffen plan, Alfred Count von Schlieffen.[152]

The Invalidenhaus's august halls harbored the superannuated, the disabled, and especially the titled. On the eve of the First World War, 400 souls lived there, 110 "wards" with their wives and children, among them 36 officers (26 from noble families), 8 sergeants, 22 non-commissioned officers, and 38 common soldiers. For the well-heeled, there were sumptuous living quarters, ten well-proportioned rooms, along with private gardens sheltered by high hedges. Ordinary soldiers fortunate enough to be admitted had to settle for more common dwellings. Yet even so, residency in the Invalidenhaus entailed considerable privileges. As Frederick the Great had specified, all of the inhabitants lived rent-free and received free medical care, coal, and uniforms. In return, they were obligated to wear military dress in public and take part in Sunday church parades. Despite its "highly sober and spare" exterior, the Invalidenhaus enjoyed a prominence befitting its residents' stature.[153] On dates of significance, generals and politicians paid their regards. Every Sunday, spectators came to watch the procession of grandly uniformed officers and hear the military bands. If they wished, members of the public were permitted to tour the renowned graveyard and climb to the top of the Warrior's Monument, a 145-foot-high Corinthian column of iron commemorating the fallen royal soldiers of the 1848–1849 revolution.[154]

Not least of the indignities that the army suffered in 1919 was the forcible removal of the Invalidenhaus from its control. Under the demilitarization mandated by the Treaty of Versailles, the Labor Ministry acquired responsibility for the house as a part of the military's pension system, but not without a spirited fight from the offices of the army ministry. In the summer of 1919, the army conceded the pensions offices but still maintained that the transfer of the Invalidenhaus "was out of the question."[155] After more than 170 years, the Invalidenhaus was an integral part of the army establishment. Moreover, General von Seeckt doubted that the army could trust the republican Labor Ministry to care adequately for their officers.[156] When the Labor Ministry gained the Ministry of Finance's support, the battle was lost. Specifying that "nothing of the previous character of the Invalidenhaus should be changed," the army surrendered its claim to the institution.[157]

For the Labor Ministry, the acquisition of the Invalidenhaus was more of a symbolic than a material triumph. The Ministry justified its interest in the House by referring to the number of apartments to be gained for the severely disabled. However, its value lay in more than housing stock. Located just down the Scharnhorststrasse from the Labor Ministry's own building, the Invalidenhaus would serve as a laboratory for the Ministry's policies—and the showpiece of its successes. Frederick the Great's Invalidenhaus would be transformed into a proud symbol of republican war victims' care. Where militarism had once prevailed, the virtues of the state's new programs would be evident. In the place of a paternalistic institution inhabited by uniform-wearing inmates, the Labor Ministry planned to construct a home for men made self-sufficient despite their severe disabilities. What had become the preserve of the elite would now benefit the common soldier.

The Labor Ministry's civil servants wasted no time in transforming the Invalidenhaus. Within a few months of its accession, the old commandant, the eighty-year-old General Lieutenant von Bergemann, was forcibly retired, along with his title (too military). In his place came the emphatically civilian "manager," the Labor Ministry's senior civil servant, Richard Stern. Under Stern's supervision, twenty widows and adult children without the right to an apartment were evicted, their palatial residences divided into smaller apartments for newcomers. The prewar Invalidenhaus had catered less to the deserving than to the well connected, but the Labor Ministry planned changes. From 1920 onward, the Invalidenhaus accepted only severely disabled veterans of the 1914–1918 war who had a wife or another female family member to look after them.[158] Officers received no special consideration, either in admission to the Invalidenhaus or in the distribution of apartments. Those with the largest families were entitled to the most spacious living quarters.

Above all, the Ministry intended the new Invalidenhaus to promote self-reliance in disabled veterans. By providing its wards with all of life's necessities, the army had fostered dependence irreconcilable with civilian life. In contrast, the Labor Ministry's civil servants aimed to encourage inhabitants' self-sufficiency. They gave priority in admission to men whom an apartment would allow a normal existence. As a rule, they preferred married men; the tenant's wife had to testify that she would take full responsibility for his day-to-day care. Single men were no longer admitted unless they lived with their mothers. Without relatives to care for him, the severely disabled Max Janik received an apartment so that he could marry.[159] Within a year, the newlywed Willi Langhanky—a former prisoner of war and double amputee, awarded the Iron Cross, first class—joined him.[160]

Although neediness served, in theory, as a criterion for admission, in practice the Ministry gave preference to those who worked over their unemployed (and less well off) counterparts.[161] Men who could demonstrate that they needed an apartment in order to keep a job were virtually assured of a place in the House. Despite tuberculosis and the loss of both hands and an eye, Erich Rehse managed to return to work at the Reichsbank. Yet because of the housing shortage, the only apartment he could find was a three-room flat in a distant northern suburb, shared with his wife, child, and parents, and located nearly an hour away from the bank. By the time that he boarded, the streetcars were usually full, and he had to stand, "which, because of my inability to hold onto the rail, is onerous for me and often embarrassing for the other passengers."[162] Under doctors' orders to conserve his strength, Rehse acknowledged he would not be able to maintain his post much longer. The Labor Ministry granted him an apartment immediately.

By admitting employed married men, the Labor Ministry's civil servants demonstrated the central principle of republican war victims' care: even the most severely of disabled men could return to productive life. Despite its name, the Invalidenhaus was not a "welfare institution."[163] The Labor Ministry conceived of the new Invalidenhaus as a housing scheme that provided the war's victims with a quiet sanctuary where they could preserve their ability to work and nurture their family life. In keeping with the House's civilian character, the Labor Ministry ended the custom of military concerts and full-dress parades. No longer would the residents receive the free uniforms, coal, or medical care granted their predecessors. To ensure that prewar residents did not suffer because of the demilitarization, the Labor Ministry paid them a considerable allowance to compensate for the loss of former privileges.

To the Invalidenhaus's collection of superannuated captains the Labor Ministry added its own protégés, handpicked by civil servants in consultation with the Main Pension Office. They were mostly young men, some of them, like Langhanky and Janik, newly married. Although there were a handful of officers among their number, the overwhelming majority were drawn from the rank and file. Most were native Berliners. Despite considerable obstacles, all but two had worked after demobilization. In comparison to their comrades on the outside, the Invalidenhaus's residents enjoyed substantial advantages. Besides proximity to government offices and businesses, they enjoyed apartments considerably more luxurious than they could otherwise have afforded. According to the American journalist Katherine Mayo, who visited the Invalidenhaus in 1933, "All of [the apartments] are ample in size, strikingly well-proportioned, airy and filled with pleasantness and sunshine."[164] A family of four could expect at least a three-room apartment (in addition to kitchen and bathroom), while couples without children generally received two rooms. Every apartment was equipped with electric lights. Most residents—not just officers—were allocated garden plots behind the house. In addition, the House provided its residents with a lecture hall, a library, a recreation room, and two chapels. A cooperative store on the ground floor of the main building sold groceries at reduced rates.

Yet to the Labor Ministry's frustration, the Invalidenhaus's new residents did not appreciate their advantages. The independence that the Ministry's civil servants sought to cultivate in their charges produced results very different from what they had intended. Instead of gratitude for the Ministry's provisions and loyalty to the state that provided them, the veterans' self-assurance manifested itself in demands for still more autonomy and special privileges. The most persistent troublemakers were not the Invalidenhaus's old residents, until 1923 still in the majority. Although they had lost accustomed privileges, the prewar residents proved less trouble than the Ministry had feared. To its civil servants' discomfort, the Ministry of Labor's most implacable foes were their ostensible charges: the severely disabled of the First World War.

The first point of conflict between the Labor Ministry and the tenants arose over the residents' council. In response to residents' demands for a role in the House's management, the Labor Ministry had agreed in 1920 to the formation of a council composed of representatives elected from the Invalidenhaus's tenants. Through the Residents' Council, the House's occupants were to be granted a voice in administration for the first time in the institution's 170-year history. Buoyed with the principle of co-determination, the Labor Ministry anticipated that a Residents' Council would "strengthen the trust between the House's administration and its occupants,...preventing conflicts among occupants, and between occupants and the House's administration."[165] According to the Labor Ministry's plans, the Council would enjoy the role of "expert witness." In critical decisions about daily management, the Invalidenhaus's director was obliged to ask the Council's opinion.

The Council's mandate appeared innocuous, but it soon became a matter of concern to the Labor Ministry's civil servants. Rarely did the Residents' Council agree with the House's management. Called to approve decisions about the amount that individual residents should pay in rent, the Council unfailingly demanded either rent reductions or total exemptions. Flat refusals provoked further evidence of insolence. Rather than respond to the director's orders, the Council presented the House's administration with demands of its own, requesting that war-disabled admitted after demilitarization be given the benefits accorded the House's prewar occupants.[166] Its petitions denied, the Council appealed to the Main Pension Office. "We occupants have the impression," its letter began, "there is little goodwill for us in the Labor Ministry."[167] Intended to promote trust, the Residents' Council had become a lightning rod for discontent.

Angered by the betrayal of a body it had itself created, the Labor Ministry called for the Council's dissolution. As the senior civil servant Oskar Karstedt noted in response to one Council petition: "Once again the Council's application...roused my misgivings whether it is able to fulfill the tasks that I had in mind when I called it into being."[168] Not only had the Council arrogated unwarranted authority to itself and proffered "incorrect and unjustified criticisms of the Labor Ministry's operating procedures and its civil servants," but it legitimated every malcontent's complaints and represented his claims. At the Labor Ministry's request, the Main Pension Office ordered the Council to disband: "Since the Residents' Council has fulfilled the tasks produced by the demilitarization of the Invalidenhaus, it has become dispensable."[169] By March 1923, the Invalidenhaus's first exercise in codetermination had come to an end.

The Labor Ministry was not let off the hook that easily. The Residents' Council had been eliminated, but the spirit of codetermination thrived within the Invalidenhaus as it did in the country as a whole. As the Ministry noted with consternation, the newest residents were especially embittered by the Council's dissolution, and throughout the last months of 1922 they staged meetings in the House's common room to demand reconsideration of their viewpoint. To placate them, the Invalidenhaus's director suggested that tenants be permitted to elect a financial support committee. It was to be a more modest endeavor than the Residents' Council, composed of representatives chosen separately by officers and enlisted men. The new committee was accorded only two duties: to judge residents' requests for house funds and to determine suitable rents for individual apartments.

Yet like the Residents' Council, the Financial Support Committee proved more than the Invalidenhaus's officials had bargained for. Three years after its founding, Stern asked the Main Pension Office to sanction dramatic changes in the committee's composition and responsibilities. Members of the Financial Support Committee, he complained, appeared to believe that it "has the same authority as the previous Residents' Council, that it is basically nothing more than a change of name and that the committee therefore has the right to participate in purely administrative affairs."[170] Particularly to blame, according to Stern, was the war-blinded, ex-sergeant Eduard Schermenske, formerly a member of the Residents' Council and a vocal representative of the Social Democratic Reichsbund: "Propped up by the most disorderly elements of the House, the person concerned believes himself...justified to act as a sea lawyer for occupants in all possible cases—against the superior authorities as well—and to run a sort of 'subsidiary government.'" This was not the sort of codetermination that the Labor Ministry had intended.

For those in the Labor Ministry who had counted on the allegiance of the Invalidenhaus's new residents, Eduard Schermenske's behavior was cause for distress. By all material indications, Schermenske should have been among the Labor Ministry's most loyal supporters. Blinded in 1917, the forty-nine-year-old Schermenske lived with his wife in a three-room apartment in the Invalidenhaus's main building. Because of the Law of the Severely Disabled, he had a secure job.[171] He also received a full pension plus supplements, 249 RM a month—more than a civil servant, fourth class, earned the same year in Berlin.[172] The welfare office supplied him with a guide dog and provided him with extra funds to feed it. Moreover, because Schermenske had been admitted to the Invalidenhaus two months before demilitarization, he was entitled to the additional allowances granted longtime residents.

Schermenske was not the Invalidenhaus's only disgruntled resident. According to Stern, he had assembled a following among his fellow disabled. Fearing that the "already so difficult to maintain peace in the House would be destroyed," Stern refused him permission to call a meeting of all residents to discuss proposed rent increases. The next day, Schermenske resigned from the Financial Support Committee and brought the war-blinded cigarette maker Georg Petrikowski, who had entered the House four years before, with him.[173] Schermenske not only petitioned the Reichsbund and the League of Blinded Soldiers for support but also used the occasion of his resignation to draw attention to his campaign. When supplementary elections were held two months later, Schermenske and his two running mates—Alfred Fick, wounded in a battle with the Red Army at Riga, and the war-blinded Friedrich Krüger—won overwhelmingly.

Schermenske's chief grievance was the issue of rents. Although Stern informed all tenants accepted after demilitarization that they should expect to pay rent for their apartments, the Residents' Council and Financial Support Committee had almost completely succeeded in blocking all levies. The Invalidenhaus's administration judged that Max Janik, with his yearly income of 14,539 M in 1921, could afford to pay 300 M a year for his sixty-square-meter apartment. The Residents' Council disagreed, claiming that Janik "is not now in a position to pay rent."[174] Unwilling to provoke a fight, the House's administration conceded the point again and again. In late 1925, the Main Pension Office noted with disapproval that the only tenant at the Invalidenhaus who paid even half of the fixed rent was the bank employee Erich Rehse.[175]

The question of rents could be postponed as long as the Invalidenhaus had at its disposal rich assets accumulated over 170 years. However, after the hyperinflation destroyed much of the House's capital, the Labor Ministry reopened the issue. In 1924, Stern informed all the tenants, including the prewar residents, that they would be charged rent according to their income and disability. Those with monthly incomes under 200 RM (for disabilities rated less than 70 percent) or 300 RM (for disabilities rated 80 percent and above) were exempt. The rest would automatically be levied a rent on a sliding scale. A man with an income of 400 to 500 RM a month, omitting children's allowances and care allowances, had to pay 30 percent of the market value of his apartment. The full rent would be assessed only on large incomes exceeding 1,100 RM.

The Invalidenhaus's residents decried as an outrage a demand that the Labor Ministry viewed as moderate. Although only a quarter of the residents were charged even half of the full rent (on average 60 to 70 RM a month), the amount of money was less important than the principle of the matter: apartments in the Invalidenhaus had always been free. It was not only the House's prewar inhabitants, promised free housing for their lifetime, who responded to the Labor Ministry's decree with "the greatest consternation and alarm."[176] The new residents greeted it with still more agitation. By fixing rents according to income, Schermenske and Fick responded that the decree penalized those who worked. No mathematical formula could measure the "gravest physical and mental exertions" that "blinded, single, double and triple amputees" endured in order to hold down a job.[177]

In their protests against rents, the Invalidenhaus's residents deployed the language of the war victims' movement. No one could understand their suffering. "Only those who have themselves sacrificed," wrote the amputee Gerhard Pump, "can measure what it means." Nothing could compensate for their injuries. Because he had made "the greatest and severest sacrifice that anyone can make, incommensurate with even the largest assets, . . . my health is irretrievably gone, my existence destroyed, everything has been lost because of the war."[178] Although the Labor Ministry's new rules would take his salary into account, they would not consider either the suffering he endured in order to work or "the fact that I've been torn from my old profession, and can no longer compete for jobs with healthy people." He acknowledged the state's poverty, "but what I do not comprehend is why we war disabled should be forced to sacrifice once again."[179]

To the Labor Ministry's civil servants, the protests of the Invalidenhaus's war-disabled residents appeared at the very least exaggerated. Given the small amount of money involved and the fact that those tenants accepted after demilitarization were informed they would have to pay rent, the Ministry rejected allegations that the "apartment reimbursement" violated residents' rights. As Stern reminded residents, disabled veterans accepted in the Invalidenhaus enjoyed substantial advantages compared with their comrades on the outside. A shopkeeper before the war, the thirty-four-year-old Pump held a secured position at a local branch of Berlin's Housing Authority and received 259 RM as a pension and 215 RM as a salary. He, his wife whom he married in 1920, and their child occupied a three-room apartment in the Invalidenhaus for a rent of 40 RM a month, less than a third of what they would have paid on the open market.[180]

For the Invalidenhaus's residents, rent was yet another sacrifice exacted from them. The Labor Ministry's civil servants, by contrast, regarded the payments as a valuable indication of self-sufficiency. By rejecting even the small rents that the Labor Ministry demanded, the Invalidenhaus's war-disabled intended, in Stern's words, to turn the place into a "welfare institution" filled with men who lived at the public's expense.[181] Stern and his Labor Ministry colleagues did not believe that free apartments should be given to those who could easily afford to pay. The residents viewed the problem differently, insisting that the standard of measurement should be what a man had already given, not what he could afford. By that criterion, the Invalidenhaus's war-disabled declared themselves exempt from further sacrifice, no matter how modest rents might be. To expect them to pay more because they worked was to punish them for their survival.

The Labor Ministry had intended to foster veterans' self-reliance, but not at the expense of its own authority. Yet the Ministry's officials were hoisted by their own petard. They had believed that men who went to work every day, and whose jobs the state secured, would become loyal citizens, content to enjoy their well-proportioned apartments. At the Invalidenhaus, as in the nation at large, just the opposite had happened. Unlike their British counterparts at the Star and Garter, forced to bury their dissatisfaction behind a cheery smile or face expulsion, the Invalidenhaus's tenants did not shrink from defending their rights, or claiming new ones. The state had given them not just jobs and pensions but also the ability to voice their discontent.

As the conflict over rents deepened, House administrators moved to reduce tenants' role in management. In Stern's opinion, the fault belonged "principally to those severely war-disabled men, who are inclined to believe that serious disciplinary measures...will not be applied to them because of their war disability."[182] With the permission of the Labor Ministry and the Main Welfare Office, the Invalidenhaus's director instituted new rules in 1926 to diminish both the Financial Support Committee's autonomy and its influence. No longer would the residents elect representatives directly. Although they could offer nominations, the right of selection belonged to the Main Pension Office. Nor would the Financial Support Committee have authority over the dispensation of House funds. While the director was obliged to take their recommendations into consideration, he retained final authority over all decisions.

To ensure the "maintenance of peace" in the House, Stern insisted on a final change. For the purposes of elections, the Invalidenhaus's residents were divided not only into officers and enlisted men, as had been the practice before, but also by the date that they entered the House. Each of the four groups (predemilitarization officers, postdemilitarization officers, predemilitarization enlisted men, postdemilitarization enlisted men) nominated three representatives, one of whom the Main Pension Office selected to sit on the Financial Support Committee. Despite the fact that the fourth group (all severely disabled veterans) contained more than double the number of men in any of the other categories, they were not accorded another representative. As Stern explained to his superiors in the Labor Ministry, the change would ensure that members of the prewar army were not outvoted by the disabled veterans.[183] To the detriment of its disabled clients, the republican Labor Ministry had made common cause with the old regime.

By casting its lot with the Invalidenhaus's old residents, the Labor Ministry entered an already well-established feud. The Invalidenhaus's disabled veterans had quarreled bitterly with the old occupants, who remained loyal to the imperial institutions of monarch and army. Disputes that began about wash days or gardens quickly took on a political color. Disturbed on Sunday by the noise of the war-disabled Schubert washing his clothes, one longtime resident denounced the newcomers as "cowardly criminals."[184] For their part, the war-disabled believed that the old residents enjoyed unfair advantages. According to the double amputee Max Janik, new tenants had to pay rent so that the officers could live free. He, at least, was a republican.[185] When a leaflet for a 1924 Reichsbund demonstration, headlined "No More War," was found inscribed "invitation for deserters and cowardly good-for-nothings," war-disabled residents blamed the prewar officers.[186]

If the old residents were ill disposed toward the Republic and its Labor Ministry, they at least agreed with the House's director that war-disabled residents had taken the principle of codetermination too far. In 1927, before the new rules had been put into effect, members of the prewar officer corps refused to vote for the Financial Support Committee so long as Schermenske remained a member. Schermenske agitated against the House's officers, they complained, and in meetings of the Financial Support Committee he "brought up every possible House matter, for which the Committee is in no way responsible." According to the ex-major Walter Stülpner, resident since 1911 and head of the Officers' Association formed in 1923, the Financial Support Committee should be disbanded. It was "superfluous, given the small amount of funds available for support, and under the present circumstances meant only a great burden for the administration and the orderly elements among the residents."[187]

The Labor Ministry's alliance with the prewar officers was a sign of desperation, not strength. To placate Stülpner and his officers, Stern assured them that the Main Pension Office would not choose Schermenske for the Financial Support Committee. Although his war-disabled constituency elected him once more, Schermenske never again sat on the committee. That problem, at least, had been put to rest. Beginning in 1927, Stern's new rules held the Financial Support Committee in check. In accordance with the director's privileges, Stern convened the committee only irregularly. If little remained of its democratic function, neither the Labor Ministry nor the House's prewar officers minded. To Stern, the maintenance of the "authority principal"—in practical terms his unchallenged control over all elements of House life—was decisive.[188] To prevent the "commotion" associated with voting, the Main Pension Office agreed in 1931 simply to confirm for a new term the candidates already in office, thereby avoiding new elections.[189]

Although Stern's administration succeeded in extinguishing collective protest, the Invalidenhaus had become a still more contentious place. The files of the Labor Ministry and the Main Pension Office swelled with complaint letters, anonymous threats, and newspaper articles hostile to the House's management. Relations between the director and his charges worsened. In 1929, ex-captain Wilhelm Boetticher, accepted into the Invalidenhaus in 1926 with a paralyzed leg, complained to the Main Pension Office that he found Stern's impoliteness intolerable.[190] Denying Boetticher's charges, the director's response encapsulated the image of the war-disabled that had come to prevail in the Labor Ministry. "He makes demands that cannot be filled, and then believes he's been dealt a great injustice.... He demands the greatest thoughtfulness for himself; however, at the same time he violates the consideration necessary for the Invalidenhaus and its administration."[191]

Instead of a proud emblem of the Labor Ministry's successes, the Invalidenhaus symbolized its failures. Not only had disabled veterans turned against the state that treated them well, but the House's inhabitants felt neglected by the public that owed them its loyalty. Like the war's other victims, they believed themselves forgotten. The visitors who had once come in great numbers to pay their respects had disappeared. The special privileges accorded the House's residents in the prewar years, including tickets to the theater and zoo and free tobacco, had ended with demilitarization. Beginning in 1924, Stern appealed to Berlin's firms and banks for Christmas donations in cash or in kind. There were a few responses. Frau Hugo Stinnes, wife of the prominent industrialist, sent 100 RM, but most declined to help.[192] They had too many requests to fill, and the Invalidenhaus's appeal was just one among a number.[193] On their own initiative, the Invalidenhaus's residents petitioned local businesses and prominent individuals for donations; invoking the Bundesrat decree of 15 February 1917, the Main Pension Office ordered them to stop.[194]

Deprived of the country's honor, the Invalidenhaus's residents courted its scandalmongers. In the spring of 1930, the *National Socialist* reported on a "disgraceful state-of-affairs at the Invalidenhaus."[195] Not only had the once-proud institution fallen into the "hands of the Jew Stern," but the House's administration appeared to believe that the "war-disabled were there at [their] pleasure." According to the article, the House's physician refused to give hospital treatment and shots to the critically ill wife of a war-disabled man on the grounds that the "state had no money." When he finally brought her to the hospital, where she died, the doctor purportedly expressed his relief that the troublesome patient had passed from his hands. Such was the lot of disabled veterans in the "Young Plan Colony Germany." "That's the way that the relatives of comrades who once defended their people and home with their life, and returned severely injured from the war are treated. 'The thanks of the Fatherland are assured to you.' "[196]

Formerly a stronghold of the Social Democratic Reichsbund, the Invalidenhaus organized one of the first chapters of the National Socialist War Victims' Association (NSKOV). By the fall of 1933, the local Invalidenhaus branch of the NSKOV had recruited nearly all the House's members to its mast. At the organization's head was Alfred Fick, one of Schermenske's former allies in the Financial Assistance Committee. With a combined salary and pension of 305 RM a month, Fick lived comfortably, but not contentedly, in the Invalidenhaus, ever alive to the injustice done him. The particular target of his ire was Stern, who "claims to have a heart for us, but we have not yet been able to discover it."[197] Deploring Stern's lack of "human feeling," he reprimanded: "That is no way to treat people who have risked their best for the state."

At least initially, the Nazis restored to Fick and his comrades the respect they felt that the Republic had denied them. In 1935, the Labor Ministry settled the long-troublesome question of "apartment reimbursements." To assess rents on the basis of residents' incomes "would not be appropriate, considering the character and purpose of the War Invalidenhaus."[198] No longer would the Ministry judge "purely arithmetically," the standard that the House's war-disabled had loathed. Instead, as Schermenske and Pump had demanded ten years before, the House's officials would take into account a man's service and suffering in setting rents, if indeed any at all were to be levied.[199] A Nazi palace of honor had replaced the republican exhibition on self-sufficiency. The Labor Ministry's officials would accord needy soldiers priority over their comrades who could work. Above all, apartments in the Invalidenhaus would be given to those who served honorably and at high personal cost. In the future, "the characteristic of honor for special service in war must be taken into account in admissions."[200]

During the Republic, the Invalidenhaus had been reduced to the ig-
nominy of invisibility.[201] However, the new regime ensured that its residents suffered no shortage of public attention. So that the Invalidenhaus's residents could attend the evening festivities on the occasion of
the 1933 Day of National Work, Goebbels ordered twenty cars to take
fifty severely disabled men from the Scharnhorststrasse to Tempelhof
Airfield. Thanking the German Automobile Club for its assistance, Stern
appraised the "worth and deep significance" of the day. By participating
in the celebration, the Invalidenhaus's residents had "gained the comforting certainty that their great sacrifice for the Fatherland had not been
in vain and was now recognized."[202] It was only the beginning. In addition to a donation from Labor Minister Seldte, intended to demonstrate
his "solidarity and comradeship with the Invalidenhaus," signed photographs of Hindenburg, and a life-size painting of Hitler, the Invalidenhaus's residents received visits from dignitaries, the best seats at parades,
and admiring profiles in the Nazi press.[203]

Yet the "authority principle" that the residents exalted spelled the
doom of their claims. Within the House, the bothersome matter of tenants' codetermination was settled quietly, behind closed doors. From
1933 onward, the Financial Support Committee was appointed solely
by the Main Pension Office without consultation with the residents. In
1937, it was dismantled altogether. Freed of the pretense of codetermination, the Labor Ministry rebuffed tenants' attempts to participate in
the House's management. When the Invalidenhaus branch of the NSKOV
requested that its representative be accorded the right to veto prospective
residents, the Ministry refused without explanation.[204] NSKOV members were free to voice their concerns about applicants, but the decision
rested with the House's administrators. Recognition of disabled veterans' sacrifices did not entitle them to participate in their own care.

Individual tenants also discovered that the new moral order was too
narrow to accommodate them. Even the most honorable service to nation and to party did not guarantee a man's tenure. Alfred Fick, the
leader of the NSKOV branch since its founding, performed his tasks well
and with enthusiasm. He was a natural recruit to the Nazi cause: seriously wounded in a battle with the Red Army, adamant foe of the
House's administration, longtime member of the controversial Financial
Support Committee. Under his stewardship, the NSKOV flourished.
Through countless "comradeship evenings," Fick's organization recruited the vast majority of the Invalidenhaus's residents to its mast and
agitated against remnants of the Weimar Republic's authority, especially

the forced payments of rents. In the invaluable but delicate task of identifying Jewish residents, Fick proved himself a passionate party member. No one escaped his detection.

There was but one problem with Fick's leadership: the head of the Invalidenhaus's NSKOV was himself a Jew. Asked to produce proof of his Aryan ancestry in 1934, Fick prevaricated. He was born illegitimately, he claimed. The head office had already obtained proof. Fick's father was Jewish. After Fick was stripped of his office, his expulsion from the House was only a matter of time. Although the National Socialists had acknowledged Jewish war veterans' service to the nation by exempting them from discriminatory laws, Jews did not merit the regime's accolades.[205] Fick's successor at the NSKOV asked for his removal: "You can be assured that it is very hard for me to suggest these measures against comrades who stood by us side by side in the battlefield, but I know that these people place absolutely no value on camaraderie."[206] Within the month, Fick had been ordered to leave. As a "front soldier," he appealed to Labor Minister Franz Seldte: "I didn't think it possible that an old West Front and Border Guard fighter, who was also always nationally minded in the postwar years, could be treated like this today."[207] By the end of 1934, Fick was gone.

Victims of history, the Invalidenhaus's residents sowed the seeds of their destruction. After the ballyhooed transfer of the Invalidenhaus to the War Ministry in 1937, the army divulged plans for the relocation of the House and its inhabitants to Berlin's northern outreaches. The Military Medical Academy wanted the buildings on the Scharnhorststrasse. Heralded in song, celebrated in speeches, the invalids were nonetheless dispensable. In Frohnau, an isolated suburb more than an hour away from Frederick the Great's original structure, the army began construction for the Invalidenhaus settlement, forty separate, freestanding houses built on a hundred acres of land. In 1938, despite their bitter protests, most of the House's residents were moved to the new buildings.[208] The productive potential that the Labor Ministry had worked so hard to cultivate was threatened. Forced to commute two hours every day in their automated tricycles, few of the House's inhabitants could keep their jobs.

After Frohnau, there was no return. In 1944, Allied bombers reduced Frederick the Great's Invalidenhaus to rubble. Nothing remained of the original building but one forlorn side wing; the famed statue was lost, the collection of old armaments destroyed. After the war, the German Democratic Republic finished the demolition, effacing the last physical evidence of the House's centuries-old tradition: the Invalid's Obelisk and the Warrior's Monument. Intended for the casualties of war, the Invalidenhaus's grounds had become a no-man's-land in the last of the twentieth century's epic struggles. The Berlin Wall ran through the once-renowned graveyard. To make room for watchtowers, large portions of the graveyard were unceremoniously uprooted. Headstones were removed, piled on the edge of the street or stacked against buildings. Among them was the stone that marked the last resting place of the Invalidenhaus's would-be protector: General von Seeckt.

The Weimar state's welfare programs secured the material integration of severely disabled veterans. Yet if individual disabled veterans fared reasonably well in the turbulent Weimar economy, they were never satisfied with the state's provisions. In return for their sacrifices, the disabled demanded the "Thanks of the Fatherland" and control over their own care. The Labor Ministry provided them with neither. To maintain the state's monopoly on benevolence, the Labor Ministry eliminated philanthropy for disabled veterans. The principle of codetermination obscured the hard facts of veterans' dependence on the state, encouraging them to envision an impossible autonomy. What began as a concession to the nation's heroes ended with an unbrookable challenge to the state's authority. For the besieged Republic, the disabled man's claims proved impossible to fulfill, his hostility equally impossible to contain.

Conclusion

Reconstruction is an attempt to realize a social ideal....The
social ideal is comprehensive; it is concerned not only with
the relations between the individual and the State, but also
with the triangular set of relations between the individual,
social groups within the community, and the State itself.

Demos, *The Meaning of Reconstruction*, 1918

In its magnitude and ferocity, the Great War was unlike any other
conflict Europeans had known. By the time it was over, the war had destroyed millions of lives and the remarkable prosperity of a European
century. More than 44 million men were mobilized to fight a war that,
the German magazine *Die Umschau* confidently assured its readers in
October 1914, would be the safest in history.[1] Only the dead and injured
returned home before Christmas. The First World War bore witness to
the destruction that industrialized countries, committing all available resources to military production, could unleash. To fuel the war machine,
the societies of Europe were fundamentally transformed. Belligerent
states arrogated unprecedented powers to regulate and coerce. They conscripted labor, rationed commodities, controlled profits, and sent men
to die. In total, 9.5 million men lost their lives in the Great War, another
8 million were permanently disabled.

Europe's twentieth century was born in Flanders fields. The fate of interwar states hinged on their ability to contain and defuse the conflicts
that the Great War had bequeathed. In contrast to the prosperous decades
that preceded the war, the majority of governments had little more than
scarcity to distribute. Few states could relieve the hardships their citizenry
had suffered. In the early 1920s, and again during the Depression, economic turmoil fed unparalleled social unrest. For those who had believed
that the war would usher in a new era of national unity and international
accord, the years that followed proved a grievous disappointment. Two

decades after the Armistice, the peace settlement reached at Versailles lay in ruins; the world hung once again on the brink of war. The "War to end all Wars" was to prove the harbinger of still worse to come.

A history of the Great War's human aftermath, this book has explored the sources of order and instability in two combatant nations. It has demonstrated that states and powerful interest groups alone could not ensure postwar stabilization. The attainment and maintenance of social peace depended ultimately on the institutions of civil society—on the dense layer of voluntary organizations that mediated between the individual and the state. Schools for the blinded, sheltered workshops, homes for paralyzed men: these were prosaic associations, the work of bereaved countesses and literary music-hall men, schoolchildren who bought penny stamps and spinsters who made annual contributions. Voluntarism's significance lay neither simply in its pioneer role nor in the much-needed services it provided. Charity had symbolic value. Each benevolent institution testified to a promise redeemed; each served to reconcile the disabled with their fellow citizens.

This project began with a paradox. Why did German veterans become alienated from a state that provided them with generous benefits, while their British counterparts—despite the neglect of successive governments—bolstered the established order? Neither the war's resolution nor different national traditions fully explain the divergence of veterans' politics. Veterans' attitudes toward their fellow citizens, more than state policies, determined the course of ex-servicemen's movements. In response to state indifference, British philanthropists reconciled the disabled with those for whom they had suffered. The gratitude of the public shielded the state from veterans' anger. In Germany, by contrast, the state regulation of charity isolated the disabled from their fellow citizens. Convinced of the public's ingratitude, veterans demanded that the Republic recognize their sacrifices with higher pensions and improved benefits. The German state's monopoly of welfare for the disabled jeopardized the very achievements its civil servants had aimed to protect.

The history of the regulation of charity testifies to important changes in German civil society from the First World War to the new Republic. On the battleground of associational life, scholars have waged long campaigns over the "modern," "bourgeois," or "democratic" nature of modern Germany.[2] Where an older literature portrayed a populace atomized and hence susceptible to Nazism's appeal, a wealth of studies have documented the enthusiasm that Germans of all classes, regions, and political affinities exhibited for voluntary associations from the 1850s through the Weimar Republic.[3] While this scholarship has refined our understanding of associational life in Germany, it has, until recently, largely neglected one of civil society's constitutive elements: philanthropy.[4] Yet attention to the charitable sphere—and the changes wrought in it from the First World War through the Weimar Republic—indicates that civil society was neither as uniformly vital nor as autonomous as studies on associational life might suggest. As the case of disabled veterans demonstrates, the state's consolidation of welfare created expectations that the Weimar Republic—to its peril—could not fulfill.

As the state's favored wards, German veterans received secured employment and the best social services the Weimar Republic had to offer. By contrast, the British disabled faced chronic unemployment and, if they married, destitution. In Britain, social peace came at the expense of individual lives. Charity was no substitute for rights. Under the watchful eye of the Ministry of Pensions' senior civil servants, the state took only the bare minimum of responsibility for the disabled; pension expenditure remained at levels acceptable to the Treasury. Victors of the Great War, British ex-servicemen pled in vain for the rights accorded their former enemies. Abandoned to the goodwill of their fellow citizens, individual disabled men learned that they had to live by philanthropists' rules. For the objects of charity, there was little security. Because the benevolence of the public supposedly compensated for the state's neglect, the wrongs suffered by individual veterans never became a matter of public debate. Philanthropy's failings were understood as idiosyncratic, not systemic. No veterans' movement could develop around what were, after all, simply the policies of particular charities.

Relegated to silence, disabled veterans in Britain became the mute objects of gratitude, rather than subjects in their own right. Their vaunted cheerfulness just as often masked despair. In August 1914, the Englishman George Ditcher went to war voluntarily. He was twenty-two and unmarried, a gas fitter by trade. At Ypres, in 1917, Ditcher was struck by a shell. Paralyzed from the waist down, he entered the Star and Garter Home the next year. Ditcher lived at the Home for fourteen years, by all accounts a model patient. "I cannot speak too highly of this man's conduct in every way," wrote the Star and Garter's commandant. "He has a very charming personality."[5] After he married in 1930, Ditcher applied for an apartment in the War Seal Foundation so that he and his wife could live together: "No matter how much one appreciates all that is done for them in Hospital, 15 years is a long time to remain in one; & I am anxious for a few Years of Home Life."[6] After a two-year wait, the

Ditchers moved into their War Seal apartment in September 1932. By 1936, however, Ditcher's condition had deteriorated, and he was forced to spend at least two days a week in bed. Ditcher was transferred to Roehampton Hospital, then, in 1939, to the Home for Seriously Disabled Sailors and Soldiers at Gifford House in Worthing.

A week after the German invasion of Poland, Ditcher wrote his wife from Worthing.[7] How exactly the letter came to be opened in the War Seal Office was not recorded. Its contents shocked the War Seal's management. The letter was vitriolic, embittered: everything that Ditcher, as they knew him, was not. He had to leave that "Grave Roehampton" and wished that his wife could rejoin him in Worthing. But his pension was not enough to support them: "The powers against anyone living a decent married life in a home of their own are bound to force stringent times wherever they can." It was the "rulers'" desire to "remain multimillionaires themselves" that explained disabled veterans' misery. The war wounded had been "persecuted" by a government that "squeezed the last halfpenny out of us to pay for their slaughtering of multitudes of Men Women & Children. Sure to prate about the Crisis they force, they will always take care of themselves." Mrs. Ditcher never received the letter. On Oswald Stoll's advice, it remained in her husband's file.

Yet if this book has chronicled philanthropy's shortcomings as well as its strengths, it has also demonstrated the limits of state action. The Weimar Republic, long celebrated as a pioneer in the provision of welfare, created Europe's most comprehensive initiatives for disabled veterans. However, the state's generous programs nonetheless failed to provide the Republic with a much-needed basis of social cohesion. As a result of the state's elimination of charity, the Weimar Republic became solely responsible for the fulfillment of veterans' demands. The state bore the full brunt of disabled men's anger. Veterans' hostility toward the state was the consequence, not the cause, of their profound alienation from society. Within a decade of the Armistice, the Republic's most bitter enemy, the National Socialists, emerged to capitalize on veterans' discontent.

Disabled veterans were the Great War's most conspicuous legacy. In decades characterized by stubborn social problems, the disabled posed a unique dilemma: their sacrifices could never be fully compensated. This book has aimed to understand two very different approaches to the task of literal reconstruction. In Britain, philanthropists brokered a social peace between the disabled and their fellow citizens. For individual men and their families, however, charity was scant protection against poverty.

In Germany, disabled veterans received the best that a defeated and nearly bankrupt state had to offer. Alienated from the society they had served, veterans helped to topple the Republic that had favored them. In both nations, reconstruction required the full participation of civil society. The Weimar Republic's framers believed that they could heal the war's rifts solely through the distribution of generous benefits. Theirs was a tragic error, for a state alone cannot promote successful reconstruction. War's wounds can only be healed by those who have suffered its fury.

Appendix

TABLE 1   ESTIMATED CASUALTIES IN THE FIRST WORLD WAR, IN THOUSANDS

	Britain and Ireland	Germany
Estimated Wounded	1,676	4,248
Permanently Disabled	755	1,537
Total Mobilized	6,147	13,200
Prewar Male Population (15–49)	11,540	16,316
Total Prewar Population	45,221	67,800

SOURCES: Urlanis, *Bilanz der Kriege*, 354; Winter, *The Great War and the British People*, 73, 75; International Labour Office, *Employment of Disabled Men*, 15; Mayo, *Soldiers What Next!* 555; Grebler and Winkler, *The Cost of the World War to Germany and Austria-Hungary*, 78; Report of the Minister of Pensions, 1 April 1922–31 March 1923, 3.

TABLE 2   TOTAL WOUNDED AND PERMANENTLY DISABLED

	Britain and Ireland	Germany
Wounded per 1,000 Mobilized	273	322
Wounded per 1,000 Males (15–49)	145	260
Wounded per 1,000 People	37	63
Total Permanently Disabled per 1,000 Mobilized	123	116
Total Permanently Disabled per 1,000 Males (15–49)	65	94
Total Permanently Disabled per 1,000 People	17	23

SOURCES: Urlanis, *Bilanz der Kriege*, 354; Winter, *The Great War and the British People*, 73, 75; International Labour Office, *Employment of Disabled Men*, 15; Mayo, *Soldiers What Next!* 555; Grebler and Winkler, *The Cost of the World War to Germany and Austria-Hungary*, 78; Report of the Minister of Pensions, 1 April 1922–31 March 1923, 3.

TABLE 3 WAR PENSION EXPENDITURE AS A PERCENTAGE OF NATIONAL BUDGETS

	Britain	Germany
1924–1925	8.7	16.3
1925–1926	8.1	26.1
1926–1927	7.5	21.9
1927–1928	7.1	21.5
1928–1929	6.9	20.6
1929–1930	6.5	20.3
1930–1931	6.0	19.6
1931–1932	5.9	20.9
1932–1933	5.7	21.3

SOURCES: Peter-Christian Witt, "Auswirkungen der Inflation auf die Finanzpolitik," in *Die Nachwirkungen der Inflation auf die deutsche Geschichte,* ed. Gerald Feldman, table 9, p. 93; Mallett and George, *British Budgets, Third Series,* 558–559; Grebler and Winkler, *The Cost of the World War to Germany and Austria-Hungary,* 78; Reichstag, *Reichshaushaltsetat für das Rechnungsjahr 1932.*

TABLE 4 RELATIVE DEGREE OF DISABILITY

Percent disability	Britain	Germany
20	29.88	n/a
30	20.12	41.90
40	12.69	15.10
50	12.66	17.00
60	8.23	8.20
70	5.33	7.20
80	3.53	3.80
90	0.70	0.80
100	6.86	6.00

SOURCES: Reichsarbeitsblatt, Nichtamtl. Teil, 1934, p. 281; 1935, p. 241; 1936, p. 341; 1937 and 1938, p. 366; Report of the Minister of Pensions, 1 April 1935 to 31 March 1936, p. 36; Rappenecker, *Das Problem der Fürsorge für die Kriegsopfer,* 32.

TABLE 5   BRITISH PENSION RATES
(Weekly Rates for Privates)[a]

Proportion of Disablement (%)	Pension (shillings)	Specific Injury
100	40	Two or more limbs; arm and eye; leg and eye; both hands; all fingers and thumbs; both feet; hand and foot; total loss of sight; total paralysis; lunacy; permanently bedridden; total permanent disablement through internal, thoracic, or abdominal organs; head and brain injuries which permanently disable; Jacksonian epilepsy; very severe facial disfigurement
90	36	Amputation of right arm through shoulder
80	32	Amputation of leg at hip or with stump of not more than 5 inches; of right arm below shoulder with stump of not more than 6 inches; of left arm through shoulder; severe facial disfigurement; total loss of speech; loss of both feet
70	28	Amputation of leg below hip (as above), but not below middle thigh; left arm not more than 6 inches below shoulder or right arm more than 6 inches below shoulder or not more than 5 inches below elbow; total deafness
60	24	Amputation of leg below middle thigh or through or not more than 4 inches below knee or of left arm more than 5 inches below shoulder through or not more than 5 inches below elbow; of right arm more than 5 inches below elbow
50	20	Amputation of leg more than 4 inches below knee or of left arm more than 5 inches below elbow; loss of vision of one eye
40	16	Loss of thumb or 4 fingers of right hand; loss of 2 toes of both feet above knuckle; Lisfranc operation, one foot
30	12	Loss of thumb or 4 fingers of left hand; loss of 3 fingers of right hand

SOURCES: Notes on War Pensions, 75–77; N. B. Dearle, Labour Cost of the World War to Great Britain, 1914–1922, 51.
[a]The Royal Warrant also provided the option of an "alternative pension." Those men who had earned more than 25s. per week before the war, but whose pension and income currently failed to meet their prewar earnings (with some allowance made for increases in the cost of living), could apply for an "alternative pension." A man's total earnings, together with the alternative pension, could not exceed £5 per week. Alternative pensions had to be claimed within twelve months of the first grant of the disability pension. Restrictions on eligibility (and the high immediate postwar inflation) meant that, in practice, the Ministry of Pensions awarded very few alternative pensions. In his 1936 report, the Minister of Pensions judged the alternative pension thus: "It has not proved a satisfactory form of compensation, and with one exception has not been copied by any other country or Dominion." Ministry of Pensions, Nineteenth Annual Report of the Minister of Pensions, 1 April 1935 to 31 March 1936, pt. II, 13.

TABLE 6 GERMAN PENSION RATES

(Monthly, with One Occupational Allowance,[a] Without Supplementary Benefits[b])

Diminution of Earning Capacity	Locality[c]	Pension for a Single Man	For a Married Man[d]			
			Without Children	With 1 Child	With 2 Children	With 3 Children
30	S	23.70	23.70	28.44	33.10	37.93
	A	22.79	22.79	27.35	31.91	36.48
	B	22.94	22.24	26.69	31.15	35.60
	C	21.51	21.51	25.82	30.13	34.43
	D	20.78	20.78	24.94	29.10	33.27
40	S	31.59	31.59	37.91	44.23	50.54
	A	30.38	30.38	36.45	42.53	48.60
	B	29.65	29.65	35.58	41.50	47.43
	C	28.67	28.67	34.41	40.14	45.88
	D	27.70	27.70	33.24	38.78	44.32
50	S	44.76	49.23	58.19	67.15	76.10
	A	43.04	47.34	55.95	64.56	73.18
	B	42.00	46.20	54.61	63.01	71.42
	C	40.63	44.69	52.82	60.95	69.08
	D	39.25	43.17	51.03	58.88	66.74
60	S	53.53	58.89	69.60	80.31	91.03
	A	51.48	56.63	66.93	77.23	87.53
	B	50.24	55.27	65.32	75.37	85.42
	C	48.59	53.45	63.18	72.90	82.62
	D	46.95	51.64	61.04	70.43	79.82
70	S	63.18	69.50	82.13	94.77	107.41
	A	60.75	66.83	78.98	91.13	103.28

	B	59.29	65.22	77.08	88.94	100.80
	C	57.35	63.08	74.55	86.02	97.49
	D	55.40	60.94	72.03	83.11	94.19
80	S	73.71	81.08	95.82	110.57	125.31
	A	70.88	77.96	92.14	106.31	120.49
	B	69.17	76.09	89.93	103.76	117.60
	C	66.91	73.60	86.98	100.36	113.74
	D	64.64	71.10	84.03	95.96	109.88
90	S	86.88	95.56	112.94	130.33	147.71
	A	83.54	91.89	108.60	125.31	142.03
	B	81.53	89.68	105.99	122.31	138.62
	C	78.86	86.74	102.52	118.30	134.07
	D	76.19	83.80	99.04	114.29	129.53
100	S	103.55	113.91	134.62	155.32	176.03
	A	99.56	109.53	129.44	149.35	169.26
	B	97.17	106.90	126.33	145.77	165.20
	C	93.99	103.39	122.19	140.99	159.78
	D	90.80	99.89	118.05	136.21	154.37

SOURCE: Renten-Tafeln zum Reichsversorgungsgesetz (1927), Anlage 3, 753–755.

[a]Approximately 83 percent of disabled men received an occupational supplement. One occupational supplement, equal to 35 percent of the basic pension and heavy disability supplement, was accorded if a man's former occupation required considerable knowledge and skill, as well as a special degree of effort and responsibility. This supplement was also granted if the man's injury was the sole cause that prevented him from pursuing his previous occupation. Managers, professionals, and others who held "positions of responsibility" received two occupational supplements, equal to 70 percent more than the basic pension. On the occupational supplement, see Rappenecker, *Das Problem der Fürsorge für die Kriegsopfer*, 21.

[b]In addition to the basic pension, disabled men were eligible for supplementary allowances. The *Zusatzrente*, or supplementary pension, was granted to those with a disability rated 50 percent and above whose income (pension plus salary) fell below a stipulated level. A Berlin man with two children received the full *Zusatzrente* if his monthly income was below 96 RM, half of the *Zusatzrente* if it was below 144 RM. For those with disabilities rated 50 to 60 percent, the full *Zusatzrente* amounted to an additional 30 RM a month; for those rated 70 to 80 percent, the full *Zusatzrente* equaled 43 RM a month; for those rated over 80 percent, the full *Zusatzrente* amounted to an additional 60 RM a month. Men who required constant attendance because of their disabilities were eligible for an additional care allowance, or *Pflegezulage*. The *Pflegezulage* was payable monthly at a rate between 50 and 125 RM.

[c]Pension rates were determined by the disabled man's place of residence. "S" denoted Sonderklasse or especially expensive cities such as Berlin.

[d]For reasons of space, this table includes only the pensions payable for the first three children. For each additional child, the man received the same allowance.

Notes

INTRODUCTION

1. On casualty statistics, Robert Weldon Whalen, *Bitter Wounds: German Victims of the Great War, 1914–1939* (Ithaca, N.Y., 1984), 40–41; International Labour Office, *Studies and Reports,* Series E, no. 2: *The Compulsory Employment of Disabled Men* (Geneva, 1921), 2; Boris Urlanis, *Bilanz der Kriege* (Berlin, 1965), 354–356.

2. Although the subject of this book is disabled veterans, many of its conclusions, as will be noted, apply to veterans more broadly. It has not always been possible to distinguish the disabled from their fellow veterans. Many veterans' associations in Germany and Britain represented both able-bodied and disabled ex-servicemen. The treatment of the disabled became a rallying point for veterans' politics. I do not treat other war victims, such as war widows and orphans, except peripherally. For an excellent history of war victims, see Whalen; Karin Hausen, "The German Nation's Obligations to the Heroes' Widows of World War I," in *Behind the Lines: Gender and the Two World Wars,* ed. Margaret Higonnet (New Haven, Conn., 1987).

3. Martin Gilbert, *The First World War* (New York, 1994), 541; Whalen, 38.

4. Francis W. Hirst, *The Consequences of the War to Britain* (London, 1934), 295; International Labour Office, *Employment of Disabled Men: Meeting of Experts for the Study of Methods of Finding Employment for Disabled Men* (Geneva, 1923), 16.

5. Henry Souttar, *A Surgeon in Belgium* (London, 1915), 22.

6. For recent important studies of psychiatric ailments, see Paul Lerner, "Hysterical Men: War, Neurosis and German Mental Medicine, 1914–1921" (Ph.D. diss., Columbia University, 1996); Bernd Ulrich, "Nerven und Krieg: Skizzierung

einer Beziehung," in *Geschichte und Psychologie,* ed. Bedrich Loewenstein (Pfaffenweiler, 1992), 163–192.

7. Jay Winter, *Sites of Memory, Sites of Mourning: The Great War in European Cultural History* (Cambridge, 1995), 46; Eugen Weber, *The Hollow Years: France in the 1930's* (New York, 1994), 13.

8. Dan Silverman, *Reconstructing Europe after the First World War* (Cambridge, 1982), esp. 118–120.

9. "The Star and Garter Home," *Daily Mail,* 11 July 1924, PH 7, Star and Garter Collection, Acc. 961, British Red Cross Archives.

10. "War Victims for Whom Time Has Stood Still," *Star,* 10 November 1931, PH 10, Star and Garter Collection, British Red Cross Archives.

11. Erich Rehse to the Labor Ministry, 4 June 1921, RAM 7757, Bundesarchiv Lichterfelde (BAL).

12. Albert Bayliss to Lord Derby, 31 March 1922, 920 DER (17) 21/5, Liverpool Record Office.

13. See, for instance, Minutes of the War Cabinet, 6 June 1919, CAB 23/577, PRO; "A Talk with Sir Oswald Stoll," *Daily Telegraph,* 18 October 1920, Cutting Book II, Stoll Foundation Archive; Dr. Paul Franke, "Die Versorgung der Kriegsinvaliden und Hinterbliebenen," *Tägliche Rundschau (Berlin),* 23 July 1919, R 755, Archiv des Deutschen Caritasverbandes (ADCV).

14. Charles Maier, *Recasting Bourgeois Europe* (Princeton, N.J., 1975); Keith Middlemas, *Politics in Industrial Society: The Experience of the British System since 1911* (London, 1979).

15. International Labour Office, *Employment of Disabled Men,* 15.

16. "Den Opfern des Krieges," *Vorwärts,* 24 November 1919, no. 600.

17. James Currie to the Minister of Labour, Minute Note of 26 July 1919, Lab 2/523/TDS 5354/1010, PRO.

18. Rehabilitation Comm. Paper No. V.T. 8, Draft Report on Vocational Training, 22 September 1938, MSS 292/146.9/2, Modern Records Centre.

19. On the disabled in Britain, see the important works of Seth Koven, "Remembering and Dismemberment: Crippled Children, Wounded Soldiers, and the Great War in Great Britain," *American Historical Review* 99 (October 1994): 1167–1202; Joanna Bourke, *Dismembering the Male: Men's Bodies, Britain and the Great War* (Chicago, 1996), 31–75; Andrew Latcham, "Journey's End: Ex-Servicemen and the State during and after the Great War" (Ph.D. thesis, Oxford, 1997), esp. chs. 6, 7; Jeffrey Reznick, "Rest, Recovery, and Rehabilitation: Healing and Identity in Great Britain in the First World War" (Ph.D. diss., Emory University, 1999).

20. See, for instance, James Cronin, *Politics of State Expansion* (London, 1991), chs. 6, 7; Anne Crowther, *British Social Policy, 1914–1939* (London, 1988), 40–74; F. M. Miller, "The Unemployment Policy of the National Government, 1931–1936," *Historical Journal* 19 (1976): 453–476; Robert Skidelsky, "Keynes and the Treasury View: The Case for and against an Active Unemployment Policy in Britain, 1920–1939," in *The Emergence of the Welfare State in Britain and Germany,* ed. W. J. Mommsen (London, 1981); John Stevenson, "The Making of Unemployment Policy, 1931–1935," in *High and Low Politics in Modern Britain,* ed. Michael Bentley and John Stevenson (Oxford, 1983), 182–213.

21. On philanthropy, see Geoffrey Finlayson, *Citizen, State, and Welfare in Britain, 1830–1990* (New York, 1994), 201–286; Frank Prochaska, "Philanthropy," in *The Cambridge Social History of Britain, 1750–1950,* ed. F. M. L. Thompson (Cambridge, 1990).

22. Georg Benckendorff et al., *Kommentar von Reichsversorgungsbeamten zum Reichsversorgungsgesetz vom 12.5.1920* (Berlin, 1929), 748–765; Reichsarbeitsministerium, *Handbuch der Reichsversorgung* (Berlin, 1932), 356–368; for wage statistics, see Gerhard Bry, *Wages in Germany, 1871–1945* (Princeton, N.J., 1960), 341, 352, 379.

23. See, for example, Landesrat Gerlach, "10 Jahre Kriegsbeschädigten- und Hinterbliebenenfürsorge in der Rheinprovinz," *Die rheinische Provinzialverwaltung, ihre Entwicklung und ihr heutiger Stand* (Düsseldorf, 1925), 298.

24. Christopher Jackson, "Infirmative Action: The Law of the Severely Disabled in Germany," *Central European History* 26 (1993): 417–455.

25. Dr. Bruno Jung, *Der Einfluß der Wirtschaftskrise auf die Durchführung des Schwerbeschädigten-Gesetzes* (Mannheim, 1932), 32–33, 39.

26. Wilhelm Groener, Minutes, National Ausschuss für Frauenarbeit im Kriege, 29 January 1917, CA XIX 15, ADCV.

27. Young-Sun Hong, *Welfare, Modernity, and the Weimar State, 1919–1933* (Princeton, N.J., 1998), esp. 16–35, 44–75, 181–202; Jochen-Christoph Kaiser, "Freie Wohlfahrtsverbände im Kaiserreich und in der Weimarer Republik: Ein Überblick," *Westfälische Forschungen* 43 (1993): 26–57; Jochen-Christoph Kaiser, *Sozialer Protestantismus im 20. Jahrhundert. Beiträge zur Geschichte der Inneren Mission 1914–1945* (Munich, 1989); Gerhard Buck, "Die Entwicklung der freien Wohlfahrtspflege von den ersten Zusammenschlüssen der freien Verbände im 19. Jahrhundert bis zur Durchsetzung des Subsidiaritätsprinzip in der Weimarer Fürsorgegesetzgebung," in *Geschichte der Sozialarbeit,* ed. Rolf Landwehr and Rüdeger Baron (Weinheim and Basel, 1983), 139–172; David Crew, *Germans on Welfare: From Weimar to Hitler* (New York, 1998), 18–21.

28. Christoph Sachße and Florian Tennstedt, *Geschichte der Armenfürsorge in Deutschland, Fürsorge und Wohlfahrtspflege, 1871 bis 1929* (Stuttgart, 1988), 2:68–87; Detlev Peukert, *Die Weimarer Republik: Krisenjahre der Klassischen Moderne* (Frankfurt, 1987), 46–52; Elizabeth Harvey, *Youth and the Welfare State in Weimar Germany* (Oxford, 1993), 152–185; Ludwig Preller, *Sozialpolitik in der Weimarer Republik* (Düsseldorf, 1978), 34–85; Werner Abelshauser, "Die Weimarer Republik—ein Wohlfahrtsstaat?" in *Die Weimarer Republik als Wohlfahrtsstaat,* ed. Werner Abelshauser (Stuttgart, 1987).

29. Index, Rep. 191, Geheimes Staatsarchiv Preußischer Kulturbesitz (GStAB).

30. For Germany, see Peter-Christian Witt, "Auswirkungen der Inflation auf die Finanzpolitik," in *Die Nachwirkungen der Inflation auf die deutsche Geschichte,* ed. Gerald Feldman (Munich, 1985), table 9, p. 93; Whalen, 16; Reichstag, Reichshaushaltsetat für das Rechnungsjahr 1932; Leo Grebler and Wilhelm Winkler, *The Cost of the World War to Germany and Austria-Hungary* (New Haven, Conn., 1940), 78. For Britain, see Sir Bernard Mallet and C. Oswald George, *British Budgets: Third Series, 1921–1922 to 1932–1933* (London, 1933), 558–559. These figures represent the total pension budget for disabled veterans and war dependents.

31. Throughout this study, I use the term *public* as British and German veterans did—to refer to their fellow citizens in the broadest possible sense. German veterans variously spoke of the *Öffentlichkeit* and the *Volk*. Despite the different connotations these words carry, disabled veterans often used them interchangeably.

32. José Harris, "Society and State in Twentieth-Century Britain," in *Cambridge Social History of Britain, 1750–1950,* ed. F. M. L. Thompson (Cambridge, 1990), 83.

33. Ross McKibbin, *The Ideologies of Class: Social Relations in Britain, 1880–1950* (Oxford, 1990), 166.

34. See especially Graham Wootton, *The Politics of Influence: British Ex-Servicemen, Cabinet Decisions, and Cultural Change* (London, 1963), 85. Notable exceptions are M. J. Daunton, "Payment and Participation: Welfare and State-Formation in Britain, 1900–1951," *Past and Present,* 150 (February 1996): 169–216; Finlayson, 201–286; Brian Harrison, *Peaceable Kingdom: Stability and Change in Modern Britain* (Oxford, 1982), 217–259; Prochaska, "Philanthropy"; Frank Prochaska, *The Voluntary Impulse: Philanthropy in Modern Britain* (London, 1988).

35. Paul Fussell, *The Great War and Modern Memory* (Oxford, 1975), esp. 82–90; J. M. Winter, *The Great War and the British People,* ch. 9; Robert Wohl, *The Generation of 1914* (London, 1980). For a contrary viewpoint, see Charles Kimball, "Ex-Service Movement in England and Wales, 1916–1930" (Ph.D. diss., Stanford University, 1991), 150–151; Bourke, 21–23. On the antagonism caused by the white feather campaign, see Nicolette Gullace, "White Feathers and Wounded Men: Female Patriotism and the Memory of the Great War," *Journal of British Studies* 36 (April 1997): 198–206.

36. See also Ewald Frie, "Vorbild oder Spiegelbild? Kriegsbeschädigtenfürsorge in Deutschland, 1914–1919," in *Der erste Weltkrieg,* ed. Wolfgang Michalka (Piper, 1993), 564.

37. Whalen, 107–124; James Diehl, "Victors or Victims? Disabled Veterans in the Third Reich," *Journal of Modern History* 59 (December 1987): 718, 719; Michael Geyer, "Ein Vorbote des Wohlfahrtsstaates: Die Kriegsopferversorgung in Frankreich, Deutschland und Großbritannien nach dem ersten Weltkrieg," *Geschichte und Gesellschaft* 9 (1983): 230–277, esp. 257–258.

38. "Zustände beim städtischen Fürsorgeamt für Kriegsbeschädigte," *Arbeiter-Zeitung,* 11 January 1923, Mag. Akte V/65, Stadtarchiv Frankfurt (StAF).

39. Whalen, 107–124. See also Douglas McMurtrie, *Evolution of National Systems of Vocational Reeducation for Disabled Soldiers and Sailors* (Washington, D.C., 1918), 179.

40. See Ward, 25–26; Latcham, 115–117.

41. Samuel Hynes, *A War Imagined: The First World War and English Culture* (New York, 1990), 255.

42. On the Dolchstoßlegende, see Wilhelm Deist, "Der militärische Zusammenbruch des Kaiserreichs: Zur Realität der Dolchstoßlegende," in *Das Unrechtsregime: Internationale Forschung über den Nationalsozialismus,* ed. Ursula Büttner, vol. 1 (Hamburg, 1986).

43. Among others, Richard Biernacki, *Fabrication of Labor: Germany and Britain, 1640–1914* (Berkeley and Los Angeles, 1995); David Blackbourn and

Geoff Eley, *The Peculiarities of German History: Bourgeois Society and Politics in Nineteenth-Century Germany* (Oxford, 1984), 10, 135–144; W.J. Mommsen, ed., *The Emergence of the Welfare State in Britain and Germany* (London, 1981); Stefan Berger, *The British Labour Party and the German Social Democrats, 1900–1931* (Oxford, 1994); John Breuilly, "Liberalism in Mid–Nineteenth Century Hamburg and Manchester," in his *Labour and Liberalism* (Manchester, 1992), 197–227; Werner Berg, *Wirtschaft und Gesellschaft in Deutschland und Großbritannien im Übergang zum "Organisierten Kapitalismus," 1850–1914* (Bielefeld, 1980); Christiane Eisenberg, *Deutsche und Englische Gewerkschaften: Entstehung und Entwicklung bis 1875 im Vergleich* (Göttingen, 1995); E.P. Hennock, *British Social Reform and German Precedents: The Case of Social Insurance, 1880–1914* (Oxford, 1987); Michael Prinz, *Brot und Dividende: Deutsches und britisches Genossensschaftswesen im Vergleich 1830–1914* (Göttingen, 1996); V. Then, *Deutsche und englische Eisenbahnunternehmer in der Industriellen Revolution: Ein preussisch/deutscher-englischer Vergleich* (Göttingen, 1996). On comparative approaches to the study of the Great War, see Winter, *Sites of Memory*, 10–11, 227–228.

44. Richard Bessel, *Germany after the First World War*, (Oxford, 1993), 85–89; "Die Heimkehr der Soldaten: Das Bild des Frontsoldaten in der Öffentlichkeit der Weimarer Republik," in *Keiner fühlt sich hier mehr als Mensch* ed. Gerhard Hirschfeld, Gerd Krumeich, and Irena Renz (Essen, 1993), 221–239.

CHAPTER 1

1. Box 6, War Seal Mansions Collection, Hammersmith & Fulham Archive Centre (HFAC).

2. On the debate over the failure of reconstruction, see Paul Barton Johnson, *Land Fit for Heroes: The Planning of British Reconstruction, 1916–1919* (Chicago, 1968), 432–499; Kenneth O. Morgan, *Consensus and Disunity: The Lloyd George Coalition, 1919–1922* (Oxford, 1979), esp. 106–108; R.H. Tawney, "The Abolition of Economic Controls, 1918–1921" (1941), in *History and Society: Essays by R.H. Tawney,* ed. J.M. Winter (London, 1978), 129–196; Peter Cline, "Winding Down the War Economy: British Plans for Peacetime Recovery, 1916–1919," in *War and the State: The Transformation of British Government, 1914–1919,* ed. Kathleen Burk (London, 1982), 157–181.

3. According to the most reliable calculations, charitable receipts and expenditure in the 1930s amounted to between £35 and £50 million annually. Constance Braithwaite, *The Voluntary Citizen: An Enquiry into the Place of Philanthropy in the Community* (London, 1938), 173–174; Finlayson, 201–286; Prochaska, *The Voluntary Impulse;* David Owen, *English Philanthropy, 1660–1960* (Cambridge, Mass., 1964), 525–531.

4. H. Schwerdt, "Englandreise," *Reichsbund der Kriegsbeschädigten, Kriegsteilnehmer, und Hinterbliebenen,* 1 June 1927 (Nr. 11, 10 Jahrgang), p. 117.

5. Ibid.

6. Robert Skidelsky, "Keynes and the Treasury View: The Case For and Against an Active Unemployment Policy in Britain, 1920–1939," in Mommsen; John Stevenson, "The Making of Unemployment Policy, 1931–1935," in Bent-

ley and Stevenson, 182–213; W.R. Garside, *British Unemployment, 1919–1939* (Cambridge, 1990), 318–357.

7. On the Treasury, see G.C. Peden, "The 'Treasury View' on Public Works and Employment in the Interwar Period," *Economic History Review* 37 (1984): 167–181; Cronin, 87–92; R.A. Chapman and J.R. Greenaway, *The Dynamics of Administrative Reform* (London, 1980), 100–114.

8. Surveying the question of employment for the disabled in 1923, the International Labour Office resolved that compulsion "would alone seem capable of achieving lasting results." International Labour Office, *Employment of Disabled Men*, 227–233, and Resolutions.

9. Cabinet, C.P. 3013, The Employment of Severely Disabled Ex-Service Men, Memorandum by the Chancellor of the Exchequer [Horne], 3 June 1921, Lab 2/224, EDX 110/7/1921, Public Record Office (PRO).

10. Joanna Bourke's view is different. See her *Dismembering the Male*, 59, 70.

11. Fussell, 86–90; Hynes, 337–404; Frank Field, *British and French Writers of the First World War* (Cambridge, 1991); Allyson Booth, *Postcards from the Trenches: Negotiating the Space between Modernism and the First World War* (New York, 1996), 30–33; John Onions, *English Fiction and the Drama of the Great War, 1918–1939* (New York, 1990); David Lloyd, *Battlefield Tourism* (Oxford, 1998), 43–47.

12. On anticharity sentiments within the labor movement, see MSS 292/20/3, Parliamentary Committee Minutes, July 1915, Modern Records Centre; National Association of Discharged Sailors and Soldiers, "Lest We Forget," Series no. 1, 1917; Latcham, 105.

13. Since the BUFs membership files are still restricted, information on the fascist rank and file is limited. See Arnd Bauernkämper, *Die radikale Rechte in Großbritannien* (Göttingen 1991), 197–213; D.S. Lewis, *Illusions of Grandeur: Mosley, Fascism and British Society, 1931–81* (Manchester, 1987), 71–75; Robert Skidelsky, *Oswald Mosley* (New York, 1975), 317–321, 322–323, 325–329; John Stevenson and Chris Cook, *Britain in the Depression: Society and Politics, 1929–1939*, 2d ed. (London, 1994), 235–239; Thomas Linehan, *East London for Mosley: The British Union of Fascists in East London and Southwest Essex, 1933–40* (London, 1996), 195–274. On ex-servicemen and hunger marches, see Peter Kingsford, *The Hunger Marchers in Britain, 1920–1940* (London, 1982), 45, 50, 84.

14. Verbatim Report of the Annual Conference of the British Legion, 20 May 1929, p. 15, British Legion Archives.

15. See, for example, "Pensions in 1923," *British Legion Journal*, October 1922, 87.

16. Sir Oswald Stoll, "The War Seal Foundation," *Graphic*, 28 June 1919, Cutting Book, January 1916–June 1920, Stoll Foundation. For an account of the treatment of returning soldiers, see Peter Reese, *Homecoming Heroes: An Account of the Reassimilation of British Military Personnel into Civilian Life* (London, 1992), chs. 2–4.

17. "The Care of the Disabled," *Morning Post*, 21 May 1915, Cutting Book I, Roehampton, Greater London Record Office. "The public cannot know even

now if the payment of the revised scale is actually being made." "The failure of the Parliament to guard the public interest and to keep watch upon administration has seldom been more conspicuous, especially as Parliament has very little else to do."

18. "What We Think," *Star,* 14 June 1916, Cutting Book, January 1916–June 1920, Stoll Foundation.

19. On the prewar system, see Latcham, 17–19.

20. Report by Dudley Myers, 6 October 1916, PIN 15/336, PRO. See also Sir Arthur Griffith-Boscawen, Memorandum of Evidence, n.d. [1917?], PIN 15/785, PRO; Hon. E.A. Parry and Lieut.-General Sir A.E. Codrington, *War Pensions: Past and Present* (London, 1918), 58.

21. "What Do War Seals Mean?" *Midland Mail,* 27 October 1915, Cutting Book, 1915, Stoll. See also Hansard, 5th series, 1914, lxviii. 401, on the presentation of a petition for "just and generous pensions," signed by 125,000.

22. Surgeon-General Sir Launcellotte Gubbins testifying to the Ministry of Pensions Sub-committee of the Select Committee on National Expenditure, Meeting no. 3, 29 January 1918, PIN 15/788, PRO.

23. Winter, *The Great War and the British People,* 225–227.

24. Actuarial Report prepared by Mr. A.W. Watson, F.I.A., in Allowances and Pensions in Respect of Seamen, Marines, and Soldiers and Their Wives, Widows and Dependants (PP 1914–1916, xi, cd. 7662), 25, 27.

25. On the Local Committees, see Statutory Committee Circular No. 7, Local Committees (27 June 1916), Procedure and Functions of Local Committees, 27 June 1916.

26. C.F.A. Hore, "State-Aided Provision of Employment—An Act of Obligation or Charity," Committee on the Employment of Severely Disabled Men, 16 December, PIN 15/33, PRO.

27. See reports of the Westminster Palace Hotel Meeting in "War Pensions: Duty of the State," *Liverpool Courier,* 24 June 1916, 361 COU 1/5, Liverpool County Record Office. See also Edward Devine, assisted by Lilian Brandt, *Disabled Soldiers and Sailors, Pensions and Training,* Carnegie Endowment for International Peace, Preliminary Economic Studies of the War, no. 12 (New York, 1919), 139.

28. Ministry of Pensions, Nineteenth Annual Report from 1st April to 31st of March, 1936. Part II: Survey of War Pensions from 1916 (London, 1937), 2–3, OPSS MIC E 291, British Library.

29. *Birmingham Despatch,* 7 March 1931, "Midland Notabilities, Dame Ethel Shakespear," Newspaper Cuttings, Birmingham Biography, vol. 18, p. 4, Local History, Central Library. Obituary, "Death of Dame Ethel Shakespear," *Birmingham Gazette,* 18 January 1946, Birmingham Biography, vol. 38, p. 195, Local History Collection, Central Library.

30. Departmental Committee of Inquiry, Local Committees Report, PIN 15/652, PRO.

31. See, for instance, cabinet memorandums circulated by Walter Long, President of the Local Government Board, 3 December 1915, 6 March 1916, 11 April 1916, PIN 15/336, PRO; cabinet memorandum circulated by Arthur Henderson, 19 September 1916, PIN 15/336, PRO; "A Cabinet Committee on Pen-

sions," *Times,* 6 October 1916, 6; "A Pensions Policy," *Times,* 12 October 1916, 9; "The Pensions Campaign," *Times,* 13 October 1916, 8.

32. Arthur Griffith-Boscawen, *Memories* (London, 1925), 196.

33. John Hodge, *Workman's Cottage to Windsor Castle* (London, 1931), 204. The Ministry's "headquarters" was itself spread throughout temporary quarters in London. It occupied buildings in Chelsea, Baker Street, as well as the Tate Gallery, the Marylebone Town Hall, and the Office of Works building. "Note on the Origin and Progress of the Ministry of Pensions," n.a. [Matthew Nathan?], 14 April 1917, produced in response to a query from the *Manchester Guardian,* PIN 15/1395.

34. In 1921, there were 100,000 cases of pension outstanding in which entitlement had not yet been reviewed by the Medical Assessors. Ministry of Pensions, Report of the Departmental Committee of Inquiry into the Machinery of Administration of the Ministry of Pensions (London, 1921), 59. For criticism of the Ministry from two members of the Pensions Appeal Tribunal, see Parry and Codrington, esp. chs. 4, 6.

35. The 1917 Royal Warrant provided that pension rates should be calculated not according to individual wages or earning capacity (the standards used since 1915) but on the degree of disablement sustained as compared to a healthy man of the same age; it also included a provision (or the alternative pension) to compensate men whose prewar earnings had far exceeded the average.

36. Hansard, 91, col. 256 (6 March 1917); George Barnes, *From Workshop to War Cabinet* (London, 1923), 146.

37. Sir Douglas Haig's evidence before the Select Committee of the House of Commons, July 1919. "Sir Douglas Haig," *Daily Telegraph,* 2 July 1919, Cutting Book, January 1916–June 1920, Stoll Foundation. See also Countess Haig, *The Man I Knew* (Edinburgh, 1936), 243–244, 317.

38. Re. fingerprinting for identification. Note on Prevention of Fraud in Respect of Disability Pensions, A Report by the Select Committee on National Expenditure, Ministry of Pensions Sub-Committee, PIN 15/789, PRO.

39. Minute Note, J.D. to Hore, 13 January 1919, PIN 15/1101, PRO. See also W. Brandford Griffith's Memorandum on the "Statutory Right" to a War Pension, 18 July 1919: "But the mere transformation of Royal favour into legal right by empowering a pensioner to sue for payment of pension awarded to him would not for a moment satisfy the thinking public, who would rapidly see that there was no substance in the apparent concession." PIN 15/1812, PRO.

40. On the attention to public opinion during the Coalition, see Morgan, ch. 6.

41. Mr. Harris, commenting during Mr. Flynn's evidence before Ministry of Pensions Sub-Committee of the Select Committee on National Expenditure, Ministry of Pensions Sub-Committee, Meeting no. 2, 23 January 1918, PIN 15/788, PRO.

42. Sir Matthew Nathan's evidence before Ministry of Pensions Sub-Committee of the Select Committee on National Expenditure, Meeting no. 6, 6 February 1918, PIN 15/788, PRO. See also Minute Note, R. J. Cole to Hore, 16 June 1923, PIN 15/1804, PRO. "Such a course would be sure to arouse antagonism on the part of the men and, I think, the general public."

43. Board of Pensions, A Review of the Present Position with Regard to Invalidity Pensions, n.d. [1916?], PIN 15/336, PRO.

44. J. A. Flynn to Sir Matthew Nathan, 22 December 1917, "New Proposals in Warrant," PIN 15/785, PRO. See Arthur Griffith-Boscawen's response: "The fact is that rightly or wrongly (I express no opinion) the House of Commons and public opinion generally hold that the past illiberal and unsatisfactory administration of pensions was due to Treasury parsimony and interference." Response by A.G.B. to J. A. Flynn's "Facts and Formulas," PIN 15/785, PRO.

45. Hodge was minister of labour from December 1916 to August 1917. At the time of his appointment to the Ministry of Labour, he was acting chairman of the Labour Party and president of the patriotic British Workers' National League.

46. Griffith-Boscawen, *Memories,* 208.

47. Hodge, 207. See also Griffith-Boscawen, *Memories,* 208–209.

48. See Griffith-Boscawen, *Memories,* 199–200. "In most of the cases we awarded pensions; but later on when John Hodge was Minister he was hauled over the coals and charged with having acted ultra vires by the Public Account Committee on account of some decisions of the Advisory Board. John Hodge, however, was quite unconcerned; he actually boasted in the country that the charge of acting ultra vires had been brought against him, and was very proud of the fact."

49. On the Treasury during the war, see Kathleen Burk, "The Treasury: From Impotence to Power," in Burk, 84–107; Cronin, 87–92.

50. "The Pensions Muddle," *Times,* 15 July 1919, Cutting Book I, Enham. On the *Times* during the Lloyd George Coalition, see Morgan, 171.

51. On the out-of-work donation, see Garside, *British Unemployment,* 35–37.

52. Quoting Laming Worthington Evans's speech, "Village Centres," *Morning Post,* 30 October 1919, Cutting Book I, Enham.

53. The Ministry of Labour complained about "the heritage of woe that the W.P.C.'s have left us." Minute Note, [Foegamy?], 18 November 1919, Lab 2/522/TDS 3970/6/1919. See also E. Marlow's Minute Note to A.G., 22 November 1919: "When one remembers the awful mess and chaos which has been transferred to this Ministry by the Ministry of Pensions, the proposal made by the Training Department is, I think, quite reasonable."

54. International Labour Office, *Training of Disabled Men,* Appendix II, "Employment of Disabled Ex-Service Men," report submitted by Mr. J. R. J. Passmore, Ministry of Labour (Geneva, 1923), 134. Many were trained through local polytechnic institutes; see Major Mitchell, "The Present Position of the Question of Training," *Recalled to Life* 3 (April 1918): 325–341.

55. James Currie's evidence before the Select Committee on Pensions, 11 November 1919, p. 449, PIN 15/381, PRO; J. A. Flynn to Matthew Nathan, 9 August 1918, PIN 15/1838, PRO. For the Treasury's role, see Cronin; P. B. Johnson; B. B. Gilbert, *British Social Policy, 1914–1939* (London, 1970).

56. James Currie to the Minister of Labour, Minute Note of 26 July 1919, Lab 2/523/TDS 5354/1010, PRO.

57. James Currie's evidence, 11 November 1919, p. 449. For a harsh assessment of the Ministry of Labour's retraining programs, see Reese, 96. See also British Legion Planning Committee [World War II], *Training of Disabled Men,* Confidential, British Legion Archive. David Englander's judgment is more optimistic: "An absolute failure cannot be spoken of." David Englander, "Die Demobilmachung in Großbritannien nach dem ersten Weltkrieg," *Geschichte und Gesellschaft* 9 (1983): 203.

58. On the French and Belgian retraining efforts, see Matthew Price, "Bodies and Souls: The Rehabilitation of Maimed Soldiers in France and Germany during the First World War," (Ph.D. diss., Stanford University, 1998), 39–98.

59. Sir Arthur Griffith-Boscawen, *Report on the Inter-Allied Conference on the After-Care of Disabled Men* (London, 1917). According to the International Labour Office, "Work is an absolute necessity for the majority of the disabled. Before the war the vast majority of them lived on their wages. Now, as disabled men, they receive pensions which in no country are adequate for their maintenance without work, even if they are very seriously injured." ILO, *The Compulsory Employment of Disabled Men, 25 April 1921, Studies and Reports,* Series E, no. 2, 3.

60. Dr. Fortescue Fox, "The Origin, History, and Ideals of the Village Centres Movement for the Restoration of Disabled Men," Address Given to the Staff at Enham, 21 April 1920, PIN 15/34, PRO.

61. Rodney Lowe, *Adjusting to Democracy: The Role of the Ministry of Labour in British Politics, 1916–1939* (Oxford, 1986), 191–237. On the Ministry of Labour, see also Gail Savage, *The Social Construction of Expertise: The English Civil Service and Its Influence, 1919–1939* (Pittsburgh, 1996), 130–157.

62. On unions and the disabled, see Kimball, 83, 85–87, 105.

63. Select Committee on Pensions, 11 November 1919, p. 449, PIN 15/381, PRO.

64. See Johnson, *Land Fit for Heroes,* esp. 444–499; Cronin, ch. 5, esp. 87–92; Harris, "Society and the State in Twentieth-Century Britain," 3:76–80.

65. Minute Note, Foegamy [?], 18 November 1919, Lab 2/522/TDS 3970/6/1919, PRO; James Currie, Select Committee on Pensions, 11 November 1919; Minute Note, E. Marlow to A.G., 22 November 1919, Lab 2/522, TDS 3970/6/1919, PRO. On the Ministry of Labour's sympathy for private charity, see Lowe, 75.

66. Laming Worthington-Evans, quoted in "Village Centres," *Morning Post,* 30 October 1919, Cutting Book I, Enham. On Worthington-Evans, see Morgan, 86.

67. Morgan, 80–108; Johnson, *Land Fit for Heroes,* 432–499; Susan Howson, "The Origins of Dear Money, 1919–1920," *Economic History Review,* 2d ser., 27, no. 1 (1974): 88–107.

68. After the government declined to support his efforts, the renowned orthopedist Sir Robert Jones opened the specialist hospital Shepherd's Bush with voluntary contributions in 1915. In 1918, presented with the spectacular results that Shepherd's Bush had achieved (75 percent of the hospital's patients had returned to the army), the War Office pledged to fund fully the hospital's curative workshops. Transferred with the rest of the military hospitals to the Ministry of Pensions, Shepherd's Bush was closed in 1924 due to lack of funds. On Shep-

herd's Bush, see Roger Cooter, *Surgery and Society in Peace and War* (London, 1983), 79ff.: Koven, 1186–1188; Reznick, 181–211.

69. Sheffield Telegraph, "A Healing Mission," 25 October 1919, Enham, Cutting Book I. On the origins of rehabilitation efforts, see Koven, 1167–1202.

70. "The nervous energy of those who had to stay at home when others went to the front seemed to find an outlet in starting brand new societies." Elizabeth Macadam, *The New Philanthropy: A Study of the Relations between the Statutory and Voluntary Social Services* (London, 1934), 57. According to H. Smith's 1915 *War Distress and War Help,* more than 110 philanthropic societies aimed to alleviate war distress.

71. W. J. Roberts to Leete, Son & Co (Liverpool) undated [1917], Box 14, War Seal Mansions, HFAC.

72. Macadam, 245; on war charities, see Simon Fowler, "War Charity Begins at Home," *History Today,* September 1999, 17–23.

73. British Women's Hospital Committee, Final Report, 1918.

74. Annual Reports, 1918.

75. For taxation, see Cronin, 61–63. In the budget of 1918–1919, the standard rate of income tax rose from 1s. 2d. to the pound to 6s. The number of people who paid income tax more than tripled.

76. FU 12, Star and Garter Collection, British Red Cross Archives.

77. Miss Ethel Hindt to Roberts, 28 June 1919, Box 8, Stoll.

78. See FU 16 (19), Jack Cornwell Ward, Star and Garter Collection, British Red Cross Archives.

79. Sister Ada Louisa, Laundry Sister, Saint Helena's Home, West Ealing, to Rudge Harding, 9 June 1917, FU 16 (19): Jack Cornwell Ward, Star and Garter Collection, British Red Cross Archives.

80. A. Branmer to Rudge Harding, 16 February 1917, FU 16 (19), Star and Garter Collection, British Red Cross Archives.

81. See Annual Report, the Star and Garter Home, 1918; Annual Report, the Village Centre Settlement at Enham, 1919. See also Star and Garter, Quarterly Report, April–June 1923: "… and 7s from an unknown friend—one of the many anonymous donors who have from time to time contributed to the funds of the Home—who, with unfailing regularity, has sent monthly for upwards of four years, a small, but welcome gift accompanied only by the words, 'From one who is thankful.'"

82. P. Morley Hodder to J. Roberts, 17 August 1917, Box 14, HFAC.

83. Where the feeling of duty was lacking, charities sought to instill it. "Do you realise what a debt of gratitude you owe to the heroes who have been disabled in the War," asked the Prince Albert Hospital for Disabled Soldiers, concluding, "But gratitude is not enough." Charity Organisation Society, *The Annual Charities Register and Digest* (London, 1920), ii.

84. Committee on Employment of the Severely-Disabled Ex-Service Man, 3 November 1920, PIN 15/37, PRO.

85. Final Report of the Employment Bureau, August 1920, Executive Committee Minutes II, Greater London Record Office.

86. "The Star and Garter," *Sunderland Echo,* 4 July 1929, PH 10, British Red Cross Archives.

87. Admission and Discharge Books, Box 19, War Seal Mansions Collection, HFAC. Among other housing schemes was Lady Derby's thirty-apartment Wavertree House in Liverpool, opened in 1925. See "The Homeless Ex-Service Man," *Daily Post,* 24 July 1925, 361 COU 1/12, pp. 139–140, Liverpool Record Office. On a scheme inspired by Stoll's War Seal Mansions, see Disabled Soldiers' and Sailors' (Hackney) Foundation, *A Brief History of the War Memorial Homes, Wattisfield Road* (London, 1930). On the War Seal Mansions and Stoll, see chapter 3.

88. On the voluntary funding of curative workshops, see "Orthopaedic Hospital," *Daily Post,* 13 July 1917, 361 COU 1/6, p. 176, Liverpool Record Office; Haslingden Official Guide, n.d. [c. 1957], p. 13, Lancashire Record Office; Joseph Trevor Jones, *History of the Corporation of Birmingham, 1915–1935,* vol. 5, pt. 1 (Birmingham, 1940), 36–37.

89. Lord Roberts' Pamphlet, Lab 2/528/TDS 3752/9/1921, pt. 2. See also Major Algernon Tudor Craig, "Lord Roberts Memorial Workshops for Disabled Soldiers and Sailors," *Recalled to Life* 2 (September 1917): 289–294.

90. Minutes, Executive Committee, 28 October 1918, Sir John Collie in attendance, Enham.

91. Report of the Chairman of the Executive Committee (Bentinck), 1926, in Annual Report, 30 April 1926, Enham Archives.

92. In March 1934, 400 men and their families were settled permanently at Enham. Form Letter Book, Secretary Reynell J.R.G. Wrexford to Potential Donor, March 1934, p. 217, Enham Archives.

93. Sir Frederick Ponsonby to Hodge, 21 June 1918, PIN 15/3650, PRO. For registers of war charities, see Char 4, PRO. Char 4/6 for Lancastershire, for instance, registered 782 war charities, though not all were for wounded soldiers. In total, 10,000 new charitable societies were founded during the war. Frank Prochaska, *Royal Bounty: The Making of a Welfare Monarchy* (New Haven, Conn., 1995), 176.

94. J. Worsfold [M.o.P.] to C.G.L. Syers, 15 November 1939, PRO.

95. In 1917, Bernard Oppenheimer, a South African diamond magnate, took an interest in the employment possibilities for disabled veterans. Diamond-cutting, he believed, could provide skilled and highly paid work even for those servicemen who had lost the use of their legs. Moreover, a diamond factory would give British industry an opening in a field that Belgium had previously monopolized. To that end, he invested an enormous sum of his own money (more than £300,000) to equip a factory in Brighton that he planned would employ 3,000. While the factory opened on time in 1918, the Slump of the early 1920s made the diamond works unprofitable, and it shut its doors early in 1922. Oppenheimer died in 1923. Although it eventually closed (the only major private initiative to do so), the Brighton diamond works nevertheless served as a highly publicized example of individual generosity. Committee on the Employment of Severely Disabled Ex-Service Men, 24 November 1920; Ethel Wood, *Robert Mitchell: A Life of Service* (London, 1934).

96. See Susan Grayzel, *Women's Identities at War: Gender, Motherhood and Politics in Britain and France during the First World War* (Chapel Hill, N.C., 1999), esp. 1–10, 102–119.

97. See chapter 3.

98. Katherine Mayo, *Soldiers What Next!* (London, 1933), 329.

99. "Rest and Recuperation for the Disabled, the Village Centres Scheme," *Reading Standard*, 5 April 1919, Cutting Book I, Enham.

100. "The Future of the Permanently Abnormal Ex-Service Man," by Dr. Fortescue Fox, PIN 15/35, PRO.

101. J. N. Macleod, Suggestions in Connection with the Adjustment, Repair, and Renewal of Artificial Limbs, General Committee Minutes, Roehampton I, GLRO. See also Chairman to Secretary of the Ministry of Pensions, 4 November 1919, H2/QM/A 17/44, Roehampton. Despite his rhetoric, Fortescue Fox also wanted closer cooperation with the state by 1920. He suggested that Enham try to follow Roehampton's example and become an official institution. "We should approach the Minister of Pensions with some definite proposals for closer co-operation than heretofore and that any competitive spirit or feeling between the Government and ourselves should be eliminated." Minutes from 9 March 1920, Executive Committee Minutes, Enham.

102. Braithwaite, *The Voluntary Citizen*, 177. See also Kimball's comparison of the Legion's expenditure, as compared with that of the Ministry of Pensions. Kimball, 141.

103. Braithwaite, 13.

104. Macadam, 245.

105. Ethel Shakespear's testimony before the Select Committee on Pensions, 20 June 1919, p. 336, PIN 15/379, PRO.

106. *Oxford Times*, 19 April 1919, Cutting Book I, Enham.

107. *Manchester Guardian*, 22 September 1919, "For Disabled Soldiers and Sailors," Cutting Book, January 1916–June 1920, Stoll.

108. For an overview of the Schwerbeschädigtengesetz, see Jackson, 417–456.

109. Morgan, 106; Lowe, 26; Gerald Feldman, "Die Demobilmachung und die Sozialordnung der Zwischenkriegszeit in Europa," *Geschichte und Gesellschaft* 9 (1983): 156–177.

110. Kimball, 97 n. 84. For the British Legion's change of heart, see J. R. Griffin, "The Case for Compulsion," *British Legion Journal*, May 1924, 338. See also J. B. Brunel Cohen, *Count Your Blessings* (London, 1956).

111. "A National Scheme for the Employment on a Percentage Basis, of Disabled Ex-Service Men," Ministry of Labour, September 1919, Lab 2/TDX 281/1919, Box 219, PRO.

112. On the Treasury's opposition to the "waste of staff entailed by the use of gummed wafers" affixed to letterhead, see R. S. Meiklejohn, Treasury Chambers to the Secretary, M.o.L., 30 October 1919, Lab 2/221/EDX 119/2/1920, PRO.

113. Passmore's report, International Labour Office, *The Employment of Disabled Men*, 140.

114. *British Legion Journal*, January 1922, 152. According to the *Journal*, this was an improvement from the autumn of 1920, when there were 20,000 firms on the King's Roll employing about 200,000 disabled ex-servicemen. On King's Roll figures, see chapter 3. According to the Select Committee on Pen-

sions, in August 1920, there were 18,650 employers with about 173,600 disabled men. "This is obviously a quite inadequate proportion of the employers of the country, being a fifth or sixth of what it might be. The Government Departments, though they are stated to employ a higher percentage of disabled men than 5 per cent., are not yet on the Roll, though the Minister of Labour informed us that the name of H. M. Treasury on behalf of the Government Departments had recently been placed upon it. Only 382 Local Authorities in England and Wales have been enrolled out of a total of 2,514 (excluding parish councils). Report from the Select Committee on Pensions, 9 August 1920, PRO. In 1932, there were 25,000 firms on the King's Roll, employing a total of 356,000 disabled men. Major J. B. Brunel Cohen, "Has the Public Forgotten?" *British Legion Journal*, November 1932.

115. Committee on the Employment of Severely Disabled Ex-Servicemen, 3 November 1920, PIN 15/37, PRO.

116. Provisional Interim Report of the Committee on Employment of Severely Disabled Ex-Service Men, 18 January 1921, PIN 15/37, PRO.

117. For criticisms of compulsion, see H. A. Longbotham, *A Proposed National Scheme for the Permanent Settlement of the Problem of Employment for Disabled Ex-Service Sailors, Soldiers and Airmen* (Sheffield, 1919), 6; J. E. Baker, Sheffield & District Engineering Trades Employers' Association to J. B. Forbes Watson, National Confederation of Employers' Organisations, 27 May 1924, MSS 200 B/3/2/243/pt. 2, Modern Records Centre. On the role of businessmen in the Coalition, see, more generally, Morgan, 294.

118. Position of the Standing Joint Committee of Mayors of London with Regard to Unemployables, 1920, PIN 15/37, PRO.

119. Committee on the Employment of Severely Disabled Ex-Service Men, 24 and 26 November, 1920. PIN 15/37, PRO.

120. Committee on the Employment of Severely Disabled Ex-Service Men, 17 November 1920, PIN 15/37, PRO.

121. Ibid.

122. On Montague Barlow, see Lowe, 31.

123. Committee on the Employment of Severely Disabled Ex-Service Men, 9 December 1920, PIN 15/37, PRO.

124. See Hore's entry in *Who Was Who*, 1941–1950.

125. C. F. A. Hore, "State-Aided Provision of Employment—An Act of Obligation or Charity," 16 December 1920, PIN 15/37, PRO.

126. Ibid.

127. See witness from Prince Albert's Workshops, who maintained that state contributions would actually be of assistance in fund-raising.

128. Hore, "State-Aided Provision of Employment," PIN 15/37, PRO.

129. See Cronin, chs. 4, 5, Lowe, 11; R. A. Chapman and J. R. Greenaway, *The Dynamics of Administrative Reform*, 109.

130. Report from the Select Committee on Training and Employment of Disabled Ex-Service Men, 2 August 1922, Parl. Papers 1922, xi, pp. 406–407.

131. "With reference to the points made by Mr. Bowers [Barlow?]," Lab 2/522/TDS 3947/7/1919. Despite the Treasury's disapproval, J. A. Barlow openly

defended subventions to workshops such as Lord Roberts, claiming that the state's pledge to help exceptionally disabled men was one "which they will have to entertain." See also Bowers to Secretary, 5 April 1921, Lab 2/224, EDX 110/7/1921, PRO. On the Ministry of Labour's relations with the Treasury, see Lowe, esp. 50–63; on Bowers, 71. See also Savage, 130–157.

132. Helen Bolderson, *Social Security, Disability and Rehabilitation: Conflicts in the Development of Social Policy, 1914–1946* (London, 1991), 39.

133. "Re. Interdepartmental Comm. on Unemployables," Report of 23 April 1921, Hore to F. Phillips, PIN 15/2923, PRO.

134. Minute Note by Hore, 26 January 1921, PIN 15/37, PRO.

135. Report of 23 April 1921, Hore to F. Phillips, PIN 15/2923, PRO.

136. On the hostility of Horne, as chancellor of the Exchequer, to capitation grants, see Bolderson, 42–43; on Horne, see Morgan, 54, 104–105.

137. J. A. Barlow to Bowers, Minute Note of 27 September 1922, Lab 2/529/TDS 3591, 1922. In 1914, Barlow was appointed private secretary to the parliamentary secretary to the Board of Education. In 1915, he was transferred to the Ministry of Munitions, where in 1916 he became private secretary to the minister. In 1918, he came to the Ministry of Labour as principal assistant secretary in charge of the Training Department. In 1933, he was appointed principal private secretary to Prime Minister Ramsay Macdonald. Later he served as the Third Secretary in the Treasury. See *Dictionary of National Biography, 1961–1970*, entry by Austin Strutt. On Alan Barlow at the Treasury, see Lowe, 50–51.

138. Barlow to Bowers, 15 August 1921, Lab 2/1568/TDS 3752/1921, PRO. According to Barlow, Sir Bertram Boyce, the manager of the Lord Roberts Workshops, was "perfectly entitled to complain of the difficulties" that the Treasury was making for the enterprise. See also F. O. Mann to Mr. Marlow, 27 October 1919, Lab 2/523 TDS 5354/4/1919, PRO. On the policy battle over the functions of the Finance Department, see Lowe, 57–59.

139. Barlow to Bowers, 15 August 1921, Lab 2/1568/TDS 3752/1921, PRO.

140. Reese, 95.

141. Report on the 1933 Accounts, Minutes, Executive Committee, Enham. As Macadam noted, "Voluntary charities are less liable than public schemes to fluctuations of policy or economy scares" (267).

142. Mayo, 370. On Poppy Day, see also Adrian Gregory, *The Silence of Memory* (London, 1994), 99–114.

143. Hannen Swaffer, "Dancing the Dance of Death," *The People*, 9 November 1924, Cutting Book IV, J. B. Brunel Cohen, Private Collection. See Gregory, 67–71. On the postwar woman, see Mary Louise Roberts, *Civilization without Sexes: Reconstructing Gender in Postwar France, 1917–1927* (Chicago, 1994); on continuities in gender roles, see Grayzel, 5–7, 86–156, 244–246.

144. Mr. J. J. McCoy to Mr. Roberts [Minister of Pensions], 17 October 1929, PIN 15/38, PRO.

145. See, for example, Alfred Havighurst, *Britain in Transition* (Chicago, 1985), 152–153; Fussell, esp. 82–90; Hynes; Arthur Marwick, *The Deluge* (London, 1966); Winter, *The Great War and the British People*, ch. 9; Wohl. On

hostility to the Home Front, see Rosa Maria Bracco, *Merchants of Hope: British Middlebrow Writers and the First World War, 1919–1939* (Providence, R.I., 1993), 101–108.

146. In the course of my research, I found very little evidence, whether published or unpublished, to support the idea that disabled ex-servicemen were hostile toward the public. From secondary sources as well as the literature of the time, I had expected bitterness, anger, or at the very least grousing. Yet in the thousands of letters from disabled veterans that I read in philanthropic and state archives, I found almost nothing of the sort. For example, in the more than 600 letters of application to the War Seal Mansions, only one man referred to the public's obligation with any sort of ire. For similar arguments, see Kimball, 9–18, 150–151; Adrian Gregory, "Lost Generations: The Impact of Military Casualties on Paris, London and Berlin," in *Capital Cities at War: Paris, London, Berlin, 1914–1919,* ed. Jay Winter and Jean-Louis Robert (Cambridge, 1997), 99; John Fuller, *Troop Morale and Popular Culture in the British and Dominion Armies, 1914–1918* (Oxford, 1990).

147. Mr. Mackenzie to Stoll, 29 January 1932, Box 6, War Seal Mansions, HFAC.

148. *Star and Garter Magazine,* 1920–1939.

149. Recording of Bill Towers, R9, Taped 29 November 1989, Imperial War Museum, Sound Records. See also Sir Adrian Carton de Wiart, *Happy Odyssey* (London, 1950), 53–55, 76.

150. Lawson, Standing Committee D, War Pensions Bill, 19 July 1921, p. 28, PIN 15/653, PRO.

151. A. G. Webb, "Spare the Pence and Spoil the Pensioner!" *British Legion Journal,* March 1923, 215. For another positive assessment of the work of the Local Committees, see Parry and Codrington, 55.

152. Webb, "Spare the Pence and Spoil the Pensioner!" 215.

153. The first to form was the National Association of Discharged Sailors and Soldiers, which organized in 1916 under Labour Party and trade union auspices. In 1917, shortly after the despised Review of Exceptions Act subjected all men under the age of thirty-one—including those who had been disabled in service—to medical examinations and possible recall, the radical Liberal M.P. from Edinburgh, James Hogge, organized the National Federation of Discharged and Demobilized Sailors and Soldiers. The Conservative response was not slow in coming; in November 1917, the new secretary of war, Lord Derby, launched his own Comrades of the Great War. The Federation was the most vigorous of the wartime organizations. Led by the indefatigable Hogge and William R. Pringle, M.P., the Federation demanded pensions as a statutory right for all ex-servicemen, claiming that neither philanthropy nor the Poor Law could acquit the state's duties. See Stephen Ward, "Land Fit for Heroes Lost," in *The War Generation,* ed. Stephen Ward (Port Washington, N.Y., 1975), 10–37; and Latcham, 117–158.

154. On the Hyde Park clash, see *Times,* 27 May 1919.

155. At the time of the Armistice, there were four veterans' organizations (including a 1918 newcomer, the conservative and imperialist Silver Badge Party), but none were actually founded by discharged soldiers themselves. As Stephen

Ward has observed, it was not until after the war that ex-servicemen's organizations took their lead from men who themselves had served. In May 1919, a splinter group from the Federation composed largely of East End veterans and led by the ex-soldiers A.E. Mander and John Beckett founded the National Union of Ex-Servicemen (NUX). That same month, another group of Federation breakaways in Glasgow formed the International Union of Ex-Servicemen (IUX), Communist-leaning and committed to "fight for the overthrow of the capitalist system." Ward, "Land Fit for Heroes Lost," 25.

156. On surveillance, see Stephen Ward, "Intelligence Surveillance of British Ex-Servicemen, 1918–1920," *Historical Journal* 16 (March 1973): 179–188.

157. Ward, "Land Fit for Heroes Lost," 27. See also Graham Wootton, *The Official History of the British Legion* (London, 1956), 54.

158. Beginning in 1920, 40s. was the pension paid to a totally disabled man whether he was single or whether his wife and children were not pensionable—in other words, the Ministry compensated men only for the "obligations" they had at the time of their wounding. If a man later married or had more children, his pension did not increase. The total disablement pension compared favorably both with workmen's compensation and with national insurance sickness and disablement benefits. For comparative salary figures, see Winter, 236; Newman and Foster, 51. In 1920, compositors made 85s. weekly in London and 79s. 6d. in Newcastle. Laborers made 71s. 5½d. in London and 64s. 8¼d. in Manchester. Between 1919 and 1921, unemployed ex-servicemen were also eligible for the out-of-work donation. Garside, 36.

159. Antoine Prost has estimated that the French veterans' associations represented between 2.7 and 3.1 million veterans—or nearly one of every two survivors. According to Prost, "almost all" war-pensioned men belonged to a veterans' club. Antoine Prost, *In the Wake of War: "Les Anciens Combattants" and French Society* (Oxford, 1991), 44–45. Joanna Bourke explains British veterans' unwillingness to join ex-servicemen's organizations as a rejection of wartime camaraderie. See Bourke, 155–156. On the membership of the German war victims' organizations, see Whalen, 128.

160. For exemplars of each school, see Graham Wootton, *The Politics of Influence* (Cambridge, 1963); as well as his *Official History of the British Legion;* Reese, 170–171. Reese's criticism relates primarily to the 1930s.

161. Ward, 64.

162. *British Legion Journal,* April 1928, 306.

163. "How We Fight the Pensioners' Battle," *British Legion Journal,* May 1932, 407.

164. *British Legion Journal,* August 1922, 45.

165. A.G. Webb, in *British Legion Journal,* January 1923, 167.

166. Ibid.; A.G. Webb, "Spare the Pence and Spoil the Pensioner!" *British Legion Journal,* March 1923, 215.

167. Pensions were stabilized for three years from April 1923; in 1926, the stabilization was extended to 1929, when it was made final. Wootton, *Official History,* 57, 81.

168. Verbatim Report of the Annual Conference (Chichester delegate), 20 May 1929, 72.

169. Verbatim Report of the Annual Conference, 20 May 1929, 20.

170. Verbatim Report of the Annual Conference, 25 May 1931, 13.

171. Verbatim Report of the Annual Conference, 28 May 1928, 11.

172. On the notion of "fictive kinship," see Winter, *Sites of Memory, Sites of Mourning*, 49–50.

173. Resolutions of the Annual Conferences of the British Legion, British Legion Archives.

174. In 1933, the Swansea delegate cited the petition's failure to justify his call for the National Executive to take a stronger stance. "It has been a cap-in-hand policy all the time, and we should tell them for the last time that we are determined, irrespective of what happens, that we will fight the cause of these men in defiance of all regulations." Verbatim Report of the Annual Conference Held in London, 4 June 1933, 50.

175. A. G., "Pension: Legion Wants Select Committee," *British Legion Journal*, February 1926, 228. See Wootton, *Official History*, 80.

176. Wootton, *Official History*, 80.

177. T. F. Lister's speech at the 1927 Conference, Verbatim report of the Annual Conference, 5 June 1927, 22–23.

178. Minute Note, Sir Adair Hore to the Minister, 21 December 1929, PIN 15/3632, PRO. For Haig's reaction, see also Lionel Halsey to Tryon, 12 August 1926, PIN 15/3651, PRO.

179. *British Legion Journal*, March 1933; quoted in Wootton, *Official History*, 150.

180. "The Ministry of Pensions: Has It Fulfilled Its Trust?" *British Legion Journal*, April 1933, 338.

181. My account of the 1933 pensions controversy draws on Legion archives, Graham Wootton's account, and the article "Ex-Soldiers' Pension Mystery," *Evening Standard*, 27 May 1933, Cutting Book, 1932–1934, J. B. B. Cohen, Private Collection. All the quotes in the following paragraph are taken from the *Evening Standard* article.

182. See Wootton, *Official History*, 151. The Metropolitan Area held its conference on 27 May 1933. In a unanimous resolution, it formally endorsed the criticisms that the *Journal*'s editor had published. According to Wootton, the Metropolitan branch, once a Federation stronghold, was one of the more radical. See *Official History*, 166.

183. Letter to the Editor of the *British Legion Journal* by Major G. E. Cohen, *British Legion Journal*, April 1933, 352.

184. Verbatim Report of the Annual Conference of the British Legion, 1933, British Legion Archives. See also the Brixton delegate's speech: "When I took up my *Journal*...I thought 'Thank God, at last the National Executive has woke up and voiced the opinion of the men.' I thought it was not too strong at all because, as one who has dealt with thousands of cases with the Ministry, I know that you have to drag everything out of them" (41).

185. Wootton, *Official History*, 154.

186. "Army Pensions," a letter to the Editor of the *Glasgow Evening Times* from "Victimised," 16 September 1936, PIN 15/33, PRO.

187. Letter to the Editor of the *Northern Echo* (Darlington), 16 October 1937, PIN 15/1411, PRO.

188. Sir Adair Hore to Chrystal, 13 December 1933, PIN 15/790, PRO.

189. H. H. Wiles to the Secretary, 21 November 1938, Lab 20/6, PRO.

190. Incident described in "Ex-Servicemen in Distressed Areas," *Sussex County Herald,* 21 January 1938, PIN 15/3021.

191. J. H. F. Ludgate [M.o.P.] to C. G. L. Syers, 11 February 1938, PRO.

192. Re. 1937 deputation: "The outstanding impression left in the minds of those present is that there is a substantial prima facie case which must be adequately enquired into and that it is not a matter which can be left to the British Legion." Colonel Joe Nall to Ramsbotham, 11 November 1937, PIN 15/1412, PRO. In 1940, Nall took the Ministry of Pensions to task for its efforts to "sidetrack" BLESMA. Colonel Sir Joseph Nall, M.P. to Sir Walter Womersley [M.o.P.], 14 August 1940, PIN 15/2605, PRO.

193. "'Bleak House,' Old Soldiers and Pensions Ministry," *Northern Daily Telegraph,* 1 November 1938, PIN 15/1417, PRO.

194. Tapes 741 and 742, William Towers, n.d., Peter Liddle Collection, Leeds.

195. F. N. Preston [M.o.P., Manchester] to Captain R. H. Webb [M.o.P., London], 28 January 1937, Personal and Confidential, PIN 15/1409, PRO.

196. F. N. Preston to Captain R. H. Webb, 1 December 1937, PIN 15/1412.

197. See PIN 15/3021 Press Cutting File. Sir Thomas Cook speaking at the Runton Branch of the British Legion, *Norfolk Chronicle,* 28 January 1938. A. G. Webb quoted in *Somerset County Gazetter,* 23 October 1937. See letter to the editor from "Gassed at 18," 3 September 1938, *Belfast Telegraph,* PIN 15/33. See "Army Pensions," letter to the editor from "Victimised," *Glasgow Evening Times,* 16 September 1936, PIN 15/33, PRO.

198. "War Pensioners' Big Increase," *Eastern Evening News,* 31 March 1937, PIN 15/3021, PRO.

199. Mayo, 382.

200. "Conservatives in Conference," *Times,* 8 October 1937, PIN 15/1412, PRO.

201. Mr. Ellis Smith (Lab), quoted in Hansard, Tuesday, 26 October 1937, vol. 328, no. 3.

202. See Kimball, 219. Although the May committee report recommended cuts in war pensions, these were never implemented.

203. Guy Routh, *Occupation and Pay in Great Britain, 1906–1979,* 2d ed. (London, 1980), 120. See also Oksana Newman and Allan Foster, *The Value of a Pound: Prices and Incomes in Britain, 1990–1993* (New York, 1995). In London a fitter and turner made 89s. 11¼d. in 1920 and only 60s. 11d. in 1924–1926. Comparable numbers for Manchester were 84s. 11¼d., as opposed to 56s. A laborer in London made 71s. 5¼d. in 1920 but only 43s. 3½d. in 1924. Comparable figures for Manchester were 64s. 8¼d. and 38s. (151). In 1930 and 1938, a compositor earned 89s. in London and 74s. 6d. in Leeds. In 1930, a fitter and turner earned 62s. 11d. in London and 58s. in Manchester; in 1938, these figures were 70s. 11d. and 66s. In 1930, a laborer earned 45s.

3½d. in London and 40s. in Manchester; in 1938, these figures were 53s. 3½d. and 49s. (78).

204. J.B. Brunel Cohen, "Has the Public Forgotten?" *British Legion Journal*, November 1932, 157.

205. Verbatim Report of the Annual Conference held in Buxton, 1 June 1936, 37. Talk of the "generous public" was not extinguished. The next year, the Wombwell delegate expressed his confidence that the "whole of the public" would support the Legion's request for a block grant. Verbatim Report of the Annual Conference, 17 May 1937, 103.

206. "The Badly-Disabled Ex-Serviceman," *Halifax Weekly Courier and Guardian*, 21 March 1936, PIN 15/1409, PRO. Note that Bell is also talking about the British Legion's Royal Charter.

207. Quoted in the *British Legion Journal*, January 1933, 235.

208. C. Walter Hickel, "Entitling Citizens: World War I Progressivism and the Origins of the American Welfare State, 1917–1928" (Ph.D. diss., Columbia University, 1999), 128–129.

209. On Australia, see G.L. Kristianson, *The Politics of Patriotism: The Pressure Group Activities of the Returned Serviceman's League* (Canberra, 1966), 198–201, 211–212.

210. McKibbin, 166.

211. "Landestreffen der Kriegsblinden," *Städtisches Anzeigeblatt*, 2 July 1937, Stadtkanzlei, 7081/6, vol. 1, StAF. See also "Die ersten Bürger des Staates," *Waldheimer Tageblatt*, 4 July 1933, Staatskanzlei, Ausschnittsammlung, nr. 1557, Sächsisches Hauptstaatsarchiv (SHAD).

CHAPTER 2

1. Gerald Feldman, *The Great Disorder: Politics, Economics, and Society in the German Inflation, 1914–1924* (New York, 1993), table 30, p. 643; Hong, *Welfare, Modernity, and the Weimar State*, 114–115; Crew, *Germans on Welfare*, 11–12.

2. Niederschrift über die Sitzung am 12 March 1923 in RAM, Verhandlungsleiter Ministerialdirektor Dr. Wölz, RAM 9164, BAL.

3. Niederschrift über die Sitzung mit Vertretern der alt- und neubesetzen Gebiete, der Spitzenverbände der Wohlfahrtspflege, des Reichsarbeitsministeriums und des Reichsministeriums des Innern über Fragen der Anstaltsfürsorge und der allgemeinen Wohlfahrtspflege, 7 April 1923, RAM 9164, BAL.

4. On expectations, see the excellent work of Crew, *Germans on Welfare*; Greg Eghigian, "Politics of Victimization: Social Pensioners and the German Social State in the Inflation of 1914–1924," *Central European History* 26 (1993): 375–404; Eghigian, *Making Security Social*, 191–288.

5. On the consolidation of welfare organizations, see Gerhard Buck, "Die Entwicklung der freien Wohlfahrtspflege von den ersten Zusammenschlüssen der freien Verbände im 19.Jahrhundert bis zur Durchsetzung des Subsidiaritätsprinzip in der Weimarer Fürsorgegesetzgebung," in Landwehr and Baron, 139–172; Hong, *Welfare, Modernity, and the Weimar State*, esp. 44–75,

181–202; Kaiser, "Freie Wohlfahrtsverbände im Kaiserreich und in der Weimarer Republik, 26–57.

6. "Zur Kriegsinvalidenfürsorge," Siegfried von Vegesack, *Tag*, 27 October 1915, R 8034 II, Landbund, nr. 2329, BAL.

7. Resolution Mehrer Hundert Kriegsopfer, Kb und Kh aus Stadt u. Krs. Fraustadt, beauftragen heute den Vorstand der Ortsgruppe des Reichsverbandes deutscher Kriegsbeschädigter und Kriegshinterbliebener [J. A. Franke] to the Reichsarbeitsministerium, n.d. [received 5 March 1924], RAM 9238—foliated, p. 139, BAL.

8. "Der wütige Kriegsblinde," *Der Kriegsblinde*, February 1929, Rep. 62/36, Landesarchiv Berlin—Aussenstelle (LAB-A).

9. Sachße and Tennstedt, *Geschichte der Armenfürsorge in Deutschland*, vol. 2, pts. 3, 4. See also Abelshauser, 9–31; Peukert, 132–148.

10. *Soziale Praxis und Archiv für Volkswohlfahrt* 24, no. 19 (4 February 1915): 448.

11. Prof. Dr. Martin Kirchner, "Verwundeten- und Krankenfürsorge im Kriege," *Illustrirte Zeitung*, 17 December 1914, 825.

12. *Illustrirte Zeitung*, 854.

13. Kirchner, 827.

14. James Diehl, "Veterans' Politics under Three Flags," in Ward, *The War Generation*, 141.

15. Ruth Underhill, "Provision for War Cripples in Germany," *Publications of the Red Cross Institute for Crippled and Disabled Men*, 8 June 1918, 3. McMurtrie, 133; see Eghigian, 159–189.

16. Ewald Frie, *Wohlfahrtsstaat und Provinz, Westfalen und Sachsen, 1880–1930* (Paderborn, 1993), 137–138.

17. This was an arrangement replicated in West Prussia, Posen, Silesia, Pommern, Saxony, Westphalia, and Hessen Nassau.

18. Leader, *Abendblatt der Frankfurter Zeitung*, 20 January 1915, Magistrat Akte S/352, Tom 1, Stadtarchiv Frankfurt (StAF). See also Dr. Neumann, "Kriegskrüppelämter," *Tag* (Berlin), 10 March 1915, Magistrat Akte, S/352, Tom 1; "Kriegsinvalidenfürsorge," 3 March 1915, R 755, ADCV.

19. On the stance of unions, see Frie, 140; and J. Kurth, Geschäftsführer des Deutschen Metallarbeiter-Verbandes, München, *Kriegsinvalidenfürsorge und Gewerkschaften* (Munich, 1916).

20. Five million marks in 1915, another 5 million in the fall of 1917, and an additional 10 million in April 1918. On the predominance of voluntary and local programs, see Garrard Harris, *The Redemption of the Disabled* (New York, 1919), 107.

21. Leader, *Abendblatt der Frankfurter Zeitung*, 20 January 1915, Magistrat Akte S/352, Tom 1, StAF; Professor Adolf Sellmann, *Das Seelenleben unserer Kriegsbeschädigten* (Witten a.d. Ruhr: Verlag "Eckart," 1916), 3; Die Kriegsbeschädigtenfürsorge in der Provinz Westfalen, n.d. [1915?], R 755, ADCV; A. Schaidler, Direktor der K. Landesblindenanstalt, "Fürsorge für die erblindeten Soldaten," R 8034 II, Landbund, nr. 2329, BAL; Andreas Langlotz, "Kriegs-Invaliden-Fürsorge," *Bayr. Landes. Zeitung*, 20 March 1916, R 8034 II, Landbund, nr. 2329, BAL.

22. Bericht über die bisherigen Leistungen und die Aufgaben des Fürsorge-vereins für Kriegsverstümmelte, Hannover, February 1916, R 755, ADCV. See also Heimatdank leaflet, "Das tat ich für Dich! Was tust Du für mich," n.d., CA XIX/10A, ADCV.

23. "Das tat ich für Dich! Was tust Du für mich," Heimatdank leaflet, n.d. [1916?], CA XIX/10A, ADCV.

24. Verein für Kommunalwirtschaft und Kommunalpolitik, "Die Kriegs-beschädigtenfürsorge," Vorträge gehalten auf der 4. Tagung des Vereins für Kommunalwirtschaft und Kommunalpolitik (Berlin, 1916), 8; Niederschrift über die 10. Sitzung des Reichsarbeitsauschusses in Berlin, 15 December 1917, RAM 8864, BAL. See also "Die Kriegsbeschädigtenfürsorge in der Provinz Westfalen," n.d. [1915?], R 755, ADCV.

25. Quoted in Frie, *Wohlfahrtsstaat und Provinz, Westfalen und Sachsen,* 148; see also page 136.

26. Ausschuß für Kb-Fürsorge im Regierungsbezirk Cassel, "Aufruf" by v. Haugwitz, stellv. kommandierender General and Hengstenberg, Kgl. Ober-präsident, n.d. [1915?], Magistrat Akte S/352, Tom I, StAF.

27. Bessel, 26–48; Bry, 434–445; Jürgen Kocka, *Facing Total War: German Society, 1914–1918* (Leamington Spa, Warwickshire, 1984), 70–86, 119–123.

28. Dr. Erwin Steinitzer, "Invaliden Wirtschaftspolitik," *Vossische Zeitung,* 31 March 1915, Magistrat Akte S/352, Tom I, StAF. For a similar sentiment, see Dr. F. Schiller, "Kriegsbeschädigtenfürsorge," *Schlesische Zeitung,* 14 Novem-ber 1915, R 8034 II Landbund nr. 2329, BAL.

29. "Die Einarmigenschule zu Dresden," Eine Denkschrift von Gustav Curt Beyer, Dresden, am Sedantag 1917, Curt Beyer Collection, SHAD.

30. "Planlose Wohlfahrtspflege," letter from the Zentralstelle für Volkswohlfahrt, the Zentrale für private Fürsorge, and the Bureau für Sozialpolitik, *Soziale Praxis* 25, no. 22 (2 March 1916): 2. See also "Die Or-ganisation der Kriegsinvalidenfürsorge," *Concordia,* 22, no. 24 (15 December 1915): 427.

31. Der Staatskommissar für die Regelung der Kriegswohlfahrtspflege in Preußen [Geheimer Ober-Regierungsrat Schneider] to the Herrn Regierungs-präsidenten, 26 October 1915, 67. Rep. 191, 3011—foliated, GStAB.

32. Between September 1915 and March 1916, the Fatherland's Fund for the Establishment of Convalescent Homes took in 145,974 M in donations and 14,600 M in yearly membership dues. Vaterlandsspende zur Errichtung Deutscher Kb-Erholungsheime, Rechnungsabschluss und Bilanz für 1915, Rep. 191, 3705—unfoliated, GStAB.

33. Das Erholungs-Alters-und Invaliden Heim für Jäger und Schützen des deutschen Heeres, Marburg, 1 July 1916, Rep. 191, 3365, GStAB.

34. Contributions Lists, Rep. 191, 3365, GStAB.

35. See Zentrale für private Fürsorge's *Tätigkeitsbericht,* 1916–1918. Although it complained about the expansion of tasks, the Zentrale's donations actually rose significantly between 1915 and 1917. In 1915, total donations, including contri-butions from city governments of 10,000 to 15,000 M amounted to 148,950; in 1916, 157,000; and in 1917, 248,000. The income of the Saxon Heimatdank reached an all-time high in 1917. "Hauptversammlung des Vereins Heimatdank,"

Dresdner Anzeiger [Morgen], 30 December 1920, Staatskanzlei Ausschnittsammlung 1555, SHAD.

36. Analysis of Contributions List, Rep. 191, 3365—unfoliated, GStAB.

37. Studienrat Prof. Dr. Koepert, "Die bürgerliche Kriegsbeschädigtenfürsorge im Königreiche Sachsen," in *Führer durch das Gesamtgebiet der Kriegsbeschädigtenfürsorge,* ed. National-Hygiene Museum (Dresden, 1917); Wirtschaftsministerium 392, SHAD. On the dramatic growth of membership in women's patriotic associations, see Quataert.

38. "Fürsorge für Kriegsverletzte in den deutschen Bundesstaaten," *Soziale Praxis* 24, no. 17 (21 January 1915): 387. Similarly, Pastor Denker, "Die Krüppel in Zivil," *Tag,* 4 February 1916, R 8034 II, Landbund nr. 2329, BAL.

39. Dr. Schaeffer, Frankfurt, "Kb- und Khfürsorge in ihrem Aufbau und ihrer Verbindung mit der öffentlichen und privaten Wohlfahrtspflege," *Soziale Praxis* 30, no. 8 (23 February 1921): 209–211.

40. Niederschrift über die Sitzung des Arbeitsausschusses des Reichsausschusses der Kriegsbeschädigten- und Kriegshinterbliebenenfürsorge, 1 April 1927, R 758, ADCV. See also a similar statement by Caritas General Secretary Franz X. Rappenecker in "Kriegsopferfürsorge und die Caritas," p. 124, F 965, Caritas Library.

41. Bessel, 85–89; "Die Heimkehr der Soldaten: Das Bild des Frontsoldaten in der Öffentlichkeit der Weimarer Republik," in Hirschfeld, 221–239.

42. Oskar Zill, "Zur Ergänzung der Eingabe vom 26 April 1917," Rep. 191, 3570—partially foliated, p. 18, GStAB.

43. Polizeipräsidium, Charlottenburg, 11 August 1917, Rep. 191, 3570—partially foliated, p. 15, GStAB.

44. Polizeipräsidium, Charlottenburg to the Regierungspräsident, Potsdam, 15 June 1917, Rep. 191, 3570—partially foliated, p. 13, GStAB.

45. Der Leiter der Reichsgeschäftsstelle [Geib], Urschriftlich mit sämtlichen Anlagen dem Herrn Regierungspräsidenten in Potsdam, 12 November 1917, Rep. 191, 3570—partially foliated, p. 30, GStAB.

46. Oskar Zill to the Herrn Staatskommissar, 4 January 1918, Rep. 191, 3570—partially foliated, n.f., GStAB.

47. Ibid.

48. Prussia's State Commissioner was the most prominent of the officials charged with the task of regulating charity. Not only did he wield control over Germany's largest state, but his decisions set the standard for other regional commissioners. Although the implementation of the February 1917 decree varied in the German states, the Prussian decisions were widely understood as a reflection of the Labor Ministry's wishes. Hamburg's State Commissioner, for instance, often consulted his Prussian counterpart and cited Berlin's decisions as justification for his own. See 351-10 I Sozialbehörde I, EF 11.10 Band I, StAH. On the administration of the decree, see Paul Frank and Siddy Wronsky, *Die Bundesratsverordnung über Wohlfahrtspflege während des Krieges vom 15. Februar 1917* (Stuttgart, 1917).

49. Some cities did have laws on the books prohibiting certain types of collection, but most dated from the mid–nineteenth century and, with the exception of prohibitions against lotteries, were rarely enforced. In Hannover, a law of 25 May 1847 made practically every collection subject to police approval. In Magdeburg, all public collections and house-to-house collections (but not gen-

eral fund-raising or tickets to charity events) had to be approved by the police. Results of Questionnaire of 17 October 1928, RAM 9075, BAL.

50. Young-Sun Hong, "The Politics of Welfare Reform and the Dynamics of the Public Sphere: Church, Society and the State in the Making of the Social-Welfare System in Germany, 1830–1930" (Ph.D. diss., University of Michigan, 1989), 9–83.

51. Stenographischer Bericht über die Verhandlungen des Deutschen Vereines für Armenpflege und Wohltätigkeit, im Abgeordnetenhause, 23 September 1917, Rep. 191, 3012, GStAB.

52. Although charities founded before the war were required to secure permission before launching public collections, they—unlike those organizations founded after the war—could advertise for members without first obtaining approval. See Abschrift für die Akten, "Gesetzliche Neuregelung der Bundesratsverordnung vom 15. Februar 1917," Preußischer Staatskommissar für die Regelung der Wohlfahrtspflege, 9 April 1923, Rep. 191/3013 [neu: 6000a]—foliated, p. 82, GStAB.

53. Gesetz zur Regelung der öffentlichen Sammlungen und sammlungsähnlichen Veranstaltungen, Reichsgesetzblatt I, p. 1086. Der Reichs- und Preußische Minister des Innern an die Landesregierung für Preußen, 7 November 1934, E 151/09, 314, Hauptstaatsarchiv Stuttgart (HStAS).

54. Stenographischer Bericht über die Verhandlungen des 35. Deutschen Vereines für Armenpflege und Wohltätigkeit, 21 and 22 September 1917, p. 133, Rep. 191, 3012, GStAB.

55. Stenographischer Bericht, p. 137, Rep. 191, 3012, GStAB.

56. Stenographischer Bericht über die Verhandlungen des Deutschen Verein für Armenpflege und Wohltätigkeit, p. 145, Rep. 191, 3012, GStAB.

57. "Zusammenstellung der unter Verwaltung stehenden Organisationen," Fritz Maercker to the Polizeipräsidium, 4 June 1921, Rep. 191, 3012, GStAB.

58. Committee on the Supervision of Charities: Report of the Home Office Departmental Committee on the Supervision of Charities, Presented to Parliament by Command of His Majesty, March 1927 (London, 1927). According to the April 1916 War Charities Act, charities had to be registered with the local council. See HO 45/10804/308566, PRO. Registration was automatic unless the council could prove that the charity was not established in good faith or would not be properly administered. As of September 1926, there were 11,950 registered war charities. Only 52 had been refused registration (14). In response to those who favored stricter regulation, the Home Office Committee replied: "There is no touchstone in the administration of charity: nobody can say positively that a departure from recognised ways is useless or dangerous until it has at least been tried." Doubting that local authorities could be "entrusted" with the task of regulation, they noted further: "We are still more doubtful whether the charitably disposed would not greatly resent any such interference with their freedom and initiative, and whether the effect of such measures would not be to paralyze a large amount of beneficial charitable effort" (26).

59. Stenographischer Bericht über die Verhandlungen des Deutschen Verein für Armenpflege und Wohltätigkeit, p. 145, Rep. 191, 3012, GStAB.

60. Gerald Feldman, *Army, Industry and Labor, 1914–1918* (Princeton, N.J., 1966), 270.

61. Minutes of the NAfFik meeting, 29 January 1917, CA XIX 15, ADCV.

62. Tennstedt and Sachße, 2:68–87; Crew, *Germans on Welfare*, 22; Peukert, 46–52; Elizabeth Harvey, *Youth and the Welfare State in Weimar Germany* (Oxford, 1993), 152–185; Preller, 34–85.

63. Hong, *Welfare, Modernity, and the Weimar State*, esp. 16–35 44–75, 181–202; Crew, *Germans on Welfare*, 18–21; Kaiser, "Freie Wohlfahrtsverbände im Kaiserreich und in der Weimarer Republik," 26–57; Buck, 139–172. The six "leading organizations" were the Protestant Inner Mission, the Catholic Caritasverband, the Central Welfare Office for German Jews, the German Red Cross, the Fifth Welfare Society, and the Central Welfare Committee of Christian Workers. Workers' Welfare refused to join the League.

64. Hong, *Welfare, Modernity, and the Weimar State*, esp. 15–16, 44–75, 181–202.

65. Tennstedt and Sachße, esp. 2:160–161; Buck, 166–171.

66. Buck, 145; Tennstedt and Sachße, 2:167–168.

67. Christoph Sachße, *Mütterlichkeit als Beruf* (Frankfurt, 1986), 182–186; Edward Dickinson, 66–68, 151–153; Hong, 53–54; Tennstedt and Sachße, 2:161–162. On the Arbeiterwohlfahrt, see Christiane Eifert, *Frauenpolitik und Wohlfahrtspflege: Zur Geschichte der sozialdemokratischen "Arbeiterwohlfahrt"* (Frankfurt, 1993); Christiane Eifert, "Coming to Terms with the State: Maternalist Politics and the Development of the Welfare State in Weimar Germany," *Central European History,* 30 (1997): 25–47.

68. Gerald Feldman, *The Great Disorder* (Oxford, 1993); Wilfried Rudloff, *Der Wohlfahrtsstaat* (Göttingen, 1998); Crew, 18.

69. Mary Nolan, *Visions of Modernity: American Business and the Modernization of Germany* (New York, 1994), 133–134.

70. Joachim von Winterfeldt, *Kriegsbeschädigtenfürsorge,* 8.

71. Staatssekretär des Reichsschatzamts [Schiffers] to the Herrn Staatssekretär des Reichsarbeitsamts, 21 January 1919, RAM 8862, BAL. In April 1919, the Republic provided a fund of 300 million marks, intended to provide means for medical care and rehabilitation efforts, as well as to pay a 40 percent inflationary supplement to pensioners, while another 10 million was divided among the provinces. In October 1919, the Reich took over a third of administrative costs. The Reichsversorgungsgesetz made employment counseling and retraining the duty of the nation. As of April 1920, the Reich paid four-fifths of the cost, while the province and city were responsible each for one-tenth. See "Die Entwicklung der sozialen Kriegsbeschädigten- und Kriegshinterbliebenenfürsorge," *Soziale Praxis* 29, no. 34 (10 May 1920): 806.

72. Dr. Schaeffer, Frankfurt, "Kriegsbeschädigten- und Kriegshinterbliebenenfürsorge in ihrem Aufbau und ihrer Verbindung mit der öffentlichen und privaten Wohlfahrtspflege," *Soziale Praxis* 30, no. 8 (23 February 1921): 211.

73. "Die Übernahme der Kriegsfürsorge durch das Reich," *Deutsche Allgemeine Zeitung* [Abend], 5 December 1919, Staatskanzlei, Ausschnittssammlung, nr. 1554, SHAD.

74. Dr. Franz Schweyer, Ministerialdirektor im Reichsarbeitsministerium, "Der Wiederaufbaugedanke in der Kriegsversorgung und Kriegsfürsorge," Sonder-Abdruck aus der Zeitschrift *Die Kriegsbeschädigten und Kriegshinterbliebenenfürsorge,* no. 6, December 1919.

75. Peter-Christian Witt, "Auswirkungen der Inflation auf die Finanzpolitik," in Feldman, table 9, p. 93.

76. Hessisches Ministerium für Arbeit und Wirtschaft, Hauptfürsorgestelle der Kriegsbeschädigten- und Kriegshinterbliebenenfürsorge, J.V., im Entw. gez. Linkenheld, beglaubigt gez. Berntheusel über das Kreiswohlfahrtsamt Dieburg, p. 99, Rep. 191, 3016, neu: 6000—foliated, GStAB.

77. On wartime opposition to the decree, see especially Der Erzbischof von Cöln [Felix Kard. v. Hartmann] to the Deutschen Reichskanzler, 20 October 1918, RAM 8869, BAL; Denkschrift des Deutschen Caritasverbandes, "Soll die Staatsaufsicht über die neue Wohlfahrtspflege in die Friedenzeit hinübergenommen werden?" 1917, pp. 9–10, Rep. 191, 3012, GStAB; Friedrich Zahn, "Staatliche Aufsicht über die freiwillige Wohlfahrtspflege," *Archiv der hamburgischen Gesellschaft für Wohltätigkeit* 8 (December 1916): 15. The Zentralstelle für Volkswohlfahrt agreed. See Gutachten über den Plan zur Errichtung eines Archivs der deutschen Stiftungen, Wi. Th. v. Erdbay, 10 February 1917, RAM 8866, BAL. *Concordia* ran a positive review of Zahn's pamphlet. See R. v. Erdberg, *Concordia* 24, no. 5 (March 1917).

78. Siddy Wronsky, "Die Regelung der privaten Wohlfahrtspflege," *Zeitschrift für das Armenwesen* 16 (1915): 182–188. The debate among supporters and opponents of state supervision is captured in Stenographischer Bericht über die Verhandlungen des 35. Deutschen Armenpflegetages des deutschen Vereins für Armenpflege und Wohltätigkeit, 21/22 September 1917 in Berlin (Munich, 1918), 114–200. See also the earlier discussion at the December 1916 meeting of the Union for Private War Welfare Work. Bericht über die Tagung der "Freien Vereinigung für Kriegswohlfahrt," in Göttingen, 9 and 10 December, 1916, Rep. 191, 3012, GStAB; "Die neue Bundesratsverordnung über Wohlfahrtspflege während des Krieges," *Soziale Praxis* 26, no. 23 (8 March 1917): 470. On postwar opposition, Reichsarbeitsminister [LW] to the Leipziger Finanzausschuß, 1 August 1919, RAM 9015, BAL; Reichsgemeinschaft von Hauptverbänden der freien Wohlfahrtspflege, Response to Polligkeit's article in *Soziale Praxis,* 18 October, n.d. [November 1922?] RAM 9236—foliated, f. 149, BAL.

79. Der Vorsitzende des Reichsarbeitsausschusses [gez. von Winterfeldt] to the Polizeipräsidium, 26 May 1917, Rep. 191, 3705, GStAB.

80. Der RAM to the Ministerium des Innern, z.Hd. des Herrn Geheimrats Gräser, 6 September 1919, Rep. 191, 3185—unfoliated, GStAB.

81. Memo, Abschrift, gez. Polizeirat Wendel, 5 September 1919; RAM [Gassner] to the Ministerium des Innern, z.Hd. des Herrn Geheimrats Gräser, 10 September 1919, Rep. 191, 3185—unfoliated, GStAB. Franz Oskar Karstedt (1884–1953) came to the National Committee as a Referent in 1918. During the

years 1906–1913, he had served in the colonial administration in German East Africa. In the fall of 1913, he was pensioned because of severe illness. In 1919, he joined the Labor Ministry as a Regierungsrat and was promoted the next year to Ministerialrat. He remained at the Labor Ministry until he retired.

82. Karstedt to Silex, n.d. [1919], Abschrift, Pr.Br. Rep. 30 Berlin C, Tit. 122, Nr. 483, Bd. 1, Brandenburgisches Landeshauptarchiv Potsdam (BLHA).

83. Protokoll der Sitzung des Gesamtvorstandes der Deutschen Kriegsblindenstiftung für Landheer und Flotte, Rep. 62/7, LAB-A.

84. On Ritter, see Crew, *Germans on Welfare*, 19.

85. Der Polizeipräsident [im Auftrage, Wollenburg] to the Herrn Preußischen Staatskommissar, 16 October 1924, RAM 9332, BAL.

86. Adolf Pochwadt to the Vorstand der Deutschen Kriegsblindenstiftung für Landheer und Flotte, 5 January 1925 [Abschrift to Staatskommissar], Rep. 191, 3185—unfoliated, GStAB.

87. Der Polizeipräsident to the Sachsen-Weimarische Staatsministerium, 28 March 1919, Rep. 191, 3185—unfoliated, GStAB.

88. Pochwadt to the Herrn Preussischen Staatskommissar für die Regelung der Wohlfahrtspflege, 27 April 1925, Rep. 191, 3185—unfoliated, GStAB. So far as I have been able to establish, Pochwadt was referring to the businessmen Georg and Heinrich Sklarz, not to the infamous Sklarek family.

89. Vermerk, Der RAM, 4 December 1919, RAM 9053, BAL.

90. Der Staatskommissar für die Regelung der Kriegswohlfahrtspflege to the Herren Oberpräsidenten, 12 November 1921, Rep. 191, 3012, GStAB.

91. Der Regierungspräsident Cassel [v. Hartmann] to the Herrn Staatskommissar, 9 August 1920, Rep. 191, 3365—unfoliated, GStAB.

92. Der RAM [Geib] to the Herrn Reichsminister der Finanzen, 31 July 1919, RAM 9043, BAL.

93. Der RAM [G.b.] to the Herrn Reichsminister der Finanzen, 13 April 1920, RAM 9043, BAL.

94. Der RAM [Geib] to the Herrn Reichsminister der Finanzen, 31 July 1919, RAM 9043, BAL.

95. Der Reichsarbeitsminister, Vermerk, 29 September 1919, RAM 9043, BAL. See also Auszug aus dem Schreiben to the Herrn Reichsminister der Finanzen vom 6 August 1919, RAM 9043, BAL.

96. Der Polizeipräsident [in Vertretung, gez. Trewendt] to the Herrn Staatskommissar, 7 August 1923, Rep. 191/3206, n.f. See also criticism from the Preuß. Staatskommissar an den Herrn RAM, 21 August 1923, Rep. 191/3206, n.f.; Der RAM [im Auftrage, gez. Knackstedt] an den Herrn Preuss. St., 28 March 1924, Rep. 191/3206, n.f., GStAB.

97. Der Preußische Minister für Volkswohlfahrt to the Herrn Reichsarbeitsminister, 9 June 1932, RAM 9114, BAL. See also Der Reichsarbeitsminister (im Auftrage, gez. Dr. Ritter) an den Herrn Preußischen Staatskommissar, 1 October 1924, Rep. 191/3206, GStAB.

98. Stadtrat Gimkiewicz to the Herrn Ministerialdirektor, 16 February 1921, Rep. 191, 3969—unfoliated, GStAB. Petitioning for a salary raise, for example, the expert Gimkiewicz cited the amount of money he had managed to "secure" for the state.

99. Staatskommissar to the Herrn Minister des Innern, 24 June 1921, Rep. 191, 3969—unfoliated, GStAB.

100. Most extraordinary of all was the State Commissioner's request that Maercker deposit the funds that he had confiscated in a bank account bearing his own name, presumably so that his salary could be paid with less difficulty. These peculiar arrangements did not go unnoticed. Throughout the early 1920s, Maercker was the target of criticism, most of it from people whose organizations he had closed down. Although an audit exonerated the chief expert, a bank account in his name, filled with confiscated funds, remained a source for damaging rumors. Maercker to the Polizeipräsident, Potsdam, 9 October 1920, Abschrift, Rep. 191, 3902, GStAB.

101. Preußischer Staatskommissar für die Regelung der Wohlfahrtspflege to the Herrn Polizeipräsidenten, Abt. 1, 20 July 1922, Rep. 191, 3902, GStAB.

102. Ibid.

103. Knut Borchardt, "Economic Causes of the Collapse of the Weimar Republic," in *Perspectives on Modern German Economic History and Policy*, ed. Knut Borchardt (Cambridge, 1991); Harold James, *The German Slump* (Oxford, 1986), 85–109, 209-213; Jürgen von Kruedener, ed., *Economic Crisis and Political Collapse: The Weimar Republic, 1924–1933* (New York, 1990).

104. See Reichsverordnung über die Fürsorgepflicht, § 5, Abs. 1–3, Denkschrift des RAMs über die Vorarbeiten zu einem Reichswohlfahrtsgesetz, Entwurf, February 1923, RAM 9234, BAL.

105. Hong, *Welfare, Modernity, and the Weimar State*, 76, 86; Kaiser, "Freie Wohlfahrtsverbände," 46.

106. Sachße and Tennstedt, 2:170. Between 1922 and 1924, the Labor Ministry distributed 1,000 million marks to organized benevolence, the largest such subvention ever awarded. Half went to institutions run by the League's members; 300,000 went to Ländern for local organizations; the Labor Ministry and the Ministry of the Interior retained control over the disbursement of an additional 200,000. On the 1923 law, see Hong, "Politics of Welfare Reform," 344–347.

107. See Sachße, *Mütterlichkeit als Beruf*, 220–221.

108. Hong, *Welfare, Modernity, and the Weimar State*, 14–15.

109. Else Wex, *Die Entwicklung der sozialen Fürsorge in Deutschland* (Berlin, 1929), 52; for similar sentiments, see Crew, *Germans on Welfare*, 29–31, 210; Hong, *Welfare, Modernity, and the Weimar State*, 217–228.

110. Ministerialrat Dr. Karstedt, "Zum Schutze der privaten Wohlfahrtspflege," n.d. [1920], p. 301, RAM 9036, BAL; published in the *Reichsarbeitsblatt* 1. Jahrgang, nr. 11, 11 October 1920. See also Der RAM [Krastedt] to the Zentralstelle des Deutschen Städtetages, 19 November 1920, Rep. 142/1, Nr. 3200 Landesarchiv Berlin-Kalckreuthstraße.

111. Ministerialrat Dr. Karstedt, "Zum Schutze der privaten Wohlfahrtspflege," n.d. [1920], p. 303, RAM 9036, BAL.

112. Deutsche Kriegsblindenstiftung für Landheer und Flotte, Schlussbericht, 30 November 1926, RAM 9332, BAL.

113. Vermerk, RAM, 21 March 1919, "Ist die private Wohlfahrtspflege für Kriegsbeschädigte und Kriegshinterbliebene überflüssig geworden?" RAM 9036,

BAL. From 1915 onward, the officials of the Fatherland Fund had complained to the State Commissioner that the Bundesrat decree diminished voluntary enthusiasm, and endangered the organization's reputation. Vaterlandsspende [Dr. Belian] to the Herrn Geheimrat Regierungsrat Schlosser, 13 September 1915; Der Vorstand der Vaterlandsspende to the Herrn Staatskommissar, 10 January 1916; Dr. Belian to the Herrn Staatskommissar, 15 August 1918, Rep. 191, 3705—unfoliated, GStAB.

114. The state commissioner noted that the courts were generally unwilling to prosecute people who collected without permission. Preußischer Staatskommissar für die Regelung der Wohlfahrtspflege [Peters] to the Herrn Reichsarbeitsminister, 22 July 1932, RAM 9075, BAL.

115. For a biography of Kreutz, see Hans-Josef Wollasch, *Benedict Kreutz* (Freiburg, 1979); Hans-Josef Wollasch, "Benedict Kreutz," in *Zeitgeschichte in Lebensbildern,* Band 5: *Aus dem deutschen Katholizismus des 19. und 20. Jahrhunderts,* ed. Jürgen Aretz, Rudolf Morsey, and Anton Rauscher (Mainz, 1982), 118–133.

116. Niederschrift über die Sitzung des Arbeitsausschusses des Reichsausschusses der Kriegsbeschädigten- und Kriegshinterbliebenenfürsorge, 1 April 1927, R 758, ADCV. For another view from Caritas, see Generalsekretär Franz X. Rappenecker, "Kriegsopferfürsorge und die Caritas," Sonderabdruck aus *Fürsorgerecht und Caritas* (Freiburg, 1917), p. 124, F 965, Caritas Library.

117. Niederschrift über die Sitzung des Arbeitsausschusses des Reichsausschusses der Kriegsbeschädigten- und Kriegshinterbliebenenfürsorge, 1 April 1927, R 758, ADCV.

118. "Öffentliche Kriegsopferhilfe: Reden und Schriften von Benedict Kreuz," 081/01-327:16, ADCV.

119. Niederschrift über die Sitzung des Arbeitsausschusses des Reichsausschusses der Kriegsbeschädigten- und Kriegshinterbliebenenfürsorge, 1 April 1927, R 758, ADCV.

120. "Prälat Dr. Kreutz über die Caritas," *Oberschlesische Rundschau,* 78, 6 April 1927, CA XIX/4, ADCV.

121. Niederschrift über die Sitzung des Arbeitsausschusses des Reichsausschusses der Kriegsbeschädigten- und Kriegshinterbliebenenfürsorge, 1 April 1927, R 758, ADCV.

122. Whalen, 128. The Social Democratic Reichsbund der Kriegsbeschädigten, Kriegsteilnehmer und Kriegshinterbliebenen (National Association of Disabled Soldiers, Veterans, and War Dependents), founded in 1917, was the largest organization, with 639,856 members in 1921. The Kyffhäuser Bund, a prewar veterans' organization, followed, with 225,392. The moderate Einheitsverband (Unity League), founded in 1919, had 209,194 members. Another 1919 founding, the conservative Zentralverband deutscher Kriegsbeschädigter und Kriegshinterbliebener (Central Association of Disabled German Veterans and War Dependents) had 156,320 members; the communist Internationaler Bund der Opfer des Krieges und der Arbeit (International Association of the Victims of War and Work), founded in 1919, 136,883; the Deutscher Offiziersbund, 27,435; the Bund erblindeter Krieger (League of Blinded Warriors), founded in 1916, 2,521. Throughout the Republic, membership in war victims' organiza-

tions fluctuated significantly, declining in most cases from 1921. In January 1924, for instance, the Reichsbund had only 245,410 members in 4,075 local branches. By December 1926, it had 324,580 members organized in 5,156 branches. Geschäftsbericht des Bundesvorstandes und Bundesausschusses für die Zeit vom 1. Januar 1924 bis 31 März 1927, *Reichsbund*, 1927, p. 5, 351-10 I, Sozialbehörde I, KO 80. 11, f. 42, Staatsarchiv Hamburg. There is a large literature on Weimar veterans. Among others, Volker Berghahn, *Der Stahlhelm: Bund der Frontsoldaten, 1918–1935* (Düsseldorf, 1966); James Diehl, *Paramilitary Politics in Weimar Germany* (Bloomington, Ind., 1977); Karl Rohe, *Das Reichsbanner Schwarz-Rot-Gold* (Düsseldorf, 1966); Kurt Schuster, *Der rote Frontkämpferbund, 1924–1929* (Düsseldorf, 1975).

123. See, for instance, "Terror der Kriegsbeschädigten in Elberfeld," *Deutsche Tageszeitung*, 28 October 1919; Eghigian, 183–189.

124. See Rudolph Karsten, *Die sächsische Sozialdemokratie vom Kaiserreich zur Republik, 1871–1923* (Cologne, 1995). On the violence of the disabled, see "Eine Demonstration im Rathaus," *General Anzeiger*, 10 December 1919, Magistrat Akte 3/352, Tom 3, StAF; "Aufschreitungen von Kriegsbeschädigten in Spandau," *Berliner Tageblatt* [Morgen], 13 December 1919, Staatskanzlei, Ausschnittssammlung, nr. 1554, SHAD; "Der Magistratskommissar für die Kriegsbeschädigten-Fürsorge in Berlin," *Zentralblatt für Kriegsbeschädigte und Kriegshinterbliebene*, 16 August 1920, 122.

125. Whalen calculates that between 1924 and 1928, if transfer payments to the states and reparations are excluded, pensions tied up at least 30 percent of the funds available to the Reich.

126. Ewald Frie, "Vorbild oder Spiegelbild? Kriegsbeschädigtenfürsorge in Deutschland, 1914–1919," in Michalka, 564.

127. Whalen, 164, 165.

128. Diehl, "Victors or Victims?" 718, 719.

129. "Die Nationalversammlung und die Kriegsopfer," *Zentralblatt für Kriegsbeschädigte und Kriegshinterbliebene*, 16 March 1920, 41–42.

130. Geyer, "Ein Vorbote des Wohlfahrtsstaates," 230–277, esp. 257–258; Frie, 144.

131. Forderungen der Lazarettkranken, *Frankfurter Zeitung*, Morgen Ausgabe, 4 September 1919, Staatskanzlei, Ausschnittssammlung, nr. 1554, SHAD.

132. Frie, 149. On demands for the socialization of charity, see Dr. Philipp Heinrich Laub, *Die Kriegsbeschädigten- und Kriegshinterbliebenenversorgung: Das grundsätzlich Neue im Reichsversorgungsgesetz vom 12. Mai 1920* (Würzburg, 1921), 51; Resolution, Reichsbund der Kriegsbeschädigten und ehemaligen Kriegsteilnehmer, Ortsgruppe Groß-Berlin, 30 November 1918, RAM 8871, BAL.

133. Niederschrift über die Sitzung des Arbeitsausschusses des Reichsausschusses der Kriegsbeschädigten- und Kriegshinterbliebenenfürsorge, 1 April 1927, R 758, ADCV; "Öffentliche Kriegsopferhilfe: Reden und Schriften von Benedict Kreuz," 081/01-327:16, ADCV.

134. "Der Dank des Vaterlandes ist Euch gewiß," *Deutsche Tageszeitung*, 14 May 1920, Staatskanzlei, Ausschnittssammlung, nr. 1554, SHAD.

135. "Die Kriegszermalmten," *Dresden-Pirnauer Tageblatt*, 23 December 1920, Staatskanzlei, Ausschnittssammlung, nr. 1555, SHAD. The Labor Min-

istry opposed all such "special collections" for men in lazarets. Martineck, Response to article by Willy Meyer, 17 February 1923, BAL.

136. Reinh. Schumann, "Der Kampfcharakter unserer Organisation," *Reichsbund*, 15 April 1921, 118.

137. "Friede den Menschen auf Erden," *Zentralblatt für Kriegsbeschädigte und Kriegshinterbliebene*, no. 2 (16 January 1920): 1–2.

138. "Oeffentliche Versammlung der Kriegsbeschädigten und Kriegshinterbliebenen," *Wurzener Tageblatt*, 16 September 1919, Staatskanzlei, Ausschnittsammlung, nr. 1554, SHAD.

139. Whalen, 128.

140. Reichsvereinigung Heimatdank E.D. [Butterbrot] an Herrn Ministerialdirektor Bracht, 29 January 1921; Der Zentralverband deutscher Kriegsbeschädigter und Kriegshinterbliebener. Herausgegeben von der Verbandsleitung, Verlag der Vaterländischen Verlags und Kunstanstalt, p. 8, Rep. 191, 4044, GStAB.

141. Der Zentralverband deutscher Kriegsbeschädigter und Kriegshinterbliebener, p. 24, Rep. 191, 4044, GStAB.

142. Ibid., 15–16.

143. Ibid., 16.

144. Quoted in Der Zentralverband deutscher Kriegsbeschädigter und Kriegshinterbliebener, p. 34, Rep. 191, 4044, GStAB. For a critique of the Reichsbund's public outreach, see "Der Kampf mit vergifteten Waffen," *Zentralblatt für Kriegsbeschädigte und Kriegshinterbliebene*, 16 May 1921, 75.

145. Reichsvereinigung, Satzungen, n.d. [Dec. 1920], Rep. 191, 4044, GStAB.

146. Ibid.

147. For the Reichsbund's opposition to the Zentralverband's campaign, see "Die Sammeltätigkeit des Zentralverbandes," *Reichsbund*, 2 October 1920, 154. Note, however, that the Reichsbund began to collect themselves. Auszug aus der Niederschrift über die Referentenbesprechung, Genehmigung einer Warenlotterie für den Reichsbund der Kriegsbeschädigten, 4 May 1926, 351-10 I, Sozialbehörde I, EF 11,10 Band 2, f. 41, Staatsarchiv Hamburg (StAH).

148. Polizeipräsident Groß-Berlin Abt. 1 [im Auftrage, Wollenburg] to the Herrn Staatskommissar, 24 May 1921, Rep. 191, 4044, GStAB.

149. See Der Staatskommissar für die Regelung der Kriegswohlfahrtspflege in Preußen to the Herrn Reichsarbeitsminister, 18 July 1921, Rep. 191, 3605, ff. 168-169, GStAB. For the Labor Ministry's point of view, see Der Reichsarbeitsminister to the Staatsministerium des Innern in Munich, in Vertretung gez. Dr. Geib, 3 January 1922 [Abschrift], Rep. 191, 3605, ff. 251–252, GStAB.

150. Oberlandesgericht, Stuttgart, Feriensenat als Strafsenat, Urteil. In der Strafsache gegen Wilhelm Wolf, Kaspar Ottersbach, Walter Weichhold, 17 September 1923 [gez. Hess, Gaupp, Koch, Schmid, Rau], RAM 9011—partially foliated, BAL.

151. Beschluß des Amtsgerichts Berlin Mitte Abt. 135, Der Antrag der Staatsanwaltschaft gegen den Geschäftsführer Karl Butterbrodt, 30 April 1921, p. 18, Rep. 191/3013 [neu:6000a]—foliated, GStAB.

152. The left-leaning war-victims' associations, including the Reichsverband and the Reichsbund, opposed the Zentralverband's campaign and the Labor

Ministry's decision. Although branches of the Reichsbund had applied many times for permission to collect on behalf of its members, its leadership protested what they saw as the Association's attempt to keep veterans out of politics. The Reichsverband feared that the Zentralverband's campaign would serve to relieve the state of its responsibilities to the disabled. See the Niederschrift über die 7. Sitzung des Reichsausschusses der Kriegsbeschädigten- und Kriegshinterbliebenenfürsorge, RAM 8907, BAL. For the organization's reactions to the new welfare law, see Der Verbandsvorsitzende, Reichsverband Deutscher Kriegsbeschädigter und Kriegshinterbliebener, Leipzig, to the RAM, 4 April 1924; Reichsbund der Kriegsbeschädigten, Kriegsteilnehmer und Kriegerhinterbliebenen, Bundesvorstand to the Reichsarbeitsministerium, RAM 9080, BAL. On the Zentralverband's later controversial campaigns, see Rep. 191, 3651, esp. ff. 27–29, 85–87, 124–136, GStAB. For the dissolution of the Reichsvereinigung Heimatdank, later Reichsvereinigung Kriegertreue, see Niederschrift der Verhandlungen der Hauptversammlung der Reichsvereinigung Kriegertreue e.V., 18 February 1926, Rep. 191, 3651, ff. 96–97, GStAB.

153. "Der Abbau der Versorgung," *Freiburger Tagespost* 60 (11 March 1923), CA XIX 10B, ADCV.

154. Paul Marx, Geschäftsführer der Ortsgruppe Dresden des Reichsbundes, "Das Los der Kriegsopfer," *Volkszeitung Dresden,* 3 December 1923, Staatskanzlei, Ausschnittsammlung, nr. 1556, SHAD.

155. "Ein Notruf unserer Kriegsbeschädigten," von Otto Thiel, *Leipziger Nachrichten,* 8 March 1922, Staatskanzlei, Ausschnittsammlung, nr. 1556, SHAD.

156. Open letter by Otto Thiel, quoted in "Wohin mit den Schwerbeschädigten?" *Schwäbischer Merkur,* Stuttgart Morgen, 26 March 1924, Staatskanzlei, Ausschnittsammlung, nr. 1556, SHAD.

157. Deutsche Kriegsblindenstiftung für Landheer und Flotte, Schlussbericht, 30 November 1926, RAM 9332, BAL. See also Bund erblindeter Krieger, "Entwicklung, Bedeutung und seine Stellung zur Rentenversorgung und Fürsorge," April 1926, R 116/331, BAK.

158. According to Sachße and Tennstedt, approximately four times as many Germans received public assistance as in prewar years (81). See Whalen, 151.

159. For an analysis of the social rifts caused and deepened by the hyperinflation see Feldman, *The Great Disorder,* 513–575, 854–858.

160. Niederschrift über die Sitzung des Arbeitsausschusses des Reichsausschusses der Kriegsbeschädigten- und Kriegshinterbliebenenfürsorge, 1 April 1927, R 758, ADCV.

161. For an example of the Fürsorgegesetz in practice, see 351-9, Kriegsbeschädigten- und Kriegshinterbliebenenfürsorge, A II b 6 e, f. 21, StAH.

162. Niederschrift über die 15.Bezirksleitersitzung, 25 October 1923, 351-9, Kriegsbeschädigten- und Kriegshinterbliebenenfürsorge, A II b 24, f. 25, StAH.

163. Resolution Mehrer Hundert Kriegsopfer, Kb und Kh aus Stadt u. Krs. Fraustadt, beauftragen heute den Vorstand der Ortsgruppe des Reichsverbandes deutscher Kriegsbeschädigter und Kriegshinterbliebener [J. A. Franke] to the Reichsarbeitsministerium, n.d. [received 5 March 1924], RAM 9238—foliated, p. 139, BAL.

164. Kreistag des Regierungsbezirks Dresden des Reichsverbandes deutscher Kriegsbeschädigter, "Kriegsopfer-Tagung," *Volkszeitung Dresden,* 31 March 1924, Staatskanzlei, Auschnittsammlung, nr. 1556, SHAD.

165. In 1930, 897,940 veterans received disability pensions, as compared with 792,143 in 1926—an increase of over 13 percent. Whalen, 168.

166. Richard J. Evans and Dick Geary, *The German Unemployed* (New York, 1987), 6.

167. "Die Rückläufigkeit der Versorgung und Fürsorge für die Kriegsopfer im Zeichen der Notverordnungen, Eine Denkschrift an die Reichsregierung und den Reichstag," Reichsbund der Kriegsbeschädigten, Kriegsteilnehmer und Kriegerhinterbliebenen," 20 November 1931, 351-10 I, Sozialbehörde I, KO 80.11, f. 84, StAH.

168. "Unverschämte Hetze gegen die Kriegsopfer," *Reichsbund,* 10 November 1930; Otto Thiel, "Unseren Gefallenen," *Zentralblatt für Kriegsbeschädigte und Kriegerhinterbliebene,* April 1930, 38. "Sparkonto; Kriegsopferversorgung," *Der Deutsche,* 5 March 1930, cited in Whalen, 218; Niederschrift über die Sitzung des Arbeitsausschusses des Reichsausschusses der Kriegsbeschädigten und Kriegshinterbliebenenfürsorge, 17 June 1930, R 758, ADCV. "Dieses Jahr müssen 1 1/2 Milliarden an die Kriegsbeschädigten gezahlt werden!" *8 Uhr Abendblatt* [Berlin], 4 January 1929, 61 Sta 1/1148, BAL. See also the many allegations about frauds. Whalen, 171. On the April 1931 Reichsbund protests, see "Eindrucksvolle Kundgebungen gewaltiger Kriegsopfermassen," *Reichsbund,* 10 May 1931, 81; "Marsch der Kriegsbeschädigten nach Berlin?" *Kreuz-Zeitung,* 27 September 1932, 61 Sta/1148, f. 16, BAL.

169. Niederschrift über die Sitzung des Arbeitsausschusses des Reichsausschusses der Kriegsbeschädigten und Kriegshinterbliebenenfürsorge, 19 November 1929, R 758, ADCV. See also Karl Müller, "Die Aenderung der Kriegsbeschädigtenversorgung," *Deutsche Allgemeine Zeitung,* 3 July 1930, R 116/102, Bundesarchiv Koblenz (BAK). For criticism of the pensions system, Georg Bernhard, "Die Sparkonten," *Vossische Zeitung,* nr. 93, cited in Otto Thiel, "Unseren Gefallenen," *Zentralblatt für Kriegsbeschädigte und Kriegshinterbliebene,* March 1930, 26.

170. "Notschrei der deutschen Kriegsopfer," n.d. [after June 1932] by the Arbeitsgemeinschaft Reichsverband und Zentralverband, ZSg. 1-345/3 (1), BAK.

171. "Zur Lage der Kriegsblinden," *Freiburger Tagespost,* 6 January 1932, CA XIX, 6B, ADCV.

172. C. A. Ottersbach, "An alle offenen und versteckten Neider," *Zentralblatt für Kriegsbeschädigte und Kriegerhinterbliebene,* October 1931, 130; Eghigian, 224–231.

173. Paul Heinrich to Hirsch, 23 June 1931, Rep. 62/169, LAB-A.

174. "Die ersten Bürger des Staates," *Zentralblatt für Kriegsbeschädigte und Kriegerhinterbliebene,* December 1932, 29. See also August Stein, "Was man den Kriegsbeschädigten in Deutschland bieten darf," *Zentralblatt für Kriegsbeschädigte und Kriegshinterbliebene,* June 1930, 74–75.

175. See, for instance, Ministerialrat Grießmeyer's radio address of 13 December 1929. "Was geschieht für die Kriegsbeschädigten?" *Zentralblatt für Kriegsbeschädigte und Kriegshinterbliebene,* January 1929.

176. "Die Renten der Kriegsopfer," *Vorwärts*, 8 February 1924, Staatskanzlei Auschnittsammlung 1556, SHAD.

177. Zweiter Jahresbericht der Stiftung Hindenburg-Spende, 1929, Erstattet von der Geschäftsführung, p. 7, RAM 9811, BAL.

178. Zweiter Jahresbericht der Stiftung Hindenburg-Spende, 1929, p. 7, RAM 9811, BAL.

179. For the history of the NSDAP's courtship of the disabled, see Diehl, "Victors or Victims?" 705–736.

180. Quoted in "Die Kriegsopfer im Dritten Reich," *Der Angriff*, 11 November 1933, 61 Sta/1150, BAL. For a critique of the war victims' organizations, see *Völk. Beobachter*, 8 September 1934, 61 Sta/1149, BAL.

181. "Die Riesenkundgebung im Berliner Sportpalast," *Reichsbund*, no. 9 (20 May 1931): 86.

182. According to Diehl, the NSKOV (National Socialist War Victims' Association) claimed 1.1 to 1.2 million members, of whom 1,082,000 were dues-paying. "Victors or Victims?" 715 n. 27.

183. Quoted in Diehl, "Victors or Victims?" 716.

184. "Mehr Großzügigkeit gegenüber Schwerkriegsbeschädigten!" *Berliner Börsen Zeitung*, 16 July 1933, 61 Sta 1/1150, f. 1, BAL; "Für die Kriegsopfer," 16 November 1933, 61 Sta 1/1150, f. 16, BAL; "Bevorzugte Plätze für Schwerkriegsbeschädigte," *Völkischer Beobachter*, 16 February 1935, 61 Sta 1/1149, f. 3, BAL; "Freikarten für Kriegsopfer," *Angriff*, 29 June 1934, 61 Sta 1/1149, BAL; Whalen, 177; "Kriegsopfer, die Ehrenbürger des Staates," *Hamburger Tageblatt*, 20 September 1933, 351-10 I, Sozialbehörde I, KO 80.22.

185. 61 Sta/1150, f. 28, BAL.

186. "Im Zeichen der Parole: Ehre und Recht," *Berl. Börs. Zeitung*, 8 September 1934, 61 Sta/1149, BAL.

CHAPTER 3

1. *Times of London*, 21 July 1919, 7. On Armistice Day, see Gregory, esp. 51–92.

2. "The Task of Peace," *Times of London*, 21 July 1919, 13.

3. "In the Mall," *Times of London*, 21 July 1919, 14.

4. "Room for the Cripples," October 1919, n.p., *Church Army Review*, Church Army Archive. See also "With the Wounded," *Times of London*, 21 July 1919, 15.

5. J. B. Brunel Cohen, "The Peace Procession," *Daily Graphic*, 21 July 1919, Cutting Book, Private Collection; on France, see Winter, *Sites of Memory, Sites of Mourning*, 22; on the Armistice, 1920 parade, see Lloyd, 78–80.

6. *British Legion Journal*, August 1934, 49.

7. "Salvaging Lives Wrecked in Battle: Hope Winning," *Daily Chronicle*, 20 May 1930, Cutting Book II, Stoll Foundation.

8. Edward Gowlland to Lionel Bailey, 22 September 1933, Box 24, War Seal Mansions, HFAC.

9. Ibid.

10. Charles Neal, Tenancy File, War Seal Mansions, HFAC.

11. See, for instance, Albert Bayliss to Lord Derby, 31 March 1922, 920 DER (17) 21/5, Liverpool Record Office.

12. The postwar boom lasted for a year, from the spring of 1919 to the spring of 1920. By mid-1921 Britain was in a severe recession. In May 1921, there were 2.4 million unemployed. Derek Aldcroft, *The British Economy: Years of Turmoil,* vol. 1 (London, 1986), 6.

13. Charles Neal to the Prince of Wales, 31 May 1932, Charles Neal Tenancy File, War Seal Mansions, HFAC.

14. On the masculinity of the wounded, see Reznick, 174, 208–209, 218–219.

15. For personal testimony of disabled ex-servicemen, especially the unemployed, see letters written to Lord Derby in response to a speech he made in 1922 in Morecambe, which veterans interpreted as an offer of help; 920 DER (17) 21/3-5, Liverpool Record Office. Derby stated that he would gladly investigate the circumstances of men who felt that they had been given the wrong pension. Between February and April 1922, he received more than 140 letters.

16. Arthur Harry William Pool, Misc. 128, Item 1992, Imperial War Museum.

17. Bourke, 162–170.

18. Jack Hogg, Tape 743, August 1989, Blesma Home, Crieff, Peter Liddle Collection, Leeds.

19. BLESMA to Prime Minister Chamberlain, 4 August 1938, PIN 15/1414, PRO. On the benefits of marriage for the disabled man, see also Bill Towers, R 8, 29 November 1989, Imperial War Museum—Sound Records; *Yorkshire Observer,* 30 October 1919, Cutting Book I, Enham; Cohen, *Count Your Blessings,* 145.

20. F.O.B. to Hore, 13 April 1917, PIN 15/39, Public Record Office.

21. "Clerks of the King's Roll," *Times,* 27 March 1928.

22. See "Pension Grants: Interpretations and Hardships," DP, 11 July 1922, 361 COU 1/10, p. 90, Liverpool Record Office. On the Eugenics Society's opposition to the Ministry's policies, see Koven, 1191.

23. According to Hore, "in a very large proportion of cases—certainly over 50%—family allowances are not being paid in addition to pension." Hore to T.W. Phillips, Ministry of Labour, 13 October 1923, PIN 15/709. "War-Disabled Men," *Manchester Guardian,* 3 June 1938, PIN 15/1414, PRO.

24. Questions and Answers, 21 April 1921, Mr. Macpherson, PIN 14/41, PRO. Annual Value of Payments Made. Disability alone: £20,146,000. Wife and children allowances: £2,200,000. Minute Note by R. Herbert [?], 2 November 1932, PIN 15/711. Dependents' allowances were added to unemployment insurance benefit after 1921. Lowe, *Adjusting to Democracy,* 185.

25. Mayo, 444.

26. On women's paid labor, see Elizabeth Roberts, *A Woman's Place: An Oral History of Working-Class Women, 1890–1940* (Oxford, 1984), 116–118, 135–147.

27. Ernest Ripley, Tenancy File, Stoll Collection, Hammersmith and Fulham Local Record Office. On the burden of caring for disabled men, see Winter, *Sites of Memory, Sites of Mourning,* 44–45.

28. "Salvaging Lives Wrecked in Battle: Hope Winning," *Daily Chronicle,* 20 May 1930, Cutting Book II, Stoll Foundation.

29. Pilgrim Trust, *Men without Work* (Cambridge, 1938), 242.

30. Interview with Mrs. West, 19 July 1995, London.

31. In Liverpool, for instance, men with families received priority over ex-servicemen. Town Clerk to R. S. Crosby [Sec'y to Lord Derby], 11 March 1922, 920 DER (17) 21/3, Liverpool Record Office. New council houses built by the Addison Housing Act of 1919 rented for 13s. to 20s. per week, putting them out of the reach of most disabled men. Pat Thane, *Foundations of the Welfare State* (London, 1982), 207.

32. See John Burnett, *A Social History of Housing, 1815–1985* (London, 1986 [1978]), esp. 221–222.

33. George Foote, Tenancy File, War Seal Mansions, HFAC.

34. George Foote to Beatrice Herring, January 1933, War Seal Mansions, HFAC.

35. Foote's Application for Admission, War Seal Mansions, HFAC.

36. In 1920, when the War Seal scheme was first publicized, the Foundation received three applications a day. See "A Talk with Sir Oswald Stoll," *Daily Telegraph,* 18 October 1920.

37. David Lalis, Tenancy File, HFAC.

38. Edward Jenkins, Tenancy File, HFAC.

39. Robert Greig, Tenancy File, HFAC.

40. Frederick Lewis to Roberts, Lewis Tenancy File, 29 March 1928, HFAC.

41. A. Fischer [Charity Organisation Society] to Roberts, 4 April 1924, Herbert Swann Tenancy File, HFAC.

42. Edward Lifford, Tenancy File, HFAC.

43. Garside, *British Unemployment,* 16–18. See also Latcham, 327–328.

44. After the First World War, Miss Annie R. Collin (founder of the Friends of the Poor and Gentlefolk's Help) established the Disabled Soldiers Embroidery Industry. See her obituary, *Times of London,* 16 July 1957; "Disabled Men's Embroidery," *Times,* 7 May 1925; "Disabled Soldiers' Embroidery," *Times,* 10 May 1927.

45. An initiative of the Ministry of Labour, the King's Roll attempted to place disabled veterans in employment. To qualify for the Roll, employers had to fill at least 5 percent of their workforce with disabled ex-servicemen; in return, they were permitted to use the King's Roll Seal on their letterhead and, after 1920, were granted preferences in government contracts. See chapter 1.

46. Short Memorandum on Work of Employment Department for Disabled Men, October 1919, Lab 2/1196/EDX 1922/1919, PRO. "King's National Roll," Hansard, vol. 324, no. 115, 3 June 1937, p. 1151, MSS 200/B/3/2/c243 pt. 2. Select Committee on Pensions, 9 August 1920, Lab 2/522/TDS 3947/7/1919, PRO; King's National Roll, Ministry of Labour, B.S. 23/14. In 1924, there were 28,524 firms on the Roll, employing 330,000 disabled men (of a total of 680,000). More than 20,000 firms (each employing 25 or more) were not on the Roll. See T. J. MacNamara, "The King's Roll," *British Legion Journal,* May 1924, 337. As of 31 December 1926, there were 27,500 employers on the King's Roll, employing

approximately 375,000 disabled ex-servicemen. Ministry of Labour, *Annual Report* (London, 1926), 25. In June 1929, there were 26,948 employers on the King's Roll; in June 1930, 26,454; in June 1931, 25,514; in December 1938, 24,526 employers. "King's Roll," Hansard, vol. 255, no. 154, Thurs. 16 July 1931; "24,526 Employers on the King's Roll," *Times*, 7 December 1938, MSS 200/B/3/2/c243 pt. 2, Modern Records Centre.

47. The statistics offered by the King's Roll must be treated cautiously. First, they do not differentiate between those in receipt of pensions and those who had been awarded gratuities. Second, local committees had the discretion to grant the King's Roll Seal on a lower basis if the circumstances warranted. Third, there was very little oversight to ensure that employers, once on the Roll, maintained their quota of disabled employees. "Unemployment," Hansard, vol. 310, no. 68, 9 April 1936, p. 2967, MSS 200/B/3/2/c243 pt. 2; E.D. Circ. 14/52 [14 December 1921] and E.D. Circ. 14/51 [2 December 1921], Lab 2/224, EDX 5308/1921, PRO; M.F. Hoare, "King's National Roll, Report on the Position of the Above on 3 October 1921," 4 October 1921, Lab 2/224, EDX 4880/1921, PRO.

48. James Sime Waterston, Chairman, "Notes on the Problem of the Disabled Ex-Service Man," Lab 2/224, EDX 993/1921, pt. 2, PRO. On problems with the King's Roll, see Bolderson, 41; Gerald de Groot, *Blighty* (London, 1996), 260–261.

49. On the ordinary register, see D. Hoare to Mr. Barltrop, 6 May 1921, Lab 2/224, EDX 993/1921, pt. 1, PRO. In 1929, the live register for disabled ex-servicemen numbered 24,000; in April 1930, 28,000; in July 1931, 41,000; in November 1933, 36,000; in April 1938, 29,512. These figures do not include those disabled ex-servicemen whose names went onto the ordinary registers. Nor, as with all unemployment statistics, do they include those men who no longer registered at exchanges. On the difficulties in calculating unemployment, see W.R. Garside, *Measurement of Unemployment* (Oxford, 1980), 33–37, 46–61; Alan Deacon, *In Search of the Scrounger,* Occasional Papers on Social Administration, no. 60 (London, 1976), 21–68, 88. "The King's Roll," *Yorkshire Post,* 28 November 1929, MSS 200 B/3/2/243 pt. 2, Modern Records Centre; "The King's Roll," *Times,* 10 April 1930, MSS 200 B/3/2/243 pt. 2, Modern Records Centre; "The King's Roll," *Times,* 1 July 1931, MSS 200 B/3/2/243 pt. 2, Modern Records Centre; "The King's Roll," *Times,* 23 November 1933, MSS 200 B/3/2/243 pt. 2, Modern Records Centre; "Disabled Ex-Service Men," Hansard, vol. 335 no. 107, 10 May 1938, MSS 200/B/3/2/c243 pt. 2.

50. Deacon, *In Search of the Scrounger,* 88; Pilgrim Trust, 63. Disabled ex-servicemen were required to make fewer contributions for standard benefit than their able-bodied counterparts. Eveline Burns, *British Unemployment Programs, 1920–1938* (Washington, D.C., 1941), 39.

51. "The King's Roll," *Times,* 18 March 1927.

52. Captain Donald Simpson, Comrades of the Great War, Committee on the Employment of Severely Disabled Ex-Service Men, 17 November 1920, PIN 15/37, PRO. Over the course of the interwar period, unemployment rarely fell below 1 million, or about 10 percent of the insured workforce.

53. Dry Toast, Letter to the Editor, "The Pension System," *Glasgow Evening Times*, 5 February 1923, PIN 15/704, PRO.

54. In August 1920, the Roehampton Employment Bureau reported that nearly 8,717 of the hospital's patients had returned to their previous employers by previous arrangement (43.7 percent of the total); 4,383 men were either passed on for further training or found work (21.9 percent); 6,850 men refused to consider work except in the vicinity of their own homes and were passed on to their Local Committees (34.3 percent). See Final Report of the Employment Bureau, August 1920, Executive Committee Minutes II, Greater London Record Office (GLRO).

55. William Towers, Tapes 741 and 742, Peter Liddle Collection, Leeds.

56. Samuel Peers, Tape 743, August 1989, Blesma Home, Crieff, Peter Liddle Collection, Leeds.

57. George Ayling to the Ministry of Labour, received 30 August 1921, Lab 2/529/TDS4433/1921. See also W. Rankine, M.o.L., to Captain Haydn Parry, Training Dept., 1 September 1921, same file; T. B. Wheeler, Divisional Director of Industrial Training to Mr. Vernon Dier, Controller, M.o.P., 5 May 1922, Lab 2/529/TDS4433/1921.

58. J. Bennett to Lord Derby, received 3 March 1922, 920 DER (17) 21/3, Liverpool Record Office.

59. E. Wight Bakke, *The Unemployed Man: A Social Study* (London, 1933), 129–130. On transportation in London, see Kimball, 220.

60. What percentage of these men were returning to prewar jobs is not stated, nor was their disability rating. Statement Relating to the Employment of Ex-Service Men in Government Offices on 1 July 1927, Cmd. 2932. For 1932, see Ex-Service Men Employed in Government Departments (London, 1932), Cmd. 4099, MSS 200/B/3/2/c243 pt. 2, Modern Records Centre; Ex-Service Men, Hansard, vol. 344, no. 50, 22 February 1939, p. 382, MSS 200/B/3/2/c243 pt. 2, Modern Records Centre. On women civil servants, see Meta Zimmeck, "Strategies and Stratagems for the Employment of Women in the British Civil Service, 1919–1939," *Historical Journal* 27 (1984): 901–924, and "The 'New Woman' in the Machinery of Government: A Spanner in the Works?" in *Government and Expertise,* ed. R. Macleod (Cambridge, 1988). EDX 217/4/1920, Lab 2, Box 221. In 1923, government offices employed 4.8 percent of disabled veterans; on 1 January 1923 there were 26,500 disabled men in permanent employment in the public services and 17,000 in temporary employment. See International Labour Office, *Employment of Disabled Men,* 18, E.D. Circ. 14/52 [14 December 1921] and E.D. Circ. 14/51 [2 December 1921], Lab 2/224, EDX 5308/1921, PRO.

61. Jack Hogg, Tape 743, August 1989, Blesma Home, Crieff, Peter Liddle Collection, Leeds.

62. Arthur Pool to M.o.P., 4 February 1937, Misc. 128, Item 1992, Imperial War Museum.

63. General Bertram Boyce to Mr. Kearn [Divisional Controller, Ministry of Labour], 18 March 1932, Lab 20/17, PRO.

64. James Currie's evidence, 11 November 1919, p. 449.

65. Foote to Beatrice Herring, January 1933, Foote Tenancy File, HFAC.

66. Provisional Interim Report of the Committee on Employment of Severely Disabled Ex-Service Men, 18 January 1921, PIN 15/37, PRO. See also Pilgrim Trust, 64, 375; Bourke, 53–54.

67. Statement submitted by Mr. David Smale, Chief Area Officer, Ministry of Pensions, Plymouth, PIN 15/706, PRO. See also Mr. R. Griffin (British Legion), Committee on Public Assistance, Minutes of Proceedings of Meeting held on 19 April 1923, p. 1, PIN 15/706, PRO, and British Legion, Evidence for the Committee on Public Assistance, PIN 15/706; evidence of Captain J. W. Newham (Chief Area Officer, Leicester Area) and Mr. D. Smale (Chief Area Officer, Plymouth Area), 2418-45, Committee on Public Assistance, Minutes of Proceedings of Meeting held on 28 March 1923, PIN 15/706, PRO. On the genuinely seeking work test, see Deacon, *In Search of the Scrounger,* 21–68.

68. "Coordination of Public Benefits: Mr. Bonar Law Promises Inquiry," *Poor Law Officers' Journal,* 2 February 1923, PIN 15/704, PRO. See Mr. R. Griffin (British Legion), Committee on Public Assistance, Minutes of Proceedings of Meeting held on 19 April 1923, p. 9, PIN 15/706, PRO.

69. Sidney Webb, Evidence before the Committee on Public Assistance, 1 March 1923, PIN 15/705, PRO; Sidney Webb to Bonar Law, 17 January 1923 [copy], PIN 15/704, PRO; Committee on Public Assistance, Statement Submitted by Mr. Sidney Webb, n.d., PIN 15/705, PRO; see Webb's evidence before the Committee on Public Assistance, 1 and 8 March 1923, PIN 15/705, PRO. See also Arthur Poole, "Where Are the Gaps?" letter to the editor of the *Manchester Guardian,* 1 February 1923, PIN 15/705, PRO.

70. "Readers' Questions: Asked and Answered," *Yarmouth Independent,* 28 April 1923, PIN 15/709.

71. Garside, *British Unemployment,* 68; "War Pensions and Means Test," *Post and Mercury,* 7 January 1932, HQ 331 8 CUT, p. 13, Liverpool Record Office. T. W. Phillips, Deputy Sec'y, M.o.L. Transitional Payments to County Councils, County Borough Councils in England and Wales, 10 November 1931, PIN 15/710, PRO; National Health Insurance, Provisions Relating to Benefits, Departmental Memo No. 239, Ministry of Health, PIN 15/704, PRO; Sir H. Betterton, House of Commons, 9 November 1932, pp. 353–354; 14 November 1932, pp. 833–834. "Transitional Payments," M.o.L. to County Councils, 24 November 1932, PIN 15/711, PRO. On allowances, semi-official letter of 27 February 1933 from Minister of Labour [Eady], PIN 15/711; Hansard, vol. 286, no. 44, 26 February 1934, p. 831, PIN 15/714, PRO.

72. "New Pension Problem: War Disabled and Old Age Awards," *Liverpool Post,* 13 September 1933, 361 COU 1/16, p. 8, Liverpool Record Office.

73. Draft Note for Prime Minister [T. W. Phillips, M.o.L.], 23 January 1923, PIN 15/705, PRO.

74. Reese, 95.

75. James Pegrum, Tenancy File, HFAC.

76. Report by Jt. Managing Director on Training and Employment, Lord Roberts, March 1919, Lab 2/528/TDS 3752/9/1921, pt. 2, PRO.

77. John Hudson to Ministry of Labour, 2 October 1933, Lab 20/17, PRO. On the strike at Lord Roberts in Liverpool in 1917, see "Disabled Soldiers' Strike," *Daily Post,* 1 October 1917, 361 COU 2/2, Liverpool Record Office.

78. Committee on the Employment of Severely Disabled Men, 9 December 1920, PIN 15/37, PRO.

79. "Can Liverpool Forget? Our Fund for the Disabled Ex-Service Men," *Liverpool Courier,* 26 January 1922; and "Liverpool Remembers," *Liverpool Courier,* 21 February 1922, 361 COU 1/10, Liverpool Record Office.

80. Lea to Roberts, 23 April 1936, William Lea Tenancy File, HFAC.

81. Neal to the Prince of Wales, 31 May 1932, Neal Tenancy File, HFAC.

82. Stoll to Major J. R. Aird, Equery to P.o.W., 7 June 1932, Neal Tenancy File, HFAC.

83. "Disobeyed the Rules," *Fulham Chronicle,* 15 December 1933, HFAC.

84. Neal to Roberts, 31 December 1933, HFAC.

85. "Model Homes for the Disabled," *Pall Mall Gazette,* 12 December 1917, Cutting Book, January 1916–June 1920, Stoll.

86. Ibid.

87. *Dictionary of National Biography,* 1941–1950, entry by Herbert Grimsditch.

88. *Bristol Gazette Times and Weekly News,* 14 September 1918, Stoll Foundation.

89. Fred Russell, obituary of Sir Oswald Stoll, *Performer,* 15 January 1942, 5.

90. "A Talk with Sir Oswald Stoll," *Daily Telegraph,* 18 October 1920, Cutting Book II, Stoll.

91. Sir Oswald Stoll, "The War Seal Foundation," *The Graphic,* 28 June 1919, Cutting Book, January 1916–June 1920, Stoll Foundation. For an account of the treatment of returning soldiers, see Reese, chs. 2–4.

92. *Daily Telegraph,* 6 May 1919, Cutting Book, January 1916–June 1920, Stoll.

93. *Financial Times,* 23 January 1917, Cutting Book, January 1916–June 1920, Stoll.

94. "A Home with Hospital Treatment," 20 July 1918, *Nursing Mirror and Midwives' Journal,* Cutting Book, January 1916–June 1920, Stoll.

95. Ibid.

96. "Stoll Picture Theatre," *Times,* 23 December 1920, Cutting Book II, Stoll. For a similar sentiment, see Demos, *The Meaning of Reconstruction* (London, n.d.), 16: "The War has brought home to us the value of the individual."

97. "Disabled in War," *Western Mail* (Cardiff), 12 August 1915, Cutting Book, 1915, Stoll.

98. John Tosh, *A Man's Place: Masculinity and the Middle-Class Home in Victorian England* (New Haven, Conn., 1999), 111.

99. W. J. Roberts to Frederick Phillips, 30 March 1922, Box 2, HFAC.

100. "Problem of the Disabled Soldier," *Oxford Chronicle,* 4 April 1919, Cutting Book I, Enham Archives.

101. Walter Witchell, Tenancy File, HFAC.

102. On friendly societies more generally, see Paul Johnson, *Saving and Spending: The Working-Class Economy in Britain, 1870–1939* (Oxford, 1985), 49–74.

103. Report on the Independent Self-Help Society, 1932, Box 6, HFAC.

104. Visitor's Report, 12 January 1927, Henry Mitchell, Tenancy File, HFAC.

105. Oswald Stoll to Members of the Council, 28 January 1932, Box 6, HFAC.

106. Open Letter by Oswald Stoll to Tenants, 28 January 1932, HFAC.

107. Independent Self-Help Society to Robert Tasker, 23 January 1932, HFAC.

108. Open Letter by Oswald Stoll to Tenants, 28 January 1932, HFAC.

109. R. Wheeler to Stoll, 29 January 1932, Box 6, HFAC.

110. J. R. Lund to Stoll, 30 January 1932, Box 6, HFAC.

111. Sir Oswald Stoll to Mr. Roberts, 12 July 1924, Box 21, HFAC.

112. "Salvaging Humanity," *Southern Daily Echo,* 3 June 1919, Cutting Book I, Enham Archives.

113. "Village Settlements for Disabled Ex-Service Men," October 1917, PIN 15/34, PRO.

114. "Industries for Disabled Men," *Northern Daily Telegraph,* 22 September 1921, Cutting Book II, Enham Archives. On government settlement schemes, see Latcham, 198–214. The 1919 Land Settlement (Facilities) Act made no provisions for the disabled; a supplementary scheme was cut in the postwar Slump.

115. "Principles of Production and Distribution," Village Settlements for Disabled Ex-Service Men, October 1917, PIN 15/34, PRO.

116. "Enham Village Centre," *Wiltshire Gazette,* 25 March 1920, Cutting Book I, Enham Archives.

117. Major A. Garthwaite, quoted in "Salvaging Humanity," *Southern Daily Echo,* 3 June 1919, Cutting Book I, Enham Archives.

118. The Origin, History, and Ideals of the Village Centres Movement, PIN 15/34, PRO. See also "Enham Village Centre," *Wiltshire Gazette,* 25 March 1920, Cutting Book I, Enham Archives.

119. Minutes, Executive Committee, Report by Charles A. Boivin, General Manager, February–March 1929, Enham Archives.

120. Special Circular No. 9, 30 August, 1930, British Legion Archives.

121. Dr. Varrier-Jones to Lord Henry Bentinck, 14 March 1929, copy, Enham Archives.

122. Lieutenant-Colonel G. R. Crosfield to Lord Henry Cavendish-Bentinck, n.d. [March 1929], Enham Archives.

123. Minutes, Executive Committee, 1 April 1930, Enham Archives. In the end, Enham's Executive Committee offered Spicer a grant of not more than £30 to open a fish-and-chips business in Pontlottyn.

124. "Aldershot Honoured," *Aldershot Gazette,* 6 June 1929, Cutting Book IV, Enham Archives.

125. "British Legion Conference," *Aldershot News,* 7 June 1929, Cutting Book IV, Enham Archives.

126. "Aldershot Honoured," *Aldershot Gazette,* 6 June 1929, Cutting Book IV, Enham Archives.

127. Minutes, Executive Committee: Report, 22 July 1932, Enham Archives.

128. British Legion Village, Preston Hall, Kent, Report by the Medical Director, 1925–1928, p. 24.

129. Addendum B: British Legion Village Branch, 15 September 1931, Royal British Legion Industries Archive, Preston Hall.

130. *Preston Hall Industries v. Lee:* Notes of Judgment, 11 May 1934, Royal British Legion Industries Archive, Preston Hall.

131. Medical Superintendent's Weekly Report [no 1, 16 March 1916–27 November 1917], ST 12, 17 April 1917, Star and Garter Collection, British Red Cross Archives.

132. "Model Homes for the Disabled," *Pall Mall Gazette,* 12 December 1917, Cutting Book, January 1916–June 1920, Stoll.

133. "For Disabled Ex-Service Men," *Yorkshire Post,* 27 October 1919, Cutting Book I, Enham Archives. "It will be run as much as possible like a home, and as unlike an institution as is possible." "A Village Centre for Disabled Ex-Service Men," *Lady's Pictorial,* 1 March 1919, 272, Cutting Book I, Enham Archives.

134. *Star and Garter Magazine,* January 1925, 28.

135. Ibid. About the temporary Home at Enbrook, the Star and Garter's commandant wrote: "Enbrook was a beautiful place, a charming spot for those in full possession of wind and limb, but for totally paralyzed men it was the last place on earth which should have been chosen, for out of the twenty-six acres there were not more than a couple of acres which the men could use." J. L. Dickie, *Comedy and Drama of a Doctor's Life* (London, 1939), 175–176.

136. *Star and Garter Magazine,* January 1925, 28.

137. "Cheerful after 15 Years of Pain," *Daily Mirror,* 7 November 1933, Cutting Book IV, GLRO.

138. "Shattered Soldier Laughs at Fate: Life Invalid Says He's Happy," *Belfast Telegraph,* 25 June 1926.

139. Mary Borden, "These Men Have Courage!" *Sunday Graphic and Sunday News,* reprinted in *Star and Garter Magazine,* December 1934, 10–13.

140. *New Statesman* 34:482 (16 January 1930).

141. Mary Borden, *The Forbidden Zone* (London, 1929), 64–65.

142. On men's clubs, see Tosh, 186–187.

143. Annual Report, Star and Garter Home, 1934.

144. On paraplegia, see Maj. Gen. Sir W. G. Macpherson et al., *Medical Services: Surgery of the War,* vol. 2, *History of Great War Based on Official Documents* (London, 1922), 118–144.

145. "A London Letter," *Yorkshire Post,* 20 December 1929, PH 10, Star and Garter Collection, British Red Cross Archives.

146. "With the Disabled: Where the Spirit of Sacrifice Still Lives," *Evening News,* 11 November 1929, PH 10, Star and Garter Collection, British Red Cross Archives.

147. Tosh, 184, 189.

148. "Gallant Gentlemen," *Finchley Press,* 22 May 1925, PH 7, Star and Garter Collection, British Red Cross Archives; see also "Introductory," *Recalled to Life* 1 (June 1917): 3.

149. "Legion of the Broken: Indelible Mark of War Inscribed on All Hearts," *Daily Sketch,* 12 November 1931, PH 10, Star and Garter Collection, British Red Cross Archives.

150. "The New 'Star and Garter,'" *Evening News,* 11 July 1924; "A London Letter," *Yorkshire Post,* 20 December 1929, PH 10, Star and Garter Collection, British Red Cross Archives.

151. "Forgotten Men and Those Who Remember Them," *Star and Garter Magazine,* April 1935, 27.

152. "A Happy Family," *Richmond Herald,* 11 July 1931, PH 10, Star and Garter Collection, British Red Cross Archives.

153. "Queen Mary's Convalescent Auxiliary Hospital," Cutting Book I, Roehampton, GLRO. "I'd have rather been killed," remembered one man whose leg was amputated after Ypres. Oral history, Bill Towers, 29 November 1989, R8, Imperial War Museum, London.

154. Mrs. Annie Bass to W. J. Roberts, 5 March 1928, Box 2, HFAC.

155. Kingsley Martin, *Father Figures: A Volume of Autobiography* (London, 1966), 72. For the young Kingsley Martin, sent to the Star and Garter with the Friends' Ambulance Unit and soon sickened by never-ending dirty sheets and "the smell of death," the place was hell: "Abandon all hope you who enter here."

156. Appendix IV, "The Case of the Paralysed Soldier," FU 27, Star and Garter Collection, British Red Cross Archives.

157. Ibid.

158. Catalog for the Star and Garter Sale, Star and Garter Home.

159. "Star and Garter Sold at Last," *Lloyd's Weekly News,* n.d., PH 12, Star and Garter Collection, British Red Cross Archives.

160. "Last of the Star & Garter Hotel," *Richmond and Twickenham Times,* 25 September 1915.

161. "The New 'Star and Garter,'" *Evening News,* 11 July 1924.

162. "The Passing of the Star & Garter: A Contrast," *Times,* 21 October 1915, PH 8, Star and Garter Collection, British Red Cross Archives.

163. Martin, 72.

164. Dickie, 158.

165. British Women's Hospital Committee, Star and Garter Building and Endowment Funds, p. 4.

166. Margaret Webster, *The Same, Only Different* (London, 1969), 253.

167. Lewis Casson, *Dictionary of National Biography, 1941–50,* ed. L. G. Wickham Legg and E. T. Williams (Oxford, 1959), 241.

168. Desmond Young, *Member for Mexico* (London, 1966), 13.

169. "At the age of fifty, a peeress, a great London hostess and the mother of four, she had to be restrained by her family from chaining herself to the railings in Whitehall with the suffragettes." In Young, 13.

170. Star and Garter ad in the *Times,* 17 January 1916.

171. Appeal by Gertrude Forbes-Robertson, undated [A/FWA/C/D296/1], GLRO.

172. "The Romance of the Star and Garter," *Woman at Home,* December 1917.

173. John Galsworthy, "Star & Garter Home," *Observer,* 19 March 1916, PH 8, Star and Garter Collection, British Red Cross Archives.

174. Lady Fulton, Overseas Appeal, FU 21, Star and Garter Collection, British Red Cross Archives.

175. Report of the British Women's Hospital Committee from the Commencement of Its Work, p. 6, FU 27, Star and Garter Collection, British Red Cross Archives.

176. Report of the British Women's Hospital Committee, p. 4, Star and Garter Collection, British Red Cross Archives.

177. Ad from British Women's Hospital Fund, 23 March 1916, PH 8, Star and Garter Collection, British Red Cross Archives.

178. Frederick Treves, "The New 'Star and Garter,'" PP 12, Star and Garter Collection, British Red Cross Archives.

179. Role of the Ladies' Committee, Presentation at Buckingham Palace, 16 November 1916, FU 20, Star and Garter Collection, British Red Cross Archives.

180. Mary Baillie to Rudge Harding, 19 September 1916, FU 16, Star and Garter Collection, British Red Cross Archives.

181. Mrs. Gladys Street to Major Dickie, 26 January 1918, FU 16, Star and Garter Collection, British Red Cross Archives.

182. Mary S. Hine to Viscountess Cowdray, 10 December 1919, in memory of her son, Lieutenant Claude Annesley Hine, killed on the Somme, October 1916, FU 16, Star and Garter Collection, British Red Cross Archives.

183. Violet Loring to Sec'y, n.d. [1917?], FU 16 [17], Star and Garter Collection, British Red Cross Archives.

184. Helen Lloyd to Harding, 14 December, n.d. [1919?], FU 16, Star and Garter Collection, British Red Cross Archives.

185. *Woman at Home*, 6.

186. "Brighton Brilliants," *Graphic*, 1 February 1919, PIN 15/129, PRO.

187. "The Star and Garter," Editorial, *Richmond and Twickenham Times*, 5 July 1924, PH 7, Star and Garter Collection, British Red Cross Archives.

188. "Their Majesties at Richmond," *Morning Post*, 11 July 1924, PH 7, Star and Garter Collection, British Red Cross Archives.

189. "King and Queen Recognise Old Soldiers at Richmond," *Daily Graphic*, 11 July 1924, PH 7, Star and Garter Collection, British Red Cross Archives.

190. "Star and Garter Home for the Disabled," *Daily Chronicle*, 11 July 1924, PH 7, Star and Garter Collection, British Red Cross Archives.

191. "The Star and Garter," *Red Cross*, October 1924, PH 7, Star and Garter Collection, British Red Cross Archives.

192. "The Star and Garter Home," *Lancet*, 1 November 1924, 928. "The profession may rest assured that here is, in fact, a worthy home for heroes."

193. "Empire Women's Memorial to the Fallen," *Birmingham Post*, 11 July 1924, PH 7, Star and Garter Collection, British Red Cross Archives.

194. "The Star and Garter Home," *Lancet*, 1 November 1924, 928.

195. "Star and Garter Home," *Times*, 11 July 1924, PH 7, Star and Garter Collection, British Red Cross Archives.

196. "A London Letter," *Yorkshire Post*, 20 December 1929, PH 10, Star and Garter Collection, British Red Cross Archives.

197. Sir Frederick Treves, "The Case of the Paralysed Soldier," FU 27, Star and Garter Collection, British Red Cross Archives.

198. "Shall They Be Forgotten," *Evening Standard*, 9 May 1931, PH 10, Star and Garter Collection, British Red Cross Archives.

199. See, for example, Kate Finzi, *18 Months in the War Zone* (London, 1916), 112; James Allardice, "The Wounded as We See Them at Home," *British Medical Journal*, 21 April 1917; Souttar, 16.

200. "Disabled Soldiers' Singing Competition," *Richmond and Twickenham Times*, 26 June 1926, PH 11, Star and Garter Collection, British Red Cross Archives.

201. Quoted in Medical Superintendent's Weekly Report, 11 October 1919, vol. 3, Star and Garter Collection, British Red Cross Archives.

202. H. Collinson Owen, "Our Broken Soldiers," *Standard*, November 1915, Cutting Book I, Roehampton, GLRO.

203. "A Home on the Hill," *Richmond and Twickenham Times*, 12 July 1924, PH 7, Star and Garter Collection, British Red Cross Archives.

204. Norah Hill, "Lads of Richmond Hill," *World's Health*, April 1925, PH 7, Star and Garter Collection, British Red Cross Archives.

205. "The Man Who Lay Still for 20 Years," *Sunday Express*, 30 January 1938, Press Cutting Book IV, Roehampton, GLRO.

206. "Shall They Be Forgotten," *Evening Standard*, 9 May 1931, PH 10, Star and Garter Collection, British Red Cross Archives.

207. Gordon Laws, "Hang Disability: We'll Show 'Em How to Smile Through," *London Opinion*, 15 November 1930, PH 10, Star and Garter Collection, British Red Cross Archives.

208. "Salvaged Lives Wrecked in Battle: Hope Winning," *Daily Chronicle*, 20 May 1930, Cutting Book II, Stoll Foundation.

209. Maud Bigge, "The Lucky Ones," *Star and Garter Magazine*, April 1937, 60.

210. "Shattered Soldier Laughs at Fate: Life Invalid Says He's Happy," *Belfast Telegraph*, 25 June 1926, PH 11, Star and Garter Collection, British Red Cross Archives.

211. *British Legion Journal*, January 1922, 149.

212. Mrs. Clarice Gardner, Memoirs, private collection.

213. W. J. Eliott, "These Men Remember," 11 November 1926, *Evening News*, Press Cutting Book IV, GLRO.

214. Tudor Jenkins, "Eighteen Years After," *Evening Standard*, 7 April 1936, Press Cutting Book IV, GLRO.

215. Tosh, 112–113.

216. John Buchan, "The Greatest War Debt," *Star and Garter Magazine*, December 1935; reprinted from *Daily Telegraph*, 4 November 1935.

217. Laws, "Hang Disability."

218. "These Men Remember," 11 November 1926, *Evening News*, Press Cutting Book IV, GLRO.

219. "The Last Companies," *Morning Post*, 21 August 1931, PH 10, Star and Garter Collection, British Red Cross Archives. See Harold Begbie's introduction to G. H. Slade, *Two Sticks* (London, 1923), 7–8. "The writer of these

pages is not a gloomy and dejected person nursing a grievance against the State and continually bewailing his hardship." "It is, surely, a matter for consolation and for gratitude to know from these pages that there exist in the heart and character of the average young man of the present day, even when overtaken by dire calamity, those qualities of cheerful courage and unbreakable fortitude which give the bravest soldier his glory and the greatest saint his beauty."

220. Bigge, "The Lucky Ones."

221. J. B. Middlebrook, Ts Transcription, Imperial War Museum. "Man Whose Face Is a Miracle: Haig Homes Tenant," *Wimbledon Borough News,* 7 August 1931. Mr. Leslie Boorman was badly burned in France during the war, disfigured beyond recognition. The Prince of Wales spoke with him when he visited Sidcup. "It was considered inadvisable to let the Prince see such a badly disfigured face, but with characteristic interest in the welfare of the soldier he insisted on visiting his bed. He chatted with Mr. Boorman for some minutes, and there were tears in his eyes when he left his bedside."

222. "Editorial," *Star and Garter Magazine,* January 1932, 177.

223. "Gallant Gentlemen," *Finchley Press,* 22 May 1925, PH 7: 1924–6, Star and Garter Collection, British Red Cross Archives.

224. *Star and Garter Magazine,* April 1931, 74.

225. "The Convenience of Cousins," *Star and Garter Magazine,* April 1925, 51.

226. At the age of seventeen, Clifford Hill, a junior clerk, enlisted as a private in the East Yorks. Wounded in the spine in June 1918, he was rendered paraplegic. Doubly incontinent, subject to bedsores, Hill spent most of his life in veterans' homes, first at St. Martin's in Cheltenham, then in the Star and Garter, and finally at the War Seal Mansions. His injury made him unemployable. In 1932, he married Miss Helen Pollard, a member of the voluntary organization of women (nicknamed "The Camel Corps") who provided entertainment for Star and Garter patients. Although the couple moved to a bungalow in the countryside "specially designed to suit the bridegroom's needs," they decided after two years to return to London.

227. "Some Adventures in an Invalid Chair, No. 2," *Star and Garter Magazine,* November 1927, 35.

228. "Our Home," By a Sheltered One, *Star and Garter Magazine,* April 1931, 71.

229. "The Beauty of the Commonplace," *Star and Garter Magazine,* April 1931, 58.

230. "Vale: Harry John Franklin," *Star and Garter Magazine,* April 1931, 62.

231. "The Lure of a Hobby," *Star and Garter Magazine,* July 1933, 15.

232. "Vale: Harry John Franklin," *Star and Garter Magazine,* April 1931, 62.

233. Of 913 Star and Garter patients, nine committed suicide. Thirty-three demonstrated evidence of mental deterioration. Star and Garter Card File, British Red Cross Archives.

234. Medical Superintendent's Report, 22 February 1922, Star and Garter Collection, British Red Cross Archives.

235. Medical Superintendent's Report, 15 April 1918, Star and Garter Home.

236. House Committee, Report-Book, May 1937; report by Sir Barry Domvile.

237. Medical Superintendent's Report, 27 December 1918. The head of the Friends' Ambulance Unit also requested a personal meeting with the commandant. The orderlies had a "grievance with regard to the patients, who are not always particularly polite to them."

238. Medical Superintendent Report, 27 April 1918, Star and Garter Home.

239. Medical Superintendent Report, 16 and 17 October 1917, Star and Garter Collection, British Red Cross Archives. The committee discussed "putting him into the street, and seeing that the police took charge of him."

240. Medical Superintendent's Report, 6 November 1920, Star and Garter Collection, British Red Cross Archives; 21 February 1921.

241. Medical Superintendent's Report, 6 November 1920, Star and Garter Collection, British Red Cross Archives.

242. Programme of Sports and Concert to be held August 6th, 1917 at 2:30 P.M., Star and Garter Collection, British Red Cross Archives.

243. H.G.B., "First Impressions," *Star and Garter Magazine*, October 1931, 167.

244. "Thoughts by the Way," *Star and Garter Magazine*, September 1933, 24.

245. J. W. Richards, "The Invisible Man," *Star and Garter Magazine*, January 1925, 31.

246. H. T., "A Dog's Life at the Star and Garter Home," *Star and Garter Magazine*, July 1927, 119.

247. "Epistle of Imahlia to the Kroks," *Star and Garter Magazine*, January 1931, 17 ("Imahlia" as in "I'm a liah").

248. Ibid., 25.

249. John Buchan, "The Greatest War Debt," *Star and Garter Magazine*, December 1935; reprinted from the *Daily Telegraph*, 4 November 1935.

250. Laws, "Hang Disability."

251. "The Last Companies," *Morning Post*, 21 August 1931, PH 10, Star and Garter Collection, British Red Cross Archives.

252. *British Legion Journal*, January 1922, 149.

253. *Star and Garter Magazine*, April 1931, 74. In the *Sunday Times*, Pandora commented on the "spirit of forgetfulness" about the war; 10 November 1929, Cutting Book IV, Enham Archives.

254. *Star and Garter Magazine*, April 1931, 74.

255. "Forgotten Men and Those Who Remember Them," *Star and Garter Magazine*, April 1935, 27.

256. W. H. Baker to the Ministry of Pensions, 1 June 1937, PIN 15/38, PRO.

257. W. F., "Why Not Long Service Pensions for the Disabled," *Star and Garter Magazine*, January 1931, 39.

CHAPTER 4

1. On George Grosz, see Barbara McCloskey, *Georg Grosz and the Communist Party: Art and Radicalism in Crisis, 1918 to 1936* (Princeton, N.J., 1997),

13–14, 48–103; Matthias Eberle, *World War I and the Weimar Artists* (New Haven, Conn., 1985); *Der Traum von einer Neuen Welt, Berlin 1910–1933*, Internationale Tage (Ingelheim, 1989); Hans Hess, *George Grosz* (London, 1974).

2. Pomeranus, "Feldgraue Bettler," *Krieger Zeitung*, 8 October 1919, RAM 9054, BAL.

3. Der Polizei-Präsident, Bekanntmachung, 23 January 1919, RAM 9054, BAL; Dr. Arthur Stern, "Die Schüttler," *Berliner Tageblatt*, 4 December 1919, RAM 9054, BAL; "Bettelnde Kriegsinvaliden," *Berliner Tageblatt*, 1 November 1919, RAM 9054, BAL; Emil Kraepelin, *Memoirs* (Berlin, 1987 [1983]), 164.

4. See, for example, one Berliner's letter to Ebert: "Walking down the Kurfürstendamm or any other busy street one's eyes sink with shame to see how our brothers, who willingly risked their lives for us in the trenches, eke out a miserable existence by begging." Frau Sabine Hesemeyer to the Büro des Reichspräsidenten, 8 October 1919, RAM 9054, BAL.

5. Reichsarbeitsminister an das Zentralkomitee der Deutschen Vereine vom Roten Kreuz, Vermerk, Mit Referat 7, 9 October 1919, RAM 9054, BAL; Abteilung für soziale Kriegsbeschädigtenfürsorge im RAM, 25 October 1919, RAM 9054, BAL.

6. Badisches Arbeitsministerium, Hauptfürsorgestelle für Kriegsbeschädigte to the Presseabteilung des Ministeriums des Innern, 20 September 1920, RAM 9055, BAL; "Kriegsbeschädigte Bettler," in *Die Kriegsbeschädigtenfürsorge*, 30 October 1919, in RAM 8915, p. 48; *Deutsche Allgemeine Zeitung*, "Chr. B.," 1 June 1921, RAM 9054, BAL; Pomeranus, "Feldgraue Bettler," *Krieger Zeitung*, 8 October 1919, RAM 9054, BAL.

7. Freiherr von Welck, "Bedürfen die Vorschriften der Reichsgewerbeordnung über den Hausierhandel, den Straßenhandel und den Betrieb eines stehenden Gewerbes durch Reisende einer Abänderung vom Standpunkte der Kriegsbeschädigtenfürsorge," *Kriegsbeschädigten- und Kriegerhinterbliebenenfürsorge*, January/February 1919, 193.

8. See also "Im Kampfe gegen die Straßenbettelei unter dem Deckmantel 'Kriegsbeschädigter,'" *Reichsbund*, no. 35 (19 July 1919): 2; Bund deutscher Kriegsbeschädigter, Sitz Hamburg to the Reichsarbeitsminister, 25 October 1919, RAM 9054, BAL; Bessel, "Die Heimkehr der Soldaten," in Hirschfeld, ed., *Keiner fühlt sich hier mehr als Mensch*, fn. 40.

9. Jackson, 417–455. See Dr. Hans Boywidt, Die Pflicht zur Beschäftigung Schwerbeschädigter, Reichsausschuß der Kriegsbeschädigtenfürsorge, *Sonderschriften*, vol. 7 (Berlin, 1919).

10. Ernst Wiechert, *Das einfache Leben* [1939] (Frankfurt am Main, 1989), 17.

11. Christian Wilhelm, "Mein Berufstätigkeit," n.d. [April 1932], Rep. 62/349, LAB Λ.

12. In 1915, the optician Paul Silex founded the Berlin School for the War-Blinded with funds from the War Ministry. The "saddest of all cases," the blind were considered at the war's outset virtually unemployable, save as basket weavers and brush makers. Silex's school defied expectations. Under the direction of Betty Hirsch, herself blinded as a young girl, the school (after 1919 supported by the Labor Ministry) graduated accomplished stenographers and typ-

ists, bookbinders and masseurs. Against all conventional wisdom, Hirsch proved that the blind could even succeed as factory workers. On specially adjusted machines, twenty of the school's graduates labored at the Siemens-Schuckert factory outside of Berlin. See Betty Hirsch, *15 Jahre Kriegsblindenschule Geheimrat Dr. Silex* (Berlin, 1929).

13. Christian Wilhelm, "Meine Berufstätigkeit," Rep. 62/349, LAB-A.

14. From a so-called base pension, calculated on the basis of an unskilled, unmarried laborer who lived in the cheapest area of the country, compensation was increased depending not only on a man's family size, prewar occupation, and place of residence, but also on how much assistance and care he required during the day. Unlike the French and British systems, which granted officers higher pensions than enlisted men, the German National Pension Law dispensed with military rank as a basis of calculation in favor of prewar occupation. Those engaged in skilled labor before the war received 35 percent more than the combined sum of the base pension and the heavy disability supplement granted the severely disabled. Managers, professionals, and others who held "positions of responsibility" received 70 percent more.

15. See Stephan Leibfried, "Existenzminimum und Fürsorge-Richtsätze in der Weimarer Republik," in *Armutspolitik und die Entstehung des Sozialstaats,* ed. Stephan Leibfried (Bremen, 1985); Feldman, *The Great Disorder,* 223, 561; Merith Niehuss, *Arbeiterschaft in Krieg und Inflation* (Berlin, 1985), 139; on the disabled as welfare clients, see Crew, *Germans on Welfare,* 68–69; on standard welfare rates, see Crew, *Germans on Welfare,* 33.

16. *Reichsbund,* 12 June 1920, 85.

17. See Reichsbund der Kriegsbeschädigten, Kriegsteilnehmer und Kriegerhinterbliebenen, *Wie Kriegsbeschädigte abgefunden sind und wie sie wohnen.* Der Reichsregierung und dem Reichstag vorgelegt vom Reichsbund (Berlin, February 1927). For a critical examination of the disability rating scheme, see the speech by Dr. Kiessling [Leiter, Hamburger Hauptfürsorgestelle] before the Reichsbund's Gautagung in Lübeck, n.d. [1920], f. 41, 351-9 Kriegsbeschädigten- und Kriegshinterbliebenenfürsorge, J II 3, f. 41, StAH.

18. James Diehl, "Change and Continuity in the Treatment of German Kriegsopfer," *Central European History* 18 (1985): 171. See also Frei, "Vorbild oder Spiegelbild?" 564; Geyer, 230–277, esp. 246–248.

19. While every disability was assigned a minimum value (for instance, 50 percent for an amputated leg), a man whose earning capacity had fallen because of his injury could expect a higher pension than one who could return to his prewar occupation. See Dr. Franz Schweyer, "Der neue Reichsversorgungsgesetz," n.d. [May 1920?], p. 41, Pr. Br. Rep. 55, VIII 1—foliated, BLHA. Laub, 6; International Labour Office, *Compensation for War Disabilities in Germany, Austria, Poland and Czecho-Slovakia,* Series and Reports, Series E, no. 3, September 1921, p. 6.

20. Although war victims' organizations recognized that some income restrictions were necessary, they argued that the levels should be raised. See also Willi Hemeyer to Hirsch, 12 October 1920, Rep. 62/172, LAB-A.

21. See Ministerialrat Kerschensteiner, "Die Berücksichtigung der Teuerungsverhältnisse bei der Versorgung der Kriegsbeschädigten und Kriegshinterbliebenen,"

Soziale Praxis, Abschrift, 28 December 1921, 351–9 Kriegsbeschädigten- und Kriegshinterbliebenenfürsorge, F II 4, f. 28, StAH.

22. On provisions for disabled men's wives, see Dr. Adolf Sellmann, "Die Frauen unserer Kriegsbeschädigten," *Hannover Kurier,* 10 November 1916, R 8034 II/2330, folios 28–29.

23. Wixt to Hirsch, 29 June 1923, Rep. 62/354, LAB-A.

24. Th. Holz to Hirsch, 3 May 1919, Rep. 62/186, LAB-A.

25. Heidrun Homburg, "From Unemployment Insurance to Compulsory Labour," in *The German Unemployed,* ed. Richard Evans and Dick Geary (New York, 1987), 73–107; Joan Campbell, *Joy in Work, German Work* (Princeton, N.J., 1989), 213–242; Anson Rabinbach, *Human Motor: Energy, Fatigue and the Origins of Modernity* (Berkeley and Los Angeles, 1992 [1990]), 189–202, 210–217; Peukert, 135–136; Biernacki, 196–197, 213–214. On work and welfare, see Crew, *Germans on Welfare,* 191–193. On rehabilitation as a means of creating new men, see Price, 10–15, 251–254, Eghigian, 117–157.

26. "Entwurf eines Gesetzes über die Beschäftigung Schwerbeschädigter," Verhandlungen der verfassunggebenden Deutschen Nationalversammlung, Bd. 340, Anlagen zu den Stenographischen Berichten, Nr. 1750, p. 1783.

27. Dr. H. Fr. Ziegler, *Die Leistungen kriegsverletzter Industriearbeiter und Vorschläge zur Kriegsbeschädigtenfürsorge* (Düsseldorf, 1919), 48. On masculinity, see Thomas Kühne, "'… aus diesem Krieg werden nicht nur harte Männer heimkehren': Kriegskameradschaft und Männlichkeit im 20.Jahrhundert," in Kühne, *Männergeschichte—Geschlechtergeschichte: Männlichkeit im Wandel der Moderne* (Frankfurt, 1996), 174–192.

28. See Dr. G. Hohmann, "Die Kriegsbeschädigten und die neue Zeit," *Münchner Neue Nachrichten,* 11 January 1919, Staatskanzlei, Auschnittsammlung, nr. 1553, SHAD; Franz Schweyer, "Der Wiederaufbaugedanke," *Die Kriegsbeschädigten- und Kriegerhinterbliebenfürsorge* 4 (December 1919): 178.

29. Dr. Wölz, quoted in International Labour Office, *Employment of Disabled Men,* 223. The Reichsbund representative, Dr. Pfänder, agreed. Merely to restore to the disabled the standard of living they enjoyed before the war was not sufficient. He said "they should be able to improve their social position by means of their work" (226). See Price, 162.

30. See, for example, *Der Tag*'s report on the Cologne conference, 20 September 1916, R 8034 II/2330, ff. 2–3; "Die deutsche Kriegsbeschädigtenfürsorge," *Reichspost,* 31 December 1916, R 8034 II/2330, f. 46; "Neue Wege in der Kriegsbeschädigtenfürsorge," *Das Volk,* 12 October 1917, R 8034 II/2330, ff. 113–114; "Die Verwendungsmöglichkeiten der Kriegsbeschädigten," *Mitteilungen des Kriegsausschusses der deutschen Industrie,* 22 April 1916, R 8034 II/2330, f. 125; Kriegsministerium [von Stein] an die sämtliche Bundesregierungen (außer Preussen, Bayern, Königreich Sachsen und Württemberg), 6 September 1918, 111–2, Senat-Kriegsakten, CII c 1 b, f. 27, StAH.

31. "Lazarett-Beratung und Berufs-Beratung," *Frankfurter Zeitschrift,* 31 October 1916, R 8034 II/2330, f. 21; C. Zetzsche, "Die Beschäftigung der Kriegsverletzten in den Lazaretten," *Das Land,* 15 January 1916, R 8034 II/2329, f. 46, BAL.

32. Konrad Biesalski, *Kriegskrüppelfürsorge: Ein Aufklärungswort zum Troste und zur Mahnung* (Leipzig, 1915). On the prewar history of Krüppelfürsorge, Klaus-Dieter Thomann; see Price, 110–117.

33. See, for instance, Gerlach, *10 Jahre;* Roman Bachmeier, *Programm und Organisation einer Heilschule für Kriegsbeschädigte* (Halle, 1916); Devine, 294, 299; McMurtrie: "As far as can be seen…the volume of work done and the efficiency of individual institutions rank extremely high" (133).

34. Gerlach, *10 Jahre,* 298.

35. For results of the Brandenburg questionnaire to employers, see Dr. H. Beckmann, *Die Schwerbeschädigtenfürsorge in der Provinz Brandenburg,* 1919. See also Hirsch, 24, Rep. 62/36, LAB-A.

36. See Jackson. Included within the Law of the Severely Disabled were also victims of industrial accidents and the peacetime blinded, approximately one-ninth of the total. However, disabled veterans were accorded preference over the peacetime disabled. Beschäftigung Schwerbeschädigter bei hamburgischen Behörden, Referent Senatsrat Schultz, February 1928 [draft], 351-10 I, Sozialbehörde I, KO 41.51 Band 2, n.f., StAH. For P. A. Tixier, writing in the *British Legion Journal,* the German law was a model. See "Employment of Disabled," *British Legion Journal,* February 1922, 175; June 1922, 274. On modification of the law, and court decisions regarding it, see Sammlung von Gerichtsentscheidungen zum Schwerbeschädigtengesetz, May 1927, f. 85, 351-10 I, Sozialbehörde, KO 41.10 Band 2, StAH.

37. Sondersitzung der Vertreter der Hauptfürsorgestellen in Reutlingen, 7 October 1921, 351-10 I, Sozialbehörde I, KO 41.50 Band I, f. 60, StAH. For employers' complaints, see W. Mielck, Schwanapotheke an Amtliche Hauptfürsorgestelle [Abschrift], 25 May 1921, 351-10 I, Sozialbehörde I, KO 41.55, f. 7, StAH. Betonbau Arbeitgeber Verband für Deutschland [Eichenauer] an die Hauptfürsorgestelle der Kriegsbeschädigten- und Hinterbliebenenfürsorge, 10 November 1920, 351-10 I, Sozialbehörde I, KO 41.50 Band I, f. 10, StAH; Der Präsident des Landesfinanzamts Düsseldorf an den Herrn Reichsminister der Finanzen, 16 November 1926, Abschrift, RAM 8921.

38. Frie, *Wohlfahrtsstaat und Provinz,* 228–229. Die Hauptfürsorgestelle für Kriegsbeschädigte, Landeswohlfahrtsamt in Hamburg an den Landeshauptmann der Provinz Westfalen, 8 February 1928, 351-10 I, Sozialbehörde I, KO 41.31 Band I, f. 109, StAH. Der Präsident der Reichsarbeitsverwaltung an die mit den Aufgaben der Hauptfürsorgestellen beauftragten Dienststellen, 9 February 1926, 351-10 I, Sozialbehörde I, KO 41.23 Band 1, f. 64.

39. Niederschrift über die Tagung des ständigen Ausschusses der Hauptfürsorgestellen am 23 und 24 April 1925, 351-9 Kriegsbeschädigten- und Kriegshinterbliebenenfürsorge C 3 b. For praise of Rhenish employers, see also Niederschrift der Besprechung über die Unterbringung Schwerbeschädigter in der Landwirtschaft im RAM, 8 November 1921, Regierungsrat Dr. Kuessner [RAM] speaking. Sondersitzung der Vertreter der Hauptfürsorgestellen in Reutlingen, 7 October 1921, 351-10 I, Sozialbehörde I, KO 41.50 Band I, f. 51, StAH.

40. Abtlg. für Schwerbeschädigte, Hamburg, 7 June 1921, Bericht, 351-10 I, Sozialbehörde I, KO 41.50 Band I, f. 10. f. 27, StAH.

41. D. B. Schmidt, "Schwerbeschädigte und Arbeitgeber," *Zentralblatt für Kriegsbeschädigte und Kriegshinterbliebene*, April 1929, 44.

42. Otto Hager to Hirsch, 5 February 1921, Rep. 62/160, LAB-A; Kurt Neuwiller to Hirsch, 6 May 1922, Rep. 62/248, LAB-A. For the employer's perspective, see Report, Gustav Heyde, Dresden, n.d. [1917?], Rep. 62/38, LAB-A.

43. Erich Heinen to Hirsch, 3 July 1919, Rep. 62/167, LAB-A.

44. Hermann Kramer to Hirsch, 17 January 1921, Rep. 62/208, LAB-A.

45. Jung, *Der Einfluß der Wirtschaftskrise*, 7.

46. Karl Noack to Hirsch, 31 March 1920, Rep. 62/251, LAB-A.

47. Wilhelm Wix to Hirsch, 17 June 1918, Rep. 62/354, LAB-A.

48. J. Behrendt to Betty Hirsch, 15 February 1920, Rep. 62/87, LAB-A.

49. "Kriegsbeschädigte und Kriegerhinterbliebene im Reichs-, Staats- und Kommunaldienst," *Reichsbund*, 1 May 1922, 109.

50. "Lebensgestaltung," *Zentralblatt für Kriegsbeschädigte und Kriegshinterbliebene*, 16 September 1920, 134; G. Nowottnick, "Der Geist Macht Lebendig," *Zentralblatt für Kriegsbeschädigte und Kriegshinterbliebene*, 1 January 1927, 2; Josef Schmidt, "Zur Berufswahl unserer Kriegsbeschädigten," *Zentralblatt für Kriegsbeschädigte und Kriegshinterbliebene*, 1 February 1920, 18.

51. K. Junghanns to Hirsch, 29 January 1920, Rep. 62/190, LAB-A.

52. Willi Hemeyer to Hirsch, 23 July 1919, Rep. 62/172, LAB-A.

53. Willi Hemeyer to Hirsch, 30 October 1919, Rep. 62/172, LAB-A.

54. Erich Heinen to Hirsch, 25 June 1920, Rep. 62/167, LAB-A.

55. Karl Noack to Hirsch, 31 March 1920, Rep. 62/251, LAB-A.

56. P. Röhr to Hirsch, 5 September 1919, Rep. 62/278, LAB-A.

57. See "Provisions for War Disabled Pensioners: Analysis of Pensioners and their Pensions," November 1937, PIN 15/1412, PRO; Department of M.P.s on War Pensions, 25 November 1937, PIN 15/1412, PRO.

58. See Der Reichsarbeitsminister [Dr. Brauns], Entwurf eines Gesetztes zur Aenderung des Gesetzes über die Beschäftigung Schwerbeschädigter, 28 November 1922, Rep. 142, Nr. 1824, LAB-K; Walther Leuner, "Praktische Erfahrungen bei der Durchführung des Schwerbeschädigtengesetzes," *Die Kriegsbeschädigten- und Kriegerhinterbliebenen-Fürsorge* 11, no. 5 (May 1921); Niederschrift der Sitzung des ständigen Ausschusses der deutschen Hauptfürsorgestellen, 20 April 1926, 351-9 Kriegsbeschädigten- und Kriegshinterbliebenfürsorge C 3 b, Staatsarchiv Hamburg; Städt. Arbeitsamt Stuttgart, "Tätigkeitsbericht der Abteilung für Kriegsbeschädigte und Erwerbsbeschr. für das Jahr 1927," Sozialamt 775, StAS. Although disabled veterans also lost jobs during the hyperinflation, they did not suffer as badly as the general male population. See figures from the Hauptfürsorgestelle, 1924, RAM 8914, BAL. Only 851 (4.4 percent) of Westphalia's 19,476 severely disabled were unemployed in July 1923. Frie, *Wohlfahrtsstaat und Provinz*, 154.

59. According to the Hamburg welfare office's figures, approximately 12 percent of severely disabled veterans occupied "invalid posts." See Gustav Tonkow, *Das Schicksal der Schwerkriegsbeschädigten in Hamburg* (Rostock, 1927), 91.

60. See Jackson, 442.

61. In the other imperial ministries, severely disabled veterans averaged 3 percent of the total staff. See Schwerbeschädigte im Bereich der Reichsbehörden,

1928, RAM 8908, BAL. In Hamburg, the quota for city offices was raised to 2.5 percent in an attempt to counter long-term unemployment. Auszug aus dem Ersten Bericht des ständigen Staatshaushaltsausschusses, June 1928, Nr. 13, Sozialbehörde I, KO 41.51 Band 2, f. 104, StAH.

62. Tonkow, 77.

63. Ibid., 48–54.

64. Ibid., 79.

65. Ibid., 81.

66. Ibid., 79.

67. Ibid., 83.

68. Ibid., 91; "Lebensgestaltung," *Zentralblatt für Kriegsbeschädigte und Kriegshinterbliebene,* 16 September 1920, 134.

69. J. Briefs, *Die Soziale Fürsorge der Schwerbeschädigten in der heutigen Gesetzgebung* (Berlin, 1931), 104. See also Johannes Teitz, Leiter der Abteilung für Erwerbsbeschränkte beim Landesberufsamt, *Berufsberatung und Eingliederung erwachsener Erwerbsbeschränkter ins Erwerbsleben* (Berlin, 1925), 30.

70. Hans Weber to Hirsch, 13 December 1921, Rep. 62/345, LAB-A.

71. Kurt Neuwiller to Hirsch, 6 May 1922, Rep. 62/248, LAB-A. For more complaints about employers, see Georg Paffhausen to Hirsch, 23 March 1926, Rep. 62/256; Fritz Koepke, Report by Betty Hirsch, 18 December 1923, Rep. 62/204, LAB-A.

72. See Sachße and Tennstedt, 81.

73. Hauptfürsorgestelle der Kriegsbeschädigten- und Kriegshinterbliebenen-Fürsorge in Mecklenburg-Strelitz [Dr. Bahlike] an den Herrn Reichsarbeitsminister, 28 April 1923, RAM 8920, f. 135. Der Minister des Innern an den Herrn Reichsarbeitsminister, 16 April 1923, f. 189, RAM 8920; Der Landeshauptmann der Provinz Sachsen, Landesfürsorgeverband (Bernau?), Urschriftlich dem Herrn RAM, Reichsarbeitsverwaltung, 27 June 1924, RAM 8921.

74. Tonkow, 41–42. On the preference accorded the severely disabled, see Der Reichsarbeitsminister an sämtliche Hauptfürsorgestellen, 7 February 1924, 351-10 I, Sozialbehörde I, KO 41.51 Band I, f. 103; Der Reichsarbeitsminister an alle Hauptfürsorgestellen, 7 March 1924, 351-10 I, Sozialbehörde I, KO 41.51 Band I, f. 117, StAH.

75. Wohlfahrtsamt Stuttgart, "Betr. Bericht über die Arbeitsfürsorge für Schwerbeschädigte in der Zeit vom 1.12.1931 bis 31.3.1932," 28 April 1932; Wohlfahrtsamt Stuttgart, "Betr. Bericht über die Arbeitsfürsorge für Schwerbeschädigte in der Zeit vom 1.4.1934 bis 30.6.1933," 20 July 1933; An den Herrn Amtsvorstand, 9 March 1938, Betr. Tätigkeitsbericht der Abt. Arbeitsfürsorge für Schwerbeschädigte in der Zeit vom 1.8.31–31.12.37; all Sozialamt 775, StAS. Georg Panzer, "Die Wirtschaftliche Lage der Schwerbeschädigten," *Zentralblatt für Kriegsbeschädigte und Kriegshinterbliebene,* January 1929, 16.

76. As Jackson notes, 6,000 veterans lost the protection of the Law of the Severely Disabled between 1931 and 1934; according to Bruno Jung, many of those were the "lightly" disabled accorded posts after longer spells of unemployment. See Jung, 32–33, 39.

77. See Petzina, "Arbeitslosigkeit der Weimarer Republik."

78. Jung, *Der Einfluß der Wirtschaftskrise*, 23–26.

79. Ibid., 39.

80. Statistisches Jahrbuch der Stadt Berlin, 1933, pp. 105, 229.

81. From 31 March 1930 to 31 March 1931, the number of unemployed severely disabled rose from 1881 to 4097. See Jung, 23; Auszug aus der Niederschrift über die Sitzung des Ständigen Ausschusses der Deutschen Hauptfürsorgestellen, 29 January 1932, 351-10 I, Sozialbehörde I, KO 41.31 Band I, f. 163, StAH.

82. Jung, *Der Einfluß der Wirtschaftskrise*, 27–28. NS-Kriegsopferversorgung, Bezirk Hamburg (Bode, Bezirksobmann) Aufruf an die Arbeitgeberschaft Hamburg, May, 1934, 351-10 I Sozialbehörde I, KO 41.50 Band 2, f. 33, StAH.

83. August Cook, Kriegsinvalide an Seine Exelens Herrn Reichspräsident v. Hindenburg, 1 September 1927, RAM 9936 BAL. See also Julius Schwanitz to the RAM, 7 December 1921, RAM 8920, f. 65.

84. H. Näther to Hirsch, 21 June 1927, Rep. 62/645, LAB-A.

85. Herr Becker to Hirsch, 29 July 1920, Rep. 62/85, LAB-A.

86. On the significance of such labels, see Eghigian, 383.

87. Quoted in Carl Schneider, "Das Kriegsbeschädigten-Problem: Warum eine Sonderorganisation?" p. 29, RAM/8866, BAL.

88. Badischer Heimatdank, Bericht über die Sitzung des Badischen Landesausschusses der Kriegsbeschädigtenfürsorge, 25 October 1917, RAM/8866, BAL; Dr. K. Schwarz, *Kriegsbeschädigtenfürsorge*, April/May 1918, p. 463.

89. "Das Wort 'Kriegsbeschädigter' als Standesbezeichnung," Niederschrift über die 9.Sitzung des Reichsarbeitsauschusses, 15 September 1917, RAM 8861, BAL.

90. "Der gute Kamerad," *Der Reichsverband*, February 1929, R 116/199, BAK.

91. See "Allgemeine Wohlfahrtspflege oder soziale Kriegsbeschädigten und Hinterbliebenenfürsorge," *Reichsbund*, 1 July 1922, 139. On welfare clients more generally, see Crew, *Germans on Welfare*, esp. 67–136, 166–187.

92. See Nowottnick, "Der Selbsthilfegedanke," 26.

93. Josef Meister, "Die Psychologie in der Rentenversorgung der Kriegsblinden," Bund erblindeter Krieger: Entwicklung, Bedeutung und seine Stellung zur Rentenversorgung und Fürsorge, 4. ordentlicher Bundestag, Bund erblindeter Krieger, 5–7 March 1926, R 116/331, BAK.

94. "Forderungen der Lazarettkranken," *Frankfurter Zeitung*, Morgen Ausgabe, 4 September 1919, Staatskanzlei, Auschnittsammlung, nr. 1554, SHAD.

95. On "Mitbestimmungsrecht," see Hans-Joachim Bieber, *Gewerkschaften in Krieg und Revolution*, vol. 2 (Hamburg, 1981), 619–624; Heinrich Potthof, *Gewerkschaften und Politik zwischen Revolution und Inflation* (Düsseldorf, 1979), 102–121; H.A. Winkler, *Von der Revolution zur Stabilisierung: Arbeiter und Arbeiterbewegung in der Weimarer Republik* (Berlin, 1984), 168–169, 191–205.

96. On this concept, see Franz X. Rappenecker, *Das Problem der Fürsorge für die Kriegsopfer* (Münster: Aschendorffschen Buchdruckerei 1928), 77–92; Crew, *Germans on Welfare*, 76–77.

97. See Ewald Frie's analysis in "Vorbild oder Spiegelbild?" 574–575. See also the correspondence concerning the appointment of Erich Rossmann, chair-

man of the Reichsbund and a senior civil servant in the Labor Ministry, to director of the Stuttgart Hauptversorgungsamt, E 130 b/3767, ff. 14–21, 45, Hauptstaatsarchiv Stuttgart.

98. See Dr. Oscar Weigert and Dr. Lothar Richter, *Die Versorgung und die soziale Fürsorge für Kriegsbeschädigte und Kriegshinterbliebene* (Berlin, 1921), 181–182.

99. Ibid., 183–184. Proceedings of the Hamburg Beirat are contained in 351-9 Kriegsbeschädigten- und Kriegshinterbliebenenfürsorge J I 2, StAH.

100. See Crew, "'Wohlfahrtsbrot ist bitteres Brot,'" 217–246, esp. 226; Crew, *Germans on Welfare,* 99–104. Konferenz der Leiter der Deutschen Hauptfürsorgestellen am 27, 29 September 1922, Breslau, 27 September 1922, 351-9 Kriegsbeschädigten- und Kriegshinterbliebenenfürsorge, C 3 a, n.f. StAH.

101. Dr. Otto Wölz, "Der Wohlfahrtsbeamte," *Die Kriegsbeschädigten- und Kriegerhinterbliebenen-Fürsorge,* 2, no. 5 (August 1920): 43; see also Jung, *Der Einfluß der Wirtschaftskrise,* 15.

102. Rappenecker, 2.

103. See Whalen, 162–165. On hostility toward the civil service among the general public, see Feldman, *The Great Disorder,* 625–626, 679–680; Jane Caplan, *Government without Administration: State and Civil Service in the Weimar Republic and Nazi Germany* (Oxford, 1988).

104. *Reichsbund,* 18 September 1924, 134.

105. See Königlicher Landrat des Kreises Nieder-Barnim [gez. von Bredow] to the Herrn Minister des Innern, 22 April 1919 [Abschrift], Pr. Br. Rep. 2A, Regierung Potsdam I SW Nr. 1390, BLHA. Pension records created under the Mannschaftsversorgungsgesetz of 1906 did not, for instance, detail prewar occupation or number of children. Denkschrift über das Versorgungswesen, aufgestellt nach dem Stande vom 1.April 1923, Reichstag, 1.Wahlperiode, 6 April 1923, RAM 9493, BAL; Hauptmann a.D. Kratz, Vorstand der Rentenabteilung des Versorgungsamts Koblenz, "Gang der Verwaltungsarbeiten im Rentenverfahren," *Zentralblatt für Kriegsbeschädigte und Kriegshinterbliebene,* 16 July 1920, 104–105. See also Frie, *Wohlfahrtsstaat und Provinz,* 150 n. 258.

106. See, for instance, Entschliessung der am 10.August 1921 im Gewerkschaftshaus versammelten Kriegsopfer Hamburgs und Begründung zu den in der Entschliessung des Beirats der Hauptfürsorgestelle vom 31.August 1921 gemachten Vorschlägen, 111-2 Senat Kricgsakten C II c 77, StAH. "Umanerkennung gleich—Nichtanerkennung!?" *Zentralblatt für Kriegsbeschädigte und Kriegshinterbliebene,* 16 September 1921, 138–139; Württ. Arbeitsministerium Abt. Soz. Volkswohlfahrt an sämtliche Bezirks- und besondere örtliche Fürsorgestellen, 9 February 1921, Sozialamt 729, StAS.

107. Denkschrift über das Versorgungswesen, RAM 9493, BAL.

108. For an angry response, see Otto Hager to Hirsch, 15 October 1919, Rep. 62/160, LAB-A.

109. See Brandenburgische Hauptfürsorgestelle to the Herrn Reichsarbeitsminister, Verfg., j.a. gez. Magnus, 11 August 1921, p. 17, Pr. Br. Rep. 55, VIII 2, BLHA.

110. Bericht über die Monatsversammlung des Reichsbundes der Kriegs-beschädigten pp. vom 19 März 1929. 351-10 I, Sozialbehörde I, KO 80.11, f. 51, StAH.

111. Denkschrift über das Versorgungswesen, aufgestellt nach dem Stande vom 1.April 1923, Reichstag, 1.Wahlperiode, 6 April 1923, RAM 9493, BAL; Dr. Georg Panzer, "Wissenschaft und Kriegsopfer," *Der Deutsche*, 11 February 1928, 61 Sta/1148, BAL.

112. On complaints about rude welfare officials more generally, see Crew, *Germans on Welfare*, 38.

113. "Zustände beim städtischen Fürsorgeamt für Kriegsbeschädigte," *Arbeiter-Zeitung*, 11 January 1923, Mag. Akte V/65, StAF. See also "Kriegsopfer und Regierung: Die Wandlung zu Objekten der Fürsorge," *Schwäb. Tagwacht*, nr. 282, 2 December 1927, E 130 b/3773, f. 551, Hauptstaatsarchiv Stuttgart.

114. "Götz von Berlichingen," "Der Gang zum Versorgungsamt," *Röthner Nachrichten*, 14 September 1925, Staatskanzlei, Auschnittsammlung, nr. 1557, SHAD. A knight-hero of the Peasant's War (and subject of a play by Goethe), Götz von Berlichingen had an iron hand and no love of the established order.

115. "Kriegsbeschädigtentagung in Hamburg," *Hamburger Anzeiger*, 23 May 1927, 351-10 I, Sozialbehörde I, KO 80.11, f. 35, StAH.

116. "Götz von Berlichingen," "Der Gang zum Versorgungsamt."

117. Koepke to Hirsch, 2 May 1924, Rep. 62/204, LAB-A.

118. Hirsch to the Reichsarbeitsministerium, Kriegsblindenfürsorgeabtei-lung, 15 June 1921, Rep. 62/350, LAB-A.

119. Robert Hammer to Hirsch, 4 May 1922, Rep. 62/162, LAB-A.

120. "Ein vorbildlicher Erlaß des RAM," *Germania*, Morgen, 30 September 1925, Staatskanzlei, Auschnittsammlung, nr. 1557, SHAD. Herr Schädlich, 2.Sitzung des Hauptfürsorgeausschusses, 24 November 1921, 351-2 II Allge-meine Armenanstalt II, f. 24. "Ministerwechsel in RAM," *Reichsbund*, 15 July 1928, p. 108. On complaints about civil servants in welfare offices, see Der Ober-bürgermeister, Berlin [gez. Dr. Sahm] an Herrn Staatsminister Dr. Hirtsiefer, 1 October 1931, RAM 9257, BAL.

121. Frau von Ihne [Kriegsblindenheim, Bellevuestr. 12], September 1915, Rep. 191, 3185, GStAB.

122. Josef Wuttke, "Es muß wider ein Wohlsein an uns kommen!" *Zentral-blatt für Kriegsbeschädigte und Kriegerhinterbliebene*, August 1932, 91.

123. "Das moralische Recht der Kriegsopfer," *Zentralblatt für Kriegs-beschädigte und Kriegerhinterbliebene*, March 1932, 25.

124. Wuttke, "Es muß wider ein Wohlsein an uns kommen!" 91.

125. See Königlicher Landrat des Kreises Nieder-Barnim [gez. von Bredow] to the Herrn Minister des Innern, 22 April 1919 [Abschrift], Pr. Br. Rep. 2A, Regierung Potsdam I SW Nr. 1390, Brandenburgische Landeshauptarchiv [BLHA]. See also Wölz, "Der Wohlfahrtsbeamte," pp. 42–43.

126. Oehme to Hirsch, 11 July 1932, Rep. 62/254.

127. For an exception, see Bund der Hirnverletzten [A. Führmann] an den Magistrat des Herrn Oberbürgermeisters Voigt, 10 March 1923, Mag. Akte V/63, StAF.

128. See, for instance, "Von Pontius zu Pilatus," *Pirnaer Volkszeitung,* 14 August 1920, Staatskanzlei, Auschnittsammlung, nr. 1555, SHAD. On the Communist critique of the welfare state, see Crew, *Germans on Welfare,* 24–25.

129. Richard Maroke, "Jenseits und diesseits der großen Geschehnisse," *Reichsbund,* 15 April 1921, 120.

130. "Schrei in Not," *Neue Leipziger Zeitung,* 21 August 1927, RAM 9936, BAL. See also "Höhere Verrücktheit oder—?" *Vorwärts,* 1 March 1919, Staatskanzlei Auschnittsammlung, nr. 1553, SHAD.

131. Ministerialrat A. Grießmeyer, "Was geschieht für die Kb?"; quoted in the *Zentralblatt,* January 1930.

132. "Götz von Berlichingen," "Der Ganz zum Versorgungsamt" (emphasis in original).

133. Wiechert, 17.

134. See Eghigian, 382.

135. C. A. Ottersbach, "An alle offenen und versteckten Neider," *Zentralblatt für Kriegsbeschädigte und Kriegerhinterbliebene,* October 1931, 130.

136. See Evans and Geary, 79.

137. "Es geht alle an," *Zentralblatt für Kriegsbeschädigte und Kriegerhinterbliebene,* August 1931, 108.

138. Diehl, "Victors or Victims?" 705–736.

139. "Schafft Arbeitsplätze für Kriegsbeschädigte," *Hamburger Anzeiger,* vol. 79, 5 April 1934, 351-10 I Sozialbehörde I, KO 41.50 Band 2, f. 21, StAH; Stellvertr. Gauleiter Schmidt; quoted in "Fragen der Kriegsopferversorgung," Ausschnitt aus dem *N.S. Kurier,* 1 May 1934, Sozialamt/800, StAS.

140. Dr. Werner Freytag, "Der Dank des Vaterlandes: Umgestaltung des Versorgungsrechts der Kriegsbeschädigten, Endlich Erfüllung einer nationalen Dankespflicht," *Wurzener Tageblatt,* 18 July 1933, Staatskanzlei, Auschnittsammlung, nr. 1557, SHAD.

141. Kamerad Bode, Gauobmann, "Kriegsopfer, die Ehrenbürger des Staates," *Hamburger Tageblatt,* 20 September 1933, 351-10 I, Sozialbehörde I, KO 80.22, StAH.

142. Hanns Oberlindober, *Ehre und Recht für die deutschen Kriegsopfer* (Berlin, 1933); cited in Diehl, 716.

143. Henry Friedlander, *The Origins of Nazi Genocide: From Euthanasia to the Final Solution* (Chapel Hill, N.C., 1995), esp. chs. 3–4. Although disabled veterans were officially exempted from Nazi euthanasia programs, some nonetheless were killed. Friedlander, 81–82, 174; Michael Burleigh, *Death and Deliverance: "Euthanasia" in Germany, 1900–1945* (Cambridge, 1994), 93–129.

144. Der RAM to the Landesregierungen, 30 December 1939, Pr. Br. Rep. 2A, Regierung Potsdam I SW, nr. 1389, BLHA. As the Labor Ministry had decided in 1933, severely disabled veterans placed in concentration camps could also receive emergency allowances. "Insofar as the disabled receives free board and shelter," the decision read, "it is to be considered whether a need for the granting of emergency allowances in the previous amount can still be recognized." Der Landesdirektor der Provinz Brandenburg, Kriegsbeschädigten- und Kriegshinterbliebenenfürsorge, 12 September 1933, Pr. Br. Rep. 55, Abt. VIII, 7, BLHA.

145. In 1933, 46,780 severely disabled were unemployed; in 1934 only 30,797. In 1939, less than 2 percent of all severely disabled were unemployed. See Jackson, 447. Stuttgart welfare officials noted in October 1933, "eine grössere Einstellungsbereitschaft seitens der Arbeitgeber." Wohlfahrtsamt Stuttgart, "Arbeitsfürsorge für Schwerbeschädigte in der Zeit vom 1.7.1933 bis 30.9.1933," gez. Aldinger, Sozialamt/775, StAS. On the Nazi campaign for the employment of the severely disabled, see "Arbeitsbeschaffung für Kriegsbeschädigte ist Ehrenpflicht," *Hamburger Nachrichten,* 7 October 1933, 351-10 I Sozialbehörde I, KO 41.50 Band 2, f. 1, StAH; "Der Dank des Vaterlandes ist ihnen gewiß," *Hamburger Tageblatt,* 24 May 1934, 351-10 I Sozialbehörde I, KO 41.50 Band 2, f. 28, "70,000 Kriegsbeschädigten fehlt Arbeit," *Hbg. Fremdenblatt,* 29 May 1934, 351-10 I Sozialbehörde I, KO 41.50 Band 2, f. 35, StAH. "Bessere Versorgung der Kriegsopfer," *Angriff,* 4 July 1934, 61 Sta 1/1149, f. 59, BAL; "Bringt Kriegsbeschädigte unter!" *Berliner Lokalanzeiger,* 28 October 1933, 61 Sta 1/1149, f. 88, BAL; Jahresbericht der Amtlichen Hauptfürsorgestelle für Kriegsbeschädigte und Kriegerhinterbliebene (Abteilung XI der Fürsorgebehörde), Hamburg, 1936, gez. Dr. Spargel, 351-10 I Sozialbehörde I, StA 27.50, ff. 39–47; "Die Zeit des Gnadentalers ist vorbei," Ausschnitt aus dem *Stuttgarter Neuen Tagblatt,* 28 September 1941, Sozialamt 800, StAS.

146. Karl Stete an das RAM, 27 October 1935, RAM/10052, BAL.

147. Johann Stasch to the Herrn Reichsarbeitsminister, 23 May 1935, RAM/10052, BAL. On complaints about welfare officials, Auszug aus der Niederschrift der Hauptabteilung des Gemeinderats vom 8.März 1935, Sozialamt 775, StAS; "Für die Kriegsopfer," 16 November 1933, 61 Sta 1/1150, f. 16, BAL; Friedrich Stepponat, Tisit an das RAM, z. Hd. des RAM Herrn Franz Seldte, 24 June 1935, RAM 10054. Louis Siebenhüner an den Führer und Reichskanzler, 22 December 1935, RAM 10054.

148. Quoted in "Ein uns heiliges Erbe Friedrich des Großen: Das Invalidenhaus zu Berlin," in *Deutsche Kriegsopferversorgung,* May 1937, RW 6/389, Bundesarchiv-Militärarchiv (BAM).

149. Richard Stern to the Hauptversorgungsamt, 6 December 1926, PH 33/11, BAM.

150. Quoted in "Ein uns heiliges Erbe Friedrich des Großen," May 1937, RW 6/389, BAM. On the Invalides, see Isser Woloch, *The French Veteran from the Revolution to the Restoration* (Chapel Hill, N.C., 1979).

151. Mayo, 284.

152. Among the prominents buried in the Invalidenhaus between the wars were Manfred von Richthofen, Ernst Troeltsch, and Hans von Seeckt.

153. *Berlin und Seine Bauten* (Berlin, 1877), 1:216.

154. Robert Springer, *Berlin* (Leipzig, 1861), 108–109.

155. Notes from the Chefbesprechung beim Reichsfinanzminister in Weimar am 19.7.19, signed J. V. Hartwich, dated 15 August 1919, RAM/7757, BAL.

156. Reichswehrminister to the Reichsarbeitsminister, 14 April 1920, RAM/7757, BAL. For the RAM's response, see Reichsarbeitsminister an das Reichswehrministerium, Chef der Heeresleitung, 14 April 1920, RAM/7757, BAL.

157. Reichswehrminister to the Reichsarbeitsminister, 14 April 1920, RAM/7757, BAL.

158. Unless they could prove that they required no daily care, single men could generally not be admitted.

159. Geiss [Hauptfürsorgestelle der Stadt Berlin für Kriegsbeschädigte und Kriegshinterbliebene] to the Hauptversorgungsamt, 9 March 1921, RAM 7756, BAL.

160. Willi Langhanky to the Hauptversorgungsamt Berlin, 6 September 1921, RAM 7757, BAL.

161. Completely blinded, deaf in one ear, his left hand partially paralyzed, and with an amputated lower leg, Ernst Veit was refused admission on the grounds that he could not work. Vermerk, 11 November 1922, RAM 7758, BAL.

162. Herr Erich Rehse to the Reichsarbeitsministerium, 4 June 1921, RAM 7757, BAL.

163. Stern to the Hauptversorgungsamt Berlin, 26 March 1926, PH 33/196, BAM.

164. Mayo, 285.

165. "Vertrauensrat des Invalidenhauses Berlin," n.d. [1920?], PH 33/155, BAM.

166. Lemke, Leut.a.D. für die Interessierten to the Fürsorgestelle für Kriegsbeschädigte, 29 May 1922, RAM 7762, BAL.

167. Der Vertrauensrat to the Hauptversorgungsamt, 4 May 1921, PH 33/464, BAM.

168. Karstedt [im Auftrage, Reichsarbeitsminister] to the Hauptversorgungsamt, 27 January 1922, PH 33/464, BAM.

169. Witzleben [H.V.A. Berlin] to the Vorsitzenden des Vertrauensrates im Invalidenhaus Herrn Rittmeister a.D. v. Rauch, 31 March 1922, PH 33/155, BAM.

170. Stern to the Hauptversorgungsamt, Berlin, 11 September 1926, PH 33/11, BAM.

171. Vertrauensrat, 30 March 1922, PH 33/464, BAM.

172. Statistisches Jahrbuch der Stadt Berlin, 1927, p. 108.

173. Stern to the Hauptversorgungsamt, 26 March 1926, PH 33/196, BAM.

174. Fragebogen, Max Janik, 13 December 1921, PH 33/546, BAM.

175. Hauptversorgungsamt to Haus- und Kassenverwaltung des Kriegsinvalidenhauses, 16 October 1925, PH 33/546, BAM.

176. Der Unterstützungsausschuss to the Reichsarbeitsministerium, 19 March 1926, PH 33/199, BAM.

177. Fick, Fröhlich, Schermenske, Moahts to Herrn Dr. Brauns, 29 March 1926, PH 33/199, BAM.

178. Gerhard Pump to the Hauptversorgungsamt, 28 February 1924, PH 33/199, BAM.

179. Ibid.

180. List of residents, PH 33/196.

181. Stern to the Hauptversorgungsamt, Berlin, 26 March 1926, PH 33/196, BAM.

182. Richard Stern, "Erläuterungen," n.d. [1926], PH 33/11, BAM.

183. Ibid.

184. Report, Hauptversorgungsamt, 5 August 1926, PH 33/199, BAM.

185. Walter Stülpner [Vorsitzender, Offiziers Vereinigung] to Stern, 23 May 1927, PH 33/377; Walter Stülpner to Hauptversorgungsamt Berlin, 30 March 1928, PH 33/377, BAM.

186. Stern to Hauptversorgungsamt, 1 August 1924, PH 33/565, BAM.

187. Stern to Hauptversorgungsamt, 10 March 1927, PH 33/11, BAM.

188. Stern to Hauptversorgungsamt, 6 December 1926, PH 33/11, BAM.

189. Stern to Hauptversorgungsamt, 24 March 1929, PH 33/11, BAM.

190. Boetticher to the Director of the Hauptversorgungsamt, 8 October 1929, PH 33/442, BAM.

191. Stern to Hauptversorgungsamt Brandenburg-Pommern, 24 October 1929, PH 33/442, BAM. See also Stern to Hauptversorgungsamt, 3 March 1925, PH 33/199, BAM.

192. Frau Hugo Stinnes to Kriegsinvalidenhaus, 18 December 1924, PH 33/368, BAM.

193. TV [Haus u. Kassenverwaltung Kriegsinvalidenhauses] to the Direktion des Zoologischen Gartens, 26 July 1926. Reply, 28 July 1926, PH 33/475, BAM. For information about donations, see PH 33/368.

194. v. Witzleben, n.d., PH 33/368, BAM.

195. "Skandalöse Zustände im Invalidenhaus," *Der National Sozialist,* 24 March 1930, PH 33/442, BAM.

196. Although many of the Invalidenhaus's residents assumed that Stern was "a baptized Jew," he was not. He remained director of the Invalidenhaus until remilitarization in 1937. See RAM [Rettig] to Hauptversorgungsamt, Brandenburg-Pommern, 10 April 1930, PH 33/442, BAM. See also Paul Peters to Hauptversorgungsamt, Berlin, 14 June 1924, RAM 7765, BAL.

197. Alfred Fick to the Labor Minister Dr. Brauns, 21 July 1924, RAM 7765, BAL.

198. RAM [Meyes] to the Rechnungshof des Deutschen Reiches, 1 February 1935, PH 3/465, BAM.

199. Reichs- und Preussische Arbeitsminister, 3 September 1935 [Abschrift], PH 33/465, BAM.

200. Reichs- und Preussische Arbeitsminister, 3 September 1935 [Abschrift], PH 33/465, BAM.

201. "Das Invalidenhaus und sein Bataillon," *Völkischer Beobachter,* 3 March 1933.

202. Stern to the Vorstand des Automobilclubs von Deutschland, 2 May 1933, PH 33/565, BAM.

203. Seldte to Stern, 16 February 1934, PH 33/368, BAM. Stern to Herrn Staatssekretär Dr. Meissner, 6 December 1933, PH 33/565, BAM.

204. NSKOV e.V. Bezirk Groß-Berlin 18 to the Bezirk XVII der NSKOV, 12 October 1934, z.H. des Pg. Zacher, 12 October 1934, RAM 7760, BAL.

205. Saul Friedländer, *Nazi Germany and the Jews,* vol. 1, *The Years of Persecution* (New York, 1997), 28–29, 117, 292–293.

206. NSKOV e.V. Bezirk Groß-Berlin 18 to the Bezirk XVII der NSKOV, 12 October 1934, z.H. des Pg. Zacher, 12 October 1934, RAM 7760, BAL.

207. Fick to Seldte, 12 November 1934, RAM 7760, BAL.

208. Der Reichskriegsopferführer [Oberlindober?] to Herrn Oberst Reinecke [Reichskriegsministerium], 7 May 1937, RW 6/391, BAM.

CONCLUSION

1. H. Günther, "Sind die Kriege gefährlicher geworden?" *Die Umschau* 18 (1914): 808–813. Cited in Bernd Ulrich, "'... als wenn nichts geschehen wäre.' Anmerkungen zur Behandlung der Kriegsopfer während des Ersten Weltkriegs," in *Keiner fühlt sich hier mehr als Mensch,* ed. Gerhard Hirschfeld, Gerd Krumeich, and Irena Renz (Essen, 1993), 118.

2. Blackbourn and Eley, 195–205, 223–227, 264–265.

3. Celia Applegate, *A Nation of Provincials* (Berkeley and Los Angeles, 1990); Peter Fritzsche, *Rehearsals for Fascism: Populism and Political Mobilization in Weimar Germany* (Oxford, 1990), 76; Rudy Koshar, *Social Life, Local Politics, and Nazism: Marburg, 1880–1935* (Chapel Hill, N.C., 1986), esp. chs. 3, 4; Thomas Nipperdey, "Verein als soziale Structur in Deutschland im späten 18. und frühen 19.Jahrhundert," in *Gesellschaft, Kultur, Theorie* (Göttingen, 1976), 174–205.

4. Similarly, Andreas Wollasch, "Tendenzen und Probleme gegenwärtiger historischer Wohlfahrtsforschung in Deutschland," *Westfälische Forschungen* 43 (1993): 12. Important recent work includes Hong, *Welfare, Modernity, and the Weimar State,* esp. 16–35; Jean Quataert, *Staging Philanthropy* (Ann Arbor, 2001); my thanks to Professor Quataert for allowing me to read chapters of her forthcoming book. Kaiser, "Freie Wohlfahrtsverbände im Kaiserreich und in der Weimarer Republik," 26–57; Kaiser, *Sozialer Protestantismus im 20. Jahrhundert;* Buck, "Die Entwicklung der freien Wohlfahrtspflege von den ersten Zusammenschlüssen der freien Verbände im 19.Jahrhundert bis zur Durchsetzung des Subsidiaritätsprinzip in der Weimarer Fürsorgegesetzgebung," 139–172; Dickinson, esp. 93–100, 174–183; Sachße and Tennstedt, *Geschichte der Armenfürsorge in Deutschland,* vol. 1, *Vom Spätmittelalter bis zum Ersten Weltkrieg,* 222–243, and vol. 2, *Fürsorge und Wohlfahrtspflege, 1871–1929,* 24–25, 152–173; Hong, "The Politics of Welfare Reform and the Dynamics of the Public Sphere," esp. 9–83.

5. Edward Gowlland to Governing Council, War Seal Foundation, 7 October 1930, George William Ditcher's file, HFAC.

6. Ditcher to Roberts, August 1932, George William Ditcher's file, HFAC.

7. Ditcher to H. Ditcher, 8 September 1939, George William Ditcher's file, HFAC.

Bibliography

ARCHIVAL SOURCES

BRITISH

Birmingham Local Record Office
British Red Cross Museum and Archives
Cambridgeshire County Record Office
Enham Archives
Greater London Record Office
Hammersmith and Fulham Archives and Local History Centre (HFAC)
Imperial War Museum
Lancashire Record Office, Preston
Liverpool Record Office
Modern Records Centre, Warwick
Peter Liddle Collection, Leeds University Library, Special Collections
Preston Hall
Public Record Office (PRO)
Richmond Poppy Factory
Royal British Legion
Royal Star and Garter Home
Sir Oswald Stoll Foundation

GERMAN

Archiv des Deutschen Caritasverbandes (ADCV)
Archiv des Diakonischen Werkes der Evangelischen Kirche
Brandenburgisches Landeshauptarchiv Potsdam (BLHA)

Bundesarchiv Koblenz (BAK)
Bundesarchiv Lichterfelde (BAL)
Bundesarchiv Militärarchiv–Freiburg (BAM)
Geheimes Staatsarchiv Preußischer Kulturbesitz (GStAB)
Hauptstaatsarchiv Stuttgart
Historisches Archiv der Stadt Köln
Landesarchiv Berlin–Breitestraße(LAB-A)
Landesarchiv Berlin–Kalkreuthstraße (LAB)
Niedersächsisches Hauptstaatsarchiv
Sächsisches Hauptstaatsarchiv (SHAD)
Staatsarchiv Hamburg (StAH)
Staatsarchiv Ludwigsburg
Stadtarchiv Frankfurt (StAF)
Stadtarchiv Stuttgart (StAS)
Thüringisches Hauptstaatsarchiv Weimar

CONTEMPORARY PRINTED SOURCES

BRITISH

Baird, H. H. C. *A Handbook for the Limbless: For the General Guidance of Ex-Servicemen Who Have Lost One or More Limbs.* London, 1921.
———. *Light Metal Limbs for the Legless.* Bridge, nr. Canterbury, 1924.
Bakke, E. Wight. *The Unemployed Man: A Social Study.* London: Nisbet and Co., 1933.
Balme, Harold. *The Unfit Made Fit: Britain Advances.* London: Longmans Green, 1943.
Barnes, Rt. Hon. Thomas. *From Workshop to War Cabinet.* London: Herbert Jenkins, 1924.
Beveridge, William. *Voluntary Action: A Report on Methods of Social Advance.* New York: Macmillan, 1948.
Beveridge, William, and Alan Frank. *The Evidence for Voluntary Action, Being Memoranda by Organizations and Individuals, and Other Material Relevant to Voluntary Action.* Westport, Conn.: Greenwood Press, 1978 [1949].
Birmingham Training Committee. *How the Maimed Can Be Trained: The Trainees Exhibition, June 14–19, 1920.* Birmingham: Birmingham Training Committee, 1920.
Bourdillon, A. F. C., ed. *Voluntary Social Services: Their Place in the Modern State.* London: Methuen, 1945.
Braithwaite, Constance. *The Voluntary Citizen: An Enquiry into the Place of Philanthropy in the Community.* London: Methuen, 1938.
Brereton, Mrs. M. A. Cloudesley. *The Future of Our Disabled Sailors and Soldiers: A Description of the Training and Instruction Classes at Queen Mary's Convalescent Auxiliary Hospitals.* London: Roehampton, n.d.
Camus, Jean. *Physical and Occupational Re-education of the Maimed.* Trans. W. F. Castle. New York: William Wood and Company, 1919.

Charity Organisation Society. *Annual Charities Register and Digest, 1920–1938.* London: COS, n.d. [1939?].

Cohen, J. B. Brunel. *Count Your Blessings.* London: Heinemann, 1956.

Collier, John, and Iain Lang. *Just the Other Day: An Informal History of Great Britain since the War.* New York: Harper and Brothers, 1931.

Committee on National Expenditure. *Report Presented to Parliament by Command of His Majesty, July 1931.* London: HMSO, 1931.

Conference on War Relief and Personal Service. Organized by Charity Organisation Societies and Guilds of Help, Caxton Hall, Westminister 10, 11, 12 June 1915. London: Longmans, Green, 1915.

Culpin, Millais. *Recent Advances in the Study of the Psychoneuroses.* London: J & A Churchill, 1931.

Demos. *The Meaning of Reconstruction.* London: George Allen and Unwin, n.d.

Devine, Edward, assisted by Lilian Brandt. *Disabled Soldiers and Sailors, Pensions and Training.* Carnegie Endowment for International Peace, Preliminary Economic Studies of the War, no. 12. New York: Oxford University Press, 1919.

Dickie, J. L. *Comedy and Drama of a Doctor's Life.* London: Heath Cranton, 1939.

Disabled Soldiers' and Sailors' (Hackney) Foundation. *A Brief History of the War Memorial Homes, Wattisfield Road.* London, 1930.

Doherty, William Brown, and Dagobert D. Runes, eds. *Rehabilitation of the War Injured: A Symposium.* New York: Philosophical Library, 1945.

Fraser, Sir Ian. *Learning to Be Blind.* London: Longmans, Green, 1943.

———. *Sir Arthur Pearson.* London, 1922.

———. *Whereas I Was Blind.* London: Hodder and Stoughton, 1942.

———, ed. *Conquest of Disability: Inspiring Accounts of Courage, Fortitude, and Adaptability in Conquering Grave Physical Handicaps.* London: Odhams Press, 1956.

Galsworthy, John, ed. *Inter-Allied Conference on the After-Care of Disabled Men.* 2d ed. London: HMSO, 1918.

Griffith-Boscawen, Sir Arthur. *Memories.* London: John Murray, 1925.

———. *Report on the Inter-Allied Conference.* London: HMSO, 1917.

Haig, Dorothy Maud. *The Man I Knew.* Edinburgh: Moray Press, 1936.

Hicks, Ursula K. *The Finance of British Government, 1920–1936.* London: Oxford University Press, 1938.

Hirst, Francis W. *The Consequences of the War to Britain.* London: Oxford University Press, 1934.

Hodge, John. *Workman's Cottage to Windsor Castle.* London: Sampson Low, Marston and Co., 1931.

Hogge, J. M. *Love Stronger Than Death and the Consecration of Sacrifice.* London: Hodder and Stoughton, 1918.

———. *War Pensions and Allowances.* London: Hodder and Stoughton, 1918.

Hopkinson, Sir Alfred K. C. *Rebuilding Britain: A Survey of Problems of Reconstruction after the World War.* London: Cassell and Company, 1918.

Howson, Geoffrey. *Handbook for the Limbless.* London: The Disabled Society, 1922.

Ince, Sir Godfrey. *The Ministry of Labour and National Service*. London: George Allen and Unwin, 1960.

International Labour Office. *The Compensation of War Victims: Medical Aid, Compensation, and War Pensions*. Series E, no. 6. London: ILO, 1940.

———. *Employment of Disabled Men: Meeting of Experts for the Study of Methods of Finding Employment for Disabled Men*. Geneva, 31 July, 1 and 2 August 1923. Geneva: ILO, 1923.

———. *Studies and Reports*, Series E, nos. 1–5. Montreal: ILO, 1921.

———. *The Training and Employment of Disabled Persons: A Preliminary Report*. Series F, no. 7. Montreal: ILO, 1945.

Jennings, Hilda. *The Private Citizen in Public Social Work*. London: G. Allen and Unwin, 1930.

Jones, Robert. *Notes on Military Orthopaedics*. New York: British Red Cross and Cassell and Co., 1917.

King, Sir Geoffrey. *The Ministry of Pensions and National Insurance*. London: George Allen and Unwin, 1958.

Kuczynski, Jürgen. *Hunger and Work*. New York: International Publishers, 1938.

Longbotham, H. A., chairman. *A Proposed National Scheme for the Permanent Settlement of the Problem of Employment for Disabled Ex-Service Sailors, Soldiers and Airmen*. Issued with the Approval of the Rotherham Local Advisory Committee. Sheffield: Carbon Chambers, 1919.

Macadam, Elizabeth. *The New Philanthropy: A Study of the Relations between the Statutory and Voluntary Social Services*. London: George Allen and Unwin, 1934.

Mallet, Sir Bernard, and C. Oswald George. *British Budgets: Third Series, 1921–1922 to 1932–1933*. London: Macmillan, 1933.

Martin, Kingsley. *Father Figures: A Volume of Autobiography*. London: Hutchinson, 1966.

Mass-Observation. *The Journey Home*. A report prepared by Mass-Observation for the Advertising Service Guild. London: John Murray, 1944.

Mayo, Katherine. *Soldiers What Next!* London: Cassell and Company, 1934.

McKenzie, R. Tait. *Reclaiming the Maimed: A Handbook of Physical Therapy*. New York: Macmillan, 1918.

McMurtrie, Douglas. *The Evolution of National Systems of Vocational Re-education for Disabled Soldiers and Sailors*. Washington, D.C.: Government Printing Office, 1918.

Mess, Henry A., and others. *Voluntary Social Services since 1918*. London: K. Paul, Trench, Trubner, 1947.

Ministry of Labour. *Report on an Investigation into the Personal Circumstances and Industrial History of 10,000 Claimants to Unemployment Benefit*. London: HMSO, 1924.

Ministry of Pensions. *Local War Pensions Committees' Handbook*. London: HMSO, 1920.

———. *Report of the Departmental Committee of Inquiry into the Machinery of Administration of the Ministry of Pensions*. London: HMSO, 1921.

Mitchell, Robert. *What Can Be Done to Train Disabled Sailors and Soldiers in Technical Institutions*. London, 1916.

Mitchell, T. J., and G. M. Smith. *Medical Services: Casualties and Medical Statistics of the Great War*. London: HMSO, 1931.

Northfield, Wilfred. *Conquest of Nerves: The Inspiring Record of a Personal Triumph over Neurasthenia*. London: Fenland Press, 1933.

Parry, E. A., and Lieutenant-General Sir A. E. Codrington. *War Pensions: Past and Present*. London: Nisbet and Co., 1918.

Pilgrim Trust. *Men without Work*. Cambridge: Cambridge University Press, 1938.

Purse, Ben. *The British Blind: A Revolution in Thought and Action*. London: Buck Bros. and Harding, 1928.

Report from the Select Committee on Pensions Together with the Proceedings of the Committee. Minutes of Evidence and Appendices. H.C. 1920, VII.

Roberts, Henry D., ed. *The Inter-Allied Exhibition on the After-Care of Disabled Men, Central Hall, Westminster, 20–25 May 1918*. Catalogue. London: Avenue Press, 1918.

Rothband, Sir Henry. *Employment for Disabled Sailors and Soldiers: A Scheme for a National Roll of Employers*. London: John Heywood, n.d.

Select Committee Report on Training and Employment of Disabled Men. H.C. 170. London: HMSO, 1923.

Slade, G. H. *Two Sticks*. London: Mills and Boon, 1923.

Souttar, Henry. *A Surgeon in Belgium*. London: E. Arnold, 1915.

Sykes, Joseph. *British Public Expenditure, 1921–1931*. London: P. S. King and Son, 1933.

Thomas, H. H. *Help for Wounded Heroes*. London, 1922.

Trevelyan, John. *Voluntary Service and the State*. London: G. Barber, 1953.

Treves, Frederick. *Elephant Man and Other Reminiscences*. London: Cassell, 1923.

War Charities Committee. *Report of the Committee on War Charities*. Cd. 8287. London: HMSO, 1916.

Watson, Frederick. *Civilization and the Cripple*. London: J. Bale, 1930.

———. *The Life of Sir Robert Jones*. London: Hodder and Stoughton, 1934.

Webster, Margaret. *Don't Put Your Daughter on the Stage*. New York: Knopf, 1972.

Whillier, Captain E. C. *The Case for the Ex-Service Man*. Lectures to the Ex-Servicemen of Birmingham at the Headquarters of the National Federation of Discharged and Demobilized Sailors and Soldiers, Autumn 1920. Birmingham: Burman, Cooper and Co., 1920.

Wood, Ethel. *Robert Mitchell: A Life of Service*. London: Frederick Miller, 1934.

GERMAN

Anon. *Die Kriegsbeschädigtenfürsorge in Steiermark*. Graz: Verlag der Steiermärkischen Landeskommission zur Fürsorge für heimkehrende Krieger, 1918.

Bachmaier, Roman. *Programm und Organisation einer Heilschule für Kriegs-beschädigte.* Halle: Carl Marhold Verlagsbuchhandlung, 1916.

Beckmann, Dr. H. *Die Schwerbeschädigtenfürsorge der Provinz Brandenburg. Aufbau und Statistik.* Berlin: Carl Heymanns Verlag, 1919.

Benckendorff, Georg, et al. *Kommentar von Reichsversorgungsbeamten zum Reichsversorgungsgesetz vom 12.5.1920.* Berlin: Hans Markert, 1929.

Biesalski, Konrad. *Kriegskrüppelfürsorge: Ein Aufklärungswort zum Troste und zur Mahnung.* Leipzig: Voss, 1915.

Brauns, Heinrich. *Wirtschaftskrisis und Sozialpolitik.* M. Gladbach: Volksver-einsverlag, 1924.

Briefs, Dr. J. *Die soziale Fürsorge der Schwerbeschädigten in der heutigen Gesetz-gebung.* Berlin: Gersbach & Sohn, 1931.

Christian, Stabsarzt a.D. Dr. Max Christian. *Psycho-physiologische Berufsber-atung der Kriegsbeschädigten.* Leipzig: Leopold Voß, 1918.

Claessens, Dr. Eugen, and R. Meinhardt. *Reichsversorgung und Fürsorge für Kriegs- und Dienstbeschädigte. Wegweiser durch die neueste Gesetzgebung.* Berlin: Kyffhäuser Verlag, 1921.

Frank, Paul, and Siddy Wronsky. *Die Bundesratsverordnung über Wohlfahrts-pflege während des Krieges vom 15 February 1918.* Stuttgart: J. Hetz, 1917.

Frankenstein, Dr. Luise. *Die soziale Kriegsbeschädigtenfürsorge während des Krieges.* Aachen: Creutzer, 1920.

Gerlach, Landesrat. *Grundsätzliche Fragen der Zusatzrentengewährung.* Berlin: Carl Heymanns Verlag, 1932.

———. "Zehn Jahre Kriegsbeschädigten- und Hinterbliebenenfürsorge in der Rheinprovinz." Sonderabdruck aus dem Werk, *Die rheinische Provinz-ialverwaltung, ihre Entwicklung und ihr heutiger Stand.* Düsseldorf: L. Schwann, 1925.

Grebler, Leo, and Wilhelm Winkler. *The Cost of the World War to Germany and Austria-Hungary.* New Haven, Conn: Yale University Press and the Carnegie Endowment for International Peace, 1940.

Handbuch der Kriegsfürsorge im Deutschen Reich. Berlin: Vahlen, 1917.

Harris, Garrard. *The Redemption of the Disabled.* New York: D. Appleton and Company, 1919.

Hegener, Heinz. "Der Wettbewerb der Kriegsbeschädigten auf dem Arbeits-markte unter besonderer Berücksichtigung der Verhältnisse bei den Werften Blohm & Voß und der Deutschen Werft in Hamburg." Hamburg diss., 1924.

Hirsch, Betty. *15 Jahre Kriegsblindenschule Geheimrat Dr. Silex.* Berlin, 1929.

Huth, Dipl.-Ing. *150 Einzelfälle aus dem ersten Jahre der Tätigkeit der Kbfür-sorge in der Rheinprovinz.* Düsseldorf: L. Schwann, n.d.

International Labor Office. *Die Arbeitsfürsorge für Kriegsbeschädigte.* Geneva: International Labor Office, 1923.

Jung, Bruno. *Der Einfluß der Wirtschaftskrise auf die Durchführung des Schwerbeschädigten-Gesetzes.* Mannheim: J. Bensheimer, 1932.

———. *Die Öffentliche und private Wohlfahrtspflege in Deutschland.* M-Glad-bach: Volksvereinsverlag, 1921.

Karstedt, Oskar, ed. *Handwörterbuch der Wohlfahrtspflege.* Berlin: Heymann, 1924.

Kerschensteiner, Anton. *Reichsversorgungsgesetz.* Munich: Schweitzer, 1921.

Köhler, Dr. A. *Die staatliche Kriegsinvalidenfürsorge.* Leipzig: Thieme, 1916.

Die Kriegsbeschädigtenfürsorge in Steiermark, 1915–1917. Graz: Verlag der Steiermärkischen Landeskommission zur Fürsorge für Heimkehrende Krieger, 1918.

Laub, Dr. Philipp Heinrich. *Die Kriegsbeschädigten- und Kriegshinterbliebenenversorgung.* Würzburg: Kabitzsch & Mönnich, 1921.

Leipart, Th. *Kriegsinvaliden und Gewerkschaften.* Berlin: Verlag der Generalkommission der Gewerkschaften, 1915.

Liebenberg, Dr. Richard. *Richtlinien für die Praxis der Berufsberatung.* Berlin: Heymann, 1925.

Mahling, D. *Die sittlichen Voraussetzungen der Wohlfahrtspflege.* Berlin: Heymann, 1925.

Muthesius, Hans. *Die Wohlfahrtpflege.* Berlin: Springer, 1925.

Oberlindober, Hanns. *Ehre und Recht für die deutschen Kriegsopfer.* Berlin, 1933.

Panzer, Dr. Georg. *Versorgungskatechismus.* Berlin: Deutsch. literarisches Institut, 1921.

Rappenecker, Franz X. *Das Problem der Fürsorge für die Kriegsopfer.* Münster: Aschendorffschen Buchdruckerei, 1928.

Reichsarbeitsministerium. *Renten-Tafeln zum Reichsversorgungsgesetz in der Fassung vom 30.Juni 1923.* Berlin: E. G. Mittler & Sohn, 1923.

Reichsbund der Kriegsbeschädigten, Kriegsteilnehmer und Kriegerhinterbliebenen. *Wie Kriegsbeschädigte abgefunden sind und wie sie wohnen. Der Reichsregierung und dem Reichstag vorgelegt vom Reichsbund.* Berlin, 1927.

———. *Notruf der Kriegsopfer. Der Reichsregierung und dem Reichstag vorgelegt vom Reichsbund.* Berlin, 1932.

Roßmann, Erich. *Ratgeber für Kriegsbeschädigte.* Berlin: Verlag Gesellschaft und Erziehung, 1919.

Schulz, Stadtrechtsrat. *Bericht über die Tätigkeit des Ortsamtes für Kriegerfürsorge zu Dresden in der Zeit vom 1.April 1925 bis 31.März 1926.* Dresden: Verlag der Buchdruckerei der Wilhelm und Bertha v. Baensch Stiftung, 1927.

———. *Bilder von den Aufgaben und dem Aufbau des Ortsamtes für Kriegerfürsorge zu Dresden.* Dresden: Verlag der Buchdruckerei der Wilhelm und Bertha v. Baensch Stiftung, 1926.

Strehl, Dr. Carl. *Die Kriegsblindenfürsorge, ein Auschnitt aus der Sozialpolitik.* Berlin: Springer, 1922.

Teitz, Johannes. *Berufsberatung und Eingliederung erwachsener Erwerbsbeschränkter ins Erwerbsleben.* Berlin: Heymann, 1925.

Tonkow, Gustav. *Das Schicksal der Schwerkriegsbeschädigten in Hamburg.* Hamburger Schriften zur Wirtschafts- und Sozialpolitik. Heft 2. Rostock: Carl Hinstorffs Verlag, 1927.

Treffehn, Max. *Auslegungen zum Reichsversorgungsgesetz.* Berlin: Mittler & Sohn, 1925.

Wex, Else. *Die Entwicklung der sozialen Fürsorge in Deutschland.* Berlin: Heymann, 1929.

Wiechert, Ernst. *Das einfache Leben.* Frankfurt am Main: Ullstein, 1989 [1939].

Winterfeldt, Joachim von. *Kriegsbeschädigtenfürsorge*. Berlin: Carl Heymanns, 1917.

Wölz, Dr. Otto. *Arbeitsbeschaffung für Schwerbeschädigte*. Berlin: Reichszentrale für Heimatdienst, 1921.

———. *Aufgaben Deutscher Wohlfahrtspolitik*. Berlin: Gersbach & Sohn, 1925.

Wölz, Dr. Otto, Fritz Ruppert, and Dr. Lothar Richter. *Die Fürsorgepflicht*. Berlin: Carl Heymanns, 1925.

Ziegler, Dr. H. Fr. *Die Leistungen kriegsverletzter Industriearbeiter und Vorschläge zur Kriegsbeschädigtenfürsorge*. Düsseldorf: A. Bagel, 1919.

Ziem, Reg. Rat. Helmut. *Der Beschädigte und Körperbehinderte im Daseinkampf einst und jetzt*. Berlin: Duncker & Humblot, 1956.

SELECTED SECONDARY WORKS

Abelshauser, Werner. "Die Weimarer Republik—ein Wohlfahrtsstaat?" In *Die Weimarer Republik als Wohlfahrtsstaat*, edited by Werner Abelshauser. Wiesbaden: Franz Steiner, 1987.

Alber, Jens. *Vom Armenhaus zum Wohlfahrtsstaat. Analysen zur Entwicklung der Sozialversicherung in Westeuropa*. Frankfurt am Main: Campus, 1982.

Aldcroft, Derek. *The British Economy: Years of Turmoil*. Brighton, Sussex: Harvester, 1986.

Alper, Helen, ed. *A History of Queen Mary's University Hospital, Roehampton*. Roehampton: Richard and Twickenham and Roehampton Healthcare NHS Trust, 1996.

Baldwin, Peter. "The Welfare State for Historians. A Review Article." *Comparative Studies in Society and History* 34 (1992): 695–707.

Barry, Jonathan, and Colin Jones, eds. *Medicine and Charity in Western Europe before the Welfare State*. London: Routledge, 1991.

Bauerkämper, Arnd. *Die radikale Recht in Großbritannien*. Göttingen: Vandenhoeck & Ruprecht, 1991.

Benewick, Robert. *The Fascist Movement in Britain*. London: Allen Lane, 1972.

Bentley, Michael, and John Stevenson, eds. *High and Low Politics in Modern Britain: Ten Studies*. Oxford: Clarendon Press, 1983.

Berger, Stefan. *The British Labour Party and the German Social Democrats, 1900–1931*. Oxford: Clarendon Press, 1994.

Berghahn, Volker. *Der Stahlhelm: Bund der Frontsoldaten, 1918–1935*. Düsseldorf: Droste, 1966.

Bessel, Richard. *Germany after the First World War*. Oxford: Clarendon Press, 1993.

Bieber, Hans-Joachim. *Gewerkschaften in Krieg und Revolution*. Vol. 2. Hamburg: Christian, 1981.

Biernacki, Richard. *Fabrication of Labor: Germany and Britain, 1640–1914*. Berkeley and Los Angeles: University of California Press, 1995.

Blackbourn, David, and Geoff Eley. *The Peculiarities of German History: Bourgeois Society and Politics in Nineteenth-Century Germany*. Oxford: Oxford University Press, 1984.

Bleker, Johanna, and Heinz-Peter Schmiedebach, eds. *Medizin und Krieg: vom Dilemma der Heilberufe 1865 bis 1985*. Frankfurt am Main: Fischer, 1987.

Bolderson, Helen. *Social Security, Disability and Rehabilitation: Conflicts in the Development of Social Policy, 1914–1946*. London: Jessica Kingsley Publishers, 1991.

Booth, Allyson. *Postcards from the Trenches: Negotiating the Space between Modernism and the First World War*. New York: Oxford University Press, 1996.

Borchardt, Knut. "Economic Causes of the Collapse of the Weimar Republic." In *Perspectives on Modern German Economic History and Policy*. Trans. Peter Lambert. Cambridge: Cambridge University Press, 1991.

Bourke, Joanna. *Dismembering the Male: Men's Bodies, Britain and the Great War*. Chicago: University of Chicago Press, 1996.

Bracco, Rose Maria. *Merchants of Hope: British Middlebrow Writers and the First World War, 1919–1939*. Oxford: Berg, 1993.

Bremner, Robert. *Giving and Charity: Philanthropy in History*. New Brunswick, N.J.: Transaction Books, 1994.

Breuilly, John. "Liberalism or Social Democracy: A Comparison of British and German Labour Politics, c. 1850–1875." *English History Quarterly* 15 (1985): 3–42.

Bry, Gerhard. *Wages in Germany, 1871–1945*. Princeton, N.J.: Princeton University Press, 1960.

Burk, Kathleen, ed. *War and the State: The Transformation of British Government, 1914–1919*. London: George Allen and Unwin, 1982.

Burleigh, Michael. *Death and Deliverance: "Euthanasia" in Germany, 1900–1945*. Cambridge: Cambridge University Press, 1994.

Calder, John. *The Vanishing Willows: The Story of Erskine Hospital*. Guildford: Biddles, 1982.

Campbell, Joan. *Joy in Work, German Work*. Princeton, N.J.: Princeton University Press, 1989.

Caplan, Jane. *Government without Administration: State and Civil Service in the Weimar Republic and Nazi Germany*. Oxford: Clarendon Press, 1988.

Carrington, Charles Edmunds. *Soldiers from the Wars Returning*. New York: MacKay, 1965.

Chapman, Richard, and J. R. Greenaway. *The Dynamics of Administrative Reform*. London: Croom Helm, 1980.

Conrad, Christoph. "Gewinner und Verlierer im Wohlfahrtsstaat: Deutsche und Internationale Tendenzen im 20.Jahrhundert." *Archiv für Sozialgeschichte* 30 (1990): 297–326.

Cooter, Roger. *Surgery and Society in Peace and War: Orthopaedics and the Organization of Modern Medicine, 1880–1948*. London: Macmillan, 1983.

Crew, David. *Germans on Welfare: From Weimar to Hitler, 1919–1933*. New York: Oxford University Press, 1998.

———. "'Wohlfahrtsbrot ist bitteres Brot,' the Elderly, the Disabled and the Local Welfare Authorities in the Weimar Republic." *Archiv für Sozialgeschichte* 30 (1990): 217–246.

Cronin, James. *The Politics of State Expansion: War, State and Society in Twentieth-Century Britain.* London: Routledge, 1991.

Crowther, Anne. *British Social Policy, 1914–1939.* London: Macmillan, 1988.

Daunton, Martin J. "Payment and Participation: Welfare and State-Formation in Britain, 1900–1951." *Past and Present* 150 (February 1996): 169–216.

———, ed. *Charity, Self-Interest and Welfare in the English Past.* New York: St. Martin's Press, 1996.

Dickinson, Edward Ross. *The Politics of Child Welfare from the Empire to the Federal Republic.* Cambridge: Harvard University Press, 1996.

Diehl, James. "Change and Continuity in the Treatment of German Kriegsopfer." *Central European History* 18 (1985): 170–187.

———. *Paramilitary Politics in Weimar Germany.* Bloomington: Indiana University Press, 1977.

———. *Thanks of the Fatherland.* Chapel Hill: University of North Carolina Press, 1994.

———. "Victors or Victims? Disabled Veterans in the Third Reich." *Journal of Modern History* 59 (1987): 705–736.

Eberle, Matthias. *World War I and the Weimar Artists: Dix, Grosz, Beckmann, Schlemmer.* Trans. J. Gabriel. New Haven, Conn.: Yale University Press, 1985.

Eckart, Wolfgang, and Christoph Gradmann. *Die Medizin und der Erste Weltkrieg.* Pfaffenweiler: Centaurus-Verlagsgesellschaft, 1996.

Eghigian, Greg. *Making Security Social: Disability, Insurance, and the Birth of the Social Entitlement State in Germany.* Ann Arbor: University of Michigan Press, 2000.

———. "Politics of Victimization: Social Pensioners and the German Social State in the Inflation of 1914–1924." *Central European History* 26 (1993): 375–404.

Eifert, Christiane. *Frauenpolitik und Wohlfahrtspflege: Zur Geschichte der sozialdemokratischen "Arbeiterwohlfahrt."* Frankfurt: Campus Verlag, 1993.

Eksteins, Modris. *Rites of Spring: The Great War and the Birth of the Modern Age.* London: Houghton Mifflin, 1989.

Englander, David. "Die Demobilmachung in Großbritannien nach dem ersten Weltkrieg." *Geschichte und Gesellschaft* 9 (1983): 195–210.

———. "The National Union of Ex-Servicemen and the Labour Movement, 1918–1920." *History* 76 (1991): 24–42.

———. "Troops and Trade Unions, 1919." *History Today* 37 (1987): 8–12.

Englander, David, and John Osborne. "Jack, Tommy, and Henry Dubb: The Armed Forces and the Working Class." *Historical Journal* 21 (1978): 593–621.

Evans, Richard, and Dick Geary. *The German Unemployed.* New York: St. Martin's Press, 1987.

Fedorowich, Kent. *Unfit for Heroes: Reconstruction and Soldier Settlement in the Empire between the Wars.* Manchester: Manchester University Press, 1995.

Feldman, Gerald. *Army, Industry, and Labor, 1914–1918.* Princeton, N.J.: Princeton University Press, 1966.

———. "Die Demobilmachung und die Sozialordnung der Zwischenkriegszeit in Europa." *Geschichte und Gesellschaft* 9 (1983): 156–177.

———. *The Great Disorder: Politics, Economics, and Society in the German Inflation, 1914–1924.* New York: Oxford University Press, 1993.

———, ed. *Die Nachwirkungen der Inflation auf die deutsche Geschichte.* Munich: Oldenbourg, 1985.

Field, Frank. *British and French Writers of the First World War.* Cambridge: Cambridge University Press, 1991.

Finlayson, Geoffrey. *Citizen, State, and Social Welfare in Britain, 1830–1990.* Oxford: Clarendon Press, 1994.

———. "A Moving Frontier; Voluntarism and the State in British Social Welfare, 1911–1949." *Twentieth-Century British History* 1 (1990): 183–206.

Flanagan, Richard. *"Parish-Fed Bastards": A History of the Politics of the Unemployed in Britain, 1884–1914.* New York: Greenwood Press, 1991.

Flora, Peter, and A. J. Heidenheimer, eds. *The Development of Welfare States in Europe and America.* New Brunswick, N.J.: Transaction Books, 1981.

Fowler, Simon. "War Charity Begins at Home." *History Today,* September 1999, 17–23.

Frederickson, George. "From Exceptionalism to Variability: Recent Developments in Cross-National Comparative History." *Journal of American History* 82 (1995): 587–604.

Frie, Ewald. "Vorbild oder Spiegelbild? Kriegsbeschädigtenfürsorge in Deutschland, 1914–1919." In *Der erste Weltkrieg,* edited by Wolfgang Michalka. Munich: Piper, 1993.

———. *Wohlfahrtsstaat und Provinz, Westfalen und Sachsen, 1880–1930.* Paderborn: F. Schöningh, 1993.

Friedlander, Henry. *The Origins of Nazi Genocide: From Euthanasia to the Final Solution.* Chapel Hill: University of North Carolina Press, 1995.

Friedländer, Saul. *Nazi Germany and the Jews.* Vol. 1, *The Years of Persecution.* New York: HarperCollins, 1997.

Fritzsche, Peter. *Rehearsals for Fascism: Populism and Political Mobilization in Weimar Germany.* Oxford: Oxford University Press, 1990.

Führer, Karl Christian. "Für das Wirtschaftsleben 'mehr oder weniger wertlose Personen.' Zur Lage von Invaliden- und Kleinrentnern in den Inflationsjahren, 1918–1924." *Archiv für Sozialgeschichte* 30 (1990): 145–180.

Fuller, John. *Troop Morale and Popular Culture in the British and Dominion Armies in the First World War, 1914–1918.* Oxford: Oxford University Press, 1990.

Fussell, Paul. *The Great War and Modern Memory.* Oxford: Oxford University Press, 1975.

Gallagher, J. P. *The Price of Charity.* London: R. Hale, 1975.

Garside, W. R. *British Unemployment, 1919–1939.* Cambridge: Cambridge University Press, 1990.

———. *Measurement of Unemployment.* Oxford: Basil Blackwell, 1980.

Geyer, Martin. *Verkehrte Welt: Revolution, Inflation und Moderne, München, 1914–1924.* Göttingen: Vandenhoeck & Ruprecht, 1998.

Geyer, Michael. "Ein Vorbote des Wohlfahrtsstaates: Die Kriegsopferver-
    sorgung in Frankreich, Deutschland und Großbritannien nach dem Ersten
    Weltkrieg." *Geschichte und Gesellschaft* 9 (1983): 230–277.
Gilbert, Bentley B. *British Social Policy.* Ithaca, N.Y.: Cornell University Press,
    1970.
Gilbert, Martin. *The First World War.* New York: Henry Holt, 1994.
Gilbert, Neil. *Capitalism and the Welfare State: Dilemmas of Social Benevo-
    lence.* New Haven, Conn.: Yale University Press, 1983.
Gillis, John. *Commemorations: The Politics of National Identity* Princeton,
    N.J.: Princeton University Press, 1994.
Ginsburg, Norman. *Divisions of Welfare. A Critical Introduction to Compara-
    tive Social Policy.* London: Sage, 1992.
Gladen, Albin. *Geschichte der Sozialpolitik in Deutschland.* Wiesbaden: Franz
    Steiner, 1974.
Gladstone, Francis. *Charity, Law and Social Justice.* London: Bedford Square,
    1982.
Grayzel, Susan. *Women's Identities at War: Gender, Motherhood and Politics in
    Britain and France during the First World War.* Chapel Hill: University of
    North Carolina Press, 1999.
Grebler, Leo, and Wilhelm Winkler. *The Cost of the World War to Germany
    and Austria-Hungary.* New Haven, Conn.: Yale University Press, 1940.
Gregory, Adrian. *The Silence of Memory: Armistice Day, 1919–1946.* Oxford:
    Berg, 1994.
Gries, Rainer. *Die Rationen-Gesellschaft. Versorgungskampf und Vergleichs-
    mentalität: Leipzig, München und Köln nach dem Kriege.* Münster: West-
    falisches Dampfboot, 1991.
Groot, Gerald de. *Blighty: British Society in the Era of the Great War.* London:
    Longman, 1996.
Gullace, Nicolette. "White Feathers and Wounded Men: Female Patriotism and
    the Memory of the Great War." *Journal of British Studies* 36 (April 1997):
    178–206.
Harris, José. "Political Thought and the Welfare State, 1870–1940: An Intel-
    lectual Framework for British Social Policy." *Past and Present* 135 (May
    1992): 116–141.
———. "Society and State in Twentieth-Century Britain." In *Cambridge Social
    History of Britain, 1750–1950,* edited by F. M. L. Thompson. Cambridge:
    Cambridge University Press, 1990.
Harrison, Brian. *Peaceable Kingdom: Stability and Change in Modern Britain.*
    Oxford: Clarendon Press, 1982.
Harvey, Elizabeth. *Youth and the Welfare State in Weimar Germany.* Oxford:
    Clarendon Press, 1993.
Hatch, Stephen. *Outside the State: Voluntary Organisations in Three English
    Towns.* London: Croom Helm, 1980.
Hausen, Karin. "The German Nation's Obligations to the Heroes' Widows of
    World War I." In *Behind the Lines: Gender and the Two World Wars,* ed-
    ited by Margaret Higonnet et al., New Haven, Conn.: Yale University Press,
    1987.

Hennock, E. P. *British Social Reform and German Precedents: The Case of Social Insurance, 1880–1914.* Oxford: Clarendon Press, 1987.

Hickel, C. Walter. "Entitling Citizens: World War I Progressivism and the Origins of the American Welfare State, 1917–1928." Ph.D. diss., Columbia University, 1999.

Higonnet, Margaret, et al., eds. *Behind the Lines: Gender and the Two World Wars.* New Haven, Conn.: Yale University Press, 1987.

Hirschfeld, Gerhard, Gerd Krumeich, and Irena Renz, eds. *Keiner fühlt sich hier mehr als Mensch.* Essen: Klartext, 1993.

Homburg, Heidrun. "Vom Arbeitslosen zum Zwangsarbeiter. Arbeitslosenpolitik und Fraktionierung der Arbeiterschaft in Deutschland, 1900–1933." *Archiv für Sozialgeschichte* 25 (1985): 251–299.

Hong, Young-Sun. "The Contradictions of Modernization in the German Welfare State: Gender and the Politics of Welfare Reform in First World War Germany." *Social History* 17 (1992): 251–270.

———. "The Politics of Welfare Reform and the Dynamics of the Public Sphere: Church, Society and the State in the Making of the Social-Welfare System in Germany, 1830–1930." Ph.D. diss., University of Michigan, 1989.

———. *Welfare, Modernity, and the Weimar State, 1919–1933.* Princeton, N.J.: Princeton University Press, 1998.

Howson, Susan. "The Origins of Dear Money, 1919–1920." *Economic History Review,* 2d ser., 27, no. 1 (1974): 88–107.

Humphries, Steve, and Pamela Gordon. *Out of Sight: The Experience of Disability, 1900–1950.* Plymouth, England: Northcote Hall, 1992.

Hynes, Samuel. *A War Imagined: The First World War and English Culture.* New York: Collier, 1990.

Jackson, Christopher. "Infirmative Action: The Law of the Severely Disabled in Germany." *Central European History* 26 (1993): 417–455.

James, Harold. *The German Slump: Politics and Economics, 1924–1936.* Oxford: Oxford University Press, 1986.

Johnson, Paul. *Saving and Spending: The Working-Class Economy in Britain, 1870–1939,* Oxford: Clarendon Press, 1985.

Johnson, Paul Barton. *Land Fit for Heroes: The Planning of British Reconstruction, 1916–1919.* Chicago: University of Chicago Press, 1968.

Jones, Joseph Trevor. *History of the Corporation of Birmingham, 1915–1935.* Vol. 5. Birmingham: General Purposes Committee, 1940.

Kaiser, Jochen-Christoph. "Freie Wohlfahrtsverbände im Kaiserreich und in der Weimarer Republik: Ein Überblick." *Westfälische Forschungen* 43 (1993): 26–57.

———. *Sozialer Protestantismus im 20. Jahrhundert. Beiträge zur Geschichte der Inneren Mission 1914–1945.* Munich: R. Oldenbourg, 1989.

Karsten, Rudolph. *Die sächsische Sozialdemokratie vom Kaiserreich zur Republik, 1871–1923.* Cologne: Böhlau Verlag, 1995.

Keegan, John. *Face of Battle.* New York: Viking Press, 1976.

Kent, Susan Kingsley. *Making Peace: The Reconstruction of Gender in Interwar Britain.* Princeton, N.J.: Princeton University Press, 1994.

Kimball, Charles. "Ex-Service Movement in England and Wales, 1916–1930." Ph.D. diss., Stanford University, 1991.

Kingsford, Peter. *The Hunger Marchers in Britain, 1920–1940.* London: Lawrence and Wishart, 1982.

Kocka, Jürgen. *Facing Total War: German Society, 1914–1918.* Trans. Barbara Weinberger. Leamington Spa, Warwickshire: Berg, 1984.

Koshar, Rudy. *From Monuments to Traces: Artifacts of German Memory, 1870–1990.* Berkeley and Los Angeles: University of California Press, 2000.

Koven, Seth. "Remembering and Dismemberment: Crippled Children, Wounded Soldiers and the Great War in Great Britain." *American Historical Review* 99 (1994): 1167–1202.

Koven, Seth, and Sonya Michel. *Mothers of a New World: Maternalist Politics and the Origins of Welfare States.* London: Routledge, 1993.

———. "Womanly Duties: Maternalist Politics and the Origins of Welfare States in France, Germany, Great Britain and the United States, 1880–1920." *American Historical Review* 95 (1990): 1076–1108.

Kühne, Thomas. *Männergeschichte—Geschlectergeschichte: Männlichkeit im Wandel der Moderne.* Frankfurt: Campus, 1996.

Landwehr, Rolf, and Rüdeger Baron, eds. *Geschichte der Sozialarbeit.* Weinheim and Basel: Beltz Verlag, 1983.

Latcham, Andrew. "Journey's End: Ex-Servicemen and the State during and after the Great War." Ph.D. thesis, Oxford University, 1997.

Laybourn, Keith. *The Guild of Help and the Changing Face of Edwardian Philanthropy: The Guild of Help, Voluntary Work and the State, 1904–1919.* Lewiston: Edwin Mellen Press, 1994.

Leed, Eric. *No Man's Land: Combat and Identity in World War One.* Cambridge: Cambridge University Press, 1979.

Leibfried, Stephan. "Existenzminimum und Fürsorge-Richtsätze in der Weimarer Republik." In *Armutspolitik und die Entstehung des Sozialstaats,* edited by Stephan Leibfried. Bremen, 1985.

Lerner, Paul. "Hysterical Men: War, Neurosis and German Mental Medicine, 1914–1921." Ph.D. diss., Columbia University, 1996.

Lewis, D. S. *Illusions of Grandeur: Mosley, Fascism and British Society, 1931–81.* Manchester: Manchester University Press, 1987.

Lindenmeyr, Adele. *Poverty Is Not a Vice: Charity, Society, and the State in Imperial Russia.* Princeton, N.J.: Princeton University Press, 1996.

Linehan, Thomas. *East London for Mosley: The British Union of Fascists in East London and Southwest Essex, 1933–1940.* London: Frank Cass, 1996.

Lloyd, David. *Battlefield Tourism.* Oxford: Berg, 1998.

Loewenstein, Bedrich, ed. *Geschichte und Psychologie.* Pfaffenweiler: Centauraus-Verlagsgesellschaft, 1992.

Lowe, Rodney. *Adjusting to Democracy: The Role of the Ministry of Labour in British Politics, 1916–1939.* Oxford: Clarendon Press, 1986.

———. "Government." In *The First World War in British History,* edited by S. Constantine et al., London: E. Arnold, 1995.

Maier, Charles. *Recasting Bourgeois Europe.* Princeton, N.J.: Princeton University Press, 1975.

————, ed. *Changing Boundaries of the Political: Essays on the Evolving Balance between State and Society, Public and Private in Europe*. Cambridge: Cambridge University Press, 1987.

Mandler, Peter, ed. *The Uses of Charity: The Poor on Relief in the Nineteenth-Century Metropolis*. Philadelphia: Pennsylvania University Press, 1990.

Marwick, Arthur. *The Deluge: War and Social Change in the Twentieth Century*. London: Macmillan, 1974.

McKibbin, Ross. *Ideologies of Class: Social Relations in Britain, 1880–1950*. Oxford: Oxford University Press, 1990.

Merkl, Peter. *The Making of a Stormtrooper*. Princeton, N.J.: Princeton University Press, 1980.

Michalka, Wolfgang, ed. *Der erste Weltkrieg*. Munich: Piper, 1993.

Middlemas, Keith. *Politics in Industrial Society: The Experience of the British System since 1911*. London: André Deutsch, 1979.

Mockenhaupt, Hubert. *Weg und Wirken des geistlichen Sozialpolitikers Heinrich Brauns*. Munich: Schöningh, 1977.

Mommsen, Wolfgang, ed. *The Emergence of the Welfare State in Britain and Germany*. London: Croom Helm, 1981.

Morgan, Kenneth O. *Consensus and Disunity: The Lloyd George Coalition Government, 1918–1922*. Oxford: Clarendon Press, 1979.

Morris, Mary. *Voluntary Work in the Welfare State*. London: Routledge and Kegan Paul, 1969.

Mosse, George. *Fallen Soldiers: Reshaping the Memory of the World Wars*. New York: Oxford University Press, 1990.

Newman, Oksana, and Allan Foster. *The Value of a Pound: Prices and Incomes in Britain, 1900–1993*. New York: Gale Research International, 1995.

Niehuss, Merith. *Arbeiterschaft in Krieg und Inflation*. Berlin: Walter de Gruyter, 1985.

Nora, Pierre. *Realms of Memory*. 3 vols. Trans. Arthur Goldhammer. New York: Columbia University Press, 1996–1998.

Onions, John. *English Fiction and the Drama of the Great War, 1918–1939*. New York: St. Martin's Press, 1990.

Orloff, Ann Shola. *The Politics of Pensions: A Comparative Analysis of Britain, Canada, and the United States, 1880–1940*. Madison: University of Wisconsin Press, 1993.

Orlow, Dietrich. *Weimar Prussia, 1925–1933: The Illusion of Strength*. Pittsburgh: University of Pittsburgh Press, 1991.

Ostrower, Francie. *Why the Wealthy Give: The Culture of Elite Philanthropy*. Princeton, N.J.: Princeton University Press, 1995.

Owen, David. *English Philanthropy, 1660–1960*. Cambridge, Mass.: Belknap Press, 1964.

Panchasi, Roxanne. "Reconstructions: Prosthetics and the Rehabilitation of the Male Body in World War I France." *Differences* 7, no. 3 (1995): 109–140.

Peacock, Alan, and Jack Wiseman. *The Growth of Public Expenditure in the United Kingdom*. Princeton, N.J.: Princeton University Press, 1961.

Peden, G. C. "The 'Treasury View' on Public Works and Employment in the Interwar Period." *Economic History Review* 37 (1984): 167–181.

Pedersen, Susan. *Family, Dependence and the Origins of the Welfare State: Britain and France, 1914–1945.* Cambridge: Cambridge University Press, 1993.

Peukert, Detlev. *Die Weimarer Republik: Krisenjahre der Klassischen Moderne.* Frankfurt: Suhrkamp, 1987.

Potthof, Heinrich. *Gewerkschaften und Politik zwischen Revolution und Inflation.* Düsseldorf: Droste, 1979.

Preller, Ludwig. *Sozialpolitik in der Weimarer Republik.* Düsseldorf: Droste, 1978 [1948].

Price, Matthew. "Bodies and Souls: The Rehabilitation of Maimed Soldiers in France and Germany during the First World War." Ph.D. diss., Stanford University, 1998.

Prochaska, Frank. "Philanthropy." In *The Cambridge Social History of Britain, 1750–1950,* edited by F. M. L. Thompson. Vol. 3, Cambridge: Cambridge University Press, 1990.

———. *Royal Bounty: The Making of a Welfare Monarchy.* New Haven, Conn.: Yale University Press, 1995.

———. *The Voluntary Impulse: Philanthropy in Modern Britain.* London: Faber and Faber, 1988.

Prost, Antoine. *In the Wake of War: "Les Anciens Combattants" and French Society.* Oxford: Berg, 1991.

Pugh, Martin. *The Making of Modern British Politics, 1867–1919.* Oxford: Oxford University Press, 1983.

Quataert, Jean. *Staging Philanthropy: Patriotic Women and the National Imagination in Dynastic Germany, 1813–1916.* Ann Arbor: University of Michigan Press, 2001.

Rabinbach, Anson. *Human Motor: Energy, Fatigue and the Origins of Modernity.* Berkeley and Los Angeles: University of California Press, 1992 [1990].

Reese, Peter. *Homecoming Heroes: An Account of the Reassimilation of British Military Personnel into Civilian Life.* London: Leo Cooper, 1992.

Rein, Martin, and Lee Rainwater, ed. *Public/Private Interplay in Social Protection: A Comparative Study.* Armonk, N.Y.: M. E. Sharpe, 1986.

Remond, René. "Les Anciens Combattents." *La Revue Française de Science Politique* 5 (1955): 267–290.

Reznick, Jeffrey. "Rest, Recovery, and Rehabilitation: Healing and Identity in Great Britain in the First World War." Ph.D. diss., Emory University, 1999.

Ritter, Gerhard. *Social Welfare in Germany and Britain: Origins and Development.* Trans. Kim Traynor. Leamington Spa: Berg, 1986 [1983].

———. *Der Sozialstaat. Entstehung und Entwicklung im internationalen Vergleich.* 2d ed. Munich: R. Oldenbourg, 1991.

Roberts, Mary Louise. *Civilization without Sexes: Reconstructing Gender in Postwar France, 1917–1927.* Chicago: University of Chicago Press, 1994.

Rooff, Madeline. *Voluntary Societies and Social Policy.* London: Routledge and Paul, 1957.

Routh, Guy. *Occupation and Pay in Great Britain, 1906–79.* London: Macmillan, 1980 [1965].

Rudloff, Wilfried. *Der Wohlfahrtsstaat.* Göttingen: Vandenhoeck & Ruprecht, 1998.

Sachße, Christoph, and Florian Tennstedt. *Geschichte der Armenfürsorge in Deutschland.* Vol. 2, *Fürsorge und Wohlfahrtspflege, 1871 bis 1929.* Stuttgart: W. Kohlhammer, 1988.

Savage, Gail. *The Social Construction of Expertise: The English Civil Service and Its Influence, 1919–1939.* Pittsburgh: University of Pittsburgh Press, 1996.

Scholliers, P., ed. *Real Wages in 19th and 20th Century Europe.* New York: Berg, 1989.

Schulze, Hagen. *Freikorps und Republik, 1918–1920.* Boppard: Harald Boldt, 1969.

Sherman, Daniel. *The Construction of Memory in Interwar France.* Chicago: University of Chicago Press, 1999.

Silverman, Dan. *Reconstructing Europe after the First World War.* Cambridge: Harvard University Press, 1982.

Skidelsky, Robert. *Oswald Mosley.* New York: Holt, Rinehart and Winston, 1975.

Skocpol, Theda, and Margaret Somers. "The Uses of Comparative History in Macrosocial Inquiry." *Comparative Studies in Society and History* 22 (1980): 174–197.

Stachura, Peter. *Political Leaders in Weimar Germany.* New York: Harvester, 1993.

Steinmetz, George. "The Local Welfare State: Two Strategies for Social Domination in Urban Imperial Germany." *American Sociological Review* 55 (1990): 891–911.

———. *Regulating the Social: The Welfare State and Local Politics in Imperial Germany.* Princeton, N.J.: Princeton University Press, 1993.

Stevenson, John, and Chris Cook. *Britain in the Depression: Society and Politics. 1929–1939.* 2d ed. London: Longman, 1994.

Thane, Pat. *The Foundations of the Welfare State.* London: Longman, 1982.

Torstendahl, Rolf. *Bureaucratization in Northwestern Europe, 1880–1985: Domination and Governance.* London: Routledge, 1991.

Tosh, John. *A Man's Place: Masculinity and the Middle-Class Home in Victorian England.* New Haven, Conn.: Yale University Press, 1999.

Ulrich, Bernd. "Anmerkungen zur Behandlung der Kriegsopfer während des Ersten Weltkrieges." In *Keiner fühlt sich hier mehr als Mensch, Erlebnis und Wirkung des Ersten Weltkriegs,* edited by Gerhard Hirschfeld. Essen: Klartext, 1993.

———. *Die Augenzeugen. Deutsche Feldpostbriefe in Kriegs- und Nachkriegszeit 1914–1933.* Essen: Klartext, 1997.

Urlanis, Boris. *Bilanz der Kriege.* Berlin: VEB, 1965.

Vincent, David. *Poor Citizens: The State and the Poor in Twentieth-Century Britain.* London: Longman, 1991.

Waite, Robert. *Vanguard of Nazism: The Free Corps Movement in Post-war Germany.* New York: Norton, 1969.

Wall, Richard, and Jay Winter. *The Upheaval of War: Family, Work, and Welfare in Europe, 1914–1918.* Cambridge: Cambridge University Press, 1988.

Ward, Stephen. "The British Veterans' Ticket of 1918." *Journal of British Studies* 8 (1968): 155–173.

———. "Intelligence Surveillance of British Ex-Servicemen, 1918–1920." *Historical Journal* 16 (March 1973): 179–188.

———, ed. *The War Generation*. Port Washington, N.Y.: Kennikat, 1975.

Weber, Eugen. *The Hollow Years: France in the 1930's*. New York: Norton, 1994.

Whalen, Robert Weldon. *Bitter Wounds: German Victims of the Great War. 1914–1939*. Ithaca, N.Y.: Cornell University Press, 1984.

Winkler, Heinrich A. *Die deutsche Staatskrise*. Munich: Oldenbourg, 1992.

———. *Von der Revolution zur Stabilisierung: Arbeiter und Arbeiterbewegung in der Weimarer Republik, 1918–1924*. Berlin: Dietz, 1984.

Winter, Denis. *Death's Men: Soldiers of the Great War*. London: Allen Lane, 1978.

Winter, J. M. *The Great War and the British People*. Basingstoke: Macmillan, 1985.

———. *Sites of Memory, Sites of Mourning: The Place of the Great War in European Cultural History*. Cambridge: Cambridge University Press, 1995.

Winter, J. M., and Jean-Louis Robert. *Capital Cities at War: Paris, London, Berlin, 1914–1919*. Cambridge: Cambridge University Press, 1997.

Winter, J. M., and Richard Wall. *The Upheaval of War: Family, Work and Welfare in Europe, 1914–1918*. Cambridge: Cambridge University Press, 1988.

Wohl, Robert. *The Generation of 1914*. Cambridge: Harvard University Press, 1979.

Wollasch, Andreas. "Tendenzen und Probleme gegenwärtiger historischer Wohlfahrtsforschung in Deutschland." *Westfälische Forschungen* 43 (1993).

Wollasch, Hans-Josef. *Benedict Kreutz*. Freiburg: Deutschen Caritasverband, 1979.

———. "Benedict Kreutz." In *Zeitgeschichte in Lebensbildern, Band 5: Aus dem deutschen Katholizismus des 19. und 20. Jahrhunderts*, edited by Jürgen Aretz, Rudolf Morsey, and Anton Rauscher. Mainz: Matthias Grünewald, 1982.

Woloch, Isser. *The French Veteran from the Revolution to the Restoration*. Chapel Hill: University of North Carolina Press, 1979.

Woodroofe, Kathleen. *From Charity to Social Work*. London: Routledge and Paul, 1962.

Wootton, Graham. *The Official History of the British Legion*. London: MacDonald and Evans, 1956.

———. *The Politics of Influence*. Cambridge: Harvard University Press, 1963.

Young, Desmond. *Member for Mexico*. London: Cassell, 1966.

Younghusband, Eileen. *Social Work in Britain, 1950–1975*. London: G. Allen and Unwin, 1978.

Ziemann, Benjamin. *Front und Heimat: Ländliche Kriegserfahrungen in südlichen Bayern 1914–1923*. Essen: Klartext, 1997.

Zimmeck, Meta. "Strategies and Stratagems for the Employment of Women in the British Civil Service, 1919–1939." *Historical Journal* 27 (1984): 901–924.

Index

Compositor: Impressions Book and Journal Services, Inc.
Text: 10/13 Sabon
Display: Sabon
Printer and Binder: Edwards Brothers, Inc.